Stubborn Poetries

Stubborn Poetries

Poetic Facticity and the Avant-Garde

Peter Quartermain

The University of Alabama Press
Tuscaloosa

The University of Alabama Press
Tuscaloosa, Alabama 35487-0380

Manufactured in the United States of America

Typeface: Minion and Goudy Sans

Cover photograph: Courtesy of Peter Quartermain
Cover design: Gary Gore

∞

The paper on which this book is printed meets the minimum requirements of American National Standard for Information Sciences—Permanence of Paper for Printed Library Materials, ANSI Z39.48-1984.

Library of Congress Cataloging-in-Publication Data

Quartermain, Peter.
Stubborn Poetries : Poetic Facticity and the Avant-Garde / Peter Quartermain.
pages cm. — (Modern and Contemporary Poetics)
Includes bibliographical references and index.
ISBN 978-0-8173-5748-1 (quality paper : alk. paper) — ISBN 978-0-8173-8671-9 (e book) 1. Experimental poetry—History and criticism. 2. Avant-garde (Aesthetics) 3. Poetics—Psychological aspects. I. Title.
PN1059.E94Q37 2013
809.1'911—dc23

2012041445

Contents

Acknowledgments

Each of the essays in this book was written for and to an occasion. Consequently, they do not as a whole pursue a central argument or explicit thesis that might pull them together into a coherent and interlocking whole. They do not attempt to cover a particular (or even a general) field. They were not written with a collection in mind, nor a book. Gathered together, as here, there is not only an *ad hoc* quality to their assemblage but, inevitably, a recurrence of names, citations, themes, and quotations that reveal some of the constants in my reading and delight—work by Basil Bunting, William Carlos Williams, and Louis Zukofsky. The nature of literary authority is a recurrent but intermittent *motif.*

Such is the nature of occasion that inclusion and omission are in part simply a matter of happenstance: the occasion for some possible essays simply didn't arise, or my efforts were simply inadequate. There are not, for instance, as many essays on women writers as I would have liked, and some pieces—on Rachel Blau DuPlessis, Kathleen Fraser, or Rosmarie Waldrop—were too slight for inclusion. Other omissions, such as the perhaps surprising lack of anything about Robert Duncan, result from slightly different circumstance: in the case of Duncan, the process of editing his collected poems, along with the fairly long introductory essays to the two volumes of his work, tempered my appetite for writing yet another. There is also the thought that with the long-delayed publication of *The H. D. Book,* the two volumes of his *Collected Poems and Plays,* and the *Collected Prose,* Duncan is becoming canonical and the need for the sort of essay I customarily write is less. I encountered a similar situation years before when I went to write about William Carlos Williams. Like Duncan, Williams (and, later, Olson) opened doors for me—Williams is for me the wellhead (I came to Ezra Pound much later)—but by the time I began to attempt an essay (in the mid-1960s) he was rapidly becoming canonical, and I found myself irresistibly drawn to the sometimes crumpled syntax of Louis Zukofsky. Questions are more engaging than answers.

I have brought references up-to-date where it seemed more or less urgently necessary, and generally made slight revisions in the interests of clarity or even grace. I warmly thank Charles Bernstein and Hank Lazer for their strong and patient encouragement to gather these essays into a book, and Stephen Collis, who, once I'd gathered the essays, gave them an initial and extremely useful copyedit, thereby saving me the expenditure of a lot of energy during a period when I was feeling somewhat overwhelmed by too many commitments. Marjorie Perloff read the whole manuscript, made detailed and useful suggestions at both local and global levels, and wisely urged me to write the introduction; I owe her much.

The essays in this book were written between 1989 and 2006. The first to be written, "Canonical Strategies and the Question of Authority: T. S. Eliot and William Carlos Williams," was delivered in much-abridged form at the Tri-University Conference, Simon Fraser University, 4 March 1989. It has not previously been printed.

"Basil Bunting: Poet of the North" is the text of a lecture given in March 1990 at the University of Durham, England; it was originally published as a chapbook by the Basil Bunting Poetry Archive in 1990. I am grateful indeed to the Basil Bunting Poetry Center at Durham University for appointing me as its first Mountjoy Fellow, and for the opportunity this afforded me to work in the substantial archive of Bunting materials in the Mountjoy collection. The late Richard Caddel and Diana Collecott of the Basil Bunting Poetry Centre deserve my special thanks, as do Tony Downes of the Society of Fellows at Durham University and Judith Draycott of English Estates North. I also owe warm thanks to Ann Caddel for valuable comments on historical matters, and to Karen Jackson for providing me with a welcome bolt-hole from the not-inconsiderable rigors of dormitory life in Collingwood College. David Burnett and Beth Rainey of Durham University Library were constantly courteous and patient, steering me through the intricacies of the archive and the local history collection, and I thank them. I must add that without the considerable support of English Estates North, Basil Bunting's papers would not have stayed in the north of England, where they belong.

A somewhat different version of essay 4 was given as a lecture in the Department of English at the University at Buffalo, State University of New York, in late 1989 at the invitation of Charles Bernstein, Gray Chair in Poetry, and in further modified form in February 1990 at the University of Durham, in England, as part of the Mountjoy Fellowship. It first appeared as "Parataxis in Basil Bunting and Louis Zukofsky," *Sharp Study and Long Toil,* Richard Caddel, ed. *Durham University Journal* special issue (March): 54–70.

Of the two essays on Louis Zukofsky, that on writing and authority in *Thanks to the Dictionary* was initially given as "Procedural Composition: The Case of Zukofsky" at the conference *The First Postmoderns: American Poets of the 1930s Generation* held at the University of Maine, Orono, in June 1993. It was subsequently published as "Writing and Authority in Louis Zukofsky's *Thanks to the Dictionary*" in *Upper Limit Speech: The Writing of Louis Zukofsky,* Mark Scroggins, ed. (Tuscaloosa University of Alabama Press, 1997) 154–174. The other Zukofsky essay, "Thinking with the Poem," is, with several small changes and with longer quotations summarized or paraphrased, the text of an address given at a plenary session of the Louis Zukofsky Centenary Conference, Columbia University, New York, September 2004. It was published by Lou Rowan in *Golden Handcuffs Review* 1.5 (Summer-Fall): 169–181, and in severely truncated form in the electronic journal *Jacket* 30 (2006).

"Reading Niedecker" was written at the behest of Jenny Penberthy in September 1992, and first appeared in her *Lorine Niedecker: Woman and Poet* (Orono: National Poetry Foundation, 1986) 219–227; an abbreviated version of " 'Take Oil / and Hum': Niedecker and Bunting" was given at a panel on "Niedecker and Company" at the *Lorine Niedecker Centenary Celebration 1903–2003,* held in Milwaukee in October 2003; it was first published in *Radical Vernacular: Lorine Niedecker and the Poetics of Place,* Elizabeth Willis, ed. (Iowa City: U of Iowa P, 2008) 271–283.

"The Mind as Frying Pan: Robin Blaser's Humor" is the text of a paper read in June 1995 at the conference "The Recovery of the Public World: The Poetry and Poetics of Robin Blaser," held at Emily Carr College, Vancouver. It was first published by Clayton Eshleman in *Sulfur* 37 (Fall 1995): 108–116, and reprinted in *The Recovery of the Public World: Essays on Poetics in Honour of Robin Blaser,* Charles Watts and Edward Byrne, ed. (Vancouver: Talonbooks, 1999) 50–57.

" 'Writing on Air for Dear Life,' " the essay on Richard Caddel, is a somewhat extensively revised combination of two pieces: the review article "Caddel," which appeared in John Tranter's electronic journal *Jacket* 20 (December 2002), and a memorial essay titled "Richard Caddel," which was read in 2002 at the conference at the University of Calgary to honor the work of Fred Wah and mark his retirement; it was subsequently published in the Fred Wah issue of *Open Letter* 12.2 (Spring 2004): 108–120. I am grateful to Meredith Quartermain for her great help in combining the two.

The essays on Mina Loy, George Oppen, Robert Creeley, Lyn Hejinian, and Steve McCaffery were all initially delivered orally at various conferences and gatherings. "The Tattle of Tongueplay" was read at the Annual Convention of the MLA, held in New York in December 1992, and subsequently published in *Mina Loy: Woman and Poet,* Maeera Shreiber and Keith Tuma, ed. (Orono: National Poetry Foundation) 75–85. "Conversation with One's Peers" was given as the Eleventh George Oppen Memorial Lecture at the First Unitarian Church, San Francisco, in December 1996, sponsored by the Poetry Center and American Poetry Archive, San Francisco State University; excerpts were originally published in *The Poetry Center and American Poetry Archives News* [San Francisco] 13 (1997): 11–14. "Momently: The Politics of the Poem" was given at the memorial conference *On Words: On the Life and Work of Robert Creeley,* in Buffalo, NY, October 2006, and published in *On Words: Robert Creeley,* Stephen Fredman and Steve McCaffery, ed. (Iowa City: U of Iowa P, 2010) 118–139.

"Syllable as Music: Lyn Hejinian's *Writing Is an Aid to Memory*" was delivered at the invitation of Marjorie Perloff at a panel on "Musicating Language" arranged by the division on Literature and the Other Arts at the Annual Convention of the MLA, San Francisco, December 1991; it was published in slightly expanded form in *Sagetrieb* 11.3 (Winter 1993): 17–31. "McCaffery's Diptych: *The Black Debt*" was originally written at the invitation of Herbert Leibowitz for a special issue of *Parnassus* on long poetry, but it was submitted too late for publication; it has not previously been published.

At the invitation of Marjorie Perloff, " 'Getting Ready to Have Been Frightened': How I Read Bruce Andrews" was originally given as a lecture at the English Department, Stanford University, in May 1991, and was published in the Bruce Andrews issue of *Aerial* 9 (1999): 161–182. The essay which follows, on Andrews's *Lip Service,* was given in April 1997 as a lecture titled "Paradise and Praxis: Dante in a Contemporary American Avant-Garde" at the conference *La Presenza di Dante Nella Poesia Contemporanea Nordamericana* sponsored by Dipartimento di Scienze, Linguistiche e Letterarie, Università "G. D'Annunzio" [Pescara] and Casa di Dante in Abruzzo [Torre de' Passeri] [Italy]. It was published in *Witz: A Journal of Contemporary Poetics* 6.2 (Summer 1998): 5–18, and in *Dante: "For Use, Now,"* Annalisa Goldoni and Andrea Mariani, ed. (Rome: *Testo e Senso* 3, 2000) 119–132. The bulk of this essay was drafted during a resident fellowship at the Rockefeller Foundation Bellagio Center in January–February 1996, when a bout of ill health obliged me to abandon the project I originally proposed for that extraordinary and very welcome stay—I am indeed grateful.

A truncated version of "Undoing the Book" was read at a session on "The

Status of Bibliography in the Profession," arranged by the Division on Methods of Literary Research, at the Annual Convention of the MLA in Toronto, December 1993. It was first published in *Text: An Interdisciplinary Annual of Textual Studies,* D. C. Greetham, W. Speed Hill, and Peter Shillingsburg, ed. (Ann Arbor: U of Michigan P, 1997) v. 9, pp. 119–134. I am grateful to the late Charles Watts, Special Collections, Simon Fraser University Library, for bibliographic information about several of the little magazines listed in this paper.

A much longer version of "Poetic Fact," with slide illustrations, was given as a lecture in the Summer Writing Program, Naropa University, in 2006, and at the Kootenay School of Writing in Vancouver in 2007.

"Sound Reading" was written in 1997 for Charles Bernstein's collection *Close Listening: Poetry and the Performed Word,* Charles Bernstein, ed. (New York: Oxford UP, 1998) 217–230, and "Paradise of Letters" in 1997 for the "letters" issue of *Chain* 6 (Summer 1999): 175–185.

I owe sincere and warm thanks to those who in one way or another have helped me at one or all stages of writing these essays. They are (in alphabetical order): Charles Agvent, Bruce Andrews, Tony Baker, Charles Bernstein, Joann Blais, Michael Boughn, Fred Bowers, David Bromige, Colin Browne, Pauline Butling, Ann Caddel, Richard Caddel, Marina Camboni, Laura Cerruti, Norma Cole, Victor Coleman, Diana Collecott, Steve Collis, Bruce Comens, Robert Creeley, Guy Davenport, Rachel Blau DuPlessis, Ulla Dydo, Clayton Eshleman, Kathleen Fraser, Peggy Gerbrecht, Harry Gilonis, Annalisa Goldoni, Hugh Kenner, Michele Leggott, Daphne Marlatt, James Maynard, Steve McCaffery, Jerome McGann, Miriam Nichols, Linda Oppen, Judy Parker, Aaron Peck, Marjorie Perloff, Mava Jo Powell, Maureen McHale Scobie, Nathaniel Tarn, Fred Wah, Ann Waldman, Dan Waterman, Charles Watts, Lorraine Weir, and Karen Yearsley.

Above all, I have benefited from careful readings and wonderful conversations with the late Robin Blaser, very dear friend, and from informed, appreciative, and occasionally astringent commentary from my beloved partner Meredith Quartermain—this book is dedicated to them.

"Ode 1.1," "Ode 5," "Ode 1.7," and an extract from *Briggflatts,* by Basil Bunting, are printed from Basil Bunting, *Complete Poems,* Richard Caddel, ed. (Bloodaxe Books, 2000) by permission.

Jargon Society Collection (PCMS-019) and the Bunting-Pickard Collection (PCMS-018) are printed by permission of the Poetry Collection of the University Libraries, University at Buffalo, the State University of New York.

Quotations from Basil Bunting's letters from the Harry Ransom Humanities Research Center, University of Texas at Austin, and the Yale Collection of American Literature, Beinecke Rare Book and Manuscript Library, Yale University, are printed by permission.

Quotations from the uncollected work of Richard Caddel appear with the permission of the estate of Richard Caddel and are printed by permission.

Quotations from the manuscripts of Cid Corman are copyright © 2012 by the Estate of Cid Corman. Permission given by Bob Arnold literary executor for the estate of Cid Corman, and by the Harry Ransom Centre University of Texas at Austin.

Poems from *The Collected Poems of Robert Creeley, 1945–1975*, by Robert Creeley, © 1982, 2006 Regents of the University of California, published by the University of California Press, and *The Collected Poems of Robert Creeley, 1975–2005*, by Robert Creeley, © 2006 Estate of Robert Creeley, published by the University of California Press, reproduced with the permission of the University of California Press.

"Guatemala" and "The Times" by Robert Creeley reproduced with the permission of Penelope Creeley.

"The Pool" by H. D. (Hilda Doolittle), from COLLECTED POEMS, 1912–1944, copyright © 1982 by the Estate of Hilda Doolittle. Reprinted by permission of New Directions Publishing Corp.

Quotations from the work of Lorine Niedecker are copyright © 2012 by the Estate of Lorine Niedecker. Permission given by Bob Arnold, literary executor for the estate of Lorine Niedecker.

"Night Scene," "The Hills," and "The Undertaking in New Jersey" by George Oppen, from COLLECTED POEMS, copyright © 1975 by George Oppen. Reprinted by permission of New Directions Publishing Corp.

"The Zulu Girl" by George Oppen, from NEW COLLECTED POEMS, copyright © 1985, 2002 by Linda Oppen. Reprinted by permission of New Directions Publishing Corp.

"Between Walls," "Chicago" by William Carlos Williams, from THE COLLECTED POEMS: VOLUME ONE, 1909–1939, copyright © 1938 by New Directions Publishing Corp. Reprinted by permission of New Directions Publishing Corp.

Stubborn Poetries

Introduction

Reading the Difficult

O marvelous! what new configuration will come next?
I am bewildered with multiplicity.
—William Carlos Williams

In 1926 Gertrude Stein suggested that "the creator of the new composition in the arts is an outlaw until he is a classic, there is hardly a moment in between,"[1] and the lure of such disobedience is compelling. If you want to talk or write about innovative writing, it challenges our vocabulary: we don't have the right words to be precise or exact. We even have great difficulty identifying at all clearly the event our reading is, because we barely recognize it (if we recognize it at all), and *that,* as the word "recognize" reminds us, is a problem of memory. "Americans," William Carlos Williams observed, "have never recognized themselves. How can they? It is impossible until someone invent the ORIGINAL terms. . . . Invent that which is new . . . and there's none to know what you have done. It is because there's no *name.*"[2] The modernist rallying cry "Make it new!" is thus at some point self-defeating if the new does not have substantial bits of the old clinging to its hem. W. B. Yeats, struck with Whitman's originality, recognized over a century ago, in 1901, that "when Walt Whitman writes in seeming defiance of a tradition, he needs tradition for protection, for the butcher and the baker and the candlestick-maker grow merry over him when they meet his work by chance."[3] That laughter is very like the scorn John Gibson Lockhart famously poured on the "calm, settled, imperturbable drivelling idiocy" of Keats's "Endymion."[4] It is echoed in the mirth of a *Life* magazine editorial in the 1930s that ridiculed William Carlos Williams's "The Red Wheelbarrow," and likewise points to responses like Cleanth Brooks's 1964 assessment of Williams's language in that poem as "quite inert. I see the white chickens and the raindrops glazing red paint. But I have to take on faith the author's statement that 'so much depends' on this scene."[5] The would-be commentator, attempting to counter such judgment, or faced with unconventional and opaque new work, is often tempted to invent special terms or redefine those already in use. But inventing language frequently leads to an arcane jargon whose complexity is comprehensible (if at all) only to specialists. Redefining terms already in use—especially if they are ordinary words—runs risks of a different sort, for the habitual usage interferes with the revised, and thereby results in a confused response if not in confused thought. Both approaches exclude the uninitiated, and the *event* of the poem disappears.

As a schoolboy in England I was an enthusiastic though unadventurous and inarticulate reader of poetry—the first book of poetry I bought off my own bat, with birthday-present money, was *The Poetical Works of John Keats,* in the Oxford Standard Authors series. It never occurred to me that Lewis Carroll's *The Hunting of the Snark*—which Mum and Dad gave for my eleventh birthday—could be read as *poem*; its agreeable nonsense wasn't serious enough and its clear narrative too simple to count—it was too much *fun.* About a year before I went to university I spread my wings a bit when, for half my weekly pocket money, I bought Kenneth Allott's anthology *Contemporary Verse,* "a collection of verse written between 1918 and 1948" in the Penguin Poets series, for 1/6d.[6] Of the poets—ranging from W. B. Yeats to Sidney Keyes (it took me a long time to notice that only three of them were women)—the only Americans were T. S. Eliot and Arthur Waley. For reasons of space, and not because the book was an anthology of *English* verse, the introduction (dated 1948) regretted the absence of "Ezra Pound, John Crowe Ransom, E.E. Cummings, Allen Tate, Frederic Prokosch, etc.," and at some length explained why it preferred Eliot to Pound, but otherwise *en passant* mentioned only Amy Lowell and Walt Whitman. The headnote prefacing Eliot's work mentioned F. O. Matthiessen, while that prefacing W. H. Auden's mentioned Randall Jarrell; the book failed altogether even to name Hart Crane, Wallace Stevens, or William Carlos Williams. The headnote for Yeats which starts the anthology identifies "the problem facing most contemporary poets" with Yeats's "insight" (in his *Autobiographies*) that "how small a fragment of our own nature can be brought to perfect expression."[7]

Allott's "Introductory Note" was thoroughly appropriate as preparation for my undergraduate education in English literature: its expression and communicative model of poetry fed into, and owed much to, the New Criticism, much in vogue in my undergraduate and graduate student days, and indeed after. Cleanth Brooks was perhaps its leading practitioner. Like the other New Critics, Brooks owed much to T. S. Eliot, and perhaps through him to I. A. Richards, whose books Eliot cited more than once in his *Selected Essays.* Everyone in our undergraduate study of English was obliged to read Richards's *Principles of Literary Criticism* (1924); his book *Practical Criticism* (1929) was the foundation of a compulsory discussion course of great vigor that met once a week for two years. Unlike the book after which it was named, the course did not so much investigate the interpretive process as train us in *explication de texte,* providing exemplary instances of acceptable understanding of the poem or prose under scrutiny. The course gave me the habit of paying close attention to the text, but I was not very good at the overall practice of the course. I continually failed to achieve the prescribed or agreed-upon interpretation ("the paradox of 'cold heaven' is the very foundation of the tension in Yeats's poem!" we were encouraged to discern) in much the same way as, when a schoolboy, I had utterly botched scansion exercises; *then,* I had been told the meter of Donne's fourteenth Holy Sonnet, "Batter my heart, three person'd God," is "obviously iambic after the first word!" though my ear *still* tells me otherwise. Under the expert guidance of our mentors, the undergraduate group would achieve interpretive consensus, sometimes excitedly, but I found the professed clarity of my peers' interpretation of the text unsatisfying, reluctantly and even agonizingly preferring my own hesitant (and as the course rolled on, increasingly unasked) questions to whatever "answers" that emerged in the guise of "understanding."

Cleanth Brooks's blindness to Williams's wheelbarrow is of the same ilk as Richards's somewhat contemptuous dismissal of H. D.'s "The Pool" as an example of "badness in poetry" because it is a "defective communication":

THE POOL

Are you alive?
I touch you.
You quiver like a sea-fish.
I cover you with my net.
What are you—banded one?[8]

Although he somewhat begrudgingly adds that "it is likely that the original experience had some value,"[9] it is clear that Richards finds the poem's "simplicity" permanently opaque and blames the brevity of the poem and the direct openness of H. D.'s spare language, with its avoidance of connotation, for the poem's ineffectiveness. Its closing question can no more be precisely answered with a clear meaning than Williams's poem can tell us precisely *what* it is that depends "so much" on the red wheelbarrow. In their apparent inconsequentiality and refusal to explain, both poems are stubbornly opaque, and they are difficult even to describe at all precisely.

A demand for such "precision"—a preciseness not only of image and metaphor but of a response identifying the tensions and paradoxes which are (or are assumed to be) the source of the poem's dynamic—is the salient hallmark of a critical method which assumes that the work of art is, in its complexity, self-sufficient, ahistorical, and atemporal: the meaning of the work can be known objectively. The task of the reader is, through detailed consideration of relationships within the text, through consideration of symbols, images, ironies, ambiguities, and the like, to discern that meaning and its movement, and through the reconciliation of jarring and even contradictory elements in the text to discover, or rather establish, the essential unity of the work. Such criteria for the identification and assessment of poetry derives from Eliot's suggestion, in his essay on "The Metaphysical Poets" (1921), "that poets in our civilization, as it exists at present, must be *difficult.* Our civilization comprehends great variety and complexity, and this variety and complexity, playing upon a refined sensibility, must produce various and complex results. The poet must become more and more comprehensive, more allusive, more indirect, in order to force, to dislocate if necessary, language into his meaning."[10] Eliot might have Pound's "Hugh Selwyn Mauberley" or his own *The Waste Land* in mind. Faced with these examples of the new, our mentors in "Practical Criticism" preferred the challenges thus offered by Eliot and Pound to the ones posed by H. D.'s pool or Williams's wheelbarrow. With their use of quotations, foreign languages, arcane reference, and (in Eliot's case) footnotes, they are so obviously "difficult" that they demand the sort of explication New Criticism called for and which now fills so many shelves in university libraries. They are puzzling poems, and the implication (at least by our mentors, if not by the poems themselves) is that their stubbornness will yield to analysis because their essential riddle can be solved. Eliot's judgment of "Mauberley," that it is "a document of an epoch," led us—and our teachers—along with countless text-anthologies—to prefer it to Pound's "Homage to Sextus Propertius." Eliot included the first ("a great poem") and excluded the second ("a most interesting study in versification") from his edition of Pound's *Selected Poems,* noting of "Propertius" that "I was doubtful of its effect upon the uninstructed reader, even with my instructions."[11]

For the poem, especially the *new* poem, to be worthwhile, for it to be what Richards called of "some value," we learned that it must offer difficulty of a similar sort, and that analytic description, untangling it detail by detail, was the way to understanding. But faced with simplicity, not that of the new like Williams or H. D. (we hadn't even *heard* of Williams, and—but for "The Pool"—hardly at all of H. D.), but that of ballads from Percy's *Reliques* or early traditional work, we were at a loss:

> Westron wynde, when wilt thou blow,
> The small raine down can raine.

Cryst, if my love were in my armes
And I in my bedde again!

Even with Quiller-Couch's regularized version to compare, there was not much to say.[12] Like the new, the simple resists description, and this poem simply lacks those dynamic qualities we were taught to notice and "appreciate." If pressed, we might resort to the kind of associative response which we scorned in Walter Pater's aesthetic effusions over the Mona Lisa. We might—and did—recite "Westron wynde" with pleasure and even glee, so instantly did its condensed loneliness move into our hearts, but it didn't lend itself to the critical act. There was nothing to describe for there was nothing to peel apart. Shakespeare's songs, and Ben Jonson's short lyrics (such as the well-worn "Drinke to me, onely, with thine eyes")[13] were equally resistant; I got no help from Eliot, who, contrasting Ben Jonson with John Donne, and with fellow playwrights (other than Shakespeare), wrote: "He is no less a poet than these men, but his poetry is of the surface. Poetry of the surface cannot be understood without study. . . . [T]he polished veneer of Jonson only reflects the lazy reader's fatuity; unconscious does not respond to unconscious; no swarms of inarticulate feelings are aroused. The immediate appeal of Jonson is to the mind; his emotional tone is not in the single verse, but in the design of the whole."[14] After untangling the difficulties, unpacking the abstruse dense referentiality, and tracking the almost gnomic epigrammatic syntax of "Hugh Selwyn Mauberley," to see Eliot praise Pound's poem for its "simplicity"[15] was, to say the least, startling and baffling. What exactly might the distinction be, between "polished veneer" and what I took to be such simplicity as H. D.'s? As I read further and further through English and American poetry it became clearer and clearer, and more and more distressing, that the critical reading-method we were learning disqualified many poems from serious critical dialogue. What could you say about "The Hunting of the Snark"? Why didn't the lectures I eventually skipped talk about William Barnes of Dorset or John Clare or even Thomas Campion? In his essay on Jonson, Eliot had suggested that this sort of poetry demanded study, demanded "intellectual saturation in his work as a whole." But, Eliot warned, "not many people are capable of discovering for themselves the beauty which is only found after labour," a stricture that, coming as it did hand in hand with the critical approaches I was being told to learn, severely undermined the great pleasure I and some of my peers took in such songs and singers by authoritatively calling that pleasure into question. It did not occur to me that the available critical vocabulary was inadequate to the task; poems like Carroll's "The Hunting of the Snark" and "You are old, father William" were spurious poems, poems for children. Like "The Red Wheelbarrow," like almost anything by Edith Sitwell or Stevie Smith or the despised Vachel Lindsay, they were "light verse," so by definition lacked Matthew Arnold's requisite "high seriousness"; they were too easy.[16] Or they were simply, as Richards had pronounced, "bad poetry." They failed to create metaphysical ambiguities and multi-layered symbols and image-patterns, failed to demand of poet and reader the reconciliation of apparent contradictions, lacked wit and recondite allusiveness. The sheer enjoyment of chant and recitation, clarity and simplicity, were not sufficient, or even indeed legitimate; nor was, finally, the discursive poetry of say Samuel Daniel or Hugh MacDiarmid, whose demands on the reader—whose difficulties—were of a quite different order.

By the time I got out of graduate school I had stopped reading poetry altogether, it had become such a task, and an onerous one at that. I knew I could not understand it and certainly had no desire to teach it. But in 1962 I found myself obliged to teach poetry in a survey course of "American Literature After 1880," and shortly after that, completely unaware of the sheer unlikeliness as well as good fortune of it, met Robert Creeley, Robert Duncan, and (a bit later) Basil Bunting, each of whom had quite some effect. Reading the old New Directions *Selected Poems* of William Carlos Williams[17] to get ready for that 1962 course, and reading those poems with dawning excitement and intense pleasure, I began to grasp how subject I had been to the tyranny of an understanding which insists that the poem meet whatever notions of appropriateness we bring to the reading of poetry, whether of manner or matter, and that all violations of protocol can be accounted for. Such necessity to understand demanded that I take from the poem a meaning I could carry over and apply some other place—that I read, as Zukofsky put it, with "predatory intention."[18] "To Daphne and Virginia," "The Desert Music," and "Asphodel That Greeny Flower"—the long poems in Williams's *Pictures from Brueghel*—were an astonishing and exciting revelation. I carried them around for days, for weeks, the way I carried "The Red Wheelbarrow" in my head it was so vividly easy to remember—like some of the hard-to-find poems of Louis Zukofsky, it haunted me. I began to suspect that Brooks's dismissal of the poem came from a failure of attention, and that his failure of attention came from a failure of vocabulary. Insistent that the poem "say something," say "something worth saying," he had no vocabulary that would permit or enable him to attend the syntactic, rhythmic, and visual play at the heart of that poem, and leave it at that. Unlike Eliot, who is a much more sympathetic and generous reader than his magisterial and *ex cathedra* tone might suggest (though he too seems not to have liked Williams), Brooks (like Richards and many New Critics) is so trapped in the protocols of his own procedures that the sheer accessibility of Williams's language, its simplicity and lucidity, undoes his ability to discuss it.[19] Williams's poems are reader-friendly, the warm and even intimate voice so inviting and (*contra* Eliot) so *personal,* the language so accessible, that it struck me *anyone* could write like that. But of course, *anyone* could not: "The smell of the heat is boxwood"—the flat statement so immediately familiar, the perhaps ruminative not-quite-conversational voice singling out the pungent telling detail, brooking in its personal and unambiguous reportage neither disagreement nor interpretation. Yet I knew instantly, on reading it for the first time, that I might well be reading "To Daphne and Virginia," "Asphodel, That Greeny Flower" and those other late poems for the rest of my life, so loaded are they with multiply suggestive meaning. As Pound said in 1928, Williams "does not 'conclude.' "[20] Many of his poems, though pointed, are nevertheless deliberately pointless, baffling the New Critical demand that a poem lead to something conclusive and definable, in Williams's view all too frequently *stopping* thought.

Like many traditional lyrics, Williams's short poems begin *in medias res;* there's not an ounce of preparation, no warm-up for the reader, no thematic or social setting of the scene. The language is blunt, even if the bluntness is somewhat tempered by subordinate clauses.

BETWEEN WALLS

the back wings
of the

hospital where
nothing

will grow lie
cinders

in which shine
the broken

pieces of a green
bottle[21]

The language is close to journalism: flat and plain, in blunt facticity. It is, if we add punctuation and ignore the line breaks, indistinguishable from prose. Any attempt to explore the connotations of "green" or the contrast between *its* suggestiveness and the sterility of the cinders on which the glass lies, leads only to the banal—the poem registers a syntax of attention, of perception.

It is a noticing. To read the syntax as "the hospital where nothing will grow" leads us away from the poem into fruitless and irrelevant speculation, since there is a straightforward and easily sorted syntax available, even if the sentence itself seems pointless and the poem seems to "lead nowhere." In this, "Between Walls" is like "The Red Wheelbarrow" even if that poem might be said in its opening words at least to gesture toward a point. For both poems, it is difficult to imagine a social context or setting for the apparently inconsequential utterance: Under what circumstances might somebody say this? And when? Yet both poems, like so many of Williams's short poems, seem to exist simply "just to say." There is implacability in the language that resists both paraphrase and explication. The language is so spare, the details so sparse, the statement so stubbornly *there* before the reader, uncompromising, that the reader's knowledge *cannot* intervene, cannot interfere with the poem; indeed it renders that knowledge irrelevant, the poem open. The poem doesn't care whether you are puzzled or not; it's an event, and you can join it, take part in, or not.

As the opening essay in this book suggests, the central issue that distinguishes Eliot from Williams—each representative of different critical and poetic conventions—is the question of authority and where it is to be found: in the social group or in the individual; in the values of high culture or the values of the street; in calculation or in spontaneity; in the canon or in poems, one at a time. Eliot is just as insistent in his desire to define and establish himself within an explicitly British and European canon of great works as Williams is to position himself outside it. Given such polarities, complex though they are, it is not a very large jump from a poem by Williams to a poem by, say, Bruce Andrews or Maggie O'Sullivan. Both suppress allusiveness, in vocabulary and rhythm playing down literary and cultural convention and even association, the words flat and plain (though frequently startling in their unusual predication and juxtapositions), the words so aggressively and uncompromisingly *there* on the page, language constitutive of experience, of a social or even a human whose existence we might not suspect. No "easy lateral sliding" (as Williams said of "the associational or sentimental value") into reference or symbol.[22] These are take-it-or-leave-it poets; language is a "What Is," inescapably and implacably opaque. There are two essays on Andrews in this book, but there is none on O'Sullivan—she's a performance poet, utterly terrific, but I haven't found a way even to talk about the pleasure her work affords me. Her work, like most of the work discussed in this book, so insistently resists the definitive that even now, fifteen to twenty years since I first heard her read, all I can do is point with pleasure: "Here. And here. And here. Look! Listen to this!" The sheer *presence* of her words, the obduracy of her language and its refusal to explain, is not unlike work by Gertrude Stein, who also drops the reader abruptly into the deep end to sink or swim in her ocean of playful indeterminacies.

nailed Eagles beryl alter vanish
Owls, Blood-bed
Bird gear turbulent
Ruled

it,

is how one poem, "Hill Figures," begins.[23] The difficulty simply even to *say* it, as well as the sheer fluidity of syntax and the indeterminacy of even paraphrasable sense or meaning, are but extensions of the kind of relentlessness I see in Williams. They compel active reading, reading as an event. Harry Mathews has gone so far as to say, prefatory to his brief discussion of the opening of *Northanger Abbey,* that "of writer and reader, the reader is the only creator" because reading is "an act of creation for which the writer provides the means."[24] Those means, Mathews says, rest largely upon successive acts of omission. In a similar vein, Zukofsky often commented that to establish the poem as thing, the essential task of the poet is not to choose what to include but to discover what to leave out. For anyone trying to write about the poem as an active object in space and time, local and immediate, right before the senses under the nose, the essential challenge is that of description.

At just about the same time I was discovering Williams I also began, with growing excitement, to read Charles Olson. In "Human Universe" Olson talked about the "dodges" of discourse which "come out as demonstration, a separating out, an act of classification, and so, a stopping":

> All that comparison ever does is set up a series of *reference* points: to compare is to take one thing and try to understand it by marking its similarities to or differences from another thing. Right here is the trouble, that each thing is not so much like or different from another thing (these likenesses and differences are apparent) but that such an analysis only accomplishes a *description,* does not come to grips with what really matters: that a thing, any thing, impinges on us by a more important fact, its self-existence, without reference to any other thing, in short . . . its particularity.[25]

Or, one might say, its inescapable *thereness,* its ineluctable presence, its facticity: that quality which resists explanation and interpretation and cannot be accounted for. Paul Celan said that for a poem to be a poem it must by necessity include the resistance of the incommunicable—the unaccountable which is beyond (or before) words.

The central and abiding question, then, is *what makes the poem the way it is*? As Olson so clearly saw, the poem is itself an event, a movement in space and time. Or as Robin Blaser puts it:

> The statement *I drive the car* is much less interesting than what the car is doing. *A key, silver-silk, gas, burns, gears, motion, outer parts, wheels, hubs, spokes, fellies, tires, Fortuna, distances: I drive.* Perhaps Amor hitches a ride. The first example is arranged according to hypotaxis,—the "subordinative expression" of what is going on in the sentence—I'm in charge. The second is "arranged according to a kind of parataxis, one thing beside another without "expression of their syntactic relation."[26]

As the third essay in this book explores at some length, one feature of parataxis, with its rejection of subordination, is that the writing establishes a field of significations. Although this field of significations may be tied together by a common theme or "subject" (we know what or rather *where* the field is—at the very least it's before our eyes), it nonetheless provides a *common*, in which items jostle one another in more-or-less companionable felicities. Meanwhile the reader, moving about in and through the field, holds "understanding" or "conclusion" in abeyance because the exact relationship between the items, each "sufficient to itself and to be valued," is necessarily indeterminate and provisional.[27] Such writing provides no explicit overarching generalization that ties it all together. Although the boundaries may be indistinct, the whole field, *all* of it, is *along with the language* inescapably and stubbornly there before us, with its uncertainties and indeterminacies, and it now moves within us as we move within it.

But how does it *now* move within us? There is a duplicity here, a doubleness. We all of us, even poets, come to the poem from the outside; the poem is a condition of language and an event in it. I. A. Richards dismissed H. D.'s "The Pool" because it did not match a (putative) "original experience"—as if the poem were the *translation of an experience into words* and not an actual *event of language*. The poets discussed in this book demand that we respond to the poem, to the language of the poem, as a *what is*, a *thereness*, a something outside. They ask us to recognize in the poem's facticity what Giorgio Agamben calls *the irreparable:* "that things are just as they are, in this or that mode, consigned without remedy to their way of being."[28] Yet once we have read the poem, indeed *as* we read it, it inescapably moves within us, is within us, and in this the poem is like the world in which we move, which moves us, and is in us whether we are conscious of that or not. Our condition in language, our condition as language animals, is irremediable, irreparable. It is beyond "repair," and doesn't permit (presuming we want it) the perfect reading Richards and others sought, in which we all acquiesce and are of one mind, "completely" understanding one another. We are inside and outside at the same time, irreparably. That phrase I used, *along with the language,* was ill-said, separating as it did the "field" from the words of which it is constituted. As Blaser comments, "we are inside the irreparable. We are as we are implications of it."[29] That is what makes us the way we are. As Agamben argues (and Blaser develops), language "is not an 'object' presupposing the human already behind it, but is itself constitutive of the human."[30] In which case any notion that language was "invented" by or somehow originated outside humans, and is thus separable from consciousness or identity, is patently absurd. We cannot somehow put language to use, a coinage, and we cannot separate ourselves from the language, step outside it, without peril. Despite what my undergraduate teachers told us, we cannot find a meaning and an activity, an understanding and a creation, a world and a doing, that is *outside,* beyond, independent of, or transcendent over language, though such was, the teachers in my undergraduate years told us, the desirable condition of all art. Each of the poets discussed in this book posits language as a condition of the human, as constitutive of it, constitutive of meaning and hence necessarily of experience, inextricably part and parcel of apperception and conduct and understanding. Language is not, then, a means, nor is it, certainly, a precondition.

And the poem? Maurice Blanchot, perhaps echoing Celan, thinks that the poem comes from that inexpressible place before words, from that gap between what might be the world and what might be words for what we find.[31] Perhaps the poem comes from that odd cusp between the two sides of language, the outside and the inside that, mostly unknowingly, we inhabit. What *is* clear is that the poem brings into being what it says, and does not know ahead of time.

Notes

Epigraph. William Carlos Williams, "At Dawn," *The Collected Poems,* A. Walton Litz and Christopher MacGowan, eds. (New York: New Directions, 1991) v. 1, 36.

1. Gertrude Stein, "Composition as Explanation," *A Stein Reader,* Ulla Dydo, ed. (Evanston: Northwestern UP, 1993) 496.

2. William Carlos Williams, *In The American Grain* (New York: New Directions, 1956) 226.

3. W. B. Yeats, "What Is 'Popular Poetry'?" *Essays and Introductions* (New York: Macmillan, 1961) 8.

4. Cornelius Webb [i.e., John Gibson Lockhart], "Cockney School of Poetry No. IV," *Blackwood's Edinburgh Magazine* 17 (August 1818): 519.

5. Cleanth Brooks, "Poetry Since *The Waste Land*," *A Shaping Joy: Studies in the Writer's Craft* (New York: Harcourt Brace Jovanovich, 1972) 64.

6. Kenneth Allott, "Introductory Note," *Contemporary Verse* (Harmondsworth: Penguin Books, 1950) 11.

7. Allott 30. The word "insight" is Allott's.

8. H. D., *Collected Poems 1912–1944*, Louis L. Martz, ed. (New York: New Directions, 1983) 56.

9. I. A. Richards, *The Principles of Literary Criticism* (London: Kegan Paul, Trench, Trubner, 1924) 199–200.

10. T. S. Eliot, *Selected Essays 1917–1932* (London: Faber and Faber, 1932) 275.

11. T. S. Eliot, "Introduction: 1928," Ezra Pound, *Selected Poems* (London: Faber and Faber, 1928) 19–20.

12. "The Lover in Winter Plaineth for the Spring," *The Oxford Book of English Verse 1250–1900*, Sir Arthur Quiller-Couch, ed. (Oxford: Clarendon, 1926) 53.

13. "Song. To Celia," *Poems*, George Burke Johnston, ed. (London: Routledge and Kegan Paul, 1954) 88.

14. Eliot, *Selected Essays* 148. Faced with a poem like the great "Epigramme" (as Jonson called it) "On my first Sonne" ("Farewell, thou child of my right hand, and joy;" *Poems*, 23) this struck me then, as it strikes me now, a quite extraordinary judgment.

15. Eliot, "Introduction: 1928" 20.

16. Matthew Arnold introduced the term "high seriousness," which became a critical catchphrase among the New Critics, in his 1880 essay "The Study of Poetry," collected in *Essays in Criticism: Second Series* (1888) and frequently reprinted.

17. William Carlos Williams, *Selected Poems*, introduction by Randall Jarrell (Norfolk, CT: New Directions, 1949).

18. Louis Zukofsky, *Prepositions + : The Collected Critical Essays*, Mark Scroggins ed. (Hanover, NH: Wesleyan UP, 2000) 18.

19. But he did try. He seems, however, to have found Williams's language completely *in*accessible. He owned, for example, all four books of the limited (and handsome) first edition of *Paterson* (New Directions, 1946–1951). In his online catalogue, the rare-book dealer Charles Agvent (Mertztown, PA) listed and described them as follows: "The first volume contains a number of notes and marks in red ink in Brooks's hand, mostly revealing an attempt not only to understand the poem but to place it in a familiar context: witness references to *The Four Quartets* and *Finnegans Wake*. Apparently, Mr. Brooks decided to give up after the first volume as there are no notes in the remaining books." In his approaches to poetry Brooks nevertheless avoids the irrelevant banalities of thematic reading dominant in the Poetry Foundation (at least in 2011)—witness its "categorization" of "The Red Wheelbarrow" according to its "subject" on the Foundation's invitation to "Discover this poem's con-

tent" on the web: "Activities, Weather, Jobs & Working, Pets, Relationships, Nature." In similar vein, the Poetry Foundation sorts "The Pool" under the subjects "Nature, Seas, Rivers & Streams, Animals." For my own reading of "The Red Wheelbarrow, see *Disjunctive Poetics: From Gertrude Stein and Louis Zukofsky to Susan Howe* (New York: Cambridge UP, 1993) 92–93.

20. Ezra Pound, "Dr. Williams' Position," *Literary Essays*, T. S. Eliot, ed. (London: Faber and Faber, 1945) 394.

21. Williams, *Collected Poems* v. 1, 453.

22. William Carlos Williams, "Prologue to *Kora in Hell*," *Imaginations*, Webster Schott, ed. (New York: New Directions, 1970) 14.

23. Maggie O'Sullivan, *In The House of the Shaman* (London: Reality Street, 1993) 54.

24. Harry Mathews, "For Prizewinners," *The Case of the Persevering Maltese: Collected Essays* (Champaign, IL: Dalkey Archive, 2003) 7.

25. Charles Olson, *Collected Prose*, Donald Allen and Ben Friedlander, eds. (Berkeley: U of California P, 1997) 157–158.

26. Robin Blaser, "The Irreparable," *The Fire: Collected Essays*, Miriam Nichols, ed. (Berkeley: U of California P, 2006) 98.

27. Williams, *Imaginations* 7.

28. Giorgio Agamben, *The Coming Community*, Michael Hardt, trans. (Minneapolis: U of Minnesota P, 1993) 90.

29. Blaser, "The Irreparable" 107.

30. Giorgio Agamben, *Infancy and History: Essays on the Destruction of Experience*, Liz Heron, trans. (London: Verso, 1993) 49.

31. Maurice Blanchot, *The Space of Literature*, Ann Smock, trans. (Lincoln: U of Nebraska P, 1969).

Canonical Strategies and the Question of Authority

Eliot and Williams

In the spring of 1919 William Carlos Williams, reading and lecturing in Chicago, had a brief affair with Marion Strobel, associate editor of *Poetry.*

> If you will come away with me
> into another state
> we can be quiet together.
> But here the sun coming up
> out of the nothing beyond the lake is
> too low in the sky,

he told her, in one of three poems he wrote her.[1] The poem was titled "Chicago," and when it was published on page 73 of the *Egoist,* December 1919, it came immediately after these words: "The emotion of art is impersonal. And the poet cannot reach this impersonality without surrendering himself wholly to the work to be done. And he is not likely to know what is to be done unless he lives in what is not merely the present, but the present moment of the past, unless he is conscious, not of what is dead, but of what is already living"—the closing words of Eliot's essay "Tradition and the Individual Talent."[2]

It has become a critical commonplace to describe the literary and critical relations of Eliot and Williams in terms of the relationship between canonical and non-canonical writing, and it does seem to be true that, as Louis Menand puts it, "Eliot did invent, for a common set of terms and judgments, a manner . . . perfectly suited to the needs of the modern academic critic."[3] It is not at all clear to me, however, that both Eliot and Williams consciously and deliberately adopted what I call canonical strategies—indeed Williams seems actively to have resisted adoption into the canon, if he thought in terms of the canon at all. In November 1917 Eliot had begun his review of *The New Poetry: An Anthology,* edited by Harriet Monroe and Alice Corbin Henderson, by referring the reader in a footnote to Pope Gregory XVI's encyclical *Singulari nos* of July 13, 1834 and the Vatican Council canon of 1870, *Si quis dixerit . . . anathema sit.*[4] It is not putting matters too simply to suggest that in the period 1917–1920, writing for the *New Statesman,* the *Egoist,* and the *Athenaeum,* Eliot was working out a critical and aesthetic position which would legitimize his place in the canon, finding its most famous expression in "Tradition and the Individual Talent," and its most characteristic in the four-part "Reflections on Contemporary Poetry" (*Egoist,* September 1917–July 1919). Eliot, legitimizing his own status within a canonical English tradition, at the very same time helped define an American poetic canon in English canonical terms, providing it with an aesthetic and cultural identity recognizable in English terms, at a time when it seemed possibly to have no identity at all. Williams would, I think, have agreed with the Eliot who said that "Keats, Shelley, and Wordsworth punish us from their graves with the annual scourge of the Georgian Anthology" and who said "it is essential that each generation should reappraise everything for itself."[5] But Williams insisted on something other than a training in "critical judgment": "it is to loosen the attention, my attention since I occupy part of the field, that I write."[6]

I wish to examine the strategies which Eliot employed to legitimize his own position in the canon, and those with which Williams sought to resist his own canonical adoption. It may indeed be true that Eliot, in legitimizing his position in the canon, expelled Williams from it,[7] but it is equally apparent that Williams deliberately sought, from the publication of Eliot's *Prufrock and Other Observations* (1917) on, to exclude himself from that canon, and adopted strategies specifically designed to resist it. It looks very much, indeed, as though Williams wrote the prologue to *Kora in Hell* in response to Eliot's success with *Prufrock*—he completed the essay on 1 September 1918. Although we cannot wholly trust Williams's own account (in his *Autobiography*) of *The Waste Land*'s impact as a "catastrophe," there can be no doubt that he viewed the work of Eliot during and immediately following World War I as canonically anomalous and sought, in his own critical writings, to subvert the canon at the same time as Eliot (and, it should be added, Pound) would define it. By a nice coincidence Williams's "Prologue: The Return of the Sun" and Eliot's "Tradition and the Individual Talent" were serialized in little magazines four months apart, in 1919, and then gathered in books published two months apart, in 1920, in *Kora in Hell,* Williams's fourth book, and in *The Sacred Wood,* Eliot's fifth.[8] At the time of their periodical publication Williams was 35 years old and Eliot was 30.

I

An index of the radical difference between Eliot's and Williams's strategies is apparent from the use of personal pronouns in these two essays. A quick count gives Eliot 33 uses of *we* and five of *our,* compared to Williams's five *we,* and one *our;* Eliot has nine *I* and one *me* or *my,* to Williams's 64 *I* and 23 *me* or *my.* In the five sentences of Eliot's opening paragraph the word *we* occurs four times, *you* once, and *it* or *its* twice; in the second paragraph's nine sentences, *we* occurs fourteen times, *our* six, *it* five, and *he* or *his* six. In the last sentence of that paragraph the word *I* makes the first of its nine appearances in the whole essay.[9] Eliot's strategy is pretty clear: the generous use of *we* in the opening two sentences invites the reader to see himself[10] as a member of a fairly exclusive but undefined group, those who "speak" in "English writing," and the first two paragraphs taken together co-opt readers *(on pain of exclusion)* into seeing themselves as adepts of criticism, discrimination, judgment. The reader becomes one of those to "praise a poet," to "dwell with satisfaction" on the poet's difference from his predecessors. The reader is thus invited to see himself as knowledgeable, capable of discovering "the best." Eliot moves this into quite a complicated little movement when, later in the essay, he refers to specific passages and episodes of the *Divina Commedia* (paragraph 14), or quotes Tourneur's *Revenger's Tragedy* without identifying it (paragraph 16). There he resorts to a species of intimidation (excluding the reader from the club)—or of flattery (confirmation of club membership)—by challenging his reader's erudition. He has already cleared the way for this strategy when he assures the reader that "I am alive to a usual objection to what is clearly a part of my programme for the *métier* of poetry. The objection is that the doctrine requires a ridiculous amount of erudition (pedantry), a claim which can be rejected by appeal to the lives of the poets in any pantheon" (paragraph 8). The appeal to the lives of the poets here serves to distinguish the reader's "mixed motives" as Eliot called them, from the poet's professionalism.[11] That to "*any* pantheon" offers a neat tautology, since poets who lack such erudition obviously cannot belong to the pantheon anyway.

This strategy is markedly different from Williams's, since Williams doesn't seem to care whether his reader has read what he's quoting or not, and, indeed, on one occasion called himself "primary and antecedent to erudition."[12]

Eliot, in quoting from or referring to well-known if not canonically secure works is (1) flattering the reader (provided of course that the reader recognize the work, or the reference); (2) distinguishing the reader reading Eliot's essay (with its unrecognized but no doubt worthy quotations) from those who have not and presumably are not likely to read it; and (3) at the same time reinforcing the canonicity of the work in question. Such strategies have, then, a snob value, and work on the same social principle as irony by inviting the audience to join an inner circle of those in the know. In naming names (Stevens, Pound, H. D., Kreymbourg, and so on) Williams makes readers feel they belong to or at least know a small and specific *named* group of *contemporary* writers, or that their precise identity does not matter since they are unknown, and his strategies are designed rather to convey to the audience a sense that the *writing* is primary, unmediated by either a set of social values or the views of the critic; its value lies in putting the reader in touch with the *authentic* feelings of the poet—authentic because originary, with the clear implication that the reader needs no special qualifications to grasp them, since the reader's own feelings are authentic and originary too. The opening clause of "Tradition and the Individual Talent" stands in marked contrast, its *we* affording a regal cachet: "In English writing we seldom speak of tradition": the voice of authority, reflecting its glory upon us. The tone is a quite remarkable combination of cajolery and bullying, since it invites the reader to join the comfortable authority of the speaker's circle while at the same time preserving that distance from the reader on which the writer's authority depends.

The authority thus invoked is English (as specifically contrasted with French), and relies for a sense of that Englishness both on an assumption of communal values and on references to a shared but only vaguely gestured at (literary) past. It is capable of generalizing about poets both alive and dead, implicitly empowers the reader to do the same thing. It talks comfortably of the dead poets "asserting their immortality most vigorously": it is, then, an authority capable of distinguishing the timeless from the temporal, and in doing so adopts metaphysical and spiritual values which at the very least gesture toward the eternal verities and an ideal world of absolutes. When early in his third paragraph Eliot calls for a sense of tradition which will not be a "simple current soon lost in the sand" he no doubt has in mind an audience hungry, at the close of a war which has devastated Europe, for the permanent and the stable, and his prose carefully cultivates balance, rationality, poise, and order. Eliot seeks, then, to reassure the reader by claiming that the certainty of literary judgment is not subject to debate.

The closing sentence of the second paragraph seeks further to reinforce Eliot's authority by introducing the notion of maturity. Eliot's claim that "I do not intend the impressionable period of adolescence, but the period of full maturity" bullies the reader into accepting his qualifications as a guide through the sands of opinion by a species of flattery: the reader is implicitly enjoined to believe himself capable of recognizing "full maturity" even if not exactly possessed of it. At the same time, that *I* quietly detaches the speaker from the *we* who are reading, and asserts the speaker's control within and over this communal discourse: "I do not intend." We are, that is to say, lulled to acquiesce with a prose which takes a superior and confident stance that, in its claim to full maturity, will make gestures of humility to disarm readers by reinforcing their sense of its meticulous care and its superior qualifications: "we are none of us infallible judges of conformity" (paragraph 5); "the point of view which I am struggling to attack" (paragraph 15).

Eliot's prose introduces us to the notion that one function of the mind is to criticize itself. Such criticism necessarily demands a degree of detachment and claims to be impersonal, objective. Hence the second paragraph, through its four-fold repetition of *its* in the second sentence,[13] attempts to detach readers from whatever feelings or emotions they might customarily associate with *nation* or *race*, just as later in the paragraph the six-fold repetition of *he* or *his* serves to distance the reader from the individuality of "the poet," inviting us along the way to consider the "peculiar *essence* of the *man*." The figure of the poet takes a representative cast, then, and by the same token so does the reader. For the reader is tacitly encouraged on the one hand to see Eliot as presenting the reader's own views (if only he could articulate them) and to see himself as Representative Man—as distinct from Representative Poet. Underlying this taxonomy is the implicit notion of a human commonality, what Eliot had two years before (in December 1917) called "the uniformity of human nature."[14] The poet is a specialized form of human being, and Eliot the expert who introduces the reader to the reader's own thought.

The reader, now co-opted into the world of the speaker, is cautioned, by such utterances as "it is true" or "in fact," not to dispute the assertions he meets. Thus in paragraph 13 the phrase "in fact" invites assent to what is essentially a nonsensical utterance: "The poet's mind is in fact a receptacle." By this point in the essay the reader has already assented to the notion of "the mind of Europe" and "the mind of his own country"—minds "which he learns in time to be much more important than his own private mind" (paragraph 6). The reader's potential objections to such propositions have been disarmed by the reflection that his failure to assent to the existence of a "mind of Europe" is a mark of his callowness and inexperience (he hasn't lived long enough to learn it yet), while his assent to the proposition reassures him and ensures that he has reached "the period of full maturity" (paragraph

2). It also, of course, reinforces assent to an idea of an authority superior to and transcending the individual. Such authority is only natural in a critical discourse which, like Eliot's, has a marked penchant for sorting, labeling, cataloguing, measuring, ranking, and ordering.[15] It establishes boundaries, definitions and frameworks, it celebrates hierarchy; though there might be movement among and between the tiered ranks, the hierarchizing principles remain immutable. The essential uniformity of human nature persists across time, as *should* the essential literary and critical enterprise.

All this is largely accomplished by means of appeals to pseudo-logic, pseudo-science, and a vaguely identified sense of "history." This is a sort of discourse in which a metaphor (the mind as receptacle) is presented as fact; in which mind is presented as a metaphysical entity; in which the reader, lulled into being *un*critical when he thinks he's being critical, is bullied into assenting to propositions that may or may not make sense but are delivered *ex cathedra:* "Whoever has approved this idea of order, of the form of European, of English literature, will not find it preposterous that the past should be altered by the present as much as the present is altered by the past" (paragraph 4). "This idea of order" manages to be vague yet to sound precise in the same instant, since it assumes not only that order exists but that it is discernible to all: "The existing order is complete before the new work arrives." While remarking as an aside that this idea of order suggests to the reader that the new must somehow be fitted into an existing framework in order for it to acquire comprehensibility and legitimacy, it is worth stressing that this comment is startlingly like others Eliot is fond of, such as the almost completely baffling advice to the poet in July 1919: "if we are to express ourselves, our variety of thoughts and feelings, on a variety of subjects with inevitable rightness, we must adapt our manner to the moment with infinite variations."[16] "What is one's manner if it is a thing infinitely adaptable?" asks Louis Menand.[17]

Eliot's rhetorical strategies reflect his assumptions, and so the prose exhibits a fondness for rhetorical pairs, for periodic and for balanced sentences, for an air of objectivity and poise. Distinguishing between creative genius and a critical genius (paragraph 2), between historical and aesthetic criticism (paragraph 4), he embraces a taxonomic method which helps to establish a reassuring sense of stability and order while at the same time his evolutionary model of literary history implies not only that current writing must not repeat the past but that the poet has a duty to improve upon it. "The analogy to science is close," he had said in July 1918. "A poet, like a scientist, is contributing toward the organic development of culture."[18] It is a vision of culture as unitary; the model of development is toward completeness, toward the whole. Consequently, it is rule-seeking, and rarely permits uncertainty to ruffle its decorum. The writing is prescriptive: you "must" obtain tradition by great labor (paragraph 3); you "cannot" value the artist alone: you "must" contrast him with the dead (paragraph 4); the poet "must" be conscious of the main current (paragraph 6); the poet "must" be aware that art never improves (paragraph 6); the poet "must" be aware that the mind of Europe changes and that the change is a development (paragraph 6); the poet "must" develop the consciousness of the past (paragraph 8); and so on—the relationship of "change," improve," and "develop" is not investigated. In an essay which was published between the two installments of "Tradition and the Individual Talent" Eliot said that "the *only* way of expressing emotion in the form of art is by finding an 'objective correlative.'"[19] So in his criticism Eliot's procedure often is to state the rule and test the poem. His procedures are deductive, where Williams's are more frequently inductive. Thus Eliot writes, in an essay on Marianne Moore, "Rhythm, of course, is a highly personal matter; it is not a verse form. It is always the real pattern in the carpet, the scheme of organization of thought, feeling and vocabulary, the way in which everything comes together. It is very uncommon. What is certain is that Miss Moore's poems always read very well aloud. That quality is something which no system of scansion can define."[20]

So we have a canonical strategy that works in binaries, in oppositions: the significant and the trivial; the fixed and the floating; the mature and the adolescent; conformity and newness; the permanent and the ephemeral; the whole and the fragmentary; the cultured and the barbaric; the wise and the ignorant; the structured and the formless; the scientific and the intuitive; the impersonal and the personal; the central and the eccentric; the focused and the scattered; the good and the bad; the poet and the man; art and life; the right and the wrong.[21] And the scales are loaded in favor of the group, in favor of the community, in favor of shared knowledge; in favor of connectedness, in favor of the social.

II

Williams is exactly the opposite of Eliot in almost every respect. Whatever authority Williams claims, it is specifically anti-literary—witness not only his determination in the prologue "to keep my mind free from the trammels of literature" (16), but also his deliberate use of cliché. "I have discovered that the thrill of first love passes!" (22) is a far cry indeed from Eliot's careful gravity in diagnosing the hackneyed phrase as "precisely the pretentious and the *un*precise, . . . this is part of its nature. It is not hackneyed because it is old, but because it is dead; and it is dead because it has lost its meaning."[22]

Eliot claims care in thought and diction; Williams does not. "We insist in the face of a hostile majority," Eliot said in July 1918, "that reading, writing, and ciphering does not complete the education of a poet."[23] "I'll write whatever I damn please, whenever I damn please and as I damn please," says Williams (11). As Marianne Moore observed, "To discuss one's friends in print may or may not be necessitated by fealty to art but . . . in citing the idiosyncrasies of friends, note his calmness."[24]

Anecdotal and gossipy, his restive discourse prizes the personal; is disjunctive and fragmentary; frankly partisan; frequently angry or scornful; at times, as Marianne Moore noted, "too abrupt . . . sometimes to follow"; perpetually asserting the authority of the individual reader over the tradition, and yet perfectly willing to be uncertain and even contradictory. In its racy gossipiness and its inclusion of personal letters (from Pound, Stevens, H.D.), in its stories about his mother and about his wife, about Maxwell Bodenheim and Alfred Kreymbourg, it declares its impatience with the decorums of public critical discourse and minimizes distinctions not only between the poet and the man, the writer and the person, but between the writer and his reader. "It is silly to go into a puckersnatch," he says, "because some brass-button-minded nincompoop in Kensington flies off the handle and speaks openly about our United States prize poems" (23). At the same time Williams refuses such large abstractions as human nature, and rarely talks about "poetry" (a word which appears 17 times in "Tradition and the Individual Talent"). As Williams was to say over and over throughout his life, "there are only poems, one at a time."[25]

By means of quotation and anecdote (and typography) Williams provides multiplicity of perspective and voice, of types of language and styles, leaving it to the reader to determine value. So his essay begins by telling us about his mother's fear of getting lost whenever she went outdoors in Rome, and her inability to learn "from benefit or disaster" (7). This parable, in its broken style, instructs the reader (but only if the reader cares to learn from its example of benefit or disaster) the great value of "seeing the thing itself without forethought or afterthought but with great intensity of perception" (8), and thus to read Williams's texts for themselves. "Flexibility of thought," Williams wrote in 1928 or so, "is so precious that sometimes it seems the only virtue of the mind—the only virtue the mind needs."[26] It stands against the kind of thought that resists experience by categorizing it, that seeks to stabilize experience by viewing it through the rigid single perspective of what Pound called "the curse of our time": the monotheistic temperament.[27] Pointing, then, to the singularity of the texts and the writers he quotes and discusses, rather than to what they share with others, Williams asserts the primacy of change, of the ephemeral, over Eliot's abstract permanences. I say *asserts*—Williams's rhetoric is usually highly metaphorical, with lots of repetition, hectoring the reader. It is abusive, impatient, and thoroughly dogmatic, and it rarely offers explanations. He is utterly infuriating.

What is striking about Williams's insistence on the local, on the autonomy of the act of reading the text, on the particular, on the variable, is that despite his dogmatic insistences, his air of abuse and irascible impatience, and the apparent narrowness of his personal views, Williams's rhetorical strategies and his notions of value are dialectical and historicist, while Eliot, despite his dialectical and historicist model of the ways in which the new work affects and is affected by the tradition, adopts a series of rhetorical strategies which are fundamentally ahistorical. Locating merit as it does in notions of permanence, of universal and enduring human nature, Eliot's view of poetry is, finally, non-historical. Williams is revisionist where Eliot is normative, and *his* rhetorical strategies, in their inconsistency, their self-parody, their sheer arbitrariness, seek to undermine that very authority his own critical writing asserts. "You think you are opposing the rich," says one of the improvisations in *Kora in Hell*, "but the truth is you're turning toward authority yourself."[28]

III

In their fundamentally different notions of authority, Eliot and Williams find themselves in radical disagreement even when their writing *(The Waste Land; Kora in Hell)* is canonically transgressive. The salient feature of canonical writing is its legitimizing strategy of claiming kinship to an established and recognizable group. It tends to respect boundaries, definitions, and existing frameworks, and asserts and defends the connectedness, continuity, wholeness, security, and certainty of the literary and critical enterprise. It is thus hardly surprising that in October 1922, when Eliot published *The Waste Land* in the first issue of the *Criterion,* he ensured that it had good canonical company: George Saintsbury, T. Sturge Moore, Herman Hesse, and Dostoevsky, Even without footnotes the poem draws upon a sense of history, tradition, language, and meaning which works to legitimize its fragmentariness by making it appear more apparent than real: it invokes an authority located outside the reader that can be confirmed or verified either through appeal to a literary-philosophical tradition and practice or to a canonical text like an encyclopedia or a dictionary. Eliot's work, that is to say, expects the reader to bring to his or her own reading of the text a series of assumptions and expectations acquired through education and associated with a normative literary culture. Williams, on the other hand, expects the reader to bring to the reading of the text her or his own history; he locates a sense of tradition in a personal experience of a world which, if shared at all, is to be found in the commonwealth of the street rather than in that of the library or the schoolroom.

Eliot's canonical discourse is anglocentric where it is not eurocentric; like all canonical discourse (probably from Samuel Johnson on) it is often prescriptive, seeking to establish control over literary and critical endeavor. It demonstrates a fondness for ranking, ordering, classifying, and cataloguing, and thus has (among other things) a taxonomic bias. Celebrating hierarchies of value, its authority is based on appeals to other authorities and to community of discourse and/or tradition, and it often makes its claims either directly or through analogy to "scientific" objectivity, claiming not only to be rational or "reasonable" but also to be "expert." It thus lays claim to a privileged social, artistic, and philosophic status. It is a discourse of mastery. Williams's noncanonical discourse is generally disjunctive and, in claiming to be "barbaric,"[29] asserts not simply that it is possible to write outside the tradition but that it is thereby reaffirming an older or purer one ("a *reply* to Greek and Latin with the bare hands" is how he put it in the epigraph to *Paterson*—my emphasis); like all non-canonical discourse (probably from William Blake on) it is in its judgments personal, frequently emotional rather than rational or "reasonable," recognizes and even insists upon the validity of discontinuity and uncertainty, and asserts (in its preference for trans-traditional and transgeneric texts) both the singularity of texts and the difficulty if not impossibility of definitively hierarchizing or even describing them. At the same time it is fiercely partisan in its insistence that reading a text is an autonomous experience (process/act) based on the authority of the individual reader and his or her own sensibility rather than on the normative weight of a tradition. It tends to eschew terms like "taste," "sensibility," and "mastery," and legitimizes itself by claiming individuated "authenticity." It is revisionist, and is a discourse of possibility. Programmatic, anarchic, resistant to control, Williams's criticism lets the reader bring to the work his own history rather than that of the culture round him, and it invites disagreement.

Notes

1. The other two poems were "A Goodnight" and "The Late Singer." See *The Collected Poems of William Carlos Williams, Volume One: 1909–1939*, A. Walton Litz and Christopher MacGowan, eds. (New York: New Directions, 1986) 495–496. "The Late Singer" also appeared in the *Egoist*, appropriately enough immediately prefacing Eliot's fourth and final installment of "Reflections on Contemporary Verse," *Egoist* 6.3 (July 1919): 38.

2. T. S. Eliot, "Tradition and the Individual Talent," *Selected Essays* (London: Faber and Faber, 1932) 22. Since this essay has been very frequently reprinted, for ease of reference in what follows I refer all quotations from this essay to their paragraph number. I am grateful to the late Maureen McHale Scobie for her help, especially but not only in sundry statistical counts, in the preparation of this essay.

3. Louis Menand, *Discovering Modernism: T. S. Eliot and His Context* (New York: Oxford UP, 1987) 155.

4. T. S. Eliot, "Reflections on Contemporary Poetry," *Egoist* 4.10 (November 1917): 151.

5. T. S. Eliot, "Observations," *Egoist* 5.5 (May 1918): 69.

6. William Carlos Williams, "Prologue: The Return of the Sun," *Imaginations: Kora in Hell, Spring and All, the Descent of Winter, the Great American Novel, a Novelette & Other Prose*, Webster Schott, ed. (New York: New Directions, 1970) 14.

7. But we only have Williams's word for it, so far as I can tell, that Eliot dismissed him as "of local interest, perhaps." See Williams, *Selected Letters,* J. C. Thirlwall, ed. (New York: McDowell Obolensky, 1957) 141.

8. "Prologue: The Return of the Sun," appeared in the *Little Review* 5.12 (April 1919): 1–10 and 6.1 (May 1919): 74–80. "Tradition and the Individual Talent" appeared in the *Egoist* 6.4 (September 1919): 54–55 and 6.5 (December 1919): 72–73. Williams's *Kora in Hell* was published in an edition of 1000 copies on 1 September 1920; Eliot's *The Sacred Wood* two months later, on 1 November. Although Eliot's essay is dated 1917 in the first edition of his *Selected Essays* (later printings of the essay date it 1919), he told his mother in a letter dated 18 December 1919 that he had "just finished" it—see *The Letters of T. S. Eliot* vol. 1 *1898–1922,* Valerie Eliot, ed. (London: Faber and Faber, 1988) 351; the prologue to *Kora in Hell* is dated 1 September 1918.

9. Of the 38 uses of "*we*" and "*our*" in Eliot's essay, only five occur in the second half (four of them in its opening paragraph (paragraph 11); "*I*" is almost evenly divided (five to four) between the two halves. Of Williams's six uses of "*we*" and "*our,*" four of them are used personally, to refer to Williams and one of his parents or his wife. The remaining two are more general uses, but rather exclude than include the reader in the group: "It is to the inventive imagination that we look for deliverance" (11) seems to refer primarily to the company of poets he has mentioned by name, while "and so we have no choice but to accept" (23) seems to refer to the human race in general.

10. I follow Eliot's practice here in thus gendering his putative "reader," but my usage is not to be read as gender specific.

11. "Apteryx" (i.e., T. S. Eliot), "Professional, or . . ." *Egoist* 5.4 (April 1918): 61.

12. William Carlos Williams, "Now I Ask You!" unpublished typescript in the Poetry Collection of the University Libraries, University at Buffalo, the State University of New York. Comparing himself to Eliot and Pound in 1952 Williams told Kenneth Burke that "I have always felt that I was sweating it out somewhere low, among the reptiles, hidden in the underbrush, hearing the monkeys overhead" (*Selected Letters* 312).

13. A striking feature of Eliot's rhetoric, exploiting as it does an impersonal tone and lots of passive verbs, is his use of the pronoun *it* to dress illogical propositions in a masquerade of logic, as propositionally sound. The word *it* appears 55 times in this essay (as published in the *Egoist;* the lightly revised version in *The Sacred Wood* has 54); of the eleven occasions when it lacks a clear nominal antecedent, six are what grammarians call the expletive use of *it:* "it is a judgment in which . . ."; "it is desirable"; "it is true"; and so forth. A clause like "it is true" is semantically empty; in logic it proposes that everything to the right of "true" has been demonstrated to fulfill the conditions of truth. Eliot uses it disarmingly in this essay, talking about a "test of value" which "it is true, can only be slowly and cautiously applied." In the course of doing so, of course, he reinforces in the reader the notion that his considerations of literary merit have truth-value. Of the remaining five uses of *it,* one is anticipatory, looking ahead to its referent ("Whoever has approved this idea . . . will not find it preposterous that the past should be altered by the present"); one, in the final paragraph of the essay, replaces a noun-infinitival clause ("To divert interest to the poet is a laudable aim, for it would conduce to a juster estimation . . ."); and the remaining three are in a class all by themselves. They are exophoric, which is to say they lack an antecedent in the text, and they thus acquire what I can only call a pseudo-expletive function. They occur in the same paragraph, Eliot's peroration before his finale:

> We must believe that "emotion recollected in tranquility" is an inexact formula. For it is neither emotion, nor recollection, nor, without distortion of meaning, tranquility. It is a concentration, and a new thing resulting from the concentration, of a very great number of experiences which to the practical and active person would not seem to be experiences at all; it is a concentration which does not happen consciously or of deliberation. (paragraph 17)

This use of *it* occurs in a paragraph which ends on a prescriptive note, and which once again bullies the reader, this time into assenting to one of the essay's most famous statements, that "Poetry is not a turning loose of emotion, but an escape from emotion; it is not the expression of personality, but an escape from personality. But, of course, only those who have personality and emotions know what it means to want to escape from these things" (paragraph 17). Of course! In 1944 Williams called this sort of prose "an affectation of authority, an offensive leaking from above" (*Selected Letters* 225).

14. T. S. Eliot, "Turgenev," *Egoist* 4.11 (December 1917): 167.

15. Witness, for example, Eliot's 1923 review of *Ulysses,* which tells us that book "has not been out long enough for any attempt at a complete measurement of its place and significance to be possible." ("Ulysses, Order, and Myth," *Dial* 75.5 [November 1923]: 480.)

16. T. S. Eliot, "Whether Rostand Had Something about Him," *Athenaeum* 4656 (25 July 1919): 665. Though Eliot (like Williams) has a fondness for gnomic and cryptic statements, he often couches them in the form of a paradox: "To conform

merely would be for the new work not really to conform at all; it would not be new, and would therefore not be a work of art." Such paradoxical phrasing is, I believe, a mark of Eliot's willingness to make concessions to his reader.

17. Louis Menand, *Discovering Modernism: T. S. Eliot and His Context* (New York: Oxford UP, 1987) 76.

18. T. S. Eliot, "Contemporanea," *Egoist* 5.6 (June-July 1918): 84. The power and unitive effect of Eliot's appeal to science is reflected in such comments as I. A. Richards's that "mixed modes of writing which enlist the reader's feeling as well as his thinking are becoming dangerous to the modern consciousness with its increasing awareness of the distinction [between them]" (*Principles of Literary Criticism* [London: Kegan Paul, 1934] 3).

19. T. S. Eliot, "Hamlet and His Problems," *Athenaeum* 4665 (26 September 1918): 940 (italics added).

20. T. S. Eliot, "Marianne Moore," *Dial* 75.6 (December 1923): 595.

21. So I read the distinction between the professional and the man of mixed motives.

22. T. S. Eliot, "Studies in Contemporary Criticism," *Egoist* 5.9 (October 1918): 114.

23. T. S. Eliot, "Contemporanea," *Egoist* 5.6 (June–July 1918): 84.

24. Marianne Moore, "Kora in Hell, by William Carlos Williams," *Contact* 4 (Summer 1921): 6; *Complete Prose of Marianne Moore*, Patricia C. Willis, ed. (New York: Viking, 1986) 57.

25. "American and English Poetry: A Questionnaire," *Focus Five: Modern American Poetry.* B. Rajan, ed. (London: Dobson, 1950) 187.

26. William Carlos Williams, *The Embodiment of Knowledge*, R. Loewinsohn, ed. (New York: New Directions, 1974) 126.

27. Ezra Pound, "Studies in Contemporary Mentality," *New Age* 22.11 (10 January 1918): 209.

28. William Carlos Williams, *Imaginations* 73.

29. In 1927 Eliot viewed Stein's *Composition as Explanation* (like the prologue to *Kora in Hell* a specimen of non-canonical critical discourse) as essentially uncivilized and dangerous: "If this is the future, then the future is, as it very likely is, of the barbarians. But this is the future in which we ought not to be interested." T. S. Eliot, "Charleston, Hey! Hey!" *Nation & Athenaeum* 40.17 (29 January 1927): 595.

Basil Bunting

Poet of the North

> A poet is just a poet, but I am a Northumbrian man, born there, and it's always been my home even when I've been living elsewhere.
>
> —Basil Bunting

> The language of a people is the fortress which the enemy first assails; and once that fortress is captured and its stones levelled with the ground, every other stronghold of nationality must inevitably fall.
>
> —Roger Casement

The history of the North of England has never been written, except by southerners.[1] I'm a southerner.

The Northumbrian coal miner poet Joseph Skipsey and his wife Sara, later to be family friends of the Buntings, were appointed custodians of Shakespeare's birthplace in Stratford-on-Avon, on the recommendation of Robert Browning, Edward Burne-Jones, Edmund Gosse, Andrew Lang, William Morris, the Rossettis, Bram Stoker, Alfred Lord Tennyson—the entire Victorian London literary establishment. And when they arrived in Stratford-upon-Avon on 24 June 1889 to take up the job they were nearly turned away from the premises because of their "pronunciation."[2] In *The Slang Dictionary*, published in London in 1864, John Camden Hotten defined *Yorkshire* as "to trick or deceive" and *North* as "cunning. The inhabitants of Yorkshire and the northern counties are supposed, like the canny Scots, to get the better of people in dealing; hence the phrase 'he's too NORTH for me,' *i.e.* too cunning for me to deal with."[3] There is no entry in that dictionary for *South* or for any of the *Home Counties* (those immediately round London). In *Pride and Prejudice* Jane Austen exiled her foolish virgin to Newcastle, the frontier barracks. The war between the North and the South has been a very long one, and it is by no means over. Anyone who dwells in the North knows what it is to live on the edge of power, on the periphery of culture, on the edge of empire, unrecognized by the "official" arbiters of taste, of wealth: to live in the margins. Basil Bunting's writing is inevitably political; he is a northern nationalist and his writing is profoundly subversive of the literary establishment.

If it is likely, as Bunting suggested, that Northumbrian culture and even nationhood might have recovered from the Viking invasion, it is surely and unhappily true that, in Bunting's words, "after the Norman conquest [Northumberland] was governed as a conquered province of Norman England for five full centuries, constantly repressed by the authorities at York"[4]—with the exception, he should have added, of the ambiguous and turbulent authority of the Prince-Bishops of Durham. Such control is not easily purchased (witness the fate of Walcher of Lorraine, first Norman Bishop of Durham, murdered in Gateshead, 15 May 1090).[5] Elizabeth moved the Council of the North from York to London, but she maintained the Norman style of government, purchasing a northern "peace" as others had before at a price that is still being paid—the attrition of Northumbrian culture and land through a policy of rarely benevolent neglect.[6] For the last eight or nine hundred years anyone living in the North has known that power is centered in London, a London which views the North as unimportant and uncivilized: Queen Elizabeth I, harried by threats from Scotland and by international Catholicism, made sure of *that,* and she never in her life traveled further north than Stamford (in Lincolnshire) and Norwich, nor further west than Bristol. But she succeeded (where earlier monarchs had failed) through the ruthlessness with which she put down the 1569 rebellion, devastating once again the North Country and its people.

The Rising of the North was sparked off by the arrival in the North of Mary Queen of Scots, the Catholic heir to the throne, and contained and quashed with virtually no bloodshed. But it was bloodily punished. It began on 14 November 1569 at four in the afternoon, when the Catholic Earls of Westmorland and Northumberland (who had feared to obey an order to attend the Royal Court), accompanied by 500 armed men and 60 horses, entered Durham Cathedral, tore up the Bibles and prayer books, unearthed the ancient relics, celebrated Mass, and then left, at 5:00 p.m. According to Lord Huntingdon's report to Sussex, there were at most some 5500 rebels, of whom 3800 were "of all sorts of footmen, the more part being unarmed, arising one lie of artificers, and the meanest sort of husbandmen." Not above 500 of the footmen were "armed to any purpose . . . ; and those only with bows and arrows, jacks and bills."[7] After the incursion into Durham Cathedral the rebels were perpetually on the retreat: they were hopelessly unorganized and underfunded, and the only battle was the so-called Battle of Hexham, on 18 December 1569. It was a skirmish between the retreating rebels and Bowes's men; so far as I can tell no one was killed. But fearful of further Catholic uprisings (Norfolk had attempted a Catholic uprising in February 1569), Elizabeth wanted systematic control, and forbade any of the ordinary forms of justice; she demanded that 700 of the rank and file be executed under martial law, and the nobles and landowners be attainted for treason or outlawed in order that their property be forfeit to the Crown. Over the next three weeks, under the orders of the Earl of Sussex, in a bitterly cold winter, the roads blocked with snow, Sir George Bowes marched "with greate zeal and loyaltie" through Tynedale and Redesdale killing plundering and destroying, saying "the best fruit a tree can beare is a dead traytour."[8] But Elizabeth was insatiable: on 11 January 1570, "we marvel that we have heard of no executions."[9]

On 1 January 1570 the Earl of Sussex, caught between his sympathies for Norfolk and his loyalty to the Queen, was complaining to Lord Cecil that everybody had declared open season on the North: "my L. of Warwick and my L. Admiral . . . have, by their warrants, seised . . . all the landes, goodes, leases and cattelles, that appertayned to any man that was betwene Newcastle and Dancaster; and their Marshall, Mr. of the campe, and other officers, have dreven all the cattell out of the contrey, and ransomed the people in such miserable sort, and made such open and common spoile, as the lik, I think, was never harde of, putting no difference between the good and the badde." Lord Willoughby "taketh all and leaveth nothing, and driveth more cattell for his owne portion than all the groundes he hath will fede, and yet he is no lieutenant." Sussex warned Cecil that "her Majestie hath loste above 10,000 poundes" because her supporters are stealing what should be forfeit to the Crown.[10]

On 4 January 1570 the Bishop of Durham reported that "the cuntre is in great mysere; and . . . the number of offendors is so grete, that few innocent are left to trie the giltie."[11] And at the end of it all (in William Hutchinson's words) "Sir George Bowes made an inhuman boast, that in a tract of country, sixty miles in length, and forty in breadth, betwixt Newcastle and Wetherby, there was scarce a town or a village wherein he had not sacrificed some of the inhabitants to his thirst for blood."[12] In Durham Sussex hanged 63 constables *at once,* at the same time;[13] he told Bowes to "mak th examples grete" in Ripon and Tadcaster: "if you find not suffycyent nombres within the townes, . . . take of other townes, and bryng them to th executyon to those places; for it is necessary that th executyon be grete in apparance."[14] The rebels were often hanged, beheaded, and quartered, in York, in Northallerton, and probably elsewhere. Thomas and Christopher Norton, two of those who led the incursion into Durham cathedral, were on 27 May 1570 hanged drawn and quartered at Tyburn, "their heads set on London bridge, and their quarters upon the sundry gates of the city of London."[15] Thomas watching Christopher's execution before suffering his own helps us remember what "ruthless" means.

By 4 February 1570 Sir Thomas Gargrave was reporting that to bring in all offenders would leave many places bare of inhabitants (500 already having been executed).[16] A quarter of a century later, travelers reported that you could travel from Carlisle to Durham without meeting any settled population.[17] When King James I of England and VI of Scotland visited Durham in 1603, "pestilence was a frequent visitor, villages were frequently unpopulated, and tillage decayed. Starving families wandered from place to place in search of food," and the whole border-country was "the resort of outlaws, vagabonds and rovers, from all parts of the kingdom, who were harboured and countenanced by the inhabitants, and lived by plunder and execution of 'black-mail.' "[18] The summary of forfeited estates that went to the Crown fills "two ponderous quarto volumes."[19] William Cobbett, in 1832, noted, "from CHESHIRE to NEWCASTLE, I have never seen *one single labourer's cottage by the side of the road!*" and commented that between Durham and Newcastle "the absence of *homesteads,* the absence of barns, and of labourers' cottages, clearly show, that agriculture is a sort of novelty."[20]

Bunting was born toward the tag end of an energetic cycle of Northumbrian chauvinism, of which the Newcastle Literary and Philosophical Society was an important center. When he was in his twenties and possibly before then, he read widely and in detail in northern history in the Lit and Phil library—and his starting point was Cuthbert Sharp's history of *The Rising in the North,* otherwise known as the Bowes papers, from which much of my brief sketch is drawn, and to which he would return shortly before the end of his life. It is scarcely surprising, then, that in *Caveat Emptor,* the typescript version of his poems that he put together in 1935, Bunting changed the title of two poems written in 1931 and grouped under the heading "Jenghis," written in 1931, from first and second "fragment" to first and second "vestige" (they are collected as "Vestiges" [CP 116–117]).[21] Those poems do not attempt to recover or retrieve or lament for a lost past; they do try to record it, each ironically counterpointing the other, with no scrap of any sort of archaeological desire to restore. "The world is one, the Khan divides with none," reads a line later excised from the first poem; both poems offer vestiges of a world wasted by conquest or faced with the problems of maintaining a monolithic and centralized political power won by conquest. And ten years later, in 1941, Bunting called his own poems "tracings from a world that's dead" (CP 129). He does so without a scrap of regret or nostalgia. "Vestige" is Latin for footprint. Poem after poem in his *Odes* and the *Overdrafts* speak of traces overwritten by time but persisting through to the present: vestiges. Vestiges of a history and a tradition once powerful and now lost, or threatened, or likely to be almost forgotten: fragments of a past, like the fragments of Northumbrian crosses and sculpture recorded between 1885 and 1930 by J. Romilly Allen and G. Baldwin Brown, and so painstakingly catalogued by Rosemary Cramp and her team in 1984.[22]

Bunting's position as a writer of English poetry in this century has been notably marginal, and, I believe, deliberately so. It is part and parcel not only of his identification of himself as a Northumbrian writer, but also of his deliberate and conscious determination to be a *modern* writer. By his own account he had reached the essential conclusions of his own poetics—or as he put it, what needs to be done in poetry now—by 1919, long before he'd even heard of either Pound or Eliot, whose aims and conclusions he found remarkably like his own: conciseness, simplicity, musicality. "The intention," he said in a lecture at Newcastle University in 1968, is "to escape from the hampering measures imposed by our memory of several centuries of English verse written to models imported from other lands."[23] But unlike Eliot, who in a series of remarkable essays written between 1916 and 1919, some of them collected in *The Sacred Wood,* carefully inscribed himself into the tradition molded on works imported from other lands—a tradition central, monolithic, and possessed of power—Bunting throughout his career carefully problematizes that tradition, problematizes the dominant ideology, problematizes the hegemony of English Letters, by asserting the primacy of sound over meaning, by changing the syntax and sound of the poem, by denying the central tenets of the Romantic heritage. For Romanticism's love of bombast, splendor, and the pursuit of the sublime, Bunting substituted the primacy of "fact." As a sixth-form boy he got into serious trouble with his schoolmaster for spending his Sunday afternoon walks crossing out all the unnecessary words in Shakespeare's sonnets (sometimes less than two dozen words were left; on one occasion, none at all). It was an exercise he would take up again. On 13 July 1931 he wrote to Harriet Monroe that "I am engaged in rewriting Shakespeare's sonnets. They can do with it. After sufficient cutting and straightening out of inversions, rather a nice poem should emerge."[24] That is a radical subversion and decimation of the English literary canon, and confirms and indeed declares Bunting's own position on its margins.

His position as a Northumbrian writer makes him turn—just as his position as a modern writer does—to the margins of the culture. Or even beyond them. So he rewrites the tradition of the great poets, incorporating into his list writers absent from Pound's, from Eliot's, and from the academician's. Some of them are almost completely unknown in the Western tradition, and only three of them are English: "Homer. Ferdosi. Dante. Wyatt. Spenser. Wordsworth. Whitman. Yeats. Pound. Zukofsky. Jones. MacDiarmid."[25] That's a hell of a list. And always central, always there, from the beginning, Wordsworth, who he denies is a Romantic poet. "I've been thinking," he told Louis Zukofsky in a letter, 6 August 1953,

> about how and where I got whatever I know and feel about poetry, and the more I think the bigger Malherbe's part in it seems. Wordsworth, when I was a small kid, showed me what it was; Rossetti's translations from the Dolce Stil people, in my teens, enlarged the scope. Horace gave me the first inkling of how it was done (odes). Malherbe produced all I afterwards found in Ez's writing except what I'd already got from Horace. Ez and Spenser, great galleries of technical accomplishment. Lucretius. Dante. And after that, Hafez for what I got from Horace (and Ez from Chinese) only more, taken further: Manuchehri, greater and more splendid gallery that Ez and Spencer: Wyatt: the Mo'Allaqat: and for sheer pleasure, when I am not out to learn or have my mind fixed, for diversion, for sheer living, Homer and Ferdosi. (TxU)

So, too, Bunting denies utterly the modernism and even the contemporaneity of such contemporaries as Auden and Spender, finding instead his closest connections and sympathy with Americans, outsiders: William Carlos Williams, Ezra Pound, and Louis Zukofsky. He identified his own peers among British writers as Hugh MacDiarmid and David Jones, a Marxist Scot and a London Welshman. I think it is difficult from the perspective of the 1990s to remember how marginal (indeed how alien) to English readers, critics, and publishers American writers besides Eliot were; notice the history not only of Ezra Pound in Britain, satirized, lampooned, attacked, but of William Carlos Williams, who did not find an English publisher until he was dead.[26] It is extremely difficult to imagine the sort of perspicacity and courage it took for a young Englishman in the early 1920s to hitch his wagon to the stars of Pound and Eliot. And even Yeats.

His adoption of a marginal position may also, of course, be an aspect of his Quakerism, for he shares with Quakers the distrust of any authority but one's own.[27] But the Quakerism itself feeds into (and on) his Northumbrianness: conquered peoples, subject races, "the conquered province of Norman England," all resist the monolithic central power, in art as in politics. The subject races reject the ideologies which serve to bolster the oppressor's power, reject, therefore, (certain sorts of) abstractions, the metaphysics which justifies their subjugation and the syntax of politics which assures that subjugation. Instead subject races, underdogs, turn to the concrete, the physical, the practical: to the flesh; they resort to fact, to the tangible, to objects. Bunting's poetry is remarkably full of *things,* of *facts.*

Isolated from the rest of England for many years, the North historically was, in the words of Robert Wood, a "closed circle of almost feudal government with its web of families and fiercely loyal dependents known to outsiders as 'the inly working North.'"[28] This is the North that Elizabeth I and her ministers sought to break. Bunting himself acknowledged that on his mother's side he was "related to most of the border families," not least of them the Charltons, "my favourites. They had fourteen of them hanged at once after a border raid."[29] In very important ways, difficult for an outsider to grasp, the North is not a part of England but is rather, as Hugh MacDiarmid once ventured,[30] almost a separate country. As recently as early Tudor times—not long before Elizabeth, then—England was still officially split into the two great mediaeval administrative and political divisions, "England" and "England beyond Trent." And the Prince Bishopric of Durham, until its dissolution in 1832, was effectively a state within a state. In the middle of the nineteenth century, when the Elizabethan State Papers began to be calendared and published, documents relating to Yorkshire and anywhere north of Yorkshire were classed as "Border Correspondence" and remained unpublished for a further 25 or 30 years. Marginal, then, and of little "real" interest, use, or importance. A hundred or so years later, on 11 June 1974, the regional director of the Northern Arts Association told Brian Swann that Bunting's work on behalf of Northumbrian art was "a bit fatuous." And he continued: "I'm not from these parts. I'm from the Home Counties. I regard my mission as bringing arts to the North. Northumberland is dead, and its so-called folk-culture. So are the pits."[31] Less than six months later, as president of the Northern Arts association, Bunting told his audience in his annual address that "the central task of this institution should be to encourage not of course imitations of ancient [Northumbrian] models, but whatever seems to be conceived in their spirit. It is useless to import southerners, however skilled they may be in their art. They can only steer us further from the course that agrees with our deepest nature. And we should try to recall our . . . schools to the study and the habit of specifically Northumbrian art."[32] Official culture has very little room for northern margins, and will not bother even to look to see what's going on. It is the nature of power to hold to concepts of Absolute Reality, which it controls, and to which it claims to be obedient: Necessity, Justice, Morality, Intelligibility, Art. At best, it views all deviations from the norms it proclaims as error; at worst, as crime, or as treason.

In this regard it is worth noting Bunting's distrust of conventional verse; he would habitually and out of belief consign meaning to the margins of poetry, preferring to foreground its formal aspects, its formal properties, in order to rescue it from its official identity and function as "discourse," "communication," and the like. This unease has its political aspects, for by moving meaning to the periphery of the poem he is seeking to avoid a centrist monologic utterance characteristic of installed power. This unease also has its aesthetic aspects, for it affects the syntax as well as the diction of the poem, and thus affects its shape as well as its intelligibility. "I do not see why people should want to 'understand' everything in a poem," he told Alan Neame in 1951.[33]

But why put intelligibility at risk? Like language, and like aesthetics, intelligibility is a social and cultural phenomenon, it's a matter of mutual though possibly unspoken agreement, a matter of convention. The tradition into which Eliot so carefully inscribed himself through the essays in *The Sacred Wood* rests on agreed habits of syntax, rhythms and sequences of thought, intonation, figurative language, and range of diction. The normative impulses of literary and linguistic tradition reinforce notions of intelligibility (and of syntax!) which themselves constitute the intellectual legitimation of political rule, of the hegemony, whose very existence resides in and relies upon tradition for its moral and cultural legitimation, if it is not to be installed and maintained by power of brute force. Writers who for one reason or another find themselves occupying a marginal position in a culture must place authorized received syntax and intelligibility on the periphery of their own work, lest that work reinforce the power structure, lest that work reinforce the cultural categories and assumptions that it seeks to challenge. To overstate it by putting it bluntly, you cannot resist evil by evil means. Characteristically, Bunting pointed to this dilemma much more concretely than I can in a letter he wrote to Ezra Pound, 21 March 1934:

> I knew several miner's leaders at one time and another, from checkweighmen to old William Straker (the chap who had found out in the course of fifty years or so of mining politics that billiards was worse than booze). I even talked once or twice to old Charley Fenwick, before he died, a man who had been a Northumberland miner's official since the middle of the last century and went down the pit to work at the age of nine. Damn it, I was brought up in all that, Joseph Skipsey is said to have dandled me when I was a baby, and he'd been down the pit before the first factory acts touched them. I was on the spot when the View Pit was flooded and forty-five men drowned, I heard what the men had to

> say about it and the whole cursed system when there wasn't any question of politics, mining or otherwise, but just sheer human commonsense. My grandfather, whom I knew pretty well when I was a kid, was a miner, son of a miner. I know the solidity of those people, and I watched it break up in 26, when I was all the time in a mining village, took the chair at one of Cook's meetings, stuck a knife in the tyres of a government strikebreaking lorry and tried unsuccessfully nearly every paper in the country to get the scandalous faked benches of magistrates who condemned the strikers to years of hard labour shown up. Not even the independent labour party's rag would publish the facts. (CtY)

A northern poet. Centralized power, especially remote centralized power, is the power of self-regard and self-interest; it is inevitably a power of cruel mismanagement, for it is divorced from the immediacy of the local. The absentee landlord. "Our only hope for our children," Bunting told Dorothy Pound on 11 December 1954, "is to destroy uniformity, centralisation, big states and big cities and big factories and give men a chance to vary and live without more interference than it is the nature of their neighbours to insist on" (CtY).

The question of dialect is crucial to this issue. Bunting ascribed the misreading of Wordsworth as a Romantic rather than an eighteenth-century poet mainly to the fact that, reading him in a southron voice, "his great contribution to the range of English sound has usually been overlooked," and the music of the poetry has been lost simply because his southern readers could not hear it. Their attention has thus been drawn by default to "real or imaginary quirks of mysticism," and they have failed to notice that Wordsworth is "the most skilful, and the most complex, of narrative poets in English": "Two hundred years ago Standard English had not been invented and there was neither a BBC nor a system of education determined to make us talk alike. Wordsworth spoke as men spoke where he was born, with broad vowels and a marked R. He kept his native tongue in spite of Cambridge & London and Somerset and Leicestershire. Southerners found it hard to follow his conversation. . . . Wordsworth did not write dialect; but he composed aloud . . . in the language he spoke, and that was not the Koiné we are all taught to use now."[34] The koiné. Standard English: the common dialect, the language used throughout the English-speaking world, a language *theoretically* free of regional and class markers, *theoretically* free of regional and class markers and identity, but in fact the language of administrative and executive political and legal power—just as Latin once was. A language which, precisely because it is "standard," establishes social, political, and cultural hierarchies in which the speaker of the language spoken where she or he was born is consigned to the lower classes, or is made to feel inferior—or both. The koiné debases living local speech into vulgarity, alienating speakers from their own tongue, thereby shaming their origins. It's the language I'm talking now.

In the spring of 1898, two years before Bunting was born, family friend Robert Spence Watson organized a series of lectures at the Newcastle Lit and Phil on *Northumbrian History, Literature, and Art.* There, in a lecture on "Dialect Speech in Northumberland," R. Oliver Heslop's most urgent necessity was to point out to his audience that the Northumbrian dialect is not a class marker, and is not properly speaking a dialect at all.[35] Spoken by folk in all stations of life, it is, he said, a language fully as versatile, subtle, and expressive as the so-called Standard "Modern Literary English," which is itself just as much a dialect as is Northumbrian. Dialect—the use of local speech. When Basil Bunting was four years old the American novelist Henry James—a voice for the unifying standardizing force of the koiné if ever there was one—called for a "tone-standard." He said, "A care for tone is part of a care for many other things besides; for the fact, for the value of good breeding. . . . The idea of good breeding . . . is one of the most precious conquests of civilization, the very core of our social heritage."[36] Now, *that* is the voice of the ruling class. And its tone is one of detachment from the messy business of daily living, the details of ordinary life, the physical world of the body, the tangibility of bodily senses, detached from sensation. Which is why Bunting hated Latinate diction, which is the language of the administrative class, so much, and why he disliked FitzGerald's *Rubaiyat of Omar Khayyam:* he found its loftiness of language a betrayal of the perceived world as well as of Omar.[37] He confessed at one point that he should have used the Northumbrian word *gathers* instead of a word from Latin when he began the preface to his *Collected Poems* with the sentence: "A man who collects his poems screws together the boards of his coffin."[38] *Gathers* has an immediacy of physical activity about it, everything pulled in by the sweep of the arms all at once, close, that *collects* has not, and it is reinforced by the half-rhyme cognate of that *together.* "A man who gathers his poems screws together the boards of his coffin."

Language. Language divorced from the immediate is language divorced from what Bunting called "our deepest nature."[39] "I prefer any dialect of English or any other *spoken* language to the six-six-sixth generation of bastard Latin," he told Louis Zukofsky on 27 April 1934 (TxU), for that is not the language people actually speak, but is the language of books. He admired the sixteenth-century French poet Malherbe because "whenever [he] had written anything he would go down to the market and get the women there to read it to him, and he would pay them if there were any words they didn't know. He didn't expect them to understand what he was aiming at or even enjoy the poem, but he wished above all things to be meticulous about keeping his language clear and plain."[40]

At a glance this has something the flavor of the Romantic notion that some words are more real than others. "There are many words which are genuine and indigenous," Thoreau wrote in his *Journal* in 1858, "and have their root in our natures, not made by scholars, and as well understood by the illiterate as others. There are also a great many words which are spurious and artificial, and can only be used in a bad sense, since the thing they signify is not fair and substantial,—such as the *church,* the *judiciary,* to *impeach,* etc., etc. They who use them do not stand on solid ground. It is vain to say they try to preserve them by attaching other words to them as the *true* church, etc. It is like towing a sinking ship with a canoe."[41] But that is too pat, too metaphysical: it suggests that the real comes in layers, or in levels. It is the voice of what William Carlos Williams in the "Prologue" to *Kora in Hell* called "an easy lateral sliding."[42] What Bunting insists on is much more difficult, for he insists on the sheer *physicality* of a world which is (in his words) "above all, opaque and complex"[43]—and that opacity cannot be evaded through the Platonic ruse of calling it a code for a "higher" meaning, a "book" which speaks of a "higher" reality, a window through which we see the "spirit" or "soul" of things—for that is to assert that the opaque is transparent. "I began," he wrote Dorothy Pound on 11 December 1954, "with a wish to limit my aims (abolish the protection of 'game' in England and extend the range of black-faced sheep), and they were still far too abstract and ambitious to do anything but harm if I persisted. I haven't, and after my first twenties I never had, any idea of setting all or most things to right by some scheme . . . because I am sure that any scheme, anything extensive or uniform, must put more and always more men under the mortmain of 'administration'" (CtY). How can you possibly "improve" a world which is above all else opaque, without seeing it as a disguise for something else, in the process denying or side-stepping its complexity. Things are like facts: they are not simple, nor are they easily seen; William Carlos Williams thought "there are not so many things in the world as we commonly imagine."[44] Bunting's hatred of abstractions, his hatred of centralized government, rests on the notion, as he told Zukofsky, 27 April 1934, that "half the evils in the world come from verbalism, i.e. imagining that abstract words have anything more than a grammatical meaning or function. Adjectives, numbers, symbols like the word God, eat away all sense of reality and land us in every kind of social and economic mess, when people begin to think they correspond to anything genuine. . . . A poet's business is to get a language that won't have to rely on anything so slipshod as Algebra" (TxU). And so in 1938 he angrily broke with Pound, whose obsessive monotheism of economics utterly contradicted Pound's own polytheist sight of the world. "If you start thinking about economics in terms of eats, drinks and sleeps it's liable to be a little less misleading," he told Pound on 6 April 1935. "Thems words wiv a meaning, not like blasted cash and credit. They got some relation to myself but money never had." (CtY)

It always comes down to the empirical, the practical, the physical, the tangible, the felt, sensed world. In a marginalized culture, governed like a conquered province, the most urgent necessity is to find out where your choices lie, what your priorities are—and those priorities are always those of survival; so they are physical. "There's really no need of any theory for what gives pleasure through the ear, music or poetry."[45] And who concocts unnecessary theory? On 1 December 1934 he told Zukofsky it was "the imbeciles who imagine philosophy is a higher wisdom than rhyme" (TxU). So in poetry he hates what he calls "the hampering haze of glory,"[46] preferring rather "to read . . . very solid lumps of *fact*. . . . I like vowels that you can open your mouth and bawl," he said. "Poetry is just making noises, you know, it's mouthfuls of air. The meaning is hardly ever of any importance."[47] And so we come back to the heresy, at least from London's point of view: "Diction is secondary to rhythm in the genesis of poetry and must give way."[48] Rhythm is physical, and therefore prior.

But there are problems. Bunting is both outside and inside the culture and the koiné at the same time, using what he subverts, subverting what he uses. But it is not an ironic relationship, and his linguistic, syntactic, and formal stance is not finally satiric. It is compositional. The Northumbrian writer, insofar as he nourishes his difference, his distinctness, his Northumbrianness, like any outcast views society politically, yet at the same time—if he is to write at all, if he is to be heard or to be read—he is obliged to work within the culture too, presenting himself perhaps as apolitical. Prefiguring subversion, his work equally signifies order. Which is why there are so many apparent contradictions, conflicts, and inconsistencies in Bunting's work: between the private personal verse, individual, and the public; between the private personal voice, individual, and the public; between the strictly local and the koiné; between the insistence on the primacy of sound and the demand that the poem have matter. And so on. It is a question of balance, and of to what end that balance is used. "Subversion in music," says Jacques Attali in *Noise:*

The Political Economy of Music, "opposes a new syntax to the existing syntax, from the point of view of which it is noise."[49] Witness Peter Dale's obsessive and idiotic ramblings about Bunting.[50] Syntax. Noise.

By and large the surface of Bunting's poetry—the noise it makes—is astonishingly turbulent: the play of consonants, the bumpiness of the sound, the pauses and accelerations afforded by the play of vowels and the play of syntax, the apparent lurches, stops, and starts, all combine to suggest something of the Northumbrian landscape. Here is the death of Bloodaxe, figure of the poet (CP 68):

> Loaded with mail of linked lies,
> what weapon can the king lift to fight
> when chance-met enemies employ sly
> sword and shoulder-piercing pike,
> pressed into the mire,
> trampled and hewn until a knife
> —in whose hand?—severs tight
> neck cords? Axe rusts . . . .

(There's a smack of Ferdosi in that description.) These lines break a lot of rules—they don't even make a "correct" sentence. The alliteration, which we expect would speed the poem up because alliteration usually does, instead slows it down so much that we scarcely notice it as *alliteration* at all, so caught up are we in its *rhythmic* effect, the clustering of those consonants. And what is surprising is not so much the shifts from voiced to unvoiced and back again (those are a habitual Bunting strategy), or that the dominance of *l* and *d* in the opening lines gives way to *s* and *t* at the end; what is surprising is first that the consonants appear to be tightly organized into patterns strongly reminiscent of Welsh *cynghanedd,* and second that a lot of the slowing of pace is brought about through the conjunction of sounds which ordinarily speed the language up: liquids *(l* and *r)* and sibilants *(s).* Breaking the rules.

Such writing is characteristic of pretty well the whole of Bunting's career, for example Ode 5, "To Helen Egli," written in 1927 (CP 101). Here too notice the consonants, but also the lovely last line, where after all that consonantal blockage almost filling two quatrains, everything at last trips forward into a quite lovely little dance:

> Empty vast days built in the waste memory seem a jail for
> Thoughts grown stale in the mind, tardy of birth, rank and inflexible:

love and slow selfpraise, even grief's cogency, all emotions
timetamed whimper and shame changes the past brought to no utterance.

Ten or ten thousand, does it much signify, Helen, how we
date fantasmal events, London or Troy? Let Polyhymnia
strong with cadence multiply song, voices enmeshed by music
respond bringing the savour of our sadness or delight again.

There's a muscularity to this speech, and the syntax is quite hard to follow until you've sorted it out, especially if you read it with the eye rather than the ear. The chunky syntax forces the reader to speak the poem.

This is especially clear, I think, in the opening sentence of "At Briggflatts Meetinghouse" (CP 145), which I take to be thoroughly representative of Bunting's verse. I also take it to be thoroughly representative of what he believed constituted the essence of Northumbrian art. Five words:

Boasts time mocks cumber Rome.

Read them with the eye only, and they make a list. And we can't tell how that list is ordered or organized. The consonants seem to offer a clue—or do they? *Boasts time*: plural/singular? Noun/verb? *Mocks cumber*: plural/singular? Noun/verb? The consonants make lovely patterns, quite complicated little patterns:

STS KSK

little symmetries:

STSTM MKSKM

almost a mirror pattern:

BSTSTM MKSKMB

—and at the very end,

RM.

And a new pattern—or a variant—will begin again, next sentence. So the mind, reading with the eye, scutters about the surface, elaborating unlikely or at any rate *abstract* because undetermined or more accurately unstable meanings. And suddenly the sense emerges:

> Boasts time mocks, cumber Rome.

Abstraction resolves into the solidity of sense. And the caesura is central, by syllable count, though not by quantity—which is why there's another word in that line, so it reads

> Boasts time mocks cumber Rome. Wren [.]

It's a perfectly clear sentence, with a *simple* meaning following the word order of speech. This, *reading,* is a compositional process, in which the elements coalesce into a pattern. Here is Bunting, describing a carpet page of the Lindisfarne Gospels: it is "a page entirely filled with interwoven patterns. . . . What you see at first sight is usually only the perpetual crisscross of lines, or perhaps some elements of the design, which may be more ribbons, or may be forms that suggest the forms of birds, animals or foliage, extraordinarily simplified and changed. . . . But as you gaze at one of these so-called carpet pages, little by little the confusion of ornament sorts itself out, you notice how carefully balanced the whole is, and a great cross emerges from the welter of ornament." And the pattern is left for the beholder "to discover it for himself."[51] This is what I mean by a compositional process, which so decentralizes the act of writing that—though Bunting's notion or general intention for the poem is more or less clear, and the pattern is of his making—finally the act of comprehension and pleasure and "understanding" is placed at the extremity of the local, in the reader. There is a relinquishing of control which you don't find in say Auden or Spender. Zukofsky called it trusting the reader. "It took me four months to get it right," Bunting wrote to Jonathan Williams on 16 March 1975, of "At Briggflatts Meetinghouse" (NBuU). And clearly, whatever else is going on here, the immense concentration, the immense condensation which gives rise to such apparently difficult syntax comes about for the sake of the sound. Look at those patterns. Diction is secondary to rhythm. Sound is primary.

Peter Makin thinks that the theme of *Briggflatts is* its activity—weaving and interweaving. Kenneth Cox, suggesting that the theme is "out and back" or something similar, at the same time fears that he is being too abstract in saying so.[52] Ornament. Elaboration. Pattern. *Sound* is primary, on the local level of the syllable and of the letter; and on the global level of the five Cantos of *Briggflatts.*

With such Northumbrian heresies I should stop. But I think Basil Bunting himself should have the final word. These words to me epitomize the poet *as* Northumbrian, epitomize Basil Bunting, poet of the North. It is from his notebook for *Briggflatts,* but it is not (or is it?) part of the poem:

> The scholar ought to be like the poet,
> an Ishmael, scanted and feared;
> a magician, impious, to be
> consulted in secrecy and shame.
> Only men rejected by men can keep
> either truth or beauty in view.
> The moment advantage has a
> part in his studies or his craft,
> his work perishes.[53]

I don't think that's gender specific. But I do think it tells the North what to do.

Notes

Quotations from Basil Bunting's letters are from materials held in various libraries, which are coded as follows:

NBuU	The Poetry Collection of the University Libraries, University at Buffalo, State University of New York; Bunting-Pickard Collection, or Jargon Society Collection, as appropriate.
TxU	Harry Ransom Humanities Research Center, University of Texas at Austin.
CtY	Yale Collection of American Literature, Beinecke Rare Book and Manuscript Library, Yale University.

Epigraphs. The first epigraph is by Basil Bunting from Eric Mottram, "Conversation with Basil Bunting on the Occasion of his 75th Birthday, 1975," broadcast by the BBC on 7 March 1975, printed in *Poetry Information* 19 (Autumn 1978): 3; partly printed also in "Out Loud," *Listener* 94 (28 August 1975): 274; the second, from Roger Casement, *The Language of the Outlaw* (Dublin? 1903?). Quoted in bookseller's *Catalogue 79: Literature, Including Recent Acquisitions* (New Haven: William Reese, 1989), item 243.

1. Bunting himself noted, in the "Afterthoughts" to *Briggflatts:* "all the school histories are written by and for Southrons" (*Complete Poems,* Richard Caddel, assoc. ed. [Newcastle upon Tyne: Bloodaxe, 2000] 226. All further references abbreviated CP and cited parenthetically in the text). In his introduction to Gerald Brenan's

A History of the House of Percy from the Earliest Times down to the Present Century, W. A. Lindsay, ed., 2 vols. (London: Freemantle, 1902), W. A. Lindsey states flatly "our popular school histories, written in the Protestant interest and to flatter the national vanity, are far—very far—from veracious" (v. 1. xiv). G. Baldwin Brown makes the similar accusation that the history of the shift in the Northern Church under Wilfrid in the seventh century from Celtic to Roman orders has been distorted to serve the interest of "the ecclesiastical power of Rome," with every scene in that history "accentuated by professional applauders" (*The Arts in Early England: The Life of Saxon England and its Relation to the Arts* [London: Murray, 1903] 159). This follows the lead of Joseph Barber Lightfoot, Bishop of Durham, who claimed in a sermon preached in 1887 that "not Augustine, but Aidan, is the true apostle of England" (*Leaders in the Northern Church: Sermons Preached in the Diocese of Durham,* 2nd ed. [London: Macmillan, 1891] 9).

2. Robert Spence Watson, *Joseph Skipsey: His Life and Work* (London: Unwin, 1909) 73.

3. John Camden Hotten, *The Slang Dictionary; or, The Vulgar Words, Street Phrases, and "Fast" Expressions of High and Low Society* (London: Hotten, 1864) 273, 189.

4. Basil Bunting, *Basil Bunting on Poetry,* Peter Makin, ed. (Baltimore: Johns Hopkins UP, 1999) 16.

5. As a result of Walcher's murder, Odo, Bishop of Bayeux, was sent by William to punish those guilty of the outrage. "Having crossed the Tyne, the chiefs of the offenders being fled at his approach, he wasted the country, put many to death, and mutilated others, who were of consanguinity to the murderers, and could not pay the price set on their heads; amongst whom many innocent wretches suffered under the avenger's sword. . . . He desolated that part of the province so as to reduce it to a dreary solitude and desert" (William Hutchinson, *The History and Antiquities of the County Palatine, of Durham* [Newcastle: Hodgson; London: Robinson, 1785–1794] v. 1, 131). There is an excellent brief account of Walcher's career and death in the *DNB.*

6. For a detailed account of the Council of the North under Henry VIII in York as a law court and as a political entity, see Rachel R. Reid, *The King's Council in the North* (London: Longmans Green, 1921). A valuable study, this book is too little known.

7. In 1833, Sir Cuthbert Sharp discovered a large collection of original letters, copies of letters and other documents relating to the rebellion of 1569 in a closet in the library at Gibside, and (with the help of a Mr. Hutt) in an old pine box in the armory of the Derwent and Gibside yeomanry. Sorted and repaired, they filled 18 folio volumes. In 1840, Sharp edited and published (in an edition of 500 copies) *Memorials of the Rebellion of 1859* (London: Bowyer Nichols and Pickering); reprinted, with a preface by Robert Wood, as *The Rising of the North: The 1569 Rebellion* (Durham: Shotton, 1975). Huntingdon's words quoted here are on pages 184, 185. All further references to this text will be abbreviated as *Rising.*

Some historians estimate that at its peak the rebellion attracted perhaps as many as 7000 followers and perhaps 600 horses but only for a period of about three days at most.

8. *State Papers and Letters of Sir Ralph Sadler, To which is added a memoir of the Life of Sir R. Sadler, with historical notes by Walter Scott,* Arthur Clifford, ed. (Edinburgh: Constable, 1809) v. 2, 82.

9. Elizabeth to Surrey. *Rising* 155.

10. Sussex to Cecil. *Rising* 130, 131.

11. Bishop of Durham to Cecil. *Rising* 135.

12. Hutchinson v. 1, 451.

13. M. A. Richardson, *The Local Historian's Table Book, of Remarkable Occurrences, Historical Facts, Legendary and Descriptive Ballads, &c. &c. connected with the counties of Newcastle-upon-Tyne, Northumberland, and Durham.* Historical Division; Legendary Division (Newcastle upon Tyne: Richardson, 1841–1846) v. 1, 44. Richardson only devotes seven pages to "The Rising in the North" (43–49), and pieces his narrative together without reference to Sharp's book.

14. Sussex to Bowes. 19 January 1570. *Rising* 160.

15. *Rising* 278, 286.

16. *Rising* 173.

17. Cuthbert Headlam, "From 1603 to the Present Time: A Brief Historical Summary," *The Three Northern Counties of England,* C. Headlam, ed. (Gateshead: Northumberland Press, 1939) 109.

18. William Fordyce, *The History and Antiquities of the County Palatine of Durham . . .* (Newcastle: Fullerton, 1857) v. 1, 70.

19. John Hodgson, *A History of Northumberland, in Three Parts: Part I: Containing the General History of the County* (Newcastle upon Tyne: Nichol, &c., 1858) v. 1, 370.

20. William Cobbett, *Rural Rides . . . Together with Tours in Scotland . . . and Letters from Ireland,* G. D. H. and M. Cole, ed., (London: Peter Davies, 1930) v. 3, 700, 696 (Cobbett's emphases). In Hexham on 1 October 1832 Cobbett remarked that "the country [between Hexham and Morpeth] seems to be almost wholly destitute of people. Immense tracks of corn-land, but neither cottages nor churches" (v. 3, 728).

21. The carbon copy of Bunting's 1935 collection, *Caveat Emptor,* is in the Ezra Pound collection at Yale University.

22. Rosemary Cramp, *Corpus of Anglo-Saxon Stone Sculpture in England. I: General Introduction to the Series; County Durham and Northumberland* (Oxford and London: Oxford UP for the British Academy, 1984).

23. Bunting, *Bunting on Poetry* 123.

24. Letter to Harriet Monroe, 13 July 1931, *Poetry* Magazine papers, 1912–1936, Box 30, Folder 23, Department of Special Collections, University of Chicago Library. Bunting told me about his sixth-form revision of Shakespeare in December 1971. Four pages of the volume described are reproduced in Massimo Bacigalupo, *Ezra Pound: Un Poeta a Rapallo* (Genoa: Edizioni San Marco dei Giustiniani, 1985) 7.

25. In his interview with Jonathan Williams, "Eighty of the Best," *Paideuma* 9.1 (Spring 1980), Bunting offered another list of master-poets writing before the twentieth century: Homer, Ferdosi, Manuchehri, Dante, Hafez, Malherbe, Aneurin, Heledd,

Wyatt, Spenser, Sidney, and Wordsworth. As Jonathan Williams remarks, only four of these wrote in English (136).

26. One of the minor ironies of modern literary history is the fact that Williams's first publication (save for his privately printed *Poems* [1909]) was in *The Poetry Review* (October 1912), with an "Introductory Note" by Ezra Pound. *The Poetry Review* later became the journal of the Poetry Society, of which Bunting would become president over sixty years later.

27. Quakerism in the North seems especially to have attracted shepherds, whose lonely, independent, and difficult lives, far from any form of authority, were especially predisposed to that belief. Describing the Westmorland Seekers of 1652, Geoffrey Hubbard comments that Fox's teachings "came to them as an illumination of their pre-existent condition" (*Quaker by Convincement* [Harmondsworth: Penguin, 1974] 27). I am indebted to Richard and Ann Caddel for this point.

28. Preface, *Rising* xii.

29. Brian Swann, "Basil Bunting of Northumberland," *St. Andrews Review* 4.2 (Spring-Summer 1977): 40.

30. Hugh MacDiarmid and Duncan Glen, "A Conversation," *Akros* 5.13 (April 1970): 9–72, but especially 27–31.

31. Swann, "Basil Bunting" 33.

32. *Presidential Addresses: An Artist's View on Regional Arts Patronage* (Newcastle: Northern Arts, 1976?) 1–2.

33. Letter to Mr. [Alan] Neame, 16 April 1951, quoted in part in bookseller's catalogue *Modern First Editions* (Warwick: R. A. Gekoski, 1984). There is a carbon copy of Bunting's typescript letter among Dorothy Pound's papers at the Lilly Library, Indiana University.

34. Bunting, *Bunting on Poetry* 103, 102, 100, 103.

35. Thomas Hodgkin, Robert Spence Watson, R. Oliver Heslop, and Richard Welford, *Lectures Delivered to the Literary and Philosophical Society of Newcastle-upon-Tyne, on Northumbrian History, Literature, and Art, Lent Term 1898* (Newcastle: Literary and Philosophical Society, 1898) 173–196.

36. Henry James, *The Question of Our Speech; The Lesson of Balzac. Two Lectures* (Boston: Houghton Mifflin, 1905) 13, 15.

37. Much of Bunting's essay "The Lion and the Lizard" (1935, but unpublished until 1993 in *Sulfur* 33 [Fall 1993]: 73–78; and reprinted in Basil Bunting, *Three Essays*, Richard Caddel, ed. [Durham: Basil Bunting Poetry Centre, 1994] 27–31) is a consideration of Fitzgerald's language.

38. Conversation, December 1971.

39. *Presidential Addresses* (1974 address) 2.

40. T. B. Webster, "Basil Bunting—a poet in his own time," *Courier* (Newcastle University: 5 February 1969): 6.

41. H. D. Thoreau, *Journal*, 1 January 1858. *Writings*, Bradford Torrey, ed., Walden Edition (Boston: Houghton Mifflin, 1906) 16. 233.

42. William Carlos Williams, *Imaginations,* Webster Schott, ed. (New York: New Directions, 1970) 14.

43. Bunting, "Lion and Lizard," *Three Essays* 31.

44. William Carlos Williams, letter to Louis Zukofsky, 2 April 1928, *Selected Letters,* John C. Thirlwall, ed. (New York: McDowell Obolensky, 1954) 94.

45. Bunting, "The Poet's Point of View," *Diary of the North-Eastern Association for the Arts* (April 1966): 2; reprinted *Three Essays* 34.

46. Bunting, "The Lion and Lizard," *Three Essays* 28.

47. Sally Beaumon, "Man of Plain Words," *Daily Telegraph Magazine* 244 (13 June 1969): 32.

48. Letter to Ezra Pound, April 1954 (CtY).

49. Jacques Attali, *Noise: The Political Economy of Music,* Brian Massumi, tr. (Minneapolis: U of Minnesota P, 1985) 34. In this paragraph I draw heavily on the first chapter of this book.

50. Peter Dale, "The Gronk and Squoggle School of Poetry," *Agenda* 16.1 (1978): 55–65; "Bunting and Villon," *Paideuma* 9.1 (Spring 1980): 101–107.

51. Bunting, *Bunting on Poetry* 10–11, 12.

52. Peter Makin, unpublished typescript "Bunting and Swinburne"; Kenneth Cox, letter to Roger Guedalla, 7 November 1970, Guedalla Collection, University of Durham.

53. Manuscript notebook for *Briggflatts,* NBuU.

Parataxis in Basil Bunting and Louis Zukofsky

> A poem is neither a tool nor a vessel nor a remedy for anything but only and just a poem—for at any rate that's what it survives by.
>
> —Basil Bunting

> Rhyme is a hedge against the arbitrary.
>
> —Le Corbusier

I begin by defining parataxis in the simplest possible terms. Parataxis is not hypotaxis. Hypotactic sentences use subordinate clauses: "The man who I saw yesterday fell down the stairs this morning": a principal clause and a subordinate clause. Hypotactic structures hierarchize discourse; parataxis does not. Aristotle attacked parataxis, saying it strung notions together like beads on a string: parataxis places clauses side by side: equivalent value. "I saw that man yesterday. That man fell down the stairs this morning." You could even say "I saw that man yesterday and he fell down the stairs this morning" and still be paratactic; there are two independent clauses and each can be pulled right out of the sentence. It's a characteristic of a great deal of the *Iliad* but not much of the *Odyssey.* It's characteristic of a great deal of lyric poetry, but generally speaking that kind of paratactic structure tends to be depressed, downplayed, or even to vanish altogether from lyric poetry in English written between roughly 1600 and 1900. Which is to say that it seems to be a medieval and modern form. Hypotaxis tends to move toward cause and effect; parataxis tends to leave cause and effect to one side; it places one event next to another event next to another event and next to another event. At first sight it looks as though what it's doing is following a straight single linear progression through time. But paratactic structures actually *suspend* linearity, and instead create a field of apprehension in prose or in poetry, in the writing, in the language.

Almost exactly coinciding with the great San Francisco earthquake of October 1989, and roughly a thousand miles north, there opened in Vancouver a quite remarkable exhibition of work by two Vancouver artists, Bill Bissett and Al Neil, and by two California artists, George Herms and Jess.[1] Jess calls his works "paste-ups." They are pictorial, and they often contain words. Drawn from great variety of printed sources, mostly but not exclusively Victorian, the pictures are usually but not always steel engravings. The collage is at first sight disconnected fragments, not making a picture, nor a singular depiction of an object; it has no apparently unified object, though the verbal text may declare a theme or subject. But such a declaration is not, in Jess's work, a means by which to control response and reception, save to position the viewer *inside* the territory of the collage.

Each fragment maintains its separateness, works in terms of its juxtapositional relation to its neighbor—so the paste-up works by a virtually indescribable syntax, an extremely complex work of a structure hard to limn. Overall, the eye rarely finds a place to stop, being insistently drawn on across and round the collage by an adjacent image, a juxtaposition, an emphatic contrast, save perhaps to pause at an eye staring back at it from the surface, or at a series of words. But there are usually so many clusters of words that the eye, having paused, moves on. Layering of readings because layering of multiple devices: bold-face words, engravings, original and altered texts, quotations surreal or nonsensical. Depths and heights, nears and fars. Transformations of space and of prioritizing, so that nothing finally can be seen to claim primacy, and within some collages there is (quite often) a series of inner frames (rather like those in a comic strip) across which the images transgress—a hedge of convention through which the apparently arbitrary breaks. They are astonishing, rich, and lovely works, in which there is no single dominant focal point, for the act of collage in Jess's work surrenders focal point to the interaction of color and texture, with no one area claiming primacy (though some colors are, in context, by their very nature assertive)—sometimes areas and images even meld and blend into the edges and frame, so that it becomes hard to tell where the collage stops.

A Jess collage is a disconcertion of images, a series of collisions, disturbances, and occasional felicitous harmonies at the local level, bewildering perhaps, areas of the grotesque in the sharp juxtaposition of the organic and the mechanical, the naturalistic and the surreal, the antique and the current; a comic and comedic multitude from the mad island of Doctor Moreau, a Caligarian cabinet of curiosities, a multiplicity, in which the eye as soon as it focuses on one image is immediately drawn away to another and to another and to another so that the eye continually strays across and through the whole work in a curious suspension of decision. Stand back a little, and the eye begins tentatively to organize these shapes into larger swirls and movements overall and to perceive figures against a ground, but the very busyness of the detail dissolves the hierarchy, and the patterns shift, the eye keeps moving. Some of his collages are laminations, layered like (and with the techniques of) an overlaid jigsaw-puzzle, using jigsaw-puzzle pieces; there's a three-dimensional or rather a bas-relief quality, and the jigsaw extends into the frame as well. The edges of the puzzle pieces run an additional and severe interference for the eye, a grey curvilinear, interlocking and branching distraction.

In his studio Jess has thousands of images carefully sorted in files under such categories as Form, Vegetation, Demonic, Worship, Ghastly, Army, Things, Astronomic. Some images will wander from file to file seeking their context, an adventure that may take years and which operates as a kind of "rehearsal" for their final role, when they are firmly glued to paper in their restless home. The uncertainty which marks their migration through Jess's files carries through to the parataxis of the final and "completed" collage, a very fluid structure in which the errant eye is incapable of error. There are layerings of readings because there are layerings of structures and frames: there's a lot of verbal activity going on in these texts—for texts they are—but if there's narrative, it is not linear.

This is true of even the most obviously narrative of Jess paste-ups, the series of strip-cartoon frames of *Tricky Cad* (1953–1959), a series taken from the newspaper strip *Dick Tracy* (of which the title is an anagram) recollaged with at first sight completely nonsensical utterances by all the standard *Dick Tracy* characters; indeed, the whole piece is an anagram of a Dick Tracy serial in which neither iconography nor language cohere, and out of which we can retrieve a curious sort of comic sense (as we can from the title, but much more severely disrupted). In the classic comic strip, frame partitions and orders spatiality and sequence, eliminating the need for interpretation or specialized competence required to relate the glyphs to some prior text—they propose or announce, that is to say, their own self-containment. But in *Tricky Cad*—rather as in a Glen Baxter cartoon—the matter, the verbal component, bursts out of "sense" and seriously disrupts the linearity: "Three longers later on the count of three" says one narrative box, "whinemeal" offers another, and the pictorial anagrams are equally disjunctive. Narrative falters, to say the least, and we are left wondering what order to read the eight rows of frames in. It subverts our notions of narrative order and especially of the weird kind of "sense" a strip-cartoon makes, yet the juxtapositions are not random. They draw our attention to their self-referentiality by comedic exophoric gesture, the final frame captioned "Tricky old cad, as soon as we've regained our significance, suppose we go topside and leave no remnants of ought still raging manananana."

The net effect is that any reading of this work (or of any Jess collage) as narrative is inevitably tentative; always indeterminate and non-definitive; we are offered minimal interpretive guidance and it is impossible to figure out (rather like the *Dick Tracy* it parodies) whether there even is a story. In similar spirit, I think, Robert Grenier complained in 1971 of Creeley's criticism that each word "means something apart from the fact of its own existence and cannot really be understood in its own terms / without reference to some other X."[2]

We must make of it what we will.

Such paratactic structuring extends beyond the graphic. Among Jess's other works are his assemblages, a form of three-dimensional collage made of objects. But Jess rarely if ever fastened his assemblages together, and consequently they are extremely fragile; very rarely have they left the studio in his and Duncan's house, and so have very rarely been exhibited. They have been photographed. They fell to pieces in the San Francisco earthquake of October 1989. It may or not be possible to put them back together, and the work is thus situated like the early work of George Herms. Herms builds his extraordinary assemblages of, as Robert Duncan puts it, "materials fallen from their original uses," things that people throw away, so he haunts places like city dumps, picking up old mattresses, discarded books, and so on, going through trash cans.[3] He works, then, with *objets trouvées.* Among his first assemblages were those composed of various materials found near his home at Hermosa Beach south of Los Angeles. In 1957, while preparing for a move to Berkeley, he gathered them all together into a kind of votive environment among the foundations of some demolished houses. Called *Secret Exhibition,* it was unannounced and simply left to destiny. Art made of the discarded, and then itself discarded.

I

Such collage and assemblage, leaving the work to its own destiny, exhibits extreme magnanimity toward it. The artist of paratactic imagination completely relinquishes control over the work once it is done, and over its reception. The paratactic writer is prepared to abandon whatever pretext and even pre-text there may have been for the work—the aims of the artist irrelevant once the work is finished. And in these terms, probably Bunting (who, like Zukofsky insisted that the artist exhibit such magnanimity toward his work) does not have a paratactic imagination, and Zukofsky probably does. For Bunting is in two minds about how he wants his work to be received. His note on *Briggflatts* ends "Let the images and events take care of themselves."[4] But it begins somewhat differently: "*Briggflatts* is a poem: it needs no explanation. The sound of the words spoken aloud is itself the meaning, just as the sound of the notes played on the proper instruments is the meaning of any piece of music. Yet I have been teased so much by people who cannot be content to listen without reasoning, and by people who think they detect in the poem notions alien to it and sometimes repulsive to me that I will set down, if I can, some hint of its maker's mind" (3). This immediately suggests that although he wants the poem to be sound only, there is also some communicative element, the poem has a referential quality, and Bunting wants to maintain some form of stability, control over it. Yet in the poem itself he writes, "Follow the clue patiently and you will understand nothing"—and I see no reason why in context this statement cannot refer to the poem itself.[5] When Warren Tallman and I interviewed him in 1970 he stated flatly that "you can take it in all sorts of ways as far as interpreting the damn thing goes. There's millions of ways."[6]

I wonder. The second edition of *The Norton Anthology of Modern Poetry* prints as an extract the complete first Canto of *Briggflatts* with footnotes. After misspelling the title of the poem (as "Briggflats") it gives a footnote explaining it: "In the north of England, 'flats' are low-lying fields along a waterway. In an interview, Bunting once remarked, 'My autobiography is Briggflats.' "[7] The sub-title of the poem, as published, is of course "An Autobiography," though in a note appended to the poem (CP 226) Bunting is careful to add the rider, "but not a record of fact."[8]

The footnotes in *The Norton Anthology* are almost all wrong; but they are consistently so, like a piano whose overall pitch is off a half-tone and has been so tuned. They thus set up a different interpretive community from the one Bunting had in mind. Glossing line two's "madrigal" as a "part-song for three or more voices" and "descant" as "the upper part of a part-song," the second footnote to the poem tells us that " 'Rawthey' is presumably the name of the itinerant mason, or stone-carver, of these lines." But the Rawthey is a river, and to read it as a man's name at line 29 when "Rawthey trembles" is to change and in Bunting's view, I believe, to misread the poem. Here is the opening of an information pamphlet published for visitors to Brigflatts Meeting House: "The hamlet of Brigflatts is 1½ miles from the small town of Sedbergh. The Meeting House is a plain stone building set in a little garden, surrounded by fields. There is a farm at the end of the land, and two other houses; the sound of the River Rawthey nearby fills the air as it hurries down to join the Lune. . . . It [is] a rough bleak country."[9] For several years from 1912 on Bunting spent part of each summer with a friend who lived in one of the houses.

It would be tedious to catalogue all the errors of these footnotes, especially since they frequently contradict Bunting's own. But I do want to make clear the kind of distortion they make, for it is one I believe Bunting would object to quite strenuously. *Fell:* "In Britain, a 'fell' is a wild field on a hill." *May:* "Flowers, pink or white, of the hawthorn tree." (Bunting's own note is much more lucid and succinctly draws our attention to linguistic features: "*May* the flower, as haw is the fruit, of the thorn" [CP 226].) *Slowworm:* "or 'blind-worm,' a small, burrowing limbless lizard." But the slow-worm *(anguis fragilis)* grows to a length of several feet; male slow-worms turn brilliantly mottled blue on their backs, blue as the sky. They're very beautiful creatures. *Bloodaxe:* "Name denoting a Norse hero (similar perhaps to Beowulf) of the pirates ('with sea-reflecting eyes') from European countries around the Baltic Sea who began invading England in 450 A.D. Their 'Baltic plainsong' refers to their rough yet rhythmic speech." But Eric Bloodaxe is a *historical* figure who was indeed (though not for long) King of Dublin, and King of Orkney, killed in battle at Stainmore. Bunting thought he could identify the rocks where Bloodaxe was killed. Bloodaxe is the doomed hero, and he is doomed because it was his task in the world to be king, but nobody wanted him to be theirs, so he wandered round looking for a tribe to king, and was eventually killed while still searching. As doomed king he is very similar to the *poète maudit,* the doomed or accursed poet, who figures through the poem, whom the poem figures, whose autobiography the poem might be; whose doom it was to turn his back on love, in the service of poetry. Bunting's own note on Bloodaxe points not only to his Norse but his Northumbrian identity: "Northumbrians should know but seldom do *Eric Bloodaxe* because all the school histories are written by or for southrons. Piece his story together from the Anglo-Saxon Chronicle, the Orkneyinga Saga, and Heimskringla, as you fancy" (CP 226). That particular note of Bunting's points to the interpretive community he had in mind for the poem. As he told his audience when he read at Harvard University in 1976, "What I write is in my own language, Northumbrian: spoken in the North of England, with vowels very different from those you customarily use, and very different from those a southern Englishman uses."[10] The *language* of the poem is scrupulously accurate, and it is that which governs the stability and control which Bunting seeks to have over his poem—the words should be recognizable, in much the same way as George Herms' old paintbrushes, mattress-springs, or mailboxes, or the elements of Jess's *Tricky Cad,* carry with them a contextual human residue.

Bunting's care in this matter (and its violation by *Norton*) is apparent from two notes the *Norton* offers on four lines from the sixth of Canto I's twelve stanzas:

Skulls cropped for steel caps
huddle round Stainmore.

Their becks ring on limestone,
whisper to peat.

Stainmore: a "desolate forest in the north of England; the 'steel caps' are helmets." There are no trees at Stainmore, though one obsolete—and, I might add, northern—meaning of "forest" is (according the OED) "a wild uncultivated waste, a wilderness." *Beck:* " 'Beck' is a dialect word for a mattock, an agricultural instrument; it would 'ring' on hard limestone, but 'whisper' cutting into soft 'peat,' or decayed vegetable tissue in the earth." Bunting's note, in an apparently doomed attempt to forestall such a gloss, points to the northernness of this Scandinavian/Icelandic word: "We have burns in the east, *becks* in the west, but no brooks or creeks" (CP 226). (These footnotes are a classic example of Graduate Student's Revenge in the face of Professor's Carelessness, achieved by reading the dictionary instead of reading the poem.)

But what would Bunting think about these footnotes? Other than dismissing them as nonsense, that is. They provide the possibility of a total botch where all these figures from the poet's and from northern history are seen as legendary or as inventions of the poet, where features of the northern landscape are seen as agricultural implements, and so on. But do they change the landscape of the poem? Theoretically, Bunting should not mind, if indeed the incidents and images are going to take care of themselves. But the notion that the incidents and images can take care of themselves rests, in Bunting's case, on a notion of their cultural or historical stability, and on the notion that the reader does indeed share with the poet an ordinary language. Why else would he provide the poem with footnotes which assert roundly the distinctions between the northern and the southern ear and culture?[11] Though it uses very few dialect words, *Briggflatts* is written in a more-or-less northern dialect which perhaps is a subset of a standard *koiné* through which it will nevertheless speak. Yet on numerous occasions Bunting complained of that very *koiné* that it deadens a culture, removes men and women from the local and the live. His delight in the poor, in the folk-songs of London, was precisely grounded on his intense dislike for the sorts of constraints imposed by polite culture and by polite letters. He distrusted the poetry of Joseph Skipsey when Skipsey permitted "occasional intrusions of what Samuel Butler called 'Wardour Street' into his vocabulary," and in insisting that the poet hold to the life he knows rather than the life he sees "distorted and on paper"[12] he is insisting that the poet hold to a language he knows and is at home in equally well. A language, that is, grounded in the local, and not standardized by Oxbridge or the BBC.

The procedures and assumptions underlying such writing are quite remote from the procedures and assumptions underlying Zukofsky's work. Zukofsky is perpetually destabilizing the language throughout his work, destabilizing the ordinariness of the incidents and images, sometimes distorting them almost beyond recognition, sometimes concealing them, frequently erasing reference. Zukofsky once wrote to Cid Corman[13] of the Wrigleys at the close of "A"-2 that the sooner readers forget who the (chewing-gum) Wrigley boys are the better, and twelve days later, discussing recurrences and patterns in "*A*," said that "as for what else in the way of *content* ten years have accumulated the sooner I can get that out of the way & buried in the music of the *whole thing* the better."[14] Bunting himself commented in 1958 that "Zukofsky gets stronger and stronger, particularly in short pieces, that don't seem to be about anything."[15] In such cases the subject matter is simply something to hang the words on, to get the words moving on the page and in the air, singing (a condition Bunting seems to aspire to in his much-quoted essay "The Poet's Point of View").

But Bunting's destabilizing procedures operate differently, and to a different end, for he seems to have something in mind for the poem radically at odds with Zukofsky's procedures in a work like the opening of "A"-15. So what does he have in mind? How does it work in the poem? What is paratactic about such writing? Here are the first five lines of the third stanza of *Briggflatts:*

> Decay thrusts the blade,
> wheat stands in excrement
> trembling. Rawthey trembles.
> Tongue stumbles, ears err
> for fear of spring. (CP 61)

The history of these lines in the manuscript drafts runs like this: Version 1:

> Can the young wheat know
> what its roots feed on?
> decay and excrement produce
> the blade?[16]

Followed by version 2:

> Can the young wheat know / feel
> decay thrusts up the blade?

or guess whatever seeks the sun
feeds of excrement?

Followed by version 3:

Decay thrusts the blade
of young wheat towards the sun
Bread out of excrement,
All green things stand in excrement.

Followed by version 4:

Decay thrusts the ~~young green~~ blade
the tall wheat stands in excrement
trembling, and trembling Rawthey
reflects the breeze
~~we tremble for fear of love~~
for fear of love we tremble
with fumbling tongue . . . .

What's curious is that this language is still without subordination, paratactic, but it is pushing toward a particular point, to express and emphasize the progress of a thought, an idea which is (obviously) developing as it expands. There's a thematic coherence to these successive versions. Version 5 is closer to the final one:

Decay thrusts the blade,
wheat stands in excrement,
trembling. Trembling,
Rawthey reflects a breeze.
We tremble for fear of love
~~with numb tongue, sanded ears~~
numb tongue stumbles, ears err.
eyes down. The mason says . . . .

And version 6 is almost identical to that finally printed:

Decay thrusts the blade,
wheat stands in excrement,
trembling. Rawthey trembles.

Tongue stumbles, ears err
for fear of spring. Rub,
rub the stones with sand

and so on, though at a further stage the repeat of "rub" will be dropped.

Bunting's revisions, as we shall see, eliminate a lot of that thread, that coherence of subject/structure. One of the devices is the substitution of key words in the text, changes in diction, vocabulary, once the draft is virtually complete, to eliminate repetitiousness and to make the thought less obvious. Thus versions 4 and 5 make explicit what notion these lines have been leading toward—"for fear of love"—and then at the end, in the final version, he substitutes the word "spring," dropping the abstraction in favor of the observable. In furthering the thematic interest he buries it, conceals it, disguises it. It is a move away from the explicit yet toward the concrete.

So let's look at another passage, this time from Canto II, a highly condensed catalogue:

Who sang, sea takes,
brawn brine, bone grit.
Keener the kittiwake.
Fells forget him.
Fathoms dull the dale,
gulfweed voices . . . (CP 66)

The suppression of the verb *takes* in the second line is a form of compression thoroughly characteristic of Bunting's verse in that it ambiguates the parts of speech, just as the lack of a verb reinforces (or even, indeed, provides) the semantic ambiguity of "keener" in the third. Here is one early version of these lines:

He who sang
                the sea must take
Tempest, tide
                his bones shall shake
Keener be
                the kittiwake.

There nor dunce
        nor dun can pester,
shame confound
        or   blister

clown contemn
    nor bully bluster
Ice floes short-
    ing as they muster
Thence the slave
    is as the master
Save the
    Northwester

Little images of drowning, little images of desolation and abandonment, but fairly explicit, fairly elaborated. But it's very difficult in the text as printed to sort out exactly what's going on in these five lines. The drafts show us that this was originally a self-lament; itself keening, it follows the form of lamentation. But it has been condensed, boiled down, eighteen lines cut to three. So let's look at a later version. Here is the first line:

(Him) who sang the sea ~~shall~~ must take

Him bracketed, Bunting's going to get rid of it perhaps. For as soon as you say "He who sang" (version 1) or "Him who sang" (version 2) you're into hypotactic structure—a relative clause: "Him who sang, the sea must take" [or "Him who sang the sea, must take"]; dropping the personal pronoun makes for a curious little syntactic ambiguity and play: "Who sang": is this subordination or not? It could just as readily be understood as the opening of an independent clause (i.e., anyone, but nevertheless a particular one, sang) as of a relative clause—at least until we get to the verb "must," which declares unequivocally that "the sea must take" is a main clause. But it does not thereby declare "who sang" to be subordinate, for what we are faced with here is a simple case of inversion: "The sea must take who sang"; I can only characterize this as a case of parataxis disguised as hypotaxis. The semantic appropriateness of this syntactic strategy (for subordination provides a falling off of voice) suggests that Bunting is revising the passage to attain a particular quality of sound, and this does indeed seem to be the bent of the successive drafts. Here, then, is the complete second version:

(Him) who sang the sea ~~shall~~ must take,
flesh to salt, and bones to ~~shake~~ powder
Keener be the kittiwake

Him who sought the fish shall find
~~Him who~~ fells forget him

Distance dulls the shining dale

~~Heavy~~ fathoms ~~of~~ dull the dale
soaked sand, ~~stills~~ the voices
watchdog ~~the~~
        whale
gulfweed ~~a~~ curtain

And this in turn is followed by a further revision:

Who sang, sea ~~must~~ takes,
~~salt~~ brine flesh, bones powder, [transposed to flesh brine]
keener the kittiwake,
Fells forget him.

Fathoms dull the dale,
~~sand~~ slime voices.
Watchdog the whale,
gulfweed curtain.

And this is followed by a fair copy, with the marginal comment "brittle?" When he sent the fair copy of this version to Zukofsky, 6 December 1964, Bunting commented that "the way [it] . . . subsides to next to nothing is intentional."[17]

Bunting starts out with a straight clear thematic concern, and in revisions the condensation/compression tends to force him into paratactic structures—there are extended stretches of *Briggflatts* which are not specially paratactic—and on the whole parataxis is the exception rather than the rule in his verse, outside lyric. But thematic drive or no, the general tendency of the lyric in no matter whose hands (the lyric catalogue) is to push toward parataxis, instancing something (love, death, whatever). Bunting's paratactic strategies as a general rule achieve thematic suppression by means of omission or of verbal substitution.

II

Bunting's revisions confirm his own claim that in the poem sound takes first place: "Poetry is seeking to make not meaning, but beauty; or if you insist on misusing words, its 'meaning' is of another kind, and lies in the relation to one another of lines and patterns of sound, perhaps harmonious, perhaps contrasting and clashing, which the hearer feels rather than understands;

lines of sound drawn in the air which stir deep emotions which have not even a name in prose."[18]

In the actual process of writing, it looks as though Bunting needs—in order to achieve such "meaning"—to pay very close attention indeed to what the poem says, and no poem by Bunting that I know offers us nonsense. The concentration provided by intense focus on the condensation of theme clarifies the voice and sharpens the eye: in a fine essay on *The Spoils* Keith Alldritt has commented on Bunting's "scrupulous accuracy in representing phenomena and responses to phenomena";[19] once the music is clear then explicit thematic matter can take second place, and even be dropped. He profoundly distrusts those intentions for the poem which embody a meaning for the poem ahead of its writing, which express a purpose, a prior idea for the poem. The poet's intention for the poem is subordinate to the poem itself as it emerges, for the intention is inevitably an abstraction, a gesturing and a retreat away from the experience of the language toward a realm of meaning which resides outside the poem and independent of it (and, by corollary, independent of the reader as well as of the poet). As Bob Perelman observes, "No poem intentionally generalizes beyond itself."[20]

"It is possible," wrote Louis Zukofsky in "A Statement for Poetry" in 1950, "in imagination to divorce speech of all possible graphic elements, to let it become a movement of sounds"—a notion remarkably similar to Bunting's.[21] Calling this a "musical horizon of poetry (which incidentally poems perhaps never reach)," Zukofsky was less sanguine than Bunting of the feasibility of reading poems as sound rather than as registers of meaning, and this may account for the radically different techniques he uses to destabilize the meaning of his poems. But he points to this musical horizon as the means by which anybody who does not know Greek can listen and get something out of Homer, thus "tuning in" to "the human tradition, to its voice which has developed among the sounds of natural things."

The opening 46 lines of "A"-15 (written 1964) are all pretty much a transliteration into English of the sounds the book of Job makes in Hebrew, at the same time playing a variety of English idioms and dialects against and with the ground swell of *Job*. In the manuscripts of the poem (in the Harry Ransom Humanities Research Center at the University of Texas at Austin) Zukofsky has written by almost every line a note specifying chapter and verse, pointing to the text being transliterated. This circumstance alone raises some important issues. The poem begins:

An
 hinny

by
 stallion
out of
 she-ass[22]

In his poetry classes at the University of British Columbia Bunting would recite poems by Goethe, Manuchehri, and Malherbe in German, Persian, and French—he knew those languages. But Zukofsky did not know Hebrew. That is to say, Bunting is working inside the language, but Zukofsky is working outside the language. When Zukofsky is working to the sound of a Hebrew he does not know, he's using it as a way of exteriorizing the English so he can look at it and remove various hierarchical authority bases from that language—so he can see it some other way. It's part of the *undoing* of the language (Bunting doesn't do this to anything like the same extent, though his syntax reflects a somewhat analogous process). I should add, however, that Zukofsky reads Yiddish, knows the Hebrew alphabet, knows what noises it makes. Later in "A"-15 ("*A*" 370) he transliterates line 781 of Sophocles' *Antigone,* though he cannot read Greek.

When he wrote "A"-15 Zukofsky was half-way through translating his *Catullus* with Celia Zukofsky—the *Catullus* which, though attacked by its detractors on the grounds that it's not written in English, is surely one of the most inventive and resourceful texts produced in English in the last half of the twentieth century. It is also, clearly, one of the most offensive: "The Hun," said Robert Conquest, "is at play—worse still, at *work*—among the ruins."[23] Calling it a failed experiment "worth the making," Bunting was more temperate: "Perhaps a reader with no Latin would get more pleasure from his translation of Catullus than I can. But . . . Zukofsky has not only failed to reproduce the Latin sounds convincingly, but to get as much of them as he can he has not only neglected and distorted the meaning, he has completely changed the whole tone of Catullus. . . . Zukofsky uses a contorted syntax, and a diction as far from the colloquial as it could get."[24] Faced with the plenitude of the poem, Conquest wills his own closure.

Zukofsky's project seems designed to test Bunting's notion that "The sound, whether it be in words or notes, is all that matters. It is perfectly possible to delight an audience by reading poetry of sufficient quality in a language it does not know," and at the same time prove wrong Pound's conviction that Catullus is untranslatable.[25] Presumably transliterating the great untranslatable Latin poet into English, giving you the sounds, the intonations, and the inflections, of the original, bodily moves the physical experience the poem offers into English. If the original is a great poem, then according to the paradigmatic model the ensuing English version will also be a great poem. Of course, it doesn't work out that way (the tonalities and inflections of voice are not even sketchily equivalent in the two languages, for instance) and in Bunting's view "the experiment fails, as of course such experiments always fail. . . . It shows some of the limits that exist to the identification of poetry and music. They're twins, but they're not identical twins."[26] *Catullus* is totally subversive of the whole academic, scholastic, and pedantic tradition of poetry as practiced in the English language in the twentieth century, and is—or was, when the Zukofskys wrote it—quite unlike any other poem in the English language.

Zukofsky's transliteration is also an act of great mischief: with no knowledge of Latin whatsoever, he is translating the entire work of the great untranslatable Roman poet. Zukofsky, who as a child learned English as a second language, working outside the Latin language and approaching the English through *it*, is thus enabled to exteriorize English and, entering the realm of English through Latin and through the dictionary, is thus freed into making English foreign again. The vocabulary of the *Catullus* is generated in part by the dictionary, consulted in response to the sound of the Latin, and the dictionary in turn confirms and authenticates the place of the poem's words in the language, no matter how strange they may sound to the ear or look to the eye. It is thus written rather than spoken language which generates the work, though the work itself is intended to demonstrate and affirm the power of sound.

Zukofsky began writing "A"-15 on 3 October 1964, taking a break from *Catullus* at Number 78 (which he translated on 20 July), and finished it on 1 December. He picked up the *Catullus* again on 26 December, and wrote straight through, finishing up at Yaddo on 1 February 1966 with the more than 400 lines of Number 64 *(Peliaco quondam)*, which he'd saved till last.[27] The opening of "A"-15, then, lies at the heart of the *Catullus*. Like the project it interrupts, it is both translation and transliteration, but from Hebrew. Here is Bunting's description: "If you allow for the fact that Hebrew has several sounds that don't exist in any of the Western languages—simply omit those—the rest of it does sound *extremely* like the original. It's a very clever piece of work. . . . Clearly it is just as much a translation as the words in the English Bible. But also just as little a translation. The one misses out the meaning, the other misses out the sound."[28] But the opening of "A"-15 is a great deal closer to the book of Job than Bunting suggests. The great ten-volume edition of the *Century Dictionary*, first published in 1889–1894, and the dictionary which Zukofsky used, gives us, almost verbatim, the first six lines of the poem. *Hinny:* "a mule by stallion out of she-ass."[29] The poem starts, then, sounding a theme by quoting the dictionary Zukofsky customarily used, the dictionary current when as a child he was learning English as a second language, the authoritative register of American English when he was growing up. "An hinny / by stallion / out of she-ass": birth, then. In line 36 *she-ass* is transformed by alliterative *shophar,* which the *Century* defines as "an ancient Hebrew musical instrument, usually made of the curved horn of a ram"—echoes sound and re-sound throughout these lines. An hinny? Or a ninny? A half-wit? A half-breed? A cross-breed. What this poem is? In defining *ninny* as "A fool, a simpleton," the *Century* quotes Shakespeare, echoing horses: "What a pied ninny's this!" Horses run all through "*A*"—the index to the poem (it is selective) lists 85 entries, some of them multiple. A hinny is a mule, and in Zukofsky's own code a mule is what he called Paul Valéry, whom he thought a complete ninny. In 1928 Valéry published in the *New York Herald Tribune* an essay called "The Future of Literature: Will It Be a Sport?" in which he said that "literature is an art which is based on the abuse of language—that is, it is based on language as a creator of illusions, and not on language as a means of transmitting of realities,"[30] and that in the future it would have the status of mere hobby—so in "A"-8 Zukofsky got on his "heigh-horse," asking "What did the mule say when the tidal-wave came . . . ?"[31] Are we then to read "A"-15 as a tale told by a neighing (naying) idiot?

But in the north of England *hinny* is a term of endearment: the *Century* tells us it is a cognate of *honey* (but it is not gender-specific). The *Scottish National Dictionary* defines it as "sweetheart, darling." Joseph Skipsey, the Northumbrian coal miner poet who died in 1903 at the age of 71, was a friend of the Bunting family—he dandled the baby Basil on his knee (Bunting was born in 1900)—and his life was part of the family lore. At the pit where Skipsey worked in 1839, when he was seven, the men and boys working the mine were raised and lowered on an endless chain with rope stirrups. He saw another seven-year-old whose hold slipped on the way up, and who called to his brother behind, "A'm gannen to faal, Jimmy." "Slide doon to me hinney," his brother said, but could not hold him. Both were killed at the shaft bottom.[32] Bunting was a devoted raconteur, and Zukofsky would have known that story.

An hinny. The *New Century Dictionary* defines it as "To neigh, whinny"; it is, then, one of "the sounds of natural things" Zukofsky talks of in "A Statement for Poetry." It looks as though Zukofsky is working for multiple suggestiveness, and as we read the opening of "A"-15 we begin a course of recognitions as well as of discoveries. The discoveries, perhaps, come about from our own recourse to the dictionary. We should start recognizing the possibilities, though, simply because of the astonishing noises this poem makes, and their multiple resolution into puns—here used as a major paratactic device. For the noises this poem makes have meaning in English, and it is very difficult to see how Zukofsky, within very broad limits, is controlling the meanings that those noises make.

> He neigh ha lie low h'who y'he gall mood
> So roar cruel hire

say the lines opening the first of four ten-line stanzas recounting and transliterating *Job.* Neigh, like a horse. Hinny. But *to say nay* is to deny. *Neigh. Mood.* There are cows as well as horses in this line: "the sounds of natural things": *low.* The "Great Cow of Heaven" will make its appearance later in "A"-15 ("*A*" 369). And to lie low is of course to hide, from Yahweh if you're Iyyob.

This stanza is I think Job's; the next, Yahweh/Jehovah's, yammering at Job. Is *this* Iyyob/Job muttering to himself, yammering at Yahweh? If so, then he who neighs is Yahweh—the raging stallion or the whinnying hinny? But cruel, higher (in Heaven, that is to say, as well as in hierarchy)—a high (heigh) horse. Hinny. He neigh. He neighs a *lie*—i.e., the thing which was not? The horses in book IV of *Gulliver's Travels* had no word for lying, and were shocked at Gulliver's ability to utter the thing which was not. Swift and Gulliver have both already appeared in the poem (as has Bunting), in "A"-14.[33] We might also reflect, of course, that in *Genesis,* by uttering the thing that was not, Jehovah created the universe. Nay a lie and you get truth? Zukofsky pushes his text.

But this does not mean that we need to know *Gulliver's Travels, Genesis,* the book of Job, Hebrew, to read the poem, to see what's going on. We probably don't even need the dictionary, though recourse to it yields some quite surprising results. For this is a text bristling with significations, and in its multidirectionality the bristling is paratactically deployed, so that it becomes impossible even to imagine a definitive reading of the text. The text rejects singularity in ways in which *Briggflatts* does not; for words are loosened from syntactic stricture and can *range.* "A"-15 is a more-or-less remote descendant of the sort of game Ezra Pound plays in "Hugh Selwyn Mauberley," whose opening stanza can be read in at least two contrary ways: as a dismissal of the person being talked about (the voice of the London pundit, of the critic, of hegemony, of power), and as a defense and justification of him (the voice of sympathetic insight and understanding). Yahweh and Iyyob are shadows of each other, each echoing back the words of the other throughout these opening stanzas of "A"-15, and they (and the whole of "A"-15) can be read as exploring and elaborating some of the complexities of duty, obedience, and love.

There are at least two counter-readings running through the poem, playing off each other. One, as Iyyob attacking and resisting and hating and dismissing Yahweh and the very concept of Yahweh and Yahweh's sheer abuse of power—in these terms Yahweh is a ninny. And the other, to say the opposite: that Yahweh is indeed the power—he is, after all, God, and it is Iyyob who is the ninny for resenting it and resisting it and rejecting it—no wonder, then, he must "lie low." So it's a little drama, a prosodic drama of disobedience, that we are witnessing here. And as we read, we discover that that opening *He* is—as in ordinary speech—what grammarians and linguists call a *shifter.* And when we start sorting out the puns and syntactic ambiguities of this poem—especially Zukofsky's use of *apo koinou*—virtually all the words become shifters, and it becomes extremely difficult to sort out exactly or definitively where or how the words fit. Even Zukofsky, in reading the poem at the University of Connecticut in 1971 and at Johns Hopkins in 1975, didn't satisfactorily sort out the italicized "*Then* I said" of the thirteenth line. He smoothed it out.[34] But it seems to me that he smoothed it out for a very important reason—to keep the assignment of value, the weight we give that word, neutral, uncommitted, so that we can read it as part of a time continuum, as narrative, or as part of a logical continuum. The shape of the discourse is thus left open, simultaneously offering both narrative and logic.

That is completely characteristic of what I think of as Zukofsky's paratactic imagination, which forces the reader into a collaborative relation with the writer: Zukofsky throws the poem at you (if you like) and *you* then read it according to however you feel at that particular time, bringing to bear on the reading whatever expertise or ignorance, experience, or innocence, you have. But this is not to say that the text is indeterminate or that the meanings are arbitrary. It is to say that more than one meaning is not only possible but enjoined upon us: there are specific and even contradictory but not indeterminate meanings, and we cannot determine *completeness.* Any number of readings is possible, I believe, but in Zukofsky—and in another way in Bunting—the specificness, the particularity, is so great that actually it directs the reader's response more closely, less ambiguously, than in more conventional poems which lean heavily upon (quite possibly open ended) metaphor. The poem exploits, that is to say, undecidability.

Where Bunting and Zukofsky differ here is on the kind of authorial control being asserted. Much of the text of "A"-15 is so-to-speak self-generated in that there seems to have been no prior determination (other than the Hebrew) to govern what comes where in the text, or even what it shall say, though clearly the book of Job has its part to play in providing a ground on and in which the meaning can play. To say that Zukofsky's writing is interrogative rather than manipulative of language is to say that Zukofsky seems to owe obedience and allegiance to the immense range of possibilities afforded by semantics, phonetics, syntax. He is attentive to the dictionary and to the niceties of grammar-books whereas Bunting seems more obedient to theme. "You know quite well," Bunting wrote to a correspondent, "that no muse, no Apollo, no Holy Ghost whispers in my ear. Nothing outside a man's mind suggests what he should write."[35] In "A"-15 Zukofsky works a complex and open-ended counterpoint in which the multiplicity of (dictionary) meanings discerned through close attention to echo, vowel-leading, consonance, assonance, orthography, syntax, line-break, and even rhyme play against and with the sound and meaning suggested by the base-text, and the poet's work is to explore, exploit, and interrogate as many possibilities as he can at the same time. The language, that is to say, functions in much the same way as might the muse, Apollo, or Holy Ghost who Bunting rejects.

This may be why Zukofsky's usual impulse, as he told me in a letter, is to write against something, a resistance for work or working-out.[36] The resistance of the material (or of the scheme, or of what I have called the base-text) generates meanings by forcing attention to those features of the language more usually neglected or overlooked. Such a procedure de-hierarchizes rather than re-hierarchizes the writing process, for the writer in certain (quite specific) ways has to relinquish a great deal of control over what the poem is going to say or how it's going to run, because that has been or is being determined elsewhere. That is, the choices are very largely determined by some agency which is not the poet's will—though obviously in choosing those things he exercised his will in the first place.

Aristotle complained of parataxis that it was beads on a string, each separate, unconnected but strictly linear. But in fact parataxis dissolves linearity; linearity demands that you know where you're going, or that cause and effect, sequence, be laid out in a particular way for a reason. Linearity is a feature of hypotactic discourse: there is an end if not in sight at least in mind, for both writer and reader. But in paratactic discourse neither writer nor reader knows where the writing is going: that is only visible when you've got the whole field. And then you can browse around in that field in whatever way you wish—and you can do so at any stage of the trip too—provided you are obedient to the features of the field itself. Parataxis, as Alan Davies and Nick Piombino have observed of "field reading," permits the writer/reader "to reshuffle experience, to see new connections than those which were thought when the mind originally thought the connections."[37] It is a species of fragmentation, in which the elements of poems only acquire full meaning in relation to one another as the parts begin to coalesce: we learn the details of a perception before we arrive at its complete expression—and even when it is complete the words and their plural connections shift and realign themselves anew. This is Olson's distinction between "language as the act of the instant and language as the act of thought about the instant"; it is the distinction between collage and discourse, parataxis and hypotaxis.[38] Multiple meanings are available in both *Briggflatts* and in "A"-15, though in the Bunting passages to far lesser extent, because Bunting is much more closely focused, thematically speaking, and has indeed an end in view. Yet both poets, surely, would nod with sympathy and agreement with Jackson Mac Low when he spoke of the great "relief to stop making artworks carry that burden of 'expression'! To let them become themselves, watch them grow & take shape without one's pushing and shoving them around too much, was and is a great pleasure."[39]

Zukofsky's and Bunting's parataxis in part rests on seemingly recoverable deletions of ordinary speech, but what is recovered is up to the reader. In its breaking away from the hierarchies of hypotaxis and its escape from linear progressions, in its fragmentation which apparently disclaims the author's (and the reader's) "responsibility" for the text, the poem admits, recognizes, and discovers roles for the aleatory, and enjoins collaborative enterprise with the reader. The necessity to relinquish authorial control, and the hierarchic relations of social power that go with it, is a necessary feature of this sort of parataxis. It is an empowerment of the reader because it is an empowerment of language.

Notes

Epigraph. Basil Bunting, letter to Louis Zukofsky, 10 May 1953, in the Harry Ransom Humanities Research Center, University of Texas at Austin. Le Corbusier, *Vers une Architecture* (1926), as quoted in Joseph Rykwert, *On Adam's House in Paradise: The Idea of the Primitive Hut in Architectural History*, 2nd ed. (Cambridge, MA: MIT P, 1981), 15. Le Corbusier is talking about using rectangles as repeats and rhymes in architectural structures.

1. *Rezoning: Collage and Assemblage Bill Bissett/George Herms/Jess/Al Neil Vancouver Art Gallery, October 19,1989 to January 1, 1990* (Vancouver: Vancouver Art Gallery, 1989). In my discussion of the work of Herms and of Jess I draw extensively on Keith Wallace's essay "Rezoning" in this exhibition catalogue and the exhibition catalogue *Translations Salvages Paste-Ups by Jess*, an exhibition organized by the Dallas Museum of Fine Arts April 6 through May 15 1977 (Dallas: Dallas Museum of Fine Arts, 1977). For reproductions of Jess's work, see also Michael Auping, *Jess: Paste-Ups (and Assemblies) 1951–1983* (Sarasota, FL: The John and Mable Ringling Museum of Art, 1983); Michael Auping, *Jess: A Grand Collage 1951–1993* (Buffalo: Albright Knox Art Gallery 1993); Ingrid Schaffner, *Jess: To and From the Printed Page* (New York: Independent Curators International, 2007).

2. Robert Grenier, "Robert Creeley: A Quick Graph." *This* 1 (Winter 1971): 85.

3. Robert Duncan, "Of George Herms, His Hermes, and His Hermetic Art," *George Herms Selected Works 1960–1973. An Exhibition Presented by the Memorial Art Gallery, University of California, Davis January 10—February 16, 1973* (Davis, CA: Memorial Art Gallery University of California, 1973).

4. Basil Bunting, *A Note on Briggflatts* (Durham: Basil Bunting Poetry Archive, 1989), unpaginated.

5. Basil Bunting, *Complete Poems,* Richard Caddel, associate ed. (Newcastle upon Tyne: Bloodaxe, 2000) 75. Hereafter cited as CP.

6. "Basil Bunting Talks about *Briggflatts,*" *Agenda* 16.1 (Spring 1978): 16.

7. *The Norton Anthology of Modern Poetry.* 2nd. ed. Richard Ellman and Robert O. Clair, ed. (New York: Norton, 1988) 637–640.

8. *Norton* omits the poem's subtitle.

9. *Brigflatts Meeting House* (Brigflatts: Brigflatts Preparative Meeting, 1983) unpaginated. Bunting's misspelling of Brigflatts is deliberate; *Norton*'s is not.

10. My thanks to the late Richard Caddel of the Basil Bunting Archive for this quotation.

11. I discuss the northern aspects of this vexed question at some length in "Basil Bunting: Poet of the North," earlier in this book.

12. "Preface," Joseph Skipsey, *Selected Poems,* Basil Bunting ed. (Sunderland: Ceolfrith Press, 1976) 12, 14.

13. Letter to Cid Corman, 13 August 1960, in the Harry Ransom Humanities Research Center, University of Texas at Austin. Part of the letter is printed in *Origin,* second series, 1 (April 1961): 62.

14. Letter to Cid Corman, 25 August 1960. *Origin,* second series, 1 (April 1961): 63.

15. Basil Bunting, Letter to Ezra Pound, 10 April 1958, in the American Literature Collection, Beinecke Rare Book and Manuscript Library, Yale University.

16. The heavily revised drafts of Cantos 1 and 2 of *Briggflatts* are in the Poetry Collection of the University Libraries, University at Buffalo, and are copyrighted by the Estate of Basil Bunting, with whose permission they are printed here.

17. The letter is in the Harry Ransom Humanities Research Center, University of Texas at Austin.

18. Basil Bunting, "The Poet's Point of View," *Three Essays,* Richard Caddel, ed. (Durham: Basil Bunting Poetry Centre, 1994) 34.

19. Keith Alldritt, *Modernism in the Second World War: The Later Poetry of Ezra Pound, T. S.Eliot, Basil Bunting, and Hugh MacDiarmid* (New York: Peter Lang, 1989) 80.

20. But, adds Perelman (echoing Bunting's remark to Zukofsky which stands at the head of this essay), "All criticism does, even the closest reading." "Criticism [symposium on critical writing]" *Ottotole* 2 (Winter 1986–1987): 147.

21. Louis Zukofsky, *Prepositions* + 20. See also "*A*" (Berkeley: U of California P, 1978) 566–571.

22. "*A*" 359.

23. Robert Conquest, "The Abomination of Moab," *Encounter* 34 (May 1970): 56. This essay, slightly revised and now naming the translators "Zukofsky," has been re-

printed as "On the Battlements of Babel" in *The Abomination of Moab* (London: Temple-Smith, 1979) 108–120.

24. Basil Bunting, *Basil Bunting on Poetry,* Peter Makin, ed. (Baltimore: Johns Hopkins UP, 1999) 160.

25. Bunting, "The Poet's Point of View" 2. In February 1916, Pound told Harriet Monroe that to translate Catullus was to "try the impossible. . . . Even Landor turned back from attempts to translate Catullus. I have failed forty times myself so I do know the matter." *The Letters of Ezra Pound 1907–1941,* D. D. Paige, ed. (New York: Harcourt Brace, 1950) 69.

26. Bunting, *Bunting on Poetry* 160.

27. Zukofsky scrupulously dated all his manuscripts, and I draw these (and subsequent) dates from them. They are housed at the Harry Ransom Humanities Research Center, University of Texas at Austin.

28. Bunting, *Bunting on Poetry* 160.

29. *The Century Dictionary and Cyclopedia* (New York: Century, 1902).

30. Paul Valéry, "The Future of Literature: Will It Be a Sport?" *New York Herald Tribune* (22 April 1928) 1. A slightly different version of this essay is collected as "The Future of Literature" in *The Collected Works of Paul Valéry,* Jackson Mathews, ed., vol. 11, *Occasions,* trans. Roger Shattuck and Frederick Brown (Princeton: Princeton UP, Bollingen Series 45.11, 1970) 151–157.

31. "*A*" 94. Zukofsky completed this passage on 7 January 1937.

32. My account is drawn from Bunting's as printed in his "Preface" to Joseph Skipsey, *Selected Poems* (Sunderland: Ceolfrith, 1976) 8.

33. Swift, "*A*" 333, 345; *Gulliver's Travels,* "*A*" 345; Bunting, "*A*" 333.

34. A tape of Zukofsky reading at the Wallace Stevens Memorial Series, University of Connecticut, Storrs, 29 April 1971, and a videotape of his 1975 reading at the Johns Hopkins University are at the Harry Ransom Humanities Research Center, University of Texas at Austin.

35. Possibly undated letter to unidentified correspondent, quoted in bookseller's catalogue *1st Editions Catalogue 62* (Eastchester, NY: Bernice Weiss Rare Books, April 1982) item 88.

36. Letter to Peter Quartermain, 18 October 1968.

37. Alan Davies and Nick Piombino, "The Indeterminate Interval: From History to Blur," *Open Letter* 5.1 / *L=A=N=G=U=A=G=E* 4 (Winter 1982): 39.

38. Charles Olson, "Human Universe," *Human Universe and Other Essays,* Donald Allen, ed. (New York: Grove, 1967) 4.

39. Jackson Mac Low, "Museletter," *L=A=N=G=U=A=G=E* 2 (April 1978): 26.

Writing and Authority in Zukofsky's *Thanks to the Dictionary*

> There will have to be a
> Redefinition of writing
> —Louis Zukofsky

In considering Zukofsky's poetics of procedural composition, as the following notes on the writer's authority must, I have in mind something along the lines of Joseph Conte's notions of "a procedural order that is proteinic and predetermined," and one that is "aleatory," random, and "protean," but I make no sharp distinctions between the two, for it appears to me that Zukofsky frequently combines them.[1] Much of the general drift especially of later parts of my discussion draws upon the English poet J. H. Prynne's remarkable essay *Stars, Tigers and the Shape of Words*.[2]

I take as key and starting point, Zukofsky's 1966 comment "That's Herrick: I want to *deduce* something as good as that" (my italics) in the *Poetry U.S.A.* film about him,[3] and his repeated determination to be a writer "representative" of his age. Zukofsky's friend the English poet Basil Bunting admired Spenser for abandoning the *Faerie Queene* after finishing only six of the poem's projected twelve books because neither the poem nor its author could keep pace with the rapidly changing late-sixteenth-century world. This is but one way of saying that the poet must be representative of his time, and that Spenser had the wit to recognize his poem's increasing inability to be so representative. It is a common artistic ambition, of course: Théophile Gautier pursued it avidly, and surely it is one of the great driving forces behind Ezra Pound's enormous economy of literary energy. Zukofsky repeatedly admired the representative quality of writers he admired (like Whitman, say, Henry Adams, or Apollinaire) and affirmed it as his own intention: "I don't want to falsify my time," he told an audience in London in 1969, "so I get it down."[4] As Zukofsky well knew,[5] it is an extremely difficult thing consciously to achieve, and the difficulty is compounded if you believe—as did say Pound or Eliot, Bunting or Zukofsky—that the poem must approximate the condition of music, that its most important feature is its sound, the form rather than the purport of the saying and the doing. The connection of the poem to music is of course very ancient indeed, as is that between music and mathematics.

Notions of the mathematical basis of the arts have indeed a long history, reaching back through Dryden and Spenser to Alberti and Piero della Francesca to Plato and beyond; none of us needs reminding that "number" and "measure" and "meter" are terms shared by mathematics and prosody. But the link enjoyed something of a revival in the 20s and 30s, John Rodker in 1926 suggesting that the "mathematical preoccupation" of Futurism "has lately touched all the arts in some degree. In music Schoenberg, . . . and in literature Miss Stein."[6] Edith Sitwell quoted with approval Eugene Jolas's praise of Stein's "mathematical" lucidity,"[7] and Zukofsky himself pointed in the early sections of "*A*" to Bach's and Mozart's "calculus." Sometime in 1937 Zukofsky remarked in a letter to Lorine Niedecker that Newton was discovering the calculus at the same time Bach was writing mathematical counterpoint, and specifically linked Bach's and Mozart's calculus to that of the just completed "calculus" section of "A"-8.[8] Such considerations of form necessarily redraw the relationship between the writer's motives and his or her desires for the finished work. Eliot thus formulated writing, in perhaps the most widely read literary essay of the century ("Tradition and the Individual Talent"), as an escape from personality.

In the early 1930s George Kingsley Zipf, an assistant professor of German at Harvard, taking a number of languages as his database (Chinese, English, German, Latin), attempted to show through "the direct application of statistical principles to the objective speech phenomena" that "the length of a word is closely related to the frequency of its usage."[9] The statistical method, he said, "may well prove itself of considerable service in studying objectively the otherwise highly subjective phenomena of meaning, value and experience" (12), and in what he called "a cautious inspection of the problems of meaning, emotion, and mental phenomena in general," his book *The Psycho-Biology of Language: An Introduction to Dynamic Philology* (1935) explicitly aimed, "through the discussion of meaning and emotion[,] to bring our new linguistic data into a rational perspective with the rest of human behavior." Noting that "in all languages under analysis the most frequent word in any sample will occur on the average once in approximately every 10 words, the second . . . in every 20 words," and so on, Zipf concluded that the distribution of words in any sample "approximates with remarkable precision an harmonic series" (xii). Acknowledging that "speech-phenomena cannot be isolated from the content of speech, nor from the personal, social, and cultural backgrounds of the speaker" (6)—that is to say that people use language for expressive and communicative purposes, and try to say what they mean—

Zipf suggested that the speaker's control of meaning was more apparent than real, subject as it was to "dynamic laws of speech with general applicability in any language" (3). Those laws, of which Zipf argued the speaker is unaware, are impersonal and highly ordered "underlying forces which impel linguistic expression" (3). How, then, be representative of your age?

It is a truism, not to say trite, to remark that time and space diminish the precision of expressive or communicative utterance, and with their passage render increasingly imperfect the expressive and communicative power of a given utterance. The expressive and communicative aspects of language are so dependent upon the circumstances which produced utterance, on the tones and gestures accompanying it, that our recollection of something someone else said lasts a matter of hours or even minutes. We have each of us in the small hours written notes to ourselves which were totally incomprehensible some few hours later. Zukofsky himself a shade ruefully talks in "A"-12 about old work,

> Much of it in pencil—blurred—other
>   notes written over it
> I can't read back thru the years— (251)

And there is a wonderful instance of Charles Olson at Goddard College in April 1962 reading a poem he'd written less than three months earlier: "I don't know, I don't even know what the hell I'm referring to—wait a minute . . . . Can you help me? What am I talking about there? Do you know what I'm talking about?"[10] As the semantic theorist John Lyons puts it, "There is much in the structure of languages that can only be explained on the assumption that they have developed for communication in face-to-face interaction."[11]

Yet if the passage of space and time may be seen to diminish the precision of utterance, it is equally true that their passage enlarges its scope and range by radically decontextualizing and recontextualizing it. Immense labors of scholarship have been devoted to determining whether a particular phrase in Catullus is lascivious or not, but no debate reckons the poems (or the phrase) worthless; there is sharp disagreement about the meaning of key passages of (say) *Billy Budd,* but there is no disagreement either that the passages are key or that *Billy Budd* is worth attending to. This is but another way of saying that such works stand the test of time and of translation, and that they do so by rather paradoxical if not baffling means. It also, I believe, reinforces Bunting's persuasion that the meaning of poetry "lies in the relation to one another of lines and patterns of sound, perhaps harmonious, perhaps contrasting and clashing, which the hearer feels rather than understands."[12] So how can the poet be representative of the age? To point to Herrick—presumably "representative" of his age—and want "to deduce something as good as that" is to point to the poem as an intellectual construct, subject to a form of analysis which can strip the poem down to its essentials.

And to do *that* is to point to composition by procedure. The 1930s was a decade of intense and astonishingly varied literary activity for Zukofsky;[13] with Jerry Reisman, he explored the means by which the poem can achieve this sort of "objective" status. Stated perhaps too simply, his concentration on procedure is an investigation into meaning by deliberately obscuring the motives of utterance, yet without, I think, relinquishing the personal in ways that Eliot had seemed to call for. I want to list three of these procedures, I shall mess up the chronology in doing so, and I shall discuss only one of them in any detail. Between them they combine certain aspects of Conte's "aleatory" and "predetermined" procedures.

1. *Counting and letter-distribution.* During the 1930s Zukofsky undertook with Jerry Reisman a series of statistical and sequential analyses of letter distribution in a number of canonical English lyric poems. Used in "A"-8, "A"-9, and indeed elsewhere. Sufficiently well-known to warrant no description here,[14] but closely connected to:
2. *Transliteration.* In answer to the question "What sound effects are you conscious of using or seeking?" in 1973 Zukofsky answered simply: "Transliteration (as in C. & L. Z. *Catullus*)."[15] Adopted as a compositional principle in "A"-15 and later works, transliteration has a long history in Zukofsky's poetics, reaching back possibly as far as "A"-7 or "A"-9, but taking a much more central place in later work, with transliterations (in alphabetical order) from Greek, Hebrew, Latin, Ojibway, and Welsh as well as (possibly) French and German.[16] Counting and transliteration procedures are both close to Zipf; the next is not, and seems in its assumptions to work against predetermined procedures.
3. *The aleatory and random. Thanks to the Dictionary,* in retelling a well-known story by arbitrarily and even randomly determined means, introduces major disruptions which severely break conventional narrative and reference while by and large observing syntactic propriety. Such behavior both diminishes the preciseness of utterance and enlarges its scope. This strategy, that is to say, both undermines and enlarges the significance of the story this "novel" tells. It explores, in J. H. Prynne's phrase, "the meaning-bearing nature of system violations" (30)—an activity Zipf had himself pointed to (though in different terms) in *The Psycho-Biology of Language*[17]—for it enables Zukofsky, by means of dis-

> ruptive processes, to explore the implications of his comment in 1931 that "the sound and pitch emphasis of a word are never apart from its meaning. In this sense each poem has its own laws" (*Prepositions* + 17).

Each of these methods may be considered accidental, each is an attack not only on *le mot juste* but on most forms of authorial control, and each may turn out to be a source of iridescence (an accidental color) for the words, as Prynne puts it, act both as agencies of expression and as narrative "substrate for smelting and re-working into new forms" (30).[18]

Zukofsky started work on *Thanks to the Dictionary* in July 1932; it would occupy him on and off until 1939, when (16 August) he at last settled on a sequential order for the piece, signed and dated it, and sent it to Lorine Niedecker for her to type. The actual writing (as opposed to arrangement) was probably pretty much completed by December 1934, when he sent an extract entitled "from *Thanks to the Dictionary*" to Kerker Quinn's magazine *Direction.*[19] In 1935 he sent a quite differently ordered (and much shorter) selection, with the title "Parts of a Novel," to Basil Bunting,[20] and in 1951 he went through the text yet again, making extracts for a projected (and aborted?) magazine somewhat ironically entitled *Possibilities.* Cid Corman's publication of "*A*" *1–12* in 1959 encouraged Zukofsky to turn to *Thanks to the Dictionary* yet again, making further extracts, and the complete work was eventually published by Corman in Japan in 1961, almost thirty years after its inception, as the final section of *It Was,* in an edition of 250 copies.[21] Off and on, then, the book engaged Zukofsky's attention for close to thirty years.

So far as we can tell, other productions of the 1930s did not, even though they too remained unpublished or remained as unobtainable as *Le Style Apollinaire,* published in Paris in 1934 in a small edition mostly destroyed in a warehouse fire. He seems not, that is to say, to have persistently attended to the fate of other works long unpublished and exactly contemporary with *Thanks to the Dictionary;* indeed he seems not to have attended to them at all. The film script of *Ulysses,* written 1932–1935 with Jerry Reisman, and his compilation *A Workers Anthology,* completed in 1935 and then abandoned, were (like the four lengthy articles and eleven radio scripts of the *Index of American Design,* written 1938–1940) not published until 2003, sixty-odd years after their completion. Even *Arise, Arise,* completed in 1936, seems to have languished in neglect until Zukofsky submitted it to Kerker Quinn's magazine *Accent* in the summer of 1953;[22] but it would remain unpublished until Lita

Hornick printed it in *Kulchur* in 1962; it was then directed by Jerry Benjamin for the New/Kinda Theatre Company in August 1965. The 1973 Grossman edition was early remaindered and has long been out of print.[23]

Why did *Thanks to the Dictionary* so engage Zukofsky's attention? Besides Michele Leggott and Barrett Watten, no one seems to have paid it any attention whatsoever,[24] and by conventional standards it is no doubt to be counted a rather unsuccessful literary experiment. It is among the most puzzling of Zukofsky's texts, extremely difficult to read, utterly resistant to paraphrase. Even if you already know the story of King David it seems to make very little sense.

About 10,000 words long, *Thanks to the Dictionary* retells the story of David, the second king of Israel, 1055–1015 B.C., as recounted in the Bible (I and II Samuel—I Kings). It consists of 29 unnumbered sections (though in manuscript drafts they were numbered) and a one-line preface, the somewhat baffling italicized sentence: "*And what will the writers do then, poor things*" (270).[25] Devoid of any immediately intelligible context, it not only starts things off *in medias res*—its anaphoric (backward pointing) *then* perhaps echoing the opening of Pound's *Cantos* ("And then went down to the ship")—but also points to what is to come: a somewhat puzzling episodic narrative organized according to no immediately discernible principle.

Five of the 29 sections have a title: Young David (271–72); Thru the Eyes of Jonathan (277); David and Michal (282–83); David and Bath-sheba (286–87); and Degrees (290–91). Each of the 29 sections draws much of its vocabulary from a page in one of two dictionaries, a 1930 *Funk and Wagnalls Practical Standard Dictionary*, and a 1917 *Webster's Collegiate Dictionary*.[26] The page determining the vocabulary of each episode was as a rule established—as the 25th section tells us—by a throw of dice. It is difficult to say how strictly Zukofsky stuck to his procedure, since the opening section draws on the opening page (page 1) of *Funk and Wagnalls*. "Degrees," the twenty-sixth section and at one time no doubt the actual preface to the work, tells us not only about the dice, but also that the dice chose page 327 (of *Webster's*), which apparently begins with the entry for *Dib*, with *Dickson City*, a borough in East Pennsylvania, among its entries.[27] The closing words of this section, in telling us that the dictionary page for the next (twenty-seventh) section was deliberately chosen (and thus a violation of procedure), hints at the possibility that this section was itself chosen because it includes the entry for *dictionary*: "on page 303, the hand has turned back, there is David" (291).

David is the subject of section 27 (291–98). Almost 3000 words, this section is the longest in *Thanks to the Dictionary*. It is also, after its opening paragraph, the only straightforward piece in the whole work, a condensation of the biblical history of David mostly in a single urgent paragraph of great narrative drive. Where the other sections of *Thanks to the Dictionary* rely upon the inclusion of apparently irrelevant matter seemingly designed to block referentiality or at least seriously impede it, this section (after its opening paragraph) relies for its urgency on the omission of detail in the interests of lucidity. The omissions come in the form of gaps, white spaces on the page, sometimes simply a space between sentences, sometimes a direct omission: "David came to Saul. He became his _____. David took a harp and played" (291); "David fled from _____, and came and said to Jonathan—What have I done?" (293); "David also took _____, and they were both of them his wives" (294). In his letter of 1 December 1934 Zukofsky told Quinn that the gaps separated episodes in the story, but this particular telling, clear and urgent as it is, full of names though it is, seems nevertheless rather to point toward Zukofsky's words in "A"-22, "History's best emptied of names' / impertinence" (511).

Zukofsky's compositional procedures are what interest me here, and the ends to which they seem to be put. Section 27 (the story of David) opens with a paragraph which draws on page 303 of *Webster's,* working (but not in alphabetical order) from Date to Dauphin to Dative to Dauber to Daughter to Datum until it reaches what appears to be the *terminus ad quem,* "David," whereupon it then settles into telling David's story in a single paragraph which is over six printed pages long.[28] In the opening paragraph (291), as in the rest of the work, Zukofsky varies his recourse to the dictionary, though not in any apparent pattern, sometimes using a term in isolation ("Dates! dates! dates!"); sometimes giving the term and its definition ("Who paints coarsely or cheaply—a dauber, a dabber"); sometimes transcribing or citing a definition without identifying or using the term ("a conceded fact"—the definition of datum). I cannot even guess what determined Zukofsky's choices here—a further throw of the dice? Impulse? An idle casting of the eye down the page? To the reader it seems almost randomly determined, so that although at times reading *Thanks to the Dictionary* may, at the local level of the episode or the sentence, feel a bit like reading something like Clark Coolidge's *The Maintains* (1974), with which its deployment of dictionary formulae seems to have something in common, it is by no means so tightly structured a work as Coolidge's.

For at the global level *Thanks to the Dictionary* is equally puzzling, equally a skirting of chaos: after the first (which begins on page 1 of the dictionary) the sections appear in no readily identifiable order. Indeed, Zukofsky's seven-or-eight-year tinkering with the order of the sections seems to have culminated in a principal of *dis*order, almost as though he felt the need to demonstrate the truth of Bunting's comment, in an essay he sent to Zukofsky on 1 May 1935, that "cacophony is at least as intricate an art as harmony."[29] An examination of the manuscripts suggests that Zukofsky did something like this: Writing the story of David in its customary chronological sequence, cast the dice, turn to the dictionary-page thus selected, incorporate what terms and/or definitions are to be incorporated, and when you've finished start the next episode of the story in a new section, casting the dice again to find a new page. And so on. Reading *Thanks to the Dictionary,* I might add, it is difficult to determine exactly what constitutes an "episode" or how its parameters are determined. When he'd finished the first draft of the whole work (sometime in 1934) Zukofsky seems initially to have ordered the narrative approximately in the sequence of the dictionary-pages used, so that the *alphabetical dictionary order* would determine the narrative sequence.[30] Such a procedure severely disturbs the chronological or "logical" sequence of the story's events, the sequence of historical narrative, reconfiguring perhaps not only our notion of story and of plot (of what happened and why), but also of how narrative meaning is constituted. Over the next half-dozen years or so (1934 to 1939 or 1940) he tinkered with the order, in the extract he sent to Bunting in 1935 omitting the preface and first section altogether and starting with what is now section 28: "There was a horse, its face bauson" (298). Though the final published version does seem vaguely to follow a chronological approximation of the story (from youth to age, at any rate) Zukofsky seems in determining the final order of *Thanks to the Dictionary* to be bent on ensuring that the work follow no clearly identifiable sequence, whether chronological in the narrative, alphabetical from the dictionary, whatever. Hence, as section 25 puts it,

> — Design!
> — Who wants a design?
> ....
> — Hey, this novel wants a design!
> — Okay!—says David—you find it! (289–90)

Words immediately followed, in the final version, by "Degrees," the section which seems most properly fitted to be the work's preface.

There are, then, two major sources of confusion, both derived from Zukofsky's application of a single procedure: the throw of the dice. In the published version the global disorder, a rupture of sequence and thus of intelligibility or at least of narrative harmony, echoes and mirrors the local disorder within the sentence, a kind of dislocation of utterance producing a species of semantic cacophony. "Who wants a design?" Section 26 answers, "Thanks to the Dictionary, this book will be prefaced. As against any dictator, there is that book containing the words of a language, modes of expression, diction" (291). As against *any* dictator? Thanks to *my* dictionary I know that a dictator is a person who speaks words aloud for someone else to write down, and/or a person whose pronouncements on some subject are meant to be taken as the final word, and/or a ruler with absolute power and authority. David the second king of Israel "became," one reference book tells me, "the pattern and standard by which all succeeding rulers were measured, the prototype of the last perfect ruler, the Messiah."[31] Here, in *Thanks to the Dictionary,* the dice and the dictionary together are now dictator, with the Bible making a Triumvirate (I shall return to this observation later). Following *their* dictates, Zukofsky-amanuensis tells a very strange story indeed, comic, grave, mad, lyrical, labored, prankish, reflective, grotesque, dramatic, horrific, ludicrous, yearning. So in section 3 "after the winter everybody in Bethlehem had the flu" David journeys (I Samuel 17) to supply his brothers and the army with such circumlocutions as "the ground and bolted substance of wheat," and such anachronisms as blancmange and vermouth (instead of parched corn, bread, and cheese) (272). Recourse to the dictionary tells us he carries *flour* and *flummery* and the *fluid extract* of wormwood.

But recourse to the dictionary does not make the passage any the more intelligible, even though the section ends "it was that way he met the Philistine" (274). What happens instead is that the dictionary provides additional and non-biblical material for the narrative, blocking reference through a series of ambiguations and seeming irrelevances. "The dense head-like clusters of the sessile florets lined up a passage for display," says one sentence in this episode (272), in its staggering ambiguity sounding remarkably like an inept translation into English. Insofar as the Bible is itself a translation, Zukofsky's activity is parodic if not emblematic, in this instance of the translation from Hebrew to English. The sentence immediately following, though it starts out more or less intelligible, quite rapidly turns into a vaguely suggestive gibberish composed of definitions culled from the dictionary by an imperfect speaker of American-English cursed with literary pretensions: "The stream was one issue, the flow-moss rising and falling with the water, and not forming a bog: imperfectly fluid, and a deformation of a solid body, but a gliding of interglobular movement such as might be rendered with an easy, gentle movement of speech—the brightest, finest, choicest of a period" (272–73). A scene impossible to visualize, and with only the vaguest associative connection—through the definition of *flower* with which it closes—to King David the Psalmist, whose story this purports to be.

Or does it? Is it not rather a *flourish,* which in music (the dictionary tells us) is "an elaborate but unmeaning passage for display, or as preparation for real performance"? Is *Thanks to the Dictionary,* then, a sort of psalm or the rehearsal of one?

The preface, "*And what will the writers do then, poor things,*" is a poor excuse for a preface; it is not until we reach the twenty-sixth section that we find something which—titled "Degrees"—might validly claim to be one. Yet the diversionary tactics with which *Thanks to the Dictionary* abounds are such that, all this flummery to the contrary, the opening of *Thanks to the Dictionary,* drawn from page 1 of *Funk and Wagnalls,* tells us a great deal and is, indeed, a perfectly adequate preface. " 'A'. Quoting the dictionary" it begins (270). "Remembering my sawhorses, my little a.'s abbreviated for afternoon, perhaps for years, this afternoon." A little masterpiece of seeming misdirection and non-sequitur, after five more sentences it ends "But David who resists all its agents is free from iridescence, and without accidentals. If there is iridescence, it will be at his toes. His name, these words till now, are almost his story." *Almost? History?* And when is *now*?

So far as the dictionary is concerned, the whole paragraph is pretty straightforward (it is only 155 words long), the only words likely to give us pause in the intervening sentences being *Ab* and *Abad,* and these perhaps because they have fallen out of most dictionaries. *Abad* is familiar to most of us as a suffix in Indian place-names; it is Hindi for—as Zukofsky tells us—peopled, cultivated, an inhabited place, especially a city. *Ab* is the eleventh month of the Jewish calendar, in which falls the holy day commemorating (with fasting) the Destruction of the Temple. Zukofsky puts it a little differently: "when the fast will not commemorate a Temple in ruins, Aaron's rod, the serpent to blossom, will grow, goldenrod." *Ab* usually falls in July and August, when goldenrod flowers; page 1 of the dictionary tells us not only that goldenrod is one name for Aaron's Rod, but also, as Michele Leggott reminds us in *Reading 80 Flowers,* that "the first mention of Aaron's rod, before it budded and flowered, appointing Aaron and his brothers keepers of the tabernacle (Num. 17:8, 18:3), occurred when he cast it down before Pharaoh and it turned into a serpent which swallowed up the rods-also-turned-serpents of the Egyptian enchanters (Exod. 7:10–12)"—hence "the serpent to blossom."[32] All this is pretty straightforward, and is, if not more or less common knowledge, at least pretty generally available in a public way.

But two other features of the first section of *Thanks to the Dictionary* deserve notice. While much of the information in this prose comes from the dictionary—a public source—some of it does not, but is completely personal. Who, among Zukofsky's readers in 1932, would recognize the sawhorses of

"A"-7, or recognize "my little a.'s"? Who, for that matter, would in 1932 notice that personal Zukofskian interjection in the identification of *Ab,* "when the fast will *not* commemorate a Temple in ruins"? Only, perhaps, the reader already familiar with "A"-4, with its lines:

> We had a speech, our children have
> evolved a jargon.
> We prayed, Open, God, gate of Psalmody,
> ....
> Deafen us, God, deafen us to their music,
> Our own children have passed over to the ostracized, . . . (12–13)

When Zukofsky began to write *Thanks to the Dictionary* the whole of "A" 1–7, had just been published in *An "Objectivists" Anthology.* It is worth noting that Zukofsky would virtually suspend work on "*A*" until he had completed *Thanks to the Dictionary,* starting "A"-8 on 5 August 1935 and finishing it on 14 July 1937. One thread running through *Thanks to the Dictionary* like a patterning of tropes is a more-or-less private and personal discourse which refers to Zukofsky's own work, in the form of horses, flowers, leaves, music, and so on. These are his little a's.

Then, too, there is the fine distinction made about David, "on his page, *not* like a slab forming the top of a capital"—which is an abacus, yet who is "not *unlike* . . . a reckoning table", which is also an abacus (270, my italics). To *reckon,* says *Funk and Wagnalls,* is to tell over by particulars, to enumerate, to count, to esteem, to come to a settlement of one's differences with another. David, on *his* page "not unlike a reckoning table telling its sums will embrace all the words of this novel." But what, then, is to be reckoned? Perhaps Zukofsky's phrasing, which is to say his use of the dictionary, including of course his use of pun: "His name, these words till now, are almost his story." Which words are *these* words—and when is *now*? The play of possibility, in which *these words* can refer exophorically, outside the text, to the dictionary, is echoed in the exophoric play in which *now* can be not this stage in the telling of the story but this stage of human history (i.e., 1932 or even the now in which the reader reads the story). There is a great deal to do with time in *Thanks to the Dictionary.* A dictionary, the dictionary tells us, is a word-book containing all the words in a language—in which case, then, section 25's "prefatory" remark that "as against any dictator, there is that book containing the words of a language" (290) opposes the dictionary, its words, the language, not only against Hitler or Mussolini (rising to power in 1932) but also against David, second king of Israel, risen to power in 1055 BC, and against Zukofsky himself, writing to power in 1932. "These words" may be *almost* his story, but they cannot be the whole thing.

That they cannot be the whole thing has to do not only with the nature of story (as contrasted, let us say, with the nature of "event") but with the nature of Zukofsky's sources and of the authorship of *Thanks to the Dictionary,* a fiction which raises important questions about the nature and identity of authority. If we consider where the actual words of *Thanks* came from—a question frequently and indissolubly linked in the interpretive critic's mind to the problem of what a work means—if we consider the question "who wrote this work?"—we are obliged to point to three possible authors, that Triumvirate I mentioned earlier, the dice, the dictionary, and the Bible, who collaboratively dictate this quite unusual tale. This, of course, brings us back to the preface: if other sources write the text, then what *will* the authors do then, poor things?

Thanks to the Dictionary exploits, even as it interrogates, the agency and authority of the triumvirate: the dice, by whose agency the (selected) vocabulary of any given section of the story is determined; the Bible, by whose agency the story in all its recorded detail is already known; and the dictionary. "A dictionary," Basil Bunting would write in 1938, talking about translation, "puts difficulties in the way."[33] There is also of course Zukofsky himself. (That there is some interference from Zukofsky-amanuensis need not argue that this transcribed text is thereby corrupt; I shall consider his role shortly.) The Bible is, of course, to many readers not only an unimpeachable authority and source of ethical, moral, and spiritual value, telling you what you *ought* to think, but also a great narrative storehouse of great instructional worth. The story of David is of central significance not only in the Jewish tradition, but in the Christian. For David, whose name traditionally means "the beloved," is the ideal king, the prototype of the Messiah; so, too, just "as Moses completed the law of Israel for all time before the people entered Canaan, so David completed the theory and contents of the Temple psalmody before the temple itself was built."[34] He is, then, a figure of great historical and cultural significance within the Judaeo-Christian framework, within, that is to say, what Prynne calls "a traceable history of interpretation" (14).

So *Thanks to the Dictionary* plays one authority against another, plays with patterns of authority: *David* the prototype human model; the *Bible* the template of sensibility and intelligibility; the *dictionary* the book of words as Bible; the *dice,* chance as decision-maker and arbitrator. Writers, of course, work by chance; they are the habitual editors of serendipity. So are thinkers: what gets thought depends on what got put in the hopper in the first place.

But the words I quoted about David came not from a dictionary but from yet another kind of authority, the encyclopedia.[35] Now the salient feature of a dictionary is that it is a word-book. It lists all (or most) of the words in a given language in an arbitrary (i.e., alphabetical) order, with definitions or explanations of meaning. It does not give details of usage, nor of context, save in the simplest ways, and it does not (in the case of most dictionaries) provide much in the way of illustrative quotation or usage. In the case of the two dictionaries Zukofsky drew upon in writing *Thanks to the Dictionary*, there is minimal information about synonyms and antonyms. The dictionary is the repository of lexical meaning; it is the repository of a vocabulary; it tells us the words for things, but it does not tell us their history or their significance, and it does not (in I. A. Richards's term)[36] "interinanimate" them. An encyclopedia does. Its etymology tells us that an *encyclopedia* is the circle of the sciences, a general system of instruction.[37] In the pedantic and somewhat solemn blather of flat-footed dictionary definition, an encyclopedia is—as we all know—"a work in which the various topics included under several or all branches of knowledge are treated separately, and usually in alphabetical order" (*Century Dictionary and Cyclopedia*, entry for Encyclopedia). Above all else the great virtue of the encyclopedia is that it is, as James Russell Lowell observed, a place "where one may learn without cost of research what things are generally known"[38] (90). The encyclopedia is the repository of general culture, it is an acculturating tool. Unlike the dictionary, but like the Bible, it is a storehouse of received ideas, it teaches the tradition.

Now language, and especially "literary" language, is a system of meanings and of meaning relations more or less (in Prynne's phrase) "inflected by semantic and cultural history" (11). But Zukofsky's book, of course, is *Thanks to the DICTIONARY*, not to the encyclopedia, and the astonishing culling of odd words and unusual definitions challenges the reader to make sense of what is being said by destroying the preordained linkages.

The very form of *Thanks to the Dictionary* is indeed crucial, for it plays the long straightforward section (section 27), which condenses at high speed and with great lucidity the story of David as recounted in I and II Samuel, against the other 28 sections, with their more or less private and personal discourse (referring to Zukofsky's work) and their randomly chosen vocabulary. *Thanks to the Dictionary* plays, then, the sacred text of public virtue against the secular text of personal accomplishment; it also plays private signification against the profane vocabulary of chance. It thus plays a narrative with pre-existent meaning against a writing which invites the reader to make meaning; a narrative the meaning of which we already know (for we have a traceable history of its interpretation) against a narrative whose meaning is not known. The writing of one text over another, however (and of course the very act of reading), seduces the reader into assuming that the aleatorically determined text is as coherent, as meaningful, as articulate, as the sacred; and the title, *Thanks to the DICTIONARY,* suggests that *its* meaning too is accessible, for it is already there, pre-existent and recoverable from the dictionary. The dictionary thus becomes an agent of recovery, by which we excavate a set of more-or-less related elements—except that once we've uncovered them they still don't tell us why they're there, and the words remain opaque. The dictionary thereby becomes a means by which to position the writer outside the culture, outside the tradition (and not, therefore, subject to it), and even (especially if we bear Zukofsky's much later working of *Catullus* in mind) outside the language. In such "insistence on the constant display and play of language,"[39] words approach the condition of *things,* and one might observe that *Thanks to the Dictionary,* insofar as it exploits the relationship of local pockets of clarity to a larger global sense, theme, structure, and environment, one long work whose beat the writer "cannot be entirely aware of" ("*A*" 214), is an anticipatory gesture toward work by such writers as Bruce Andrews, Clark Coolidge, David Melnick, or Steve McCaffery. *Thanks to the Dictionary,* however, avoids the acute semantic inertia characteristic of these writers.

One drama *Thanks to the Dictionary* affords, then, is that between what words *actually* mean (in the narrative) and what we think they *ought* to mean. The work exploits, then, the tension between two views of language: language as arbitrary (in which meaning is in the system and the context) and language as motivated (in which meaning is in the words). Either words have "real" meanings (Adam was the perfect man because he knew the real name of things), or they don't. Either there is a necessary and inherent "natural" connection between the word and its meaning, so that words *of themselves* tell you something of what they say, or there isn't. Either the disruption of meaning is sense-bearing, or it is not. *Thanks to the Dictionary* thus points to the theme of Plato's *Cratylus,* which concludes that the two views can only be reconciled by recourse not to words but to things; it also points to the difference between ordinary language, which treats words more or less as transparencies, counters for communicative and expressive purposes, and literary language, which, using defamiliarizing techniques, develops system-violations which make sense, disruptions which are sense-bearing, thereby treating words as objects for meditative and exploratory purposes.

All of this is parallel to that larger social and public drama, between what one thinks and what one ought to think: the moral imperative of Authority here becomes a drama encapsulating the moral imperative of Authorship. That there is some interference from Zukofsky himself in the telling need not argue that this text is "corrupt." But of course that is entirely the wrong way of putting it, since the notion of corruption entails a prior condition of "purity." Whether we add Zukofsky's name or not to the authorial triumvirate of Bible, Dice, and Dictionary, it is quite clear that Zukofsky's procedural strategy in compiling this text is designed to obscure its origin; that in so doing it undercuts the divine origin of the sacred text is incidental. More to the point is that the originary motives for this text, and indeed for all texts and for language itself (to say nothing of meaning), are irrecoverable, lost, not only to readers but also to writers. Opposed to the dictatorial intent which would "overleap all particulars" (including David, including Zukofsky, including the reader) "and fasten on the *end itself*"[40] (that end itself a mental construct, a logical construct, standing in dualistic relation to the material world), stands the language itself and the arbitrarily ordered dictionary which indeed, as Bunting said, "puts difficulties in the way." It may or may not be an accident, but it is certainly remarkably fitting that Zukofsky carried his "original" outline and plan of "*A*" around with him in his pocket for so long that the words literally wore off the paper.[41] Such literal undoing of the origins is, surely, a trope for Zukofsky's enterprise. "To begin a song," says "A"-12,

> if you cannot recall,
> Forget. (140)

Notes

Epigraph. Louis Zukofsky, "*A*" (Berkeley: U of California P, 1978) 292. Hereafter cited parenthetically in the text.

1. Joseph M. Conte, *Unending Design: The Forms of Postmodern Poetry* (Ithaca: Cornell UP, 1991) 11.

2. J. H. Prynne, *Stars, Tigers and the Shape of Words: The William Matthews Lectures 1992 Delivered at Birkbeck College, London,* (London: Birkbeck College) 1993. Cited parenthetically in text as Prynne.

3. *Poetry U.S.A.*, Louis Zukofsky, video, PBS, 1966, filmed 16 March 1966. I am indebted to WNET for providing a dub of the soundtrack in September 1966.

4. Louis Zukofsky, *Prepositions +: The Collected Critical Essays,* Mark Scroggins, ed. (Hanover: Wesleyan UP, 2000) 170. Hereafter cited parenthetically in text.

5. Witness his quotation (with elisions as indicated) from Gibbon towards the end of "A"-15: "The poet or philosopher illustrates his age and / country by the ef-

forts of a *single* mind; / but these superior powers of reason or fancy / are but rare and spontaneous productions; /and the genius of Homer . . . or Newton / would excite less admiration / if they could be created / by the will of . . . a preceptor" (373).

6. John Rodker, *The Future of Futurism* (London: Kegan Paul, Trench, Trubner, 1926) 11.

7. Edith Sitwell, *Aspects of Modern Poetry* (London: Duckworth, 1926) 217.

8. Lorine Niedecker, undated (1937) letter to Zukofsky, in the Zukofsky collection at the Harry Ransom Humanities Research Center, University of Texas at Austin (hereafter cited as TxU).

9. George Kingsley Zipf, *The Psycho-Biology of Language: An Introduction to Dynamic Philology* (1935), George A. Miller, introduction (Cambridge: MIT Press, 1965) xi. Subsequent references cited parenthetically in text. My thanks to Fred Bowers for telling me about this book and lending it to me.

10. Charles Olson, "Readings at Goddard College, 12–14 April 1962," *Minutes of the Charles Olson Society* 2 (June 1993): 17–27 (24–25).

11. John Lyons, *Semantics* (Cambridge: Cambridge UP, 1978) 637–38.

12. Basil Bunting, "The Poet's Point of View," *Three Essays,* Richard Caddel, ed., 34. Reinforces, yes, but as this essay I hope shows, Bunting's view requires enlargement. The stress in my formulation would be on *patterns* rather than, with Bunting, on *sound.*

13. Work of the 1930s includes: *1930:* "A" 5, 6, 7; *1931:* editing the "Objectivist" issue of *Poetry; 1932:* completing (19 April) *The Writing of Guillaume Apollinaire;* July–16 August: *Thanks to the Dictionary* (first draft); *An "Objectivists Anthology; 1932–35:* (with Jerry Reisman) film script of *Ulysses; 1935:* completes *A Workers Anthology;* 5 August begins "A"-8 (completed 14 July 1937); begins *A Test of Poetry* (completed 1940); *1936: Arise, Arise; 1937:* 12 November proposal/outline for *Index of American Design* (four articles written 1938, seven radio scripts 1939, and four radio scripts in 1940). During this period, too, Zukofsky taught for a year at the University of Wisconsin (and a summer at Berkeley), collaborated with William Carlos Williams on *The First President,* acted irregularly as informal poetry editor for *Hound and Horn* and possibly *Pagany,* and wrote and published reviews, essays, and shorter poems. And, of course, he worked for a living, at a variety of more-or-less unpleasant jobs for more-or-less unpleasant pay.

14. Marcella Booth reproduces some notes in Reisman's and Zukofsky's hands in *A Catalogue of the Louis Zukofsky Manuscript Collection* (Austin: U of Texas, 1975); a useful discussion of the letter distribution in "A"-9 is in Barry Ahearn, *Zukofsky's "A": An Introduction* (Berkeley: U of California P, 1983) 231–241.

15. "Supplement: On Rhythm: from America. A Questionnaire," *Agenda* 11.2–3 (Spring-Summer 1973): 37, 66; and see also "Correction," *Agenda* 11.4–12.1 (1974): 102 (66).

16. For a detailed discussion of late transliterative effects in Zukofsky, see Michele J. Leggott, *Reading Zukofsky's 80 Flowers* (Baltimore: Johns Hopkins UP, 1989).

17. Zipf postulated (287–291) that symbols are constructed of "genes of meaning"

(symbol *X* "means *abcde*"); since many different symbols have genes in common, he speculated, poetic and "bookish" language might result in such system violations as the seemingly arbitrary or incorrect mixing of semantic fields apparent in "dormant baby and sleeping rose-bush" (290n).

18. The first section of *Thanks to the Dictionary* reminds us (via the dictionary) that iridescence is an accidental color; in *The First Half of "A"-9* Zukofsky speaks of his "intention to have the poem fluoresce as it were in the light of seven centuries of interrelated thought."

19. Calling it a work in progress, Zukofsky originally sent Quinn some handwritten pages from *Thanks to the Dictionary* in August 1934; Quinn liked them well enough to type some, and in a letter on 1 December Zukofsky gave detailed instructions for typing the long section 27 (the sixth of this version's eleven sections), and explained that in the printed version each section should bear as title the page number of the dictionary from which the section was drawn. (Materials at the University Library, University of Illinois at Urbana/Champaign.)

20. "Parts of a Novel," a 17-page typescript in the Basil Bunting archive at Durham University, is undated, but was sent from 149 East 37th Street, an address Zukofsky seems to have used only for the first few months of 1935.

21. Louis Zukofsky, "Thanks to the Dictionary," *It Was* (Kyoto: Origin, 1961), 99–130. There are a very few misprints in this edition, principally to do with the spacing in the longest section (27). Despite the fact that (occasionally quite severe) misprints were introduced into the typographically infelicitous reprint in Zukofsky's *Collected Fiction* (Elmwood Park, IL: Dalkey Archive, 1990) 270–300, for ease of reference page numbers in parentheses refer to this edition, on the grounds of its greater availability.

22. Letter to Quinn, 24 August 1953, at the University of Illinois at Urbana/Champaign.

23. "Arise, Arise," *Kulchur* 6 (Summer 1962): 66–100; the production by Jerry Benjamin took place at the Cinemathèque Theatre, 85 East 4th Street, New York, on August 6, 7, 12, 13, 14, 19, 20, 21 and 27 1965; it appeared as a book in 1973.

24. Barrett Watten, *The Constructivist Moment: From Material Text to Cultural Poetics* (Middletown, CT: Wesleyan UP, 2003) 25–29.

25. In the MS version (TxU) "And what will the writers do then, poor things" is followed by a pair of initials.

26. Letter to Quinn, 1 December 1934, at the University of Illinois at Urbana/Champaign.

27. In the TxU manuscript, each section after the preface is headed with a number and a code, usually "F&W" but in six instances "W.C.D." When Zukofsky sent his abbreviated but still coded version to Quinn's magazine in December 1934, he identified the dictionaries from which *Thanks to the Dictionary* is drawn (see note 20 above). The first section of *Thanks to the Dictionary* (270) tells us that Zukofsky is retelling the story of David using a vocabulary in part determined by casting dice to find the dictionary page number—in this case, *Funk and Wagnalls* page 327, which seems to cover *Dib* through *Dictionary*. My statement of the range of entries on the page is a

guess, derived from the text, since I have not been able to examine either of the dictionaries in the edition Zukofsky used. Each section in the TxU manuscript also bears two or three (crossed out) numbers revising the order of the sequence.

28. In the manuscript. The breaks on pages 292 and 293 of *Collected Fiction* are not authorized in any manuscript that I have examined.

29. Basil Bunting, "The Lion and The Lizard," *Three Essays,* Richard Caddel, ed. (Durham: Basil Bunting Poetry Centre, 1994) 27–31 (30); also in *Sulfur* 33 (Fall 1993): 73–78.

30. In the manuscript (at TxU) fifteen of the sections were originally ordered in strict alphabetical sequence according to the dictionary page upon which they draw. Thus the thirteenth manuscript section drew on *Webster's* page 327 (Dicta-Dicti), the fourteenth *Funk and Wagnalls* 342 (Dist), the fifteenth *F&W* 350 (Doo-Don), the sixteenth *F&W* 351 (Dos), and so on. In the final published version these are sections 26, 4, 7, and 9 respectively.

31. *Century Dictionary and Cyclopedia,* (New York: Century, 1897) v. 9, *Century Cyclopedia of Names,* s.v. "David."

32. Leggott, *Reading 80 Flowers,* 312–13.

33. Basil Bunting, "Verse Translations," *Criterion* 17 (April 1938): (558).

34. *Encyclopædia Britannica* 13th ed., 22: 535, entry for "Psalms, Book of." The *Century* entry for David calls him "[t]he actual founder of a sanctifying, divine worship, refining and enriching it by the influence of music and psalmody."

35. In what follows, the distinctions I draw between dictionaries and encyclopedias have much in common with those made for somewhat different ends by both Prynne and Watten.

36. Chapter 3 of I. A. Richards, *The Philosophy of Rhetoric* (London: Oxford UP, 1936) is titled "The Interinanimation of Words."

37. Greek ἐνκύκλιος in a circle, circular, periodic, general (as in encyclic), and παιδεία, education, from παῖς, child. An encyclopedia is, then, a general system of instruction in several or all parts of knowledge, which is to say the circle of the sciences (of what is known).

38. James Russell Lowell, "Books and Libraries," *The Writings of James Russell Lowell: Literary and Political Addresses,* Riverside ed. (Boston: Houghton Mifflin, 1894) v. 6, 90.

39. Louis Zukofsky and René Taupin, *The Writing of Guillaume Apollinaire: Le Style Apollinaire,* Serge Gavronsky, ed. and trans. (Hanover: Wesleyan UP, 2004) 192.

40. Zukofsky, *Collected Fiction* 290 (Zukofsky's italics). The Dalkey Archive edition unfortunately prints "overlaps" for "overleaps." See *It Was* 121, and the MSS at both Illinois and Texas.

41. The paper in question is at TxU. For a description, see Ahearn *Zukofsky's "A"* 38.

Thinking with the Poem

Louis Zukofsky

"Poems are only acts upon particulars," Zukofsky said in 1930, and "only through such activity do they become particulars themselves."[1] Thinking with the poem, I'm going to belabor the obvious, and I'm going view some of those particulars very narrowly indeed. I begin with vowels.

A. E. I. O. U. *aeiou. ah eh ih oh uh.* Vowels can be muscular, or slack. "[T]hi• has the sound of tree," as Robert Duncan put it, "and thə has the sound of nut."[2] Sometimes you get to choose; sometimes you don't. We all, Zukofsky included, call his long poem "*A*" (ēi), and we do so without instruction and without thought. But that *A* of the title is in quotes because it's the first line of the poem ("A / Round of fiddles playing Bach"), and so the title really should be *Uh* (ə). His first poem of some length is closely similar—you might call it "Poem beginning *Thee*" (Thi•), as Zukofsky did; but if you pay attention to the first line you might prefer to call it "Poem beginning *Thuh*" (Thə)—again, the title gives the complete first line of the poem ("The / voice of Jesus I. Rush singing." So, provided you pay attention, "*A*" (ēi) probably rhymes with *The* [Thə], and *Uh* [ə] with *Thee* [Thi•]. Zukofsky's a trickster, and he thinks like one; that sort of play is everywhere. It requires you to think as well as notice. And it requires you to listen. The vowels *ah eh ih oh uh* and their many variants and combinations determine tone—in March 1948 Pound instructed younger poets to be "vitally aware of the duration of syllables, of melodic coherence, and of the tone leading of vowels."[3] And the consonants? Consonants have to do with pace.

Here's three words: *Hedge-crickets sing.* Basil Bunting thought that half-line from the ode "To Autumn" the only thing worth bothering with in the whole of Keats's work; it's the only bit of Keats that Zukofsky included in *A Test of Poetry.*[4] The movement of the mouth, the shifts the tongue and the breath undergo (I'm talking about poems as mouthfuls of air) as you go from the close of *hedge* to the start of *crickets,* the unavoidable break in the breath (juncture) as you go from *crickets* to *sing,* is quite energetic.

Here's three more words: *A torch surged.*[5] That's the third line of "A"-12; the italicized first line, with its little consonant clusters *f-d* and *p-n* neatly sets it up: "*Out of deep need*" moving into the smoother flow of the second: "Four trombones and the organ in the nave"—that third line, "A torch surged—" might be a kind of antiphonal response to Keats. The fourth, "Timed the theme Bach's name," bolsters, for those with sleepy ears, the poem's intense interest on how it sounds—the hesitations and accelerations of quantity, the cadence of inflection. *A torch surged:* the vowel sounds in that line prolonged by those barely-if-at-all-sounded *r*'s in *torch surged* (Zukofsky didn't roll his *r*'s). The vowels move—there's nothing slack in that shift from *uh* to *or* to *ur,* the tones—I mean the tune—dipping down (to *torch*) and then rising on *surge,* a word which drags the torch *up* along with it: here the movement of the vowels and consonants gives rise to image, moves into image, conjures the image. This movement—and possibly the flickering of the surging torchlight—is reinforced first by the drastic slowing down of the line through the consonant clusters, and second by Zukofsky's inverted patterning of the consonants, in a brief *cynghanedd* sequence which the ear registers, though it might well slide right past the eye, in the shifts from *ch* to *dg,* and *t* to *d.* The move from *torch* to *surged* is a move from unvoiced to voiced, catching the eye through the ear. Particularity, as Zukofsky puts it in *Bottom,* here resolving "tensions of *melody* and *sight.*"[6] Thinking with the *poem*? This is thinking with the *ear,* whereby the words take on a *physical* form. Thinking with the poem? One might think of this as thinking with the *body,* and language as *sense*-able. At the Gotham Book Mart in 1931 Zukofsky spoke of "poets who see with their ears, hear with their eyes, move with their noses and speak and breathe with their feet" (*Prepositions* + 17, 212). Thinking with the body connects to "the detail, not mirage, of seeing, of thinking with the things as they exist, and of directing them along a line of melody" (*Prepositions* + 12).

"The sound of words," Zukofsky says in *A Test of Poetry,* "is sometimes 95% of poetic presentation" (58). After an evening at a friend's listening to records of Bach and Mozart, Zukofsky found (as usual) that the music gave him an awful itch to get back to writing—in this case, writing "A"-8.[7] What he repeatedly called the "music" of poetry really does have close connections to played music. Bunting commented that "when [Zukofsky] wanted to imitate a fugue, he determined that the actual sounds"—rather than thematic recurrences or reiterative rhythm—"should be the substance of it" and stated flatly that "no other [twentieth-century] poet has stated or followed more clearly the closeness of poetry to music."[8]

There may be a "music of ideas" in Zukofsky's poetry, but there's also an *actual* music. Culturally we are nevertheless so in the habit of reading poems for their "meaning" that we still (though there is a vast literature) down-play the immensely complex relationship of poems to music.[9] Critics and readers pay so little attention to the tone-value of vowels that they forget how difficult it is even to *say* the vowels A E I O U in a flat monotone—to sound them that way takes hard practice and great concentration. There is quite explicitly and distinctly a music in speech, each vowel sounding its own note. But we don't have a vocabulary to trace the subtle interactions and patterns of pitch, stress, duration, the movements of breath through voice, and we certainly don't have a notation. All we have is the ear. Part 2 of *Bottom: On Shakespeare* gives us 62 detailed pages (33–94) on prosody considered as speech, the music of speaking. A footnote on page 37 tells us that Celia Thaew (Zukofsky's) setting of *Pericles* is "the one excuse for all that follows in this part." In October 1963, after *Bottom* had been published, Zukofsky told Cid Corman "yes I mean that footnote . . . & will mean it more & more as the world understands less & less how much I mean it."[10]

But reader after reader has remarked on the "genuine difficulty" (the phrase is Bunting's) and general impenetrability of Zukofsky's poems— "semantically dense" says one critic;[11] "opaque and annoying to a remarkable degree" says a contemporary poet;[12] some of the poems drive one nuts. What makes it worse is Zukofsky's repeated assertion that they're clear. There's not just his expostulations in letters to Cid Corman that "*A*" is always direct (17 August 1959, TxU) and to Lorine Niedecker that his poems are, to a careful reader, clear (1941, TxU); there's also the half-humorous half-mocking but certainly not wholly ironic claim in *Anew* 42: "I will not regret it one day / That I am plain to the simplest" (CSP 99). But if he's so clear, how come we can't see what he's up to? What's going on? Mark Scroggins has suggested that it is the "tactics of juxtaposition and montage" that "pose formidable difficulties for the average reader" of Zukofsky's poems of the 1930s.[13] Leaving the question of "the average reader" to one side, the difficulties are far more pervasive than he suggests.

In 1962 Ian Hamilton Finlay wondered how serious Zukofsky was in sending his poem "The" (CSP 232) for Finlay to publish in the sixth issue of *Poor.Old.Tired.Horse* (May 1963). He was puzzled and dubious. "THE"—a one-word title followed by four one-word lines, the first line repeating the title: "The"—and a minuscule pause before the next line's single word, "desire"—but desire *of*, the third line tells us, not "for." It is the last line's simple "towing" that has the desire, and there's no closing period, no internal punctuation. Zukofsky had to explain that he'd been thinking of tugboats, which *tow* very seriously; and he pointed out that none of the vowels in the poem repeat.[14] But I'm not so sure about that—when Zukofsky read the poem on tape not long after he wrote it, he repeated *schwa* three or possibly even four times. But of course there are various ways to sound the poem, there are so many ways to think it/hear it.[15]

And that's the difficulty. It's a simple enough little poem, I guess, but what does it sound like? What noises *does* it make? How can we tell? Thinking with the ear? *Whose* ear? Your own, of course, but I think Guy Davenport somewhat overstates the case when he says, "His obscurity is in the reader's mind, not in the poem."[16] It is of course true that the assumptions you bring to your reading determine the difficulties the poems raise, and it follows that the nature of the difficulties varies from reader to reader. But very often Zukofsky's writing seems to constitute a pretty direct assault on collective reading habits. A study group in Berkeley was in June 2004 scratching its collective head over a possible gloss for the opening line of Zukofsky's 1941 poem *Anew* 38 (MS dated 7 April): "Belly Locks Shnooks Oakie" (CSP 97).[17] That line might, I suppose, have something in common with the well-known utterance from *The Meaning of Meaning,* "The gostak distims the doshes,"[18] published in 1923 and still (2004) enjoying wide circulation. But *there* it's obvious that *distimming* is something *gostaks* do to *doshes* (and so on, by permutation)—there *is* a syntax in that sentence which, unlike Zukofsky's opening line follows a familiar grammar. The parts of speech in "Belly Locks Shnooks Oakie" are so unstable that syntax disappears, we can't tell whether there's a verb at all. If there's one verb among those four opening words there's quite possibly even two, but which is which is up for grabs, and the line might just as readily be a simple list of names,[19] a notion reinforced only when you get to the second line: "When he awoke, he"—but even then—since the first line is unpunctuated—grammar and syntax remain uncertain.

However you understand that opening line—and surely you have to keep the options open—it's clear that that line generated the sheer playfulness of the whole poem, the *sound* of it, and the echoes (Oakie / He awoke, he / some oak, he) fundamentally constitute the poem. But here there's a problem: how does it sound? What noise *does* it make? What noise, exactly, *does* the complete poem make? Starting each line in this poem with a capital letter confuses the coding if we expect consistency, for the initial "When" of "When he awoke" strongly suggests that we back-read the first line as grammatically complete (and hence, perhaps, a sentence) whereas the third's "Scared all the spooks. He" severely undermines any presumed clarity such a reading might have. There's a strong jingle or maybe singsong effect, firmly encouraged by the playful rhyme (Oakie / he / He) of the first three lines, culminating in the fourth line's "was some oak, he"—but that singsong (if that's what to call it) is totally disrupted by the indented fifth line, with its single and blunt word "Was." What sort of weight do we give that final *Was*? He was some oak, *he* was? or He was some oak. He *was*? The punctuation encourages the former; the line-break and indentation the latter. And does that *Shnooks/spooks* in their surround suggest the word *smoke* emerging from that *some oak*? And so on. There's a range of possible voicings here, and the many echoes make the whole poem—from a sonic point of view—extremely unstable.

Now, I take as a truism that meaning determines tone, and meaning determines quantity—tone, pacing, and rhythm are intimately connected, and in traditional or conventional verse the sense of the words, their meaning, is the governing, determining factor. To note that there is a connection between voicing and thinking belabors the obvious, but if the poem is there for the *music,* then the question "How *should* this poem sound?" demands *thought,* and it tempts one into interpretation. "Thinking's the lowest rung," says the close of "A"-12 (260), but it *is* a rung, and necessary: Get the meaning clear and you can get the tone clear, get the tone clear and you get the sound right. And interpretation—in the sense of coming up with a paraphrasable meaning or summary of the poem—is very tempting; indeed the opening line invites it.[20] It's worth noting that the suggestive uncertainties of reference in the first line of the poem raise the spooks that we meet in line three when he scared them all, but that reflection doesn't get the meaning clear, nor even the multiplicities of meaning clear, they proliferate so, and the sound the poem makes is still variable. Although the poem seems to settle into a fairly secure voicing in its middle three lines (mainly because of the kind of sound-pattern invited by a clause beginning "When"), and the syntax and grammar pretty clear even if the semantic field is still obscure, the sounds the poem makes nevertheless have an improvisational quality, a different sound each time you say it. It might even be—as Meredith Quartermain suggested in conversation—that the multiplicity of possible voicings, simultaneously held in the poet's—and perhaps the reader's—head, begin to feel a bit like voices all sounding at once: the poem as chorus. Zukofsky achieves that effect not simply by making the poem "difficult" or "opaque" but by deliberately withholding the meaning—I mean, by making sure it's more-or-less incomprehensible—while at the same time enjoining you to think (*and* speak). That double push—the carrot always held out of reach on the stick, the hermeneutic promise of meaning dangled before the reader's nose—is a characteristic Zukofsky move.

So. If he's withholding the meaning, to that extent he's withholding the poem by cultivating its inaccessibility. But why? Why is he so opaque? A quick answer might be that if the world, the events and objects in it, is essentially opaque, if "writing occurs which is the detail, not mirage, of seeing, of thinking with the things as they exist, and of directing them along a line of melody" (*Prepositions* + 12)[21] and if poetry "is an object or affects the mind as such" (*Prepositions* + 13) then necessarily the poem, if it is to be an object in the world, if it is to be a "particular," will resist what we think of as "understanding." (In 1928 Williams congratulated Zukofsky on his achievement in "Poem Beginning The": "It escapes me in its analysis (thank God) and strikes against me a thing (thank God). There are not so many things in the world as we commonly imagine. Plenty of debris, plenty of smudges."[22]) But that quick answer's too simple. Again and again in his critical writing Zukofsky is scornful of what he calls "the predatory intent" (*Prepositions* + 18), and—to put it bluntly—he cultivates opacity because he wants to change the way we read, he wants to make predatory reading impossible.[23] In this, he's like Stein. "What is the difference between a fig and an apple" Stein asked, and answered "the one precedes the other."[24]

Zukofsky is at times more cryptic even than Stein, as in, for instance, the recurrence (in early movements of "*A*") of billboards advertising Wrigley's chewing gum. They come up three times, in "A"-2 (8), "A"-5 (19), and "A"-6. The last of these reads:

Jesus bless, too, that lady's avoirdupois
Great as of outlasting song,
Also her tiny daughter hoiden
Outwriggling the wriggly Wrigley boys. (21)

—lines which puzzled Cid Corman, who complained that "certain references . . . certainly are almost meaningless for any readers younger than I. The Wrigley advertisements, for example. (I have to dig back into memory for that.) It is NOT the personal allusions that vanish, for you establish them perfectly . . . but the highly local (even Gracie Allen or Fred Allen)" (4 January 1960 [TxU]). Zukofsky's impulse is to remove reference and force attention to the movement of the words. And he told Corman (7 January 1960 [TxU]) that he can't explain, for it has nothing to do with what people call reasons: it's a matter of feeling, that the "wriggle" in "Wrigleys" will last, when the name has lost its local or historical reference, its context, for as long as print. *Sound* is primary, so half a year later he would exclaim, in another letter to Corman (25 August 1960 [*Origin* 63]), that as for "*content*, . . . the sooner I can get that out of the way & buried in the music of *the whole thing* the better."[25] The uncertainty—of "Belly Locks Shnooks Oakie," "The desire of towing," "the wriggly Wrigley boys"—is part of the poem and essential. Zukofsky withholds reference and meaning because he wants you to think *through* the uncertainty, *by means of it.* The uncertainty is itself the material and the ground of thought, for uncertainty is, when all's said and done, how we go through the world in which those particulars we call objects are, finally, inscrutable. The poem is a way of being in the world without claiming power over it.

Corman seeks what Zukofsky once called "the horror of explanation";[26] the need for such explanation is symptomatic of what Williams called "an easy lateral sliding":[27] reading the language as instrument of another will, moving outside the poem. In this, his reading is predatory, akin to Henry Ford's, whom Zukofsky quoted scornfully in "A"-6:

> "I read poetry, and I enjoy it
> If it says anything,
> But so often it doesn't say anything,"
> says Henry.[28]

But what would one want a poem to *say*? What is the value of certainty, and of assertion? Bunting had the right of it when he told Pound in 1958 that "Zukofsky gets stronger and stronger, particularly in short pieces, that dont seem to be about anything."[29]

I can't find a word that adequately identifies or describes "non-predatory" reading—and, I must add, non-predatory writing.[30] It has to do with getting rid of unquestioned habits of mind and assumptions that we customarily bring to the act of reading. In Part 1 of *Bottom: On Shakespeare* Zukofsky tells of taking a four-year-old to see Cocteau's "Beauty and the Beast." After sitting through most of the film the child asks, "When will the beast become fancy?" Zukofsky explains that "he means, of course, when will the good Beast look as good as he is."[31] I'm still not at all sure I understand this, but I take him to mean the child seeks a match between appearance and reality, or—to put it another way—that *words should mean what they say.* Zukofsky is discussing the difference between hallucination and imagination—he's talking about Ovid's *Metamorphoses*—and says it is "more salutary" to read literally than to "cower" in the figurative. "One will see," he had said in "A"-6 (27), "gravel in gravel"—no symbolism here. In these terms, language as figuration constitutes a retreat from language itself, an evasion, a refusal to see and hear what is before us, *and it is a refusal to engage the imagination.*

Our sympathies, in the interlude which brings *A Midsummer Night's Dream* to a close, are with the "rude mechanicals," for the demands of the play of Pyramus and Thisby are that Snout *be* a wall, so he *is* one, and those hands held in the air *make* a chink through which Bottom-Pyramus may see, speak, and attempt to kiss. Snout is transformed into Wall (though he is still Snout), and Wall, in a play within a play, is by turns transformed to "lovely" (line 172), "wicked" (line 178), and "vile" (line 198), transformed into a state of which "the eye . . . hath not heard, the ear . . . hath not seen, [the] hand is not able to taste, [the] tongue to conceive, nor [the] heart to report."[32] Imagination transforms the world—this is not a matter of illusion, precisely—it is a *making*, a *seeing*—we see Snout and think or *feel* Wall (I'd take *feel* to be Zukofsky's preferred term): in part 1 of *Bottom* Zukofsky suggests that "furthering the same theme over and over and multiplying reflecting hallucinations of it . . . make it literal."[33] It is the literal we are after, in our non-predatory reading. That *a torch surged* with which I began conjures an *imagined* event which we perceive and feel, and our perception is a perception of language, an act of conjuration attentive to possibilities of meaning, possibilities of pun, possibilities in which the literal fact, the poetic fact and the imagined fact merge in a complex of make-believe. Attentive to transformations of which language is the agent and of which language is the subject, making up a world, making it up.[34] "The order of all poetry is to approach a state of music wherein the ideas present themselves sensuously and intelligently and are of no predatory intent" (*Prepositions* + 18). Physical and emotional. Musical.

Notes

1. Louis Zukofsky, *Prepositions* +, Mark Scroggins ed. (Hanover: U of New England/Wesleyan UP, 2000) 18. Hereafter cited in text as *Prepositions* +.

2. Robert Duncan, "Structure of Rime X," *The Opening of the Field* (New York: Grove, 1960) 72.

3. Ezra Pound, "Cleaners Manifesto," *Four Pages* 3 (March 1948): 3. (Summarized in part in Robert Duncan, "The Venice Poem," *The First Decade: Selected Poems 1940–1950* [London: Fulcrum, 1968] 91; the full text quoted in Dallam Simpson [as "Dallam Flynn"], "Preface" to Basil Bunting, *Poems: 1950* [Galveston: Cleaners Press, 1950)] ii-iii).

4. Louis Zukofsky, *A Test of Poetry* (New York: Jargon/Corinth, 1964) 41.

5. Louis Zukofsky, "*A*" (Berkeley: U of California P, 1978) 126. Hereafter cited in text.

6. Louis Zukofsky, *Bottom: On Shakespeare*, 2 vols. (Austin, TX: Ark P, 1963) 424.

7. Letter to Lorine Niedecker, dated (in Zukofsky's hand) "'36–37"; quoted in part in Barry Ahearn, *Zukofsky's "A": An Introduction* (Berkeley: U of California P, 1982), 234, where he cites it as "undated." Zukofsky directly acknowledges the connection between some of his shorter poems and specific musical works—the earliest I can

identify is "Song Theme" (Louis Zukofsky, *The Complete Shorter Poems* [Baltimore: Johns Hopkins UP, 1991], 33—hereafter cited in-text as CSP); the manuscript, at the Harry Ransom Humanities Research Center, U of Texas at Austin (TxU), is dated 26 January 1927.

8. Basil Bunting, *Basil Bunting on Poetry,* Peter Makin, ed. (Baltimore: Johns Hopkins UP, 1999) 155.

9. "The sound and pitch emphasis of a word are never apart from its meaning," Zukofsky wrote in "An Objective" (*Prepositions* + 18). In "Poetry: For My Son When He Can Read" he would remark on "how much what is sounded by words has to do with what is seen by them and how much what is at once sounded and seen by them cross-cuts an interplay among themselves" (*Prepositions* + 8).

10. Quoted in Cid Corman, "At: Bottom," *Word for Word: Essays on the Arts of Language,* v. 1 (Santa Barbara: Black Sparrow, 1977) 168. This was written 1963 and originally published in Bloomington, Indiana, by Clayton Eshleman as the second of his "Caterpillar" series of pamphlets in May 1966.

11. Kent Johnson, "A Fractal Music: Some Notes on Zukofsky's Flowers," Mark Scroggins, ed., *Upper Limit Music: The Writing of Louis Zukofsky,* Mark Scroggins, ed., (Tuscaloosa: University of Alabama Press, 1997) 257.

12. Rachel Blau DuPlessis, personal communication 8 August 2004.

13. Mark Scroggins, "The Revolutionary Word: Louis Zukofsky, New Masses, and Political Radicalism in the 1930s," *Upper Limit Music,* Scroggins, ed., 54.

14. Finlay thought enough of the poem, following Zukofsky's explanation, to reprint it alongside his own version as a Christmas card twenty-two years later, in 1985. Finlay's version reads "THE / The / attire / of / snowing" and is assigned to "Uncollected Embers."

15. "Thə Thə dəsire əf towing" is how it sounds to my ear (a copy of the recording is in the Zukofsky collection at TxU). He wrote the poem on 21 June 1962 (MS date, TxU). Stan Phillips taped Zukofsky reading this poem on 28 August 1962, less than a month before he wrote the letter I cite.

16. Guy Davenport, "Zukofsky," *The Geography of the Imagination: Forty Essays* (San Francisco: North Point, 1981) 106

17. J. Scappetone, Lyn Hejinian, Jean D., Ruth J., and Colin D.; e-mail enquiry to Buffalo Poetics List 9 June 2004.

18. C. K. Ogden and I. A. Richards, *The Meaning of Meaning* (1923), 8th ed. (London: Routledge and Kegan Paul, 1946) 46.

19. *Belly lox,* as Rachel Blau DuPlessis reminds me, "is the best quality smoked salmon, just what you want with your bagel and cream cheese. Trés trés culturally Jewish. That used to be obscure too!" (personal communication)—not to mention "snook" since at least the 1690s a name for various kinds of fish, edible and otherwise. A preliminary (limerick-like) draft of the poem, printed in "Discarded Poems," in *Louis Zukofsky: Man and Poet,* Carroll F. Terrell, ed., (Orono, ME: National Poetry Foundation, 1979) 159, begins "Belly Lox Shnooks Oaky"; *snoek* is a food-fish in the mackerel family, common in the southern hemisphere.

20. Oakie might be Jack Oakie (1903–1978), say, film star and comedian; or even

one of the Okies in Steinbeck's *Grapes of Wrath*—which won the Pulitzer Prize in 1940, the year before Zukofsky wrote the poem; or it might be, well, whatever—one cannot list all the possibilities the first line brings to mind.

21. "Thinking with things as they exist" is so abstract as to be almost incomprehensible—besides the question of what "things" might here be, one is driven to ask "as they exist *where*?" (to say nothing of that difficult term "exist"). But if the poem under hand is indeed a *thing,* then writing the poem might very well become a case of thinking *with* things *before* they exist—a reflection which perhaps needlessly complicates an already complicated issue.

22. *The Correspondence of William Carlos Williams and Louis Zukofsky,* Barry Ahearn, ed. (Middletown: Wesleyan UP, 2003) 5.

23. The "predatory intent" (*Prepositions* + 18) Zukofsky abhors in both reading and writing is far more pervasive than what Mark Scroggins calls "the propagandistic advocacy" so beloved of the writers in *New Masses* and elsewhere ("Revolutionary Word" 53). What Zukofsky had in mind with that word *predatory* is far more complex than I can suggest in this paper. A fuller treatment would involve detailed consideration of Zukofsky's views on the nature of poetry, the "poetic fact," and poetic language.

24. Gertrude Stein, "Patriarchal Poetry," *Yale Gertrude Stein,* Richard Kostelanetz, ed. (New Haven: Yale UP, 1980) 128.

25. *Origin* second series 1 (April 1961): 63; also in Corman, "In the Event of Words," in Terrell, *Louis Zukofsky* 326. Zukofsky's remark is strongly similar to Francis Ponge's distinction, in his "Ardens Organum, Selections from Pour un Malherbe" (Francis Ponge, *The Power of Language: Texts and Translations,* Serge Gavronsky, ed. and trans. [Berkeley: U of California P, 1979] 248–249), between reason *(raison)* and *réson,* a pun scarcely available in English but, surely, highly pertinent to Zukofsky's poetics.

26. *Poetry U.S.A.: Louis Zukofsky,* video, PBS, 1966, filmed 16 March 1966. I am indebted to WNET for providing a dub of the soundtrack in September 1966.

27. William Carlos Williams, "Prologue to Kora in Hell," *Imaginations,* Webster Schott, ed., (New York: New Directions, 1970) 14.

28. The version printed in "*A*" omits the last two words quoted here. The speaker is identified as "Henry" in "A"-6 as printed in both *Active Anthology,* Ezra Pound, ed. (London: Faber and Faber, 1930) 137 and *An "Objectivists" Anthology,* Louis Zukofsky, ed. (Le Beausset, Var: To Publishers, 1932) 138–139.

29. Basil Bunting, letter to Ezra Pound, 10 April 1958 (CtY).

30. A possible term might be "behavioural" reading as Bruce Andrews offers the term in *Paradise & Method: Poetics & Praxis* (Evanston: Northwestern UP, 1996) 157–158. Andrews distinguishes its openness and multiplicity from what he calls the "control" of "hermeneutic" reading, though his sense of the term emphasizes the role of bodily behavior (eye movement, breath, arm gesture, and so on), possibly downplaying the cognitive as I think of it in reading Zukofsky, whose complex poetics of the non-predatory also includes the physical, though in a different inflection: how the words seem to behave in relation to one another as we process the reading, how

muscular and oral activity in conjunction with syntactic, aural, and other linguistic aspects and effects determine (and often problematize) the cognitive process.

31. Zukofsky, *Bottom: On Shakespeare,* 21.

32. William Shakespeare, *A Midsummer Night's Dream,* Madeleine Doran, ed. (Pelican Shakespeare; Baltimore: Penguin, 1959) 4.1, 210ff. In "Recencies" Zukofsky talked of "poets who see with their ears, hear with their eyes, move with their noses and speak and breathe with their feet" (*Prepositions* + 17, 212).

33. Zukofsky, *Bottom: On Shakespeare* 23.

34. "Events," Basil Bunting wrote in an essay he sent to Zukofsky in 1934, "make up the world." ("The Lion and the Lizard," *Three Essays,* Richard Caddel, ed. [Durham: Basil Bunting Poetry Centre, 1994] 29. I take the pun there to be deliberate.

Reading Niedecker

> "Writing should generate ideas into matter, not the other way round."
> —Robert Smithson

Gossip. v. intrans. To talk idly, especially about other people; *noun.* Idle talk, as of one friend or acquaintance to another; especially, confidential or minutely personal remarks about other people.[1]

> Mr. Van Ess bought 14 washcloths?
> Fourteen washrags, Ed Van Ess?
> Must be going to give em
> to the church I guess.
>
> He drinks, you know. The day we moved
> he came into the kitchen stewed,
> mixed things up for my sister Grace—
> put the spices in the wrong place. (95)

The air of lucidity and inconsequentiality makes this hard to talk about—as if we knew the speaker, and could weigh the possible affront afforded Grace; nothing's explained, and the implications are left hanging, a gesture toward metaphor turning misplaced spices into a joke and reinforcing the tone, mildly ironic and comic. Affectionate. If it is gossip, it is deprived of all malice. Niedecker has given us a virtually decontextualized bit of speech, yet it feels highly context-specific. An earlier version of the poem suggested the Methodist church as getting the washrags,[2] but that adjectival Methodist makes the context a bit fuzzy (for in its putative specificness it actually *withholds* information from the reader by making her feel that she ought to know that particular church). It also seriously affects the rhythm, hurrying up that fourth line, diminishing the silence the fourth and fifth lines so neatly frame.

The air of lucidity is deceptive, and some of Niedecker's poems are extremely difficult to follow, since we don't know the local references. What do we make of "LZ," for instance (289–290), which seems so personal and private as to deny accessibility altogether? The risks she takes are quite extraordinary: her poems reject the grandiose, have not an ounce of pretense; there is not the slightest hint that what is said may not be what is meant. It is, as a result, easy to discount them as inconsequential, to rest satisfied with the I think inaccurate notion that Niedecker is a poet of quiet pleasures, and even, if we demand explanations for what the poem will not explain, to dismiss them as meaningless. Niedecker's poems are so extremely difficult to talk about not simply because paraphrase seems impossible, but because there seems to be no *need* for any. Yet combine this with Niedecker's scrupulous attention to sound, and the complex play forces us to let go of the manic compulsion, so deeply ingrained in most readers, to zoom in on the meaning. Poems like "Mr. Van Ess" are hard to describe, and make us wonder why we'd want to. The lucidity, that is to say, may disadvantage many readers.

Gossip, verb and noun both, has a nice duality about it: everyday speech, talk, chatter; finding (as it does) significance in trifles, it is an agent of transformation. It is *blab,* the *Century Dictionary* tells us in a cross-reference to *tattle. Gossip, noun.* An idle tattler; a trifling or groundless report; A friend or neighbor, an intimate companion; A chatterer who carries idle tales; A sponsor, one who answers for a child in baptism. *To gossip* is to be a boon companion. "I don't know how the old time poets did it," Niedecker wrote to Louis Zukofsky in May 1948; "—the poetic vein was the soft-spoken, hushed, sweet-worded kind of thing, almost artificial, but maybe in their time it was earthy enough for poetry . . . now I find when one hasn't been writing for awhile, you start in something like that soft vein, but as soon as you get used to writing again, you pick up everything for poetry, get into everyday speech etc." (147). Her poetry is full of transformations, and at some stage of the reading we are invariably drawn to Niedecker's amazing management of *sound,* and the ways in which she uses sound to manage sense. Like the first four lines of "Darwin," for instance, to pick a late poem:

His holy
            slowly
                        mulled over
 matter (295)

Niedecker's irony tempers the tributary meditative tone. What, exactly, is being called "holy" here? Darwin, whose theories of evolution turned the church on its hip? His mulling over of matter? The matter itself? All three, perhaps. It is extremely skilful. The line break after "holy" shifts the emphasis of our expectations by delaying the anticipated noun until we wonder if indeed it has not been withheld altogether, so that we understand it as modifying everything that follows: "slowly," "mulled," "mulled-over-matter"; at the same time the rhyme with "slowly" (and perhaps the *W* in that word) reinforces the aurally glimpsed homonym "wholly," and the adjective transforms into adverb, suggesting care and reverence to accompany *slowly's* caution (and if we read "mulled" as verb rather than adjective, then *holy* syntactically transforms into a noun). The whole combination reinforces the appropriateness of *holy* as applicable to Darwin and his activity, while at the same time undercutting it. All this is accomplished through the vowel-leading; the rhyme/part-rhyme of holy/slowly/ over, and of matter/over; the consonantal and alliterative play with *H, M* and especially *L* (surely her favorite letter); the light echo, in mulled/matter, of mind over matter (a control which Darwin sought, after all). And there is of course a lexical element: Niedecker's plays are with meaning too. *To mull* doesn't simply mean to turn over in one's mind, to cogitate upon—indeed that's a fairly recent usage, American slang being adopted into standard speech. It means to reduce to small pieces, to crumble into dust, to confuse, mix up, and muddle; to make a mess of. Is this "holy," then, what got pulverized over the material, the matter and stuff of Darwin's thought and investigation? Or is it the pulverized and moiled subject-matter? But "matter" after all is not simply material or occasion for thought, a ground of importance, or even what things are composed of; it is also purulent or suppurative. Hence, as the next stanza of the poem tells us,

> not all "delirium
>   of delight"
>   as were the forests
> of Brazil

Then too, mulling is heating and stirring wine or ale with spices—something to be savored. Each line is like a string which unravels, unfolding possibilities, and resisting the quick cursory reader. Later in the poem the sounds of "delirium" and "delight" inform "Desire" and those of "Brazil" inform "the billiard table." Unfolding nuance and probability, the sound tells us that we never are really all in one place, our attention completely focused on one reality, a single thread of intelligibility and order. The sound, that is to say, mulls matter, roils sense, rejects the singularity of purpose, argument, or understanding symptomatic of the language of control. It is transformative.

This is true even of Niedecker's most obviously unified (and hence seemingly least characteristic) work, like for instance "Club 26" (196, first published as "Place to Dine"), which seems single-mindedly to trace a theme. Everything in this poem seems to bend toward a single purpose, a final unified meaning; it seems quite conventional. Yet it is full of transforms, and, on reflection, refuses to stabilize finally into a settled meaning. Despite the closeness with which the poem attends the erotic, it is quite open-ended, and in *that* it is both characteristic of Niedecker, and deceptively alluring—it seems more conventional than it is. It's also very good indeed.

CLUB 26

Our talk, our books
riled the shore like bullheads
at the roots of the luscious
large water lily

Then we entered the lily
built white on a red carpet

the circular quiet
cool bar

glass stems to caress

We stayed till the stamens trembled

"Then we entered the lily" is startling enough a transformation, perhaps, but it is only the most obvious one in this really quite ravishing poem in which theory (talk, books) metamorphoses through a pattern of sexual anticipations and delays into erotic action and satisfaction. Like "Mr. Van Ess," this poem's simplicity is only apparent, and the poem takes considerable risks in its quite complex movement. For on one hand it skirts the whimsical (a club set up inside a water lily), and on the other it invokes metaphorical and even symbolic suggestions and meanings in order virtually to reject and then restore them. It plays the literal, that is to say, against the metaphorical and symbolic, until they merge, in so doing echoes and parallels the sexual delight the poem recounts. The title, and the second line, *parade* literary devices whose artificiality the poem then undercuts by parading the artificiality of a club built like a lily, only to reinforce the almost rapturous figuration of the poem's close.

The *words* "Club 26" gesture (however slightly) beyond the literal (which I take to be the name of an actual club) toward the metaphorical or even the symbolic. A club is, after all, a society with limited membership, in some sense exclusive. And 26 is not exactly a random number: it can be somebody's age; it is the number of letters in the alphabet (an association reinforced, perhaps, by the shift from talk to books in the opening line). That gesture is reinforced by the poem's only overt simile, in its second line: "Our talk, our books / riled the shore like bullheads," much as the repeated "our" suggests exclusiveness. And the simile takes up three of the poem's remaining nine lines, only to be radically and severely undercut in the fifth line's surprising "Then we entered the lily"—a line which not only betrays (parades) the simile's source, but also invites us to read "luscious / large water lily" *literally* instead of metaphorically. The flat, almost banal "built white on a red carpet," neutral description, further emphasizes the literal and yet at the same time elaborates a sexual suggestiveness. "Club 26" is a night club built to look like a water lily, and "Club 26" is a poem, Niedecker is telling us, in which the literal and the metaphorical are almost inextricably intertwined. Is it possible, then, that "our talk, our books" *literally* "riled" the shore?

Rile. v. trans. (dialectal variant of *roil:* vex, disturb, beat, particularly as roll in the sense of wander): 1. To render turbid by stirring up dregs or sediment, as to roil wine, cider, or other liquor in casks or bottles; 2. To excite some degree of anger, annoy, vex; 3. To perplex. All these meanings seem to apply. Bullheads, if that word means some sort of more-or-less wedge-shaped fish like a sculpin, or even if it means tadpoles, club-headed, certainly roil the mud around the roots of water lilies. Bullheads, if that word means (consulting the dictionary) "a stupid fellow, a blunderer, a lubber," and especially if it means (by analogy with the adjective bullheaded) obstinate, blunderingly aggressive, stupid, are indeed a disturbance in any erotic idyll, vexatious and even perplexing (is it at all *à propos* to recall that fish see only the dark tangled underside of the "luscious lily"?) The almost comic intrusion of the bullheads, the seemingly aimless aggression of "riled," is smoothed out in the alliterated close of the first stanza, the disruption ending abruptly with the line breaks. The talk and the disruptive movement settle almost into banality with the adjectival "*built* white on a red carpet," and the seemingly aimless intrusiveness of the talk and books gives way to the purposiveness of glass stems supplied in order to caress. The stanzas slowly ebb away, from four lines to two, to two, to one, to one, sparse, unhurried, the pace slowed by the incremental white space surrounding the lines, slowed by consonantal clusters, slowed by the line breaks, slowed by the almost languid *apo koinou* of "circular quiet / cool bar." The quiet is circular, the cool is quiet, the bar is circular, quiet and cool. In such surround, glass stems transform to stamens, stayed transforms to trembles—shifts effected in part (like much of this poem) through a consistency of vowel-leading and consonantal echo which makes the metamorphoses of sense as inevitable as the erotic progress of the poem.

The sheer aptness, the very rightness of that word "stamens" is astonishing. As the plural of *stamen* its meaning is restricted to the biological sense, the male or fertilizing organ of flowering plants. The alternative (and more common) plural form of stamen is *stamina:* "The support or mainstay of a body, the fixed, firm part of a body, which supports or gives it its strength and solidity, as, the bones are the stamina of animal bodies; Whatever constitutes the principal strength or support of anything, power of endurance, staying power, lasting strength or vigor" (*Century,* entry for Stamen). We *stayed* till the stamens trembled. The delay, the unhurried prolongation of erotic desire and gratification, the pleasures and the fragility of foreplay. Glass stems, with *stems* as a verb. Such transformation of a word from one part of speech to another is largely accomplished through Niedecker's skilful management of sound in order to suggest or elaborate pun. And this is essential to the poem's enterprise, for "Club 26" is a poem in which talk, books, the cerebral, words, bullheaded, metamorphose into action, move from the mental to the physical, from the cerebral to the sexual. It is a poem in which the intensity of words gives way to the intensity of experience, in which the personae of the poem move from the *outside* world of talk to the inside world of club and lily: from word to thing. Entering the world, and excluding it too. *Club* 26.

It is essential to the poem's enterprise that its words take on many of the attributes of things, that they have solidity and weight, substance and sound. The letter *L* sounds seven times in the first four lines of the poem; the letter *O* appears (as does *L*) nine times in the same four lines. "*Our . . . our . . . shore*" lap like waves or a caress. *B*ooks, *B*ullheads, *B*uilt, *B*ar. This is a poem about words and how they enter our lives, and the reverse. It sets up the artificial world of talk, books, as invading the natural world (riling the shore), and it sets up the natural world (the lily) as artificial (built white on a red carpet), an artifice in which the natural can be found. In announcing the primacy of the senses over language it at the same time declares the prime characteristic of language to be its *physicality.* Emotion, passion, and understanding come from looking, touching, and feeling, this poem tells us, not from words, not from books, not from dictionaries. And it tells us so in words. It is a kind of imitative form in which the poem (like a sexual encounter?) begins with talking, books, perhaps even awkwardness to start, a reliance on words; but the need for outside linguistic support diminishes, the lines grow shorter, charged with sexual energy as the poem proceeds from the empty disruptive noise of talk to the subdued yet expressed physical passion. Yet at the same time the poem celebrates itself as a verbal construct. It finds, then, that the verbal and the physical, the natural and the artificial, the literal and the figurative, are one the same, stems/stamens. And that our hold on that perception is fragile—the first verb of the poem is *riled;* the last, is *trembled,* which is also the poem's last word. The poem is, then, a commingling.

This commingling includes that specialized form of metaphor we call cliché, and plays with its inversion or its reinvention and redefinition. "We stayed till the stamens trembled." A man like a flower—reversing the cliché Williams played in *Paterson* with his man like a city and woman like a flower. "Club 26" is a water lily, and it is white. Lily white, that is to say. Pure. Mentioning the poem in a letter to Zukofsky in September 1962 Niedecker called it "a mongrel poem—has both sentence—melodic line, and fragment of sentence. But something got achieved there—ecstasy, why go any further" (322). Ecstasy: to say love blossoms like a flower is to diminish it. For it is in the meeting, or rather, in the winding in of contraries that the poem draws its power. On the page it looks like a poem, but the language is everyday, and to the casual ear it sounds like ordinary speech. It skirts cliché, it skirts whimsy. It draws attention to itself by parading simile, yet uses that simile to declare its closeness to the language of everyday reality and speech: "as soon as you get used to writing again, you pick up everything for poetry, get into everyday speech etc." Gossip, that is to say, working (as gossip so often does) as much by what is not said as by what is.

It seems to me that one great distinction of Niedecker's poetry (her chiefest is her sound) is precisely in this doubleness, this multiplicity of effect, this simultaneous elaboration and demolition. Darwin the holy-unholy moiler-muller-roller; Club 26 the great repository of artifice and nature, of talk and action, of thought and feeling, of the fake and the real. It is not that Niedecker wishes to distinguish between these contraries, but that this is *how she sees,* this is how she *thinks,* this is how she *feels,* and the poems are celebrations, expositions, and elaborations of that complex mode of seeing, thinking, feeling. Metaphor is not, that is to say, a literary device but a recognition, and our awareness always includes what is not immediately before the senses. It is not a matter of looking at a club as though it were a water lily; it is a matter of looking at a club which *is* one. "In not / looking for metaphor," Louis Zukofsky wrote in 1964,

> our worlds do
> fly together: if
> there are not
>
> too many words.[3]

Identity, the perception of identity, is a construct, like the poem, like language, like speech, like the "natural" world. Perceive the world so, and it becomes essential to the matter of the writing that it be unobtrusive, unpretentious, self-effacing. With never, as Bunting said of Scarlatti, a boast or a see-here. Robert Smithson, in the essay I quote as epigraph to this note, commented that "a work of art when placed in a gallery loses its charge, and becomes a portable object or surface disengaged from the outside world." So too the poem. Words enter the life, the life enters the words.

Notes

The (as a rule fragmentary) originals of Niedecker's letters to Zukofsky are in the Harry Ransom Humanities Research Center, University of Texas at Austin; the passages I quote are from Jenny Penberthy, ed., *Niedecker and the Correspondence with Zukofsky 1931–70* (New York: Cambridge University Press, 1992). All quotations from Niedecker's poetry are from her *Collected Works,* Jenny Penberthy, ed. (Berkeley: U of California P, 2002).

Epigraph. Robert Smithson, "Cultural Confinement," *The Writings of Robert Smithson,* Nancy Holt, ed. (New York: New York UP, 1979), 133.

1. *The Century Dictionary and Cyclopedia* (New York: Century, 1889–1895), summarized from entry for "gossip." The *Century* is, for my purposes, preferable to the *Oxford* simply on the grounds that it is an American dictionary of English, widely accessible in most public libraries throughout the continental United States in the first half of this century and later; Niedecker's close connection with Zukofsky may well have encouraged her to consider the *Century* her first choice, since Zukofsky himself frequently made reference to it. Definitions given in this essay come from the *Century,* usually in summary form.

2. In *New Goose* (Prairie City: James A. Decker, 1946) 17, the fourth line reads "to the Methodist Church, I guess."

3. Louis Zukofsky. "A"-14, "*A*" (Berkeley: U of California P, 1978) 355.

“Take Oil / and Hum”

Niedecker and Bunting

Here are two poems. The first is by Basil Bunting.

> The day being Whitsun we had pigeon for dinner;
> but Richmond in the pitted river saw
> mudmirrored mackintosh, a wet southwest
> wiped and smeared dampness over Twickenham.
>
> Pools on the bustop’s buttoned tarpaulin.
> Wimbledon, Wandsworth, Clapham, the Oval. ‘Lo,
> Westminster Palace where the asses jaw!’
>
> Endless disappointed buckshee-hunt!
> Suburb and city giftless garden and street,
> and the sky alight of an evening stubborn
> and mute by day and never *rei novae*
> *inter rudes artium homines.*
> never a spark of sedition
> amongst the uneducated workingmen.
>
> Ode 1.7

And this is by Lorine Niedecker:

> I rose from marsh mud,
> algae, equisetum, willows,
> sweet green, noisy
> birds and frogs
>
> to see her wed in the rich
> rich silence of the church,

> the little white slave-girl
> in her diamond fronds.
>
> In aisle and arch
> the satin secret collects.
> United for life to serve
> silver. Possessed.[1]

They're such very different poets you'd never mistake one for the other. Niedecker's language is unmistakably spoken, conversational, at times almost casual—don't get me wrong, she's an extremely careful writer of very great skill indeed—but she does not *display* her consciousness of her art. Bunting's a different story. He started out as more-or-less a satirist, more-or-less focusing in his earliest odes on social and political absurdities, the passage of time and how we waste it, his own desolate condition having turned his back on love. A bit of posturing about some of those earlier poems, something of the *poète maudit,* the doomed poet, a self-conscious literariness about it all. "Everybody says it is extremely disagreeable of me," he wrote to Pound in 1928, "to be unpleasant about sunrise and the loud chorus of complaints encourages me to think that I must have done something of my own at last."[2] Four years before that he wrote the opening poem of the *First Book of Odes:*

> Weeping oaks grieve, chestnuts raise
> mournful candles. Sad is spring
> to perpetuate, sad to trace
> immortalities never changing.
>
> Weary on the sea
> for sight of land
> gazing past the coming wave we
> see the same wave;
>
> drift on merciless iteration of years;
> descry no death; but spring
> is everlasting
> resurrection.
>
> Ode 1.1 (CP 97)

Could he perhaps be feeling a little sorry for himself, a little rueful, the last lines an attempt to lift the poem out of that particular rut? That depends at least in part on whether you read the opening sentence as imperative or indicative. In 1970 he would point to this poem as an example of how to write in quatrains—instructive as a technical example.

There's a highly formal quality, almost oratorical, to his language—it may be, as he put it, words in their natural order (whatever that may mean), but it's not the language of ordinary speech—indeed I'm not at all sure that the inversion of "sad is spring" doesn't violate Bunting's own "natural" order. Bunting's language—syntax and vocabulary—is more like that of formal *public* speech, though too compressed for that, and overall his poems have something close to the flavor of the periodic and balanced sentences of the prose writers he so admired, Halifax and Swift—satirists both. Perhaps there's a touch, too, of the prose of David Hume's essays. There's a strong deliberative quality in his poems, purposiveness, control.

In choosing which poems to put in *Writing* 6 in 1970 (it was a generous selection, 22 pieces altogether), he clearly had one eye firmly on their usefulness to young poets learning their craft.[3] He chose three to demonstrate "Technical: The Quatrain" and three, "Technical: Quantity."[4] A year later (25 November 1971) he talked about one of the "quantity" poems, the ode "To Helen Egli," which has an almost display-case opening:

> Empty vast days built in the waste memory seem a jail for
> thoughts grown stale in the mind, tardy of birth, rank and inflexible:
> love and slow self-praise, even grief's cogency, all emotions
> timetamed whimper and shame changes the past brought to no
> utterance.
>
> Ode 1.5 (CP 101)

"Greater Sapphics," he said, which "are not used much in Greek even. But they have a kind of terse hardness"; and a month after *that,* with a quietly mischievous gleam he told me that when he read it to Pound (Bunting was with Pound in Rapallo when he wrote it) "Ezra just grunted; he couldn't make out what it was," and looked at the text. "He just sat there, and I could see him counting it out on his fingers" and he laughed. "It's a Sapphic," he said, "turned upside down. It reverses the Greek. I never told Ezra about *that* in the poem. He never asked" (20 December 1971).

That sort of story is a long way from Niedecker. But then Bunting had a pretty strict formal education that included Latin and Greek, French and German, and in his bookishness he is mischievous and controlling—the quotation in Latin in the Whitsun poem is not hard to puzzle out if you know a little Latin: "a new thing to [*or* among] men unacquainted with the arts" is one reading; his closing lines offer another.[5] When the poem was at last published, in 1950, Bunting included a footnote he'd added (so far as I can tell) in 1935, but it's not at all the sort of thing you find in Niedecker's work. Jonathan Williams in 1976 remembered Bunting saying that "Pound's generation, and perhaps mine, were a little too bookish." "I think that's true," Bunting responded. "The world doesn't spend all its time reading books, and we all assumed that they do. We have far too many references to things."[6] Niedecker has her own bookishness, of course, but she will *not* be bullied, especially by her reading.[7] In her delighted trust in lives, letters, biographies, casual utterance, she is Emerson's Reader. She does not place her trust in books as Authorities (with a capital A) but as companions, as direct voices in her life. Even in late poems like "Darwin" or "His Carpets Flowered" she does not seem to have embarked on a Project, "I am going to write about X, therefore I must get on with some research." Such poems arise out of her reading;[8] the short poems I think without exception arise from direct experience—what happened today—a visit with Al Millen to a nightclub built in the shape of a lily; seeing Winston Churchill's funeral on TV; a trip to a big fancy wedding in church—and she hangs the poem on that.[9] Books offer direct experience, because *words* offer direct experience—witness the play of parts of speech in "collects" (verb/noun) and the syntactic ambiguities in "united for life to serve." Reading, for Niedecker, is an activity, a conversation, and books are simply something she's doing, like listening to gossip in the street about Ed Van Ess (CW 95) perhaps. She takes whatever's to hand, she writes what is under her nose, no pretension, no disguise, and her attention is focused on the objects under hand, eye, ear—language, and the poem, "saying the lines to myself before sleep at night and on waking" (CW 414) to get the sound right.

Bunting's pretty close to that—these are both poets of the ear—and especially in his early work relies on traditional and classical (English, Latin, Greek, French) forms and metrics even as he plays around with them. But in a poem like "The day being Whitsun" I get the notion that the trigger for the poem was quite possibly the quote from Livy, possibly popping into his head the way things do after a miserable rainy day, penniless jobless Bunting out for lunch at someone's house, the wet cold bus ride back to his digs at 5, Osnaburgh Terrace, London NW1, his job as music critic for the *Outlook* down the tubes now that the magazine's folded, him scrambling to make ends meet, worried.[10] I very much doubt, at any rate, that he spent days or even hours scrambling through Livy looking for those words or words like them. He too is using what comes to hand, but the inclusion of Livy is a gesture towards "making something out of that," enlarging the significance of the poem, linking it to larger social issues, sharpening the satiric edge. It's a young man's poem, and the method of composition seems to me somewhat different from Niedecker's. Her techniques are far less obtrusive. It has something to do with what they think poems are, how they work or ought to work.

Bunting's footnote hides far more than it reveals: "The quotation might not be readily identified without a hint. It is from Livy."[11] That's a trick he learned from Pound, and it's characteristic of Bunting's desire to maintain a fairly complex sort of control over the reader, like Pound (and Zukofsky later) partially withholding the poem from the reader in ways which Niedecker cheerfully and I think constantly declines. It may be that the practice of withholding matter from the reader is designed to force the reader's attention to the sound, but it also has the effect of subordinating the reader to the writer in a way that Niedecker generally shuns. It is a privileging of the poet, and an implicit claim to mastery.

In this respect, Bunting's conscious and deliberate dedication to poetry as a formal craft is crucial: through the 1920s and 30s, frequently if not constantly living—after his father died in 1925—in great poverty,[12] he devoted himself pretty well full time to learning poetry in a kind of apprenticeship in London, in Paris, and in New York, including some years at the Ezuversity in Rapallo; "poet appointed dare not decline / to walk among the bogus," says the opening of *Briggflatts*, Canto II, "nothing to authenticate / the mission imposed . . ." (CP 65). And it flavors the work. Late in 1971, embroiled in what he called a "hellish year" in that "foul place" Victoria, he read through his *Collected Poems* and identified Ode 21, "Two Photographs," as the "central work." Written in 1932, it was a "turning point" in his writing, he told me; "before that, if it comes off, it's pretty much almost by accident, you could say. They hit it by chance." But in "Two Photographs,"—I quote his conversation—"and in every subsequent poem, I knew what I was doing; the poem does what I want it to do. It's the first poem I wrote that does *exactly* what it's intended to do. And all the rest, after that, do that too" (20 December 1971). But the poems didn't necessarily come easy. It took him, he said, "six months or more" to find the last half of a line in *The Spoils*, the three words "Halt, both, lament" (CP 49)—it's a translation from the *Mu'allaqát* of 'Amr al Qais, he said, two Arabic words to his three English, though "four syllables in somewhat the same rhythm."[13] And again and again, in interviews, he pooh-poohs the notion of writing as discovery. "I have never supposed a poem to be organic at all. I don't think the thing grows, it's built and put together by a craftsman," he told Dale Reagan in 1977. "The nearer you can stick to the plan you've started with the more likely the poem is to have a real balance, an effective kind of architecture"(78).[14] But "there is no doubt," he told Paul Johnstone in 1975, "many things coalesce at the time of writing that you are not fully aware of before you sit down to write."[15] And he scorns the personal: "I don't go in for personal confessions. I like describing things I see, but if it goes beyond that, you can be fairly sure it's not necessarily me that's supposed to be making these remarks. . . . I don't give a damn whether I falsify experience or not. I'm out to make a good poem. I'm not there to provide raw material for psychologists."[16]

All this is a far cry from Niedecker, who frequently opts for openness and the untidiness of possible meanings rather than strict control of meaning and response. "Very delicate," Bunting commented of her work, "many implications, none obvious."[17] And Niedecker is very far indeed from claiming mastery, witness among other things her to my mind quite astonishing remark, in a letter to Cid Corman, 2 July 1965, on the two lines

I picked a
leaf up

"Yes, I see—'I picked a / leaf up'—I get for the first time that meaning has something to do with song—one hesitates a bit longer with some words in some lines for the thought or the vision—but I'd say mostly, of course, cadence, measure make song. And a kind of shine (or somber tone) that is of the same intensity throughout the poem. And the thing moves. But as in all poems everywhere, depth of emotion condensed, I'd say."[18]

Bunting and Niedecker are startlingly different. So why and how do we link them together? In what ways might they be kindred spirits?

Well, there's some pretty obvious and superficial connections and parallels, most of them implicit in what I've already said. And there's a Wisconsin connection, of course—Bunting's marriage to Marian Culver, from Eau Claire;[19] his children growing up there after their separation in 1937; his two visits in 1966 and 1967; his first and only meeting with Niedecker in 1967; his brief and abortive plan in early 1938 to set up a carp-fishing business with Niedecker's father; and even, some time in the late 1960s or was it in 1970, his being made an Honorary Citizen of the State of Wisconsin—part of *Briggflatts* was read into the state Congressional Record. There's his and Niedecker's mutual high regard for each other's work, the letters they wrote each other (now lost), the poems they wrote for each other.[20] There's the role of sound in their poetry (I'm not going to talk about that—it's a pretty familiar topic). There's their shared experience of poverty, both coming from fairly comfortable lives in their youth, Niedecker as an adult reading proof for *Hoard's Dairyman* and then after her eyesight deteriorates, washing hospital floors; Bunting after his return from Persia in the 1950s relying in part on food parcels sent by Pound from St. Elizabeths Hospital for the Criminally Insane, reading proofs of railway timetables, and after that working as "a night-shift drudge" (Makin 317) on Newcastle newspapers until obliged to retire—after which he was virtually blinded by cataracts.[21] Frugal necessity had its effect on their poetry, which—whatever else it may be—is pretty clear of all sentimentality, is hard-headed, practical, suspicious of government and institutions, and remarkably free of abstraction—there's a close but not necessarily obvious connection between their writing and their life.

And there's the isolation and neglect. Bunting did indeed achieve considerable fame and celebrity late in his lifetime while Niedecker did not. Niedecker spoke of "my overloaded loneliness" (23 March 1956 to LZ—*NCZ* 227), and Bunting said of her ten years later (11 December 1966, to Jonathan Williams) that "nobody else has been buried quite so deep."[22] But Bunting was almost completely isolated and unknown until the publication of *Briggflatts* (1966): stuck in the Canaries in the 1930s, unable to find a publisher, rejected by Eliot at Faber who, he understood, would help him—the work in *Caveat Emptor,* sent to Eliot in 1935, remained unpublished until *Poems 1950* was finally published by an obscure press in Texas and then again rejected by Peter Russell in London. It got only one review in Britain (by G. S. Fraser in Peter Russell's little magazine *Nine*).[23] But nevertheless, like Niedecker, Bunting appeared in the pages of *Poetry* and similar magazines. "You and I," he wrote to Zukofsky 12 November 1950, "have more than the whole ruck of others who have done well out of poetry. And I'm not even noticeably eccentric on the page! Why? What has dogged us?" (TxU). Niedecker—like many another poet we might name—struck some (male) readers as trivial—no rich thick cadence, no finely wrought phrase, no grand significant themes, no high seriousness as found in the canonical masters. And Bunting? Lightweight. Referring to his "Aus Dem Zweiten Reich" (CP 36–38) without saying so, and certainly without noticing that the poem offers a sharply satiric view of life in the Weimar Republic, an early reviewer of Bunting's *Collected Poems* (1968) dismissed the early poems as merely about kissing girls in the back of taxicabs, not worth bothering with.

But if inattention has its price, life on the outside its penalties, there are compensations. Richard Caddel, another writer on the outside, thought that a major advantage of working outside the mainstream is that you're thereby free to pursue your own devices, over a period of years perhaps, without continual and in his view damaging interference. You end up driven to your own resources—always a risky business—and if you lack the company of your fellow writers, if you lack the conversation and stimulus of let's call them your peers, working alone, you can't (or don't wish) to hang onto the coat-tails of others, you *have* to make do with what you find around you, you *have* to accept the situation in which you find yourself. And you write, you *have* to write, "toward silence."[24] This makes perhaps for a certain kind of bookishness; in Bunting and Niedecker's case it makes for an affinity with borders and border creatures, the overlooked and the unrespectable—"a kinship," as Elizabeth Robinson says, "with persons on the edge."[25] It also makes for constant struggle; you "slug it out" (George Oppen's phrasing)[26] with letters, words, sounds, rhythms, sense, to get it right, confronting the very nature of your text in order to disseminate it at all.[27] Not, that is to say, to get it right in the eyes of others, but in one's own, an absolute reliance on one's own ear and eye. "I was born," says one of Niedecker's poems, "with eyes and a house" (CW 172). The price an attentive eye (ear) might pay is subjection to the immediate: it is attentive to it, and vulnerable to it, to the particularity of things, their quiddity and presence.

Her poetry is so grounded in physical detail, crammed with the names of things and people, colours and creatures and scraps of conversation overheard or made, that—along with her meticulous attention to sound—the poems inescapably place before us and within us the materiality of words, the materiality of language. As do Bunting's, through concreteness of reference and turbulence of consonantal clusters. "Can knowledge be conveyed that isn't felt?" Niedecker asks in a poem (CW 150), and she comments (of a summary she sent to Zukofsky along with a couple of nuggets from Leibniz) that "what they say is all I know about philosophy after all my vast reading on the universe and its animals and us. Can anybody feel surer or know more about all this? Materialist (not much purpose) but as Santayana said the material is wonderful" (29 Nov 1959, NCZ 258)—what Rachel Blau DuPlessis called, following Niedecker, the "Materialist sublime."[28] "I feel," said Niedecker, "that I think this way not *thought* but everything in a movement of words" (NCZ 84–85, 157)—and I take that word *feel* literally, its connection of *sense* to the senses. "Abstraction is the enemy of poetry at all times," Bunting ruled, and continued: "a word like sincerity seems to me to be almost without any assignable meaning at all."[29] Both writers, clearly, have a profound distrust of philosophy, Niedecker (as Jenny Penberthy notes [NCZ 84]) characteristically undercutting such "high seriousness" in her work, Bunting dismissing with scorn "the imbeciles who imagine philosophy is a higher wisdom than rhyme" (to LZ, 1 December 1947—TxU)[30] and deriding, in a letter to Pound, "the common lunatic notion that abstract nouns have other than a grammatical significance" (1934 CtY).

Neither, too, can abide the notion of rules. For Niedecker it is a matter of feeling it out—that letter to Corman I quoted earlier on, about line-breaks—"I get for the first time that meaning has something to do with song—one hesitates a bit longer with some words in some lines for the thought or the vision—

but I'd say mostly, of course, cadence, measure make song. And a kind of shine (or sombre tone) that is of the same intensity throughout the poem. And the thing moves." Understanding comes from looking, touching, listening, thinking, not from dictionaries and discussion, not from laying down the law. And Bunting harks back in *Briggflatts* to the time of Aneurin and Taliesin, "before rules made poetry a pedant's game" (CP 75).

Hence, I believe, both poets firmly resisted the temptation publicly to explain what they were up to. So far as I know, Niedecker never wrote any general or even specific statement of poetics outside occasional sentences or paragraphs in letters, or in other than sundry private expostulations. And Bunting I think possibly came to regret "The Poet's Point of View," which to all intents and purposes is the only essay on poetics he wrote. It is, at any rate, the only one that anybody ever paid any attention to while he was alive, he seems to have written it on demand,[31] and he seems subsequently to have distrusted it. Distrusted it because nobody seems to have understood what he said—or, perhaps, what he meant. "I've never said that poetry consists *only* of sound. I said again and again that the *essential* thing is the sound. Without the sound, there isn't any poetry. But having established it and kept it clear that the sound is the essential, the main thing, you can add all sorts of stuff if you want to."[32] And he did indeed have to say it, again and again, with more or with less impatience: "I've said often enough that without the sound there isn't a poem; but if you want to involve some sense in the sound and have the skill to do it, why not?"[33]

Bunting famously said that "there is no excuse for literary criticism."[34] It's true, surely, that no (good) poem generalizes beyond itself. And it's certainly true, after all, that any statement *about* any poem is inevitably more abstract, more general than the poem under view. Any such statement is, finally, a retreat from the poem. Neither Niedecker nor Bunting theorized a poetics, theorized their position.[35] I think it was impossible for them to do so, and I think that impossibility freed them into writing the poetry they were indeed able to write. Would that there were more such.

Notes

1. Basil Bunting, *Complete Poems,* Richard Caddel, ed. (Newcastle upon Tyne: Bloodaxe, 2000) 103. Hereafter abbreviated CP and cited parenthetically in text. Lorine Niedecker, *Collected Works,* Jenny Penberthy, ed. (Berkeley: U of California P, 2002) 170 (hereafter abbreviated CW and cited parenthetically in text); see also notes, CW 414–15, and Jenny Penberthy, ed., *Niedecker and the Correspondence with Zukofsky 1931–1970* (Cambridge: Cambridge UP, 1993), 151 (hereafter abbreviated NCZ

and cited parenthetically in text). The quotation in my title is from Lorine Niedecker (CW 197).

2. Quotations from Bunting's letters and manuscripts are from the American Literature Collection, Beinecke Rare Book and Manuscript Library, Yale University (abbreviated CtY), or from the Bunting papers in the Louis Zukofsky papers, Harry Ransom Humanities Research Center, University of Texas at Austin (abbreviated TxU).

3. *Writing* (Vancouver, B.C.: *Georgia Straight Writing Supplement*) 6: *Basil Bunting* (November 18–25 1970), edited by Peter Quartermain.

4. *Technical: The Quatrain:* "Weeping oaks grieve" (97); "To Helen Egli" (101); and "Dear be still!" (105); *Technical: Quantity:* "Two Photographs" (118); "Fruits breaking the branches" (115); "Mesh cast for mackerel" (119).

5. The typescript of *Caveat Emptor* (CtY), sent to Pound and to Eliot in 1935, places the final two lines at the bottom of the page, suggestive of a footnote and implying their status as translation of the Livy.

6. Jonathan Williams and Tom Meyer, "A Conversation with Basil Bunting," *St. Andrews Review* 4.2 (Spring/Summer 1977): 21–32. Reprinted in *Poetry Information* 19 (Autumn 1978): 37–47; 40 (abbreviated PI hereafter).

7. Ron Silliman wondered on his blog, August 29, 2003, whether one can "write usefully from 'book learning,' or, for that matter, any mode of secondary material?" and called Niedecker's "Thomas Jefferson" (CW 275–282) a "noble shipwreck" of a poem. Silliman's Blog. *http://ronsilliman.blogspot.com/* Last accessed August 8, 2012.

8. With Al Millen's destruction of most of Niedecker's archive, this assertion is necessarily somewhat speculative. As Jenny Penberthy reports ("Writing Lake Superior," *Radical Vernacular: Lorine Niedecker and the Poetics of Place,* Elizabeth Willis, ed. [Iowa City: U of Iowa P, 2008], 61–79), over 270 pages of research notes for "Lake Superior" are extant; they may have originated in her plans to explore the northern shores of the lake with Al Millen, but it is clear that they rapidly became a large project intended to lead to a long poem. The relationship between the finished poem and the notes is rather unclear.

9. "Club 26" (CW 196; see also NCZ 317); "Churchill's Death" (CW 219–220); "I rose from marsh mud" (CW 170; see also 414–416).

10. Whit Sunday (the seventh Sunday after Easter) in 1928 was on 27th May; the *Outlook* ceased publication earlier that month.

11. And was identified by Karl Müller, *Die Lyrik Basil Buntings* 152, who reports that the context adds nothing to the meaning of Bunting's poem (cited in Peter Makin, *Bunting: The Shaping of His Verse* [Oxford: Clarendon, 1992] 58n; and by Barbara L. Lesch, *Basil Bunting: A Major British Modernist* PhD Dissertation, [U of Wisconsin-Madison, 1979] 51). Lesch points out that Evander (whose name *Euandros* is Greek for Good Man), to whom Livy's words refer, was (according to Livy) "revered for his wonderful invention of letters, a new thing to men unacquainted with the arts, and even more revered because of the divinity which men attributed to his mother Carmenta, whom the tribes admired as a prophetess before the Sibyl's coming into Italy" (Livy, *Ab Urbe Condita Libri,* B. O. Foster, trans. (Loeb Classical Library,

1, 29). Evander "taught the rude inhabitants of the country writing, music, and other arts" according to Seyffert's *Dictionary of Classical Antiquities* (the standard reference in Bunting's youth), and governed his region "more through personal influence than through sovereign power." As Lesch observes (52), the quoted Latin links Evander the inventor of the Roman alphabet to the arts, which grew out of his wisdom; he is the man/god whose activity made possible the existence of man as poet.

12. Bunting had—at least until his father died in 1925—an allowance of £10 a week.

13. 20 December 1971. See also Makin *Bunting* 111n29.

14. Dale Reagan, "An Interview with Basil Bunting," *Montemora* 3 (1977): 78.

15. Paul Johnstone, "Basil Bunting: Taken from Two Interviews, recorded by Paul Johnstone in April 1974 and April 1975," *Meantime* (April 1977): 79

16. Reagan "Interview" 77, 78.

17. Basil Bunting to Tom Pickard 28 August 1967, quoted in *Basil Bunting on Poetry,* Peter Makin, ed. (Baltimore: Johns Hopkins UP, 1999) 180 n82.

18. "*Between Your House and Mine": The Letters of Lorine Niedecker and Cid Corman, 1960 to 1970,* Lisa Pater Faranda, ed. (Durham, NC: Duke UP, 1986) 64.

19. On 9 July 1930, in Riverhead, Long Island, Bunting married Marian Culver, the daughter of an Eau Claire, Wisconsin, merchant. They had met in Venice in 1929. When Marian returned to Eau Clair in 1937 she was pregnant with their son Rustam, whom Bunting never saw; their daughters Roudaba and Bourtai, though Bunting rarely saw them after 1937, spent a great part of their lives there.

20. "Ballad of Basil" LN CW 282–3; "To abate what swells" BB CP 198.

21. Makin, *Bunting* 317. One removed in California in 1967, one in England the following year.

22. *Some Jazz From the Baz: Excerpts from Basil Bunting's Letters to Jonathan Williams: 1963–1985,* Jonathan Williams, ed., (Scaly Mountain, NC: Press of Otis the Lamed-Vovnik, 2000) np.

23. There were six reviews altogether in North America (two of them in Canada), principally in little magazines such as *Montevallo Review, Imagi,* and the *Northern Review of Writing and the Arts in Canada.* There was a brief notice in *Sewanee Review* (by Vivienne Koch), and just over four pages by Hugh Kenner along with an unsigned note, in *Poetry.* See Roger Guedalla, "Basil Bunting: A Bibliography of Works and Criticism." *Poetry Information* 19 (Autumn 1978): 73–89; 79–80.

24. George Oppen, "The Philosophy of the Astonished. Selections from the Working Papers," Rachel Blau DuPlessis, ed., *Sulfur* 27 (1990): 215.

25. Elizabeth Robinson, "Music Becomes Story: Lyric and Narrative Patterning in the Work of Lorine Niedecker," in Willis 126.

26. George Oppen, "The Circumstances: A Selection from George Oppen's Uncollected Writing," Rachel Blau DuPlessis, ed., *Sulfur* 25 (1989): 12.

27. For further discussion, see Richard Caddel and Peter Quartermain, "Introduction: A Fair Field Full of Folk," *Other: British and Irish Poetry since 1970* (Hanover and London: Wesleyan UP/UP of New England, 1999) xvi and *passim.* George Oppen—another outsider—put it this way: "If a man—or a woman, of course; you'll forgive

the generic 'man'—goes rowing in the park, tho he may row as well as anyone who ever lived, tho he may row so well that he seems to be ice-skating, waltzing round the lake to the strains of the Blue Danube—still, he cannot row around and around that lake forever. But suppose he sets sail across a sea which, so far as he knows, has never been crossed—I am thinking of Columbus, of course, but a Columbus alone in a small boat. He too may turn back after a while, but if he does so it can only be a failure of nerve. He will be tempted to turn back, but he will also be tempted not to. And he will not be tempted to continue only by the hope of approval. He will want to keep going, if only his nerve does not fail, even tho he has only his bare and anxious self in the boat. ¶ Like the poet, if he becomes distracted by the desire to display his virtue, his grace, his anything at all—he will not get there. Because what he has to do is slug it out. A voyage in the open sea—unlike a row in the park—is no joke. It is also not virtuous. Nor can he recommend it to the world at large. If he makes the trip, that's his own affair, and in his heart he knows it." ("Circumstances" 12–13). Bunting commented that the poet must be "pretty clear about himself, about what he has to say" (Reagan "Interview" 76).

28. Rachel Blau DuPlessis, "Lorine Niedecker's 'Paean to Place' and Its Reflective Fusions," Willis 173.

29. Johnstone, "Basil Bunting" 74, 75.

30. "Zukofsky has always had a very warm spot for philosophers; I have nothing but the coldest dislike for the most part. My philosophy is English eclecticism—Locke, and Hume who proved that they all knew nothing; in fact one could say the same almost of Wittgenstein's *Tractatus,* which I read when it was first published and was immensely struck by." (Johnstone, "Basil Bunting" 72)

31. He did, of course, in his early years write two others: "Some Limitations of English" (which appeared, October 1932, in an obscure magazine that died a year later and was virtually impossible to find before the reprint in *Three Essays,* Richard Caddel., ed. [Durham: Basil Bunting Poetry Centre, 1994,]), and "The Lion and the Lizard," not published until more than a decade after his death. Other than sundry private expostulations against abstraction in letters to Zukofsky (and less often to Pound), Bunting's only statement of what nowadays is called poetics was in 1965, "The Poet's Point of View."

32. Eric Mottram, "Conversations with Basil Bunting on the Occasion of his 75th Birthday," *Poetry Information* 19 (Autumn 1978): 5.

33. Michael Heyward and Peter Craven, "An Interview with Basil Bunting," *Scripsi* 1.3–4 (April 1982): 28.

34. Reported by Jonathan Williams, "Note One," *Descant on Rawthey's Madrigal: Conversations with Basil Bunting,* Jonathan Williams, ed. (Lexington, KY: Gnomon Press, 1968) np.

35. "There is no need of any theory for what gives pleasure through the ear, music or poetry," said Bunting in "The Poet's Point of View" (*Three Essays* 34).

The Mind as Frying Pan

Robin Blaser's Humor

> The vices of the mind are not to be underestimated.
> —Robin Blaser, Letter to Anne Waldman, 1992

> He said he was surprised and he said laughing is coughing.
> —Gertrude Stein, "Pink Melon Joy"

> A being radically devoid of any representable identity would be absolutely irrelevant to the State.
> —Giorgio Agamben, *The Coming Community*

What I have to say draws in part upon very interesting observations and reflections on laughter by Jean-Luc Nancy, in *The Birth to Presence;* by Catherine Clément, in *Syncope: The Philosophy of Rapture;* and most of all by David Appelbaum, in his really quite extraordinary book *Voice.*[1] That acknowledgment alone should be sufficient notice that an alternative title, and certainly an unspoken refrain throughout this paper, is Robin Blaser's own recurrent "The truth is laughter."

My title comes from Blaser's poem "hard, gemlike flame":

> I've always liked the idea of the mind as a
> frying pan
> What's in it is neither true nor false.[2]

It's a pretty weird poem, I guess. The title comes from Walter Pater's famous sentence at the conclusion to *The Renaissance:* "To burn always with this hard, gemlike flame, to maintain this ecstasy, is success in life."[3] Is this the flame that heats the (I guess cast-iron) frying pan, temporary holding ground for mixes of one sort or another, some things there perhaps by design, the bulk of them there by chance, stirred up together, some a little bit scorched, some perhaps half-cooked, the rubbing sliding rolling heating hurly-burly of the frying pan intensely physical, an ecstasy possibly without transcendence? Whatever it is, it's neither good or bad: what's in it is simply *there,* itself, becoming perhaps something else, shifting about, tumbling among flavors and aromas, seasoning the pan itself, leaving something behind, emerging with bits of whatever it has acquired from the pan itself in its earlier uses, yet still its self. A fried egg, after all, is still an egg, I guess. But as I hope we shall see, it's a little more complicated than this, and not easily susceptible of explication. Maybe it ceases to be an egg at all; let's just say for now that whatever it is, it is still its *whatever—that* is what I shall come back to. And the poem makes me laugh, its incongruities making for continuing surprise.

The main drift of my argument is very simple indeed and really quite obvious. It goes like this: that Blaser is a very funny man, blessed (cursed) with great wit, a great sense of mischief, and a great outrage. It is precisely through humor, through laughter (closely related as it is to the cough), that two realms can meet in this, the only world we've got. And the realms? The realm of the body, where as Allen Ginsberg reminds us we are simply meat talking to meat; and the realm of the spirit, also known as the world of the imagination, as deeply rooted into our historicized meat as is our body itself. Laughter—like other syncopes and interruptions of the breath, such as the stutter—dissolves the dualisms of body and spirit, body and imagination, body and mind. An interjection of the body, laughter (like the cough) "shocks the cognitive apparatus in its brute reminder of organic experience" (Appelbaum 8), "deprives the body of its obedience to the mind" (Clément 7). Laughter affirms our subjection to flesh and thus to time, momentarily negating the mind's life so that—as Blaser's poem puts it—"what's in it is neither true nor false." Laughter is essential to, indeed, quintessential of, Blaser's "fundamental struggle for the nature of the real."

I once asked Robin Blaser which of the old Aristotelian or medieval humors was his. Without any hesitation at all, he replied: "melancholic."[4] When you consider the alternatives available—the sanguine, the phlegmatic, and the choleric—the speed of his reply is perhaps not too surprising. But listen to this: "The physiological syndrome of . . . abundance of melancholy includes darkening of the skin, blood, and urine, hardening of the pulse, burning in the gut, flatulence, acid burping, whistling in the left ear, constipation or excess of feces, and gloomy dreams; among the diseases it can induce are hysteria, dementia, epilepsy, leprosy, hemorrhoids, scabies, and suicidal mania."[5] In the middle of the fifteenth century Leon Battista Alberti offered a kind of solace for those afflicted with this condition, in an explanation as pertinent to the poet as to the painters he's talking about: "Painters become melancholics because, wishing to imitate, they must retain the phantasms fixed in the intellect, so that afterward they can express them in the way they first saw them when present; and, being their work, this occurs not only once but continually. They keep their minds so much abstracted and separated from nature that consequently melancholy derives from it. Aristotle says, however, that this signifies genius and prudence, because almost all the ingenious and prudent have been melancholic" (quoted by Agamben, *Stanzas* 25). Melancholia: grief for the loss of what you never had and which never even existed in the first place. The mind, hungering for the ordered harmonies of angelic space, hungering for the smoothly undisturbed stability of pristine, soulful, eternal bliss, for the securities of control, the self-calmed melancholic mind in its affliction of desire. Melancholia, obsessed with Becoming, forgetful of Being,

> as if the earth under our feet
> were
> an excrement of some sky
>
> and we degraded prisoners
> destined
> to hunger until we eat filth
>
> while the imagination strains
> after deer
> going by fields of goldenrod in
>
> the stifling heat of September
> Somehow
> it seems to destroy us[6]

Melancholia, erasing the body, rejecting the now. Melancholia, which Giorgio Agamben diagnoses as a condition of possession and loss at the same time. Its gravidity is absurdly vulnerable to the sabotage of the body's stutters, laughs, and pratfalls. No wonder, then, that "the truth is laughter," and that those four words are so persistent a refrain through Blaser's poetry. No wonder then, that another melancholic, William Carlos Williams, could reflect, late in his life, that, "The mind is the cause of our distresses."[7] Laughter, like the cough, the stutter, and the sneeze, restores us to our Being.

Yet—as the long description I just read reminds us—Melancholia is not exactly a silent condition. Indeed it's emphatically physical: flatulence; burping; whistling in the left ear. That burning in the gut no doubt gives rise to sorts of subterranean stomachic gurgles, groans, rales, hiccups, moans, wheezes, clicks, squirps, and rasps, now and again emerging as voiced burps, and belches and farts, coughs, stutters, stammers, sneezes, sputters, hesitations, and even laughs, little physical and vocal anguishes and reliefs which polite society tries not to notice, and which poems rarely if ever record and which have been utterly banished from reasonable discourse. The sounds of the body digesting, breathing, moving, sniffing, starving, tasting, drinking, spurting, chewing, shitting. The sheer restlessness of the body while we think. The sheer surprise of the body, announcing its presence to its own ear, but unrecognized, denied, and even erased by the mind.

Historically, the sounds of the body have been eliminated (if that's the word I want!) from speech, from discourse, from the poem, from signification. If, as Aristotle thought, "spoken words are the symbols of mental experience," then what sort of mental experience is a sneeze? If, as John Locke suggested, words "stand for nothing but *the ideas in the mind of him that uses them,*"[8] then what idea in the mind does a cough stand for? What sort of word is a cough and what is its meaning? At some concerts or at the opera a cough means you're bored, but what kind of cough is it anyway? What does it sound like? "Ungrammared sound stops thought," says Appelbaum (18). What is a stutter but the body, coming to thought, body's insistence calling to mind, flesh claiming possession of thought, disrupting it in its coming, resistances conjoined in the struggle of breath's interruption and thought's urgency. (The truth is laughter.)

We are so used, in our culture and in our experience, to Cartesian dualities of body and mind, flesh and spirit, that we rarely question them. Our language—and our notions of language—reinforce the distinction we draw between (to adopt an older vocabulary) the soul and its house the flesh. But the "Plan is the body," says a Creeley poem, picking at that separation of mind and body so pandemic in Western thought, worrying away at its erasure:

> Plan is the body. The mind
> is the plan.[9]

Readers familiar with the magazines *Wired* and *Mondo 2000,* with their assiduous worship of an irresistible technology, know a different story, reversing it, erasing the authority of the flesh. Technology accelerates the moves of body into mind, or the divorce of mind from body. As Scott Bukatman observes, "The hands appear *here,* while the wording appears *there.* Typing produces an information space divorced from the body: a proto-cyberspace."[10] One feature of the "WANDAH" program developed at the University of California Los Angeles between 1978 and 1984 and marketed in 1986 as the *HBJ Writer for the Computer* was "Invisible Writing" where the writing appears *nowhere.* The program doesn't let you see what you type because "not seeing what you type will force you to concentrate exclusively on your thoughts."

Writing and thinking thus lose almost all apparent corporeal being.[11] The body is the mind, says the cyberfreak, lusting for cybersex, panting after his (the genderization here is deliberate) multimedia teledildonics (a term apparently coined by Howard Rheingold in his 1991 book *Virtual Reality*). In the discourse of cyberspace thought and sex are virtually indistinguishable,[12] and among "the artificial intelligentsia" (the label is Louis Fein's)[13] the move toward ultimate but nevertheless earthly disembodiment gathers momentum. Marvin Minsky, in *The Society of Mind,* suggests replicating the individual by replacing each brain cell with a computer chip, and asks, "Would that machine be the same as you? It would be impractical," he concedes, "to duplicate with absolute fidelity all the interactions in a brain,"[14] but these microscopic differences would not make the duplicate different from your mind because you yourself are constantly changing and are never exactly the same as you were a moment ago.

The truth is laughter. In 1989 Hans Moravec, director of the Mobile Robot Laboratory at Carnegie Mellon University, hoped that "it will some day be possible for mental functions to be surgically extracted from the human brain and transferred to computer software. . . . The useless human body would then be discarded." As Claudia Springer put it (163), this means that human consciousness would be stored in computers except for the occasional outing in mobile robots.[15] Moravec calls this process "transmigration," and I wonder: has he ever laughed? Anyone who followed George Bush's conquest of Saddam Hussein in the Gulf War on a television screen has a very clear sense, surely, of the extent to which public and political discourse assumes the expendability and irrelevance of the human body in its quest for a paradise of the mind. Has nobody read Thomas Mann's *The Transposed Heads*?

It is astonishing how few phonemic representations we have of the laugh, how impoverished the vocabulary of mirth. What a surprise, for instance, to read this, in the *I Ching*—and how do we read it?:

> Laughing words—ha, ha! The shock terrifies for a hundred miles.[16]

What sort of laugh is that *ha, ha!*? Divine? Mad? Innocent? Devious? Malevolent? Is it the laugh that terrifies, or the "laughing words"? Is the one who laughs terrified too, or just those who hear it? We have so few words to record or register the laugh, in writing, that mostly we don't bother—once you've said "ha ha" or "teehee" you've pretty well exhausted the lexicon. Those we do have for laughter tend to be descriptive rather than mimetic—or their mimesis is vague. They don't, that is to say, tell us exactly what the sound of it is.[17]

"The vices of the mind are not to be underestimated," wrote Blaser to

Anne Waldman, but he is too smart to disturb his poem with a transcribed laugh; the sort of disturbance offered by transcription is too equivocal, too ambiguous, too bent on forcing the reading—and it is not, let's face it, a laugh. His poetry does not have the imprecise but predictable fixity of a "ha ha!" or a "teehee!" but instead undertakes the unpredictable risk of *the reader's* laughter, which arises as we read, conjured at a place and in a mode beyond both his and our control, and beyond or outside the score the written text is. In this he is transgressive, for the *reader's* voiced but ungrammared interruptions enter and disturb the syntax of the poem, disrupting the smooth continuity of cognitive thought, breaking the focused concentration the text demands, removing us from the act of *reading* so that we have to find our way back to it again. Blaser brings into the poem, that is to say, what historically we have expunged from discourse, from articulated speech, and from "the life of the mind"—the sounds of the body. That is to say, the sounds of our own mortality, our own subjection to the flesh.

"He said he was surprised and he said laughing is coughing." Gertrude Stein was right to link the two: Laughter always bursts, it always comes as a surprise, you really cannot plan to laugh any more than you can plan to cough—though of course you can fake it, the way lecturers cultivate a sputtery cough to buy time or to pretend to think, the way Winston Churchill practiced his oratorical stutter in order to engage his hearers. But the laughter I have in mind comes in fits, and is no more under control than is an epileptic seizure: in the midst of a laugh we do nothing but serve a spasmodic expulsion of sound. Our voice, indeed our whole being, is subservient to and even identical with that upwelling turbulent whirlwind beginning where? In the belly or the bowels, from the cavities of the thorax through the lungs and larynx out of the throat and mouth, the body in its convulsions forcing us into our *organic* intelligence. In Tibet, says a Persian tale, there is the laughing stone. "Those who set eyes upon it fall into violent laughter which continues till they die."[18] What do we really remember in the middle of a laugh? In such brute manifestations of organic experience, Edmund Husserl complained, "one man communicates nothing to another: their utterance involves no intent to put certain 'thoughts' on record expressively, whether for the man himself, in his solitary state, or for others. Such 'expressions,' in short, have properly speaking, no meaning."[19] But of course they all have meaning. Making focus vanish, the laugh takes us back into the now, into the world of the involuntary, of chance, of disruption, the world of what Giorgio Agamben calls the *whatever,* where there is no *thus,* nothing outside the immediacy of the event which holds us in its grip. The divisions of meaning-unmeaning, voluntary-involuntary, mundane-sacred, good-bad, momentarily dissolve, for the cognitive world which created these divisions has been completely destabilized; at such a point we don't even know especially that we are, or that we are "in" a body. Such matters are irrelevant. "Whatever singularity," remarks Giorgio Agamben, "rejects all identity and every condition of belonging, is the principal enemy of the State" (88).

And of course (is this a paradox?) the *impulse to laugh* (I do not mean the laugh itself) is triggered by the mind—it is a mental event. "The mind is the cause of our distresses," Williams wrote, "but of it we can build anew." And the building?

NOMAD

the grounds shift   all
          the time
                    as paradises must[20]

What a shock of recognition and discovery to recall—as does the poet in this astonishingly physical poem——that "must" is—as one dictionary so restrainedly puts it—"a condition of strong nervous excitement or frenzy to which elephants are subject, the paroxysms being marked by a dangerous irascibility"—that is to say, sexual frenzy.[21] The laughter and the satisfaction of discovering *that,* and that "must" is also mold or mustiness and is also newly pressed grape juice not yet fermented wine, is precisely the work of the mind moving into corporeality.

The kind of building I have in mind is precisely that effected in the midst of laughter, that curious stoppage of the breath in which we dwell in *the already,* wherein the flesh does not stand *between* us and the world because it *is* the world, in which the seer and the seen are in some odd sense one—a world without divisions and dichotomies, complete in its immediacy, then—and at the same time, completely and utterly itself, a singularity. To be such is to enter Agamben's *irreparable:*

images exit from Plato's
kismet   and other irreparable
absolutes (*Nomad* lines 4–6)

Laughter is its own determination; it does not point outside itself to an identity; it is not subject to an identity. The laugh is a singularity, a singularity without identity—I do not laugh as a Canadian, or as a man in his early sixties, or as an entity named Peter Quartermain. I laugh as a laugher. How does Appelbaum put it? "The laugh . . . makes the name that I call myself . . . the butt of laughter. That a person is known in essence as such and such a name, is born, dies, is acclaimed, upbraided, cajoled and vilified by a particular phonemic assemblage—and believes himself to *be* that name—is a joke of such magnitude that only a full-blooded laugh can explode it" (19, italics added). A farewell to inhibiting reason, laughter is its stoppage—and it is also, as Thomas Hobbes famously phrased it in *Human Nature* and again in *Leviathan*, "a sudden glory."

But we can no more spend our lives caught in the middle of a perpetual never-ending laugh than we can spend it in the middle of a perpetual cough, or in the suspension (Clément's syncope) between stutters, between breaths, that curious cessation of becoming—where, in this world, we can unequivocally BE. That we cannot *live* there is inescapable cause for melancholy; that we can be there at all is equally inescapable cause for mirth, and for joy. The body claims our awareness for its own, subject to no dogma, no identity, no claim of the State. The truth *is* laughter.

Notes

Epigraphs. Robin Blaser, quoted by Anne Waldman on 3 June 1995 in her paper, "Deviant Identities," at the Robin Blaser Conference; Gertrude Stein, "Pink Melon Joy," *A Stein Reader*, Ulla Dydo, ed. (Evanston: Northwestern UP, 1993), 305. Giorgio Agamben, *The Coming Community*, trans. Michael Hardt (Minneapolis: U of Minnesota P, 1993) 86.

1. Jean-Luc Nancy, "Laughter, Presence," *The Birth to Presence*, trans. Brian Holmes et al. (Stanford: Stanford UP, 1993) 368–392; Catherine Clément, *Syncope: The Philosophy of Rapture*, trans. Sally O'Driscoll and Deirdre M. Mahoney (Minneapolis: U of Minnesota Press, 1994); David Appelbaum, *Voice* (Albany: SUNY P, 1990). I thank Michael Boughn for calling my attention to Clément's work.

2. Robin Blaser, *The Holy Forest: Collected Poems*, rev., Miriam Nichols, ed. (Berkeley: U of California P, 2006) 323.

3. "Not the fruit of experience, but experience itself, is the end," said Pater, in *The Renaissance: Studies in Art and Poetry* (London: Macmillan, 1922) 236.

4. Conversation with Robin Blaser, 22 May 1995.

5. Quoted Giorgio Agamben, *Stanzas: Word and Phantom in Western Culture*, trans. R. L. Martinez (Minneapolis: U of Minnesota P, 1993) 11.

6. William Carlos Williams, "Spring and All XVIII. To Elsie," *The Collected Poems of William Carlos Williams*, A. Walton Litz and Christopher MacGowan, eds. (New York: New Directions, 1986) v. 1, 217.

7. William Carlos Williams, "To Daphne and Virginia," *The Collected Poems of William Carlos Williams*, Christopher MacGowan, ed. (New York: New Directions, 1988) v. 2, 247.

8. Aristotle, *De Interpretatione* I 16a, trans. E.M. Edghill (*The Works of Aristotle*

Translated into English, ed. W.D. Ross, v. 1 (London: Oxford UP, 1928); John Locke, *An Essay Concerning Human Understanding* Book III, chapter 2 (London, Dent: Everyman's Library, 1947) 204 (his italics).

9. Robert Creeley, *The Collected Poems 1945–1975* (Berkeley: U of California P, 1982) 602.

10. Scott Bukatman, "Gibson's Typewriter," *Flame Wars: The Discourse of Cyberculture,* Mark Dery, ed. (Durham: Duke UP, 1994) 79.

11. *HBJ Writer User's Manual* (San Diego: Harcourt Brace Jovanovich, 1986) 42.

12. "The only thing better than making love like a machine, it seems, is making love with a machine," suggests Mark Dery, "Sex Machine, Machine Sex: Mechano-Eroticism and Robo-Copulation." *Mondo 2000* 5 (n.d.): 42–43.

13. Louis Fein, quoted in Joseph Weizenbaum, *Computer Power and Human Reason: From Judgment to Calculation* (San Francisco: Freeman, 1976) 179.

14. Marvin Minsky, *The Society of Mind* (New York: Simon and Schuster, 1986) 289.

15. Much of the material in this and the previous paragraph is drawn from Claudia Springer's excellent article "Sex, Memories, and Angry Women" (in Dery, *Flame Wars*).

16. *I Ching,* trans. Richard Wolheim (Princeton: Bollingen, 1950) 197.

17. The list is not much enlarged if we think of the adjectival forms, or of synonyms for laugh and laughter: bellow, cackle, chortle, chuckle, exhilaration, giggle, grin, guffaw, hilarity, jocundity, joviality, merriment, mirth, roar, simper, smile, smirk, snicker, snigger, titter, waggishness, etc. Most phrases describing the laugh are just that: descriptions ("burst his breeches," "rolling on the floor," and so forth)—the fact of the laugh is more important than its sound.

18. Basil Bunting, *Complete Poems,* Richard Caddel, assoc. ed. (Newcastle upon Tyne: Bloodaxe, 2000) 226.

19. Edmund Husserl, *Logical Investigations,* J. N. Findlay, trans. (London: Routledge & Kegan Paul, 1970), v. 1, 275.

20. Robin Blaser, *Nomad* (Vancouver: Conference on the Recovery of the Public World, 1995); *Holy Forest* 429.

21. *The Century Dictionary and Cyclopedia* (New York: Century, 1896) entry for "must."

"Writing on Air for Dear Life"

Richard Caddel

> nothing is finished until it works out loud.
>
> —Richard Caddel

> I had no intention of writing for impatient people
>
> —Richard Caddel

> Art's purpose is to sober and quiet the mind so that it is in accord with what happens, the world around it open rather than closed
>
> —John Cage

A subtitle for this paper might be "Untidy Poetics." Canadian or U.S. visitors to England often comment on the smoothness of the landscape with its neat hedgerows and rolling fields, picture perfect after centuries of cultivation. But in the English North, that smoothness is disturbed, the sporadic turbulence and abruptness of the landscape reflecting, perhaps, the long turbulence and abruptness of northern history. We've been trained to like the smooth, the mellifluous, the tidy, and even the magnificent. Some readers talk of the Sublime as essential to poetry. The untidy disrupts; early modernists such as Mina Loy distrusted the graceful, Basil Bunting talked of the need to escape what he called "the hampering measures imposed by our memory of several centuries of English verse."[1] Both writers point towards what Robert Kroetsch calls the "derangement at the heart of . . . thinking."[2] As does Richard Caddel.

Caddel was 53 when he died in 2003 of chronic lymphocytic leukemia. Between them, his two books *Magpie Words: Selected Poems 1970–2000* (2002) and *Writing in the Dark* (posthumously published the following year), constitute what I take to be his Collected Works.[3] His poetic career was certainly inconclusive—what Antonio Tabucchi calls "a story without a solution."[4] But Caddel staunchly resisted conclusions anyway, was skeptical of certainty. "I like untidy edges," he told Tony Flowers, "the scratchmarks that show there's been a human around."[5] In 1998 he said that the act of writing poems, like attending to music, was like "going for a walk" in which "the revelations on offer to me would be in direct proportion to my ability to pay attention bar by bar, step by step, to whatever conclusions and over whatever terrain."[6]

When he went to the University of Newcastle in the late 1960s, Caddel was a music student studying composition; he played the classical viola, and saw himself as a songwriter. Basil Bunting was in residence then, and Bunting confirmed in Caddel his excitement in the physical impact of words colliding together; what he learned from Bunting led him to add English and history to his degree.

Caddel found, perhaps always heard, music at the heart of thinking (I adopt the phrase from Fred Wah).[7] "A fixed point in my work," he said in 1999, "has been my intent to sound it aloud. Even my shortest structures, some of them less than ten words long, are, I'd say, little aural events waiting to happen, and can only be comprehended in their passage through time. Sometimes I've accumulated these sound shards into longer groups—sequences, or suites, in a musical sense, and sometimes I've written genuinely longer structures. But the intention is the same, to make a sound which works on the air over the passage of time."[8] Hearing, Erin Mouré observes, is "outside" or "alongside" understanding; she notes that "understanding" is a form of possession, it tidies up the unruly world.[9]

The title of this essay, "Writing on air for dear life," comes from the title-poem (written in 1993) of his third major collection, *Larksong Signal,* a poem which acknowledges a connection with William Carlos Williams by nodding mischievously in his direction:

LARKSONG SIGNAL

Arcane and isolate breathing
acts of faith—longstone
to blind fiddler. High song
patient in rain. *Sing it—*

no ideas but in tunes—
'sounds we haven't heard
that the birds know about'—
writing on air for dear life[10]

Larksong Signal: the faint insistence of that *signal,* carrying its trace of imperative over into the noun, tells us something of Caddel's mind and look—ignore that signal at your peril. And the signal itself? In a note to the poem Caddel says, "Nearly all this short poem is derived from quotation in some form or other" (181). He tells us that the two lines in quotes are from the Ghanaian drummer Obo Addy. "Sounds we haven't heard / that the birds know about" point to let's call it the animal world, instinctual and indecipherable but not after all so Other as we might think, and the poem, so innocuous at first sight that it quite possibly slides right on by, has a few burrs, it clings. It's extraordinarily compact and not a little sneaky in its range of gestural possibilities.

That last line, "writing on air for dear life," sounding a little corny perhaps, calls forth all meanings of *air.* Equally, it calls forth all meanings of *dear,* in a life purchased at some cost by a poet whose "isolate breathing," as Tony Baker reminds us in his "Memoir," was sometimes, because of Caddel's chronic asthma, negotiated with great difficulty.[11] Then, too, there is the sheer unlikelihood of the poet's task, to enlarge our sense of life by means of the sheer fragility of the poem and the ephemerality of sound, to maintain the quality and range of consciousness under severe threat (*dear life* indeed) in a world devoted to such lifeless but poisonous abstractions as Order and Profit, Production and Efficiency, Freedom and Democracy, the nature and meaning of those abstractions determined by what can only be loathsome, a Committee. Caddel's poems are performative in that they do what they talk of, and he generally reserves Latinate diction—"committee," "endorse," "guidelines," and the like—for the objects of his scorn, preferring instead the world of scarlet berries, burnet rose, water-mint, or—as the poem "Flock" lists them—turf, birdsong, light cloud, wind. "The heart pounds on" (50). "Nothing holds, endures, but / in small things," says "Changes/The Great Rush" (a poem not gathered in *Magpie Words):*

> From the road we watch
> shafts, streams, furze,
> fire in the sun
> the streams burn
> & the moors
> recur.[12]

An early motto for Pig Press, which he and his wife Ann founded in 1972, was "Retaking the Language." "Larksong Signal" does some of that.

The poem's structure is musical—that *air* in the last line of the poem pushes us back to the *tunes* three lines before, and perhaps to *blind fiddler* before that—to say nothing of *High song,* which at careless glance might seem to diminish over the course of the next two lines to mere *tune.* "High Art" and (why not?) "Low Art," or even Pop. Blind fiddlers have a long history in British culture: one historian, I forget who, calls the blind fiddler a survivor from the era of collective music (whenever that might have been), and Caddel's *blind fiddler* in the poem evokes the stock figure of folklore, the perhaps magical or enchanted wandering musician, the ubiquitous itinerant minstrel, of years earlier than ours. In his *Diary* Samuel Pepys mentions a "very merry" dinner on April 1st 1665 at which Sir George Carteret, Vice-Chamberlain to King Charles II, Treasurer of the Navy and Member of Parliament for Portsmouth "did go to the doore and lead the blind fiddler by the hand in";[13] there's a virtuoso blind fiddler, Wandering Willie, in *Redgauntlet,* Sir Walter Scott's 1824 novel about late-eighteenth-century Jacobites; Charles Manby Smith in *Curiosities of London* (1854) presented the blind fiddler as an exemplum of "a use and a signification which discontented respectability, cushioned in its easy-chair, may do well to ponder."[14] There's the blind fiddler from Orkney, James Barnett (1847–1898), and dozens and dozens of others. There's a Kentucky folk song "The Blind Fiddler" as well as a ballad, Pete Seeger sings an American Industrial/Labour Movement version of it; Stephen Stills of Crosby, Stills and Nash sings another version. There's a quite famous, certainly popular and often reproduced 1806 painting, "The Blind Fiddler" by Sir David Wilkie (1785–1841), in the Tate Gallery in London—it's to be found easily enough on several sites on the net, and also on fine china of all sorts: it shows folk gathered round the fiddler as he plays before the cottage fire. The boundaries of highbrow and lowbrow begin to blur and merge. *The Blind Fiddler* is a 48-minute song-cycle written in 1976 "for mezzo-soprano and instrumental ensemble" by Sir Peter Maxwell Davies, text drawn from a play, *A Spell For Green Corn,* by the Orkney poet George Mackay Brown—this is the realm of Art Song, maybe what the poem calls *High song,* the self-conscious deliberate merger of musical and poetical composition, drawing on sources rich in folklore and destined for formal public performance. The High Art of Maxwell Davies meets the Kitsch Art of china plates.

High art? Low art? Fringe art? Before pursuing that, let's look at the poem's phrase "longstone to blind fiddler." There's *Longstone,* a musical group which, according to *Future Music* magazine in a 2001 interview and note, "exist[s] beneath the vagaries of the pop world's glitzy detritus." The group is actually two people, Mike Cross and Mike Ward; their second album, *auto://genous,* and I quote, "is an inventive concoction that draws from electronica, avant rock and ambient abstraction, and just occasionally bursts into the kind of futuristic butt-shaking that all intelligent clubs should be spinning. Overlooked by all but music obsessives, [its] efforts only fleetingly invigorate late night airwaves. The mainstream doesn't much care for Longstone"[15]—in that neglect they're a bit like Caddel himself, whose works have all been published by small or fringe presses,[16] and who argues that a major advantage of working outside the mainstream is that you're thereby free to pursue your own devices, over a period of years perhaps, without continual and in his view damaging interference. That word "isolate" so early in the poem gestures in that direction. Caddel's collaborator the English poet and musician Tony Baker has written movingly of Caddel's "affinity with borders and border creatures that Caddel made a primary political and aesthetic concern in his writing. It's not by accident that his work has been translated, not into the more likely European languages, but principally into Czech, Estonian, Lithuanian, Polish and Dutch,[17] regions either linguistically enclosed by more dominant tongues or sited on the frontier between an east and a west where local cultures have a long history of vulnerability to distant, dominant forces."[18]

On the other hand, the OED defines *longstone* as "a menhir," and tells us *menhir* is from Cornish and Welsh, *maen* (stone) and *hir* (long). The Blind Fiddler is the name of a menhir associated with a bronze-age stone circle on the coast of Cornwall—that is to say, it's a pre-historic (Archaic) standing stone, a megalith, a *long stone,* upended and rough. There are quite a few places named longstone in Britain, all associated with stone circles and megaliths—a megalith is a rough piece of rock, neither cut nor carved, but erected (the OED says "constructed")—Crude Art, you might say, something closer to the *sounds we haven't heard but the birds know about,* perhaps, in contrast to the High Art of Sir Peter Maxwell Davies's or Sir David Wilkie's Blind Fiddler or the highly technical art of the Longstone techno-musicians. Does it matter at all that *that* Longstone came into existence (so far as I can tell) some five or six years after Caddel wrote his poem? I think not. In a talk Caddel spoke of his desire "to make a sound which works on the air over the passage of time."[19]

That desire also challenges notions of congealed knowledge. "I've come to have a great distrust of certainty these days," Caddel said.[20] "Larksong Signal" *undoes* certainty. Its continually opening multiplicity of reference has a gestural quality in that it can't be precisely pinned down, narrowed; instead it opens up a range of possibilities, contrasting and supplementary echoes and resonances bouncing back and forth, a range which—whether we know anything about longstone or blind fiddlers—we take on faith. And there we are, back to the second line of the poem: "acts of faith." A *hymn* is an act of faith, if by that "of" we mean agency or motive. A hymn is an air, a song, Folk Art one might even call it—or some hymns anyway—and it begins to look as though the first line and a half of this poem ("Arcane and isolate breathing / acts of faith"), invoking perhaps an asthmatic sleepless night, talking about writing and reading, refer also to the act of writing a poem, along with the larksong of the title invoking music.

Caddel's determination is close to Bunting's, that poetry is sound, and the means and end of his scrutiny are musical. As the close of "Fantasia in the English Choral Tradition" puts it: "back in thought / in the hills / with scope / to sing / the things I love / as they occur / this instant" (49). *As they occur.* The randomness of that. *This instant.* The very nowness of occurrence, *present* presence, "existent or happening." Further recourse to the OED reminds us that in addition to "the present moment," an "instant" is an "example, brought forward in support of a general assertion or an argument, or in illustration of a general truth." The connections and perturbances get more and more seemingly arcane. But what may be most striking about those immediate presences in the poem, perhaps inescapably coming into the (poet's) mind (and therefore adamantly in the poem), is that they are (teasing or arcane as they may be) utterly everyday, and their strangeness is largely unobtrusive. We have to be told in an endnote to *Magpie Words* that the quotation is from Obo Addy, and who he is. Caddel remarked of his work that "it's all experiential, not out of books";[21] it's all quite ordinary. Close and concentrated attention to the ordinary defamiliarizes and transforms it, of course, and one person's ordinary is another's exotic—a condition we're especially vulnerable to, perhaps, in North America, where we might indeed hear Obo Addy on the radio, but we would have to walk far indeed to come across a menhir.[22] The poem bounces back and forth—or the mind does, and the eye, and the ear—between time and place; between what is now the twenty-first century and the archaic; between highbrow and lowbrow; studio and folk art; monument and menhir; town and country; human and bird; Britain and Africa. Attend to the details and the echoes run and run, bounce us back and forth in patterns; there's a music there, can we but hear it. And a dissolution of the artificial boundaries between the "human" and the "animal," between "culture" and "nature." The details, as the poem comes to dwell in us, get more and more detailed, proliferate, lock us into a kind of meditative present-ness. The poem reminds us of our own presentness, our life in the now of things.

Disturbance, disruption, and accidental off-beat resonance are at work throughout *Magpie Words,* Caddel's last major collection, which includes "Larksong Signal." The poem "Parsley" for example was written in 1982, and in *Uncertain Time* (1990) it was the middle of a triptych sequence, "Jackdaw in Spare Bedroom," one of 53 songs ("some of" which, as Caddel there quotes Charles Ives, "cannot be sung").[23] In *Magpie Words* it has the lovely extravagance of a page all to itself:

PARSLEY

Evening: smell of parsley
thinned in late May after rain (108)

Familiar territory, perhaps, at a glance maybe looking a bit old-fashioned, one of those careful quick takes Caddel is so good at: the quiet contemplative observation, utterly unpretentious, a tiny lyric catalogue, a bit like the music of Morton Feldman. The unobtrusive internal rhyme in the last line, the nicety of the movement through and in the vowels, the consonant play—here alliterative, there clustered juncture—determining pace, all matched by the precise specificity of that moment, the pungency caught in that otherwise humdrum "thinned" with the *length* of its single syllable—the exactness of "*late* May," and that telling "after," picking up as it does (if you pronounce the way some English people do) the first vowel of "parsley," a small resonance like the keen lingering scent. The intense fragility of the familiar and even perhaps ordinary moment, savored, available to contemplation and meditation. A little song, with an ear as exact as Creeley's, celebrating small things. It is a memory device.

But there's more: to the alert reader, "Parsley" might seem familiar, for the poems in *Magpie Words* are arranged alphabetically by title, and thus disturb chronology as well as theme. By happy accident that 1982 poem comes almost exactly sixty pages after lines which were written three years later, in 1985; it is quoted in the penultimate section of Caddel's first published attempt at a poem of some length, "Fantasia in the English Choral Tradition." I shall have more to say about the disturbance of chronology in *Magpie Words* later on; here I attend the play of memory:

it's important
          to make mistakes
in a way, once
in a way
parsley
reaching for the measure
the song wavered   recalling
  evening
          smell of parsley
thinned in late may after rain
turning
over and over
          air shifting over ground
violin, skylarks wilder. (48–49)

The shifts in lineation and spacing, the breaking-up and interruption of the original sequence, and the denser context, even in this short extract packed with abrupt transitions and disjointed sequence, make for a quite extraordinary transformation, and the act of recollection—both of the earlier short (and let's face it unruffled) poem and of the slight and more-or-less ordinary commonplace event which it registered—opens up a range of possibilities. There is the play of "measure," for instance, against the name of a common kitchen herb; but that play is modulated by the connections between "reaching for the measure"—which have to do not only with cooking but with music and poetry (with both of which "Fantasia" has been concerned in its seven or so pages so far, and which that "violin" and "skylark" nicely complicate—evoking, as they do, both the blind fiddler and the bird of "Larksong Signal")—and by the "air shifting over ground," a phrase in this particular context suggestive say of Shelley and of English Romantic violin music. The impact of the repetition, "in a way, once / in a way," along with that crucial placing of "once" just before the line break, plays up ambiguities and possibilities, not the least of which is the injunction that "it's important to make mistakes . . . *once*" as well as "once in a way" (the multiplicity of meanings the repetition makes possible serves to undermine the limitations implied in that repeated *once*).

There's an element of surprise in memory, as there is in any closely attended everyday event, an element of the unexpected. But in the book, in *Magpie Words,* it is of course *the poet* who recalls the poem, for the reader hasn't met it yet. Because we get it in reverse compositional order, it is the short, separate, quick take of "Parsley" on page 108 that acquires an otherwise unwarranted and certainly unanticipated resonance, the poem unobtrusively moving beyond the ordinariness of commonplace as it is so indirectly disturbed by the smoothing out of slightly turbulent recollection. The reader's act of remembering replays the poet's "recall" some sixty pages ago (but three years later)—such funny stuff going on with time as well as memory—with history, call it. This sort of play of repeat and surprise, where (as Gertrude Stein reminded us) repetition is never exactly repetition, is very much akin to a musical play of structure, and informs the whole book, echoes resonating back and forth among the poems. In the larger (book-length) musical structure it is as much a potentiality of repetition as it is its accomplishment, a kind of music of memory in which anticipation figures and prefigures, just as so many of the poems are, each by each, a looking forward as well as a casting back. Harry Gilonis has acutely observed (aptly quoting Zukofsky) that Caddel is interested in "the future of what has perished" as well as in "the past of what has survived,"[24] and it is with this in mind that we should recollect that remark to Tony Flowers that "it's all experiential, not out of books," the work an invitation to the reader to participate. "Without that," Caddel tells Flowers, "it's a sterile pulpit craft which I want none of."[25] Hence, Caddel's insistence on what he calls "untidy edges"; it's hardly surprising to hear that "the distractions of daily life, family, job, world, are generally very welcome . . . , recognized as part of the process."[26] If it's important to make mistakes, it's just as important to pay attention to the details, the minutiae. How telling, that nowhere in *Magpie Words* is "everyday" written "every day," adjective followed by noun.[27]

In Caddel's imagination, *everyday* points to the quality of our experience of and in the world, and calls for observation, elaboration, and investigation: "everyday / no more / than is needed" as one poem puts it (*Magpie Words* 114). And that investigation ranges from the apparently simple to the complex—from work like "Larksong Signal," or "Ramsons" (111), say, to longer poems like any of the highly flexible "Rigmaroles" or "Ground."

RAMSONS

a calm, a
  red sun low
in my driving mirror.
  pale moon.
smell I can't drop, or
  song, chance, wild
garlic, a weather
  beaten sail.

Like *throstle* (for thrush) or *spuggie* (for sparrow) *ramsons* (a plural) is current in speech though uncommon in written work, persistent like the smell the poem records. It comes from OE *hramsan*, the plural form of *hramsa*, wild broad-leafed garlic, *allium ursinum*, it is a pluralized plural, and the poem is an act of retrieval, a reminder of the world outside the book. The now of things, the everyday—the apparently casual throwaway that eludes discard—inescapably includes memory, lingers in possession, and in possessing carries with it history, memory, that weather-beaten sail.

Despite Caddel's insistence on the experiential rather than books as his sources, some poems, like the 1980 sequence "A Short Climate-Atlas of the Soul" are cut-ups, they do come out of books—as do, surprisingly, the following dense and untidy (yet highly organized) lines, the entire third section of "Underwriter" (a sequence of 14 sections, 207 lines in three-line stanzas):

horsehair viola bread -
chaff in the bright morning -
bread broken asunder (160)

No ideas but in tunes, and entuning can be complex, as in the elaborate compositional procedures of "Underwriter," which began life as a set of phonic translations from Paul Celan, so transformed by the process that Caddel himself could no longer precisely or perhaps at all identify the sources, and he certainly thought there was nothing to be gained from doing so. Here is the second (unnumbered) section of the poem:

it's weird—night in your eye
and text-frame, nose
into unsure silence

below Stonypath Ltd.—full
ships' stores in everlasting. Come
buy your stars anyway

here gripping the stone of winter
here underwriter stalling
in sound over coppice.

Fallowfrost print on
the week, so glib, nothing but
moonlight forgotten out there.

And glibly on common way
over stubble the scarf the
waymark unstill

over sleepingsickness
over turf of the law hear
heartsong down morning. (159–160)

"Underwriter" is an extraordinary poem; it can stand beside almost anything written in English in the last quarter of the twentieth century.[28] The complex of ironies lurking behind the title mitigate the overall bleakness, but the gloom is never wholly dispelled by the poem's alert wit and feeling. In its rueful shrug the poem conjures Agamemnon when, in *Troilus and Cressida,* he told Patroclus to "underwrite in an observing kind" Achilles' "humorous predominance" (2.3.138–139), to put up with it, and the language of "Underwriter," akin to such retrievals as *ramsons* and *throstle* (which Caddel points us to in his note on "Ground"), in its attentiveness to world and to word undoes the bleak, liberates the spirit, re-minds things. It is not the sort of "literary" language where metaphors or iconic figures of speech come from outside, shoveled over the experience the poem seeks to register in an attempt to "enrich" it, a language applied after the fact, after the now, neutralizing it into bland artificiality. "Underwriter" is chock full of figurative language, and this is a poem unremittingly concentrated from the inside, a writing that makes absolutely no distinction between writing and living, language and experience—responsiveness to the text at hand, looking into the ear wherein we read. We only understand what we know; as Erin Mouré puts it, if we used only words we understand, we would fall into silence. Hence the wonderful syntax of, say, those lines I already quoted,

> Fallowfrost print on
> the week, so glib, nothing but
> moonlight forgotten out there.

—the sheer *lucidity* of that, and the way in which abstractions (of which we have been forewarned by the title of this poem) are not abstract at all: One cannot be unaware of the line breaks and their power. The final two stanzas I quoted are astonishing (I hear Clare and Smart floating around somewhere) and in their wonderful play of possible meanings their compression declares kinship with Creeley, Zukofsky, Bunting. The surprises in this poem, the way they open up into the world of want, poverty, indifference to it/them, coming back to sadnesses we all are subject to and live with.

> . . . .   Memory
>
> cranks up astern in
> untidy never still legend, lover
> you fled from, your parents, your
>
> passage creature painting
> bent feet alive stops your
> wet starsight forever (162)

(that's the close of the fourth section). The sadnesses we all are subject to, but the poem faces them, underwrites in an observing kind: the vectors of deep and impossible-to-define-because-perpetually-shifting powers and subjections (abjections?) in that *passage creature* lets them flavor and intensify the we-must-work-with-what-we've-got which the poem accepts and finally finds consolation and even pleasure in. Such pleasure is deep and difficult. Real sound shines out, yes yes yes, but a sense of conundrum (I borrow the term from Robert Kroetsch) walks on.[29]

Such complex entuning is unobtrusively present throughout the work, even in the cut-ups of "Short Climate-Atlas of the Soul," the subtractive methodologies of "The Feet of Dafydd ap Gwilym Tapping to the Triads of Dr. Williams" and the first part of the astonishing "For The Fallen," which with its powerful condensation and concentration of sound, thought, and feeling amounts to an extraordinarily potent reworking of Aneurin, a great lamentation over the death of the poet's son Tom. Distillations. As in the syntax of this stanza from "Counter" (35):

> wasted lyric in sickness
> our words gone from us into that chimney
> mistake, imagining a singing loss so that a
> creature down and miles out of
> things for the lack of which the
> world dies daily

—"that chimney mistake" is remarkable indeed, but there are other astonishments in these six lines: the aural risk in that "imagining a singing" and that other kind of risk in the play on "down and out." "Counter" winds it all in, dense complexities of movement, the echo of Williams in the last of these lines resonating against and with, as a note on page 180 tells us, "a number of works on the dance-language of bees, and diseases of the blood," perhaps the poet's own sickness, perhaps the loss of his son (who when he died was learning to be a musician, like his father at that age), but perhaps, too, what pompous critics like to call "the situation of poetry at the present time." *Counter:* one who reckons; a table or board on which money is counted; contrary reckoning. It is also a term in music, and a defence or retaliation. Overall the poem has a musical structure, playing alternating forms and chants, refrains invocations and lyric stanzas, a complex Charm or Spell in which lament turns into prayer turns into praise.

"Counter" begins with two quotes, the first, as Caddel tells us in the note on page 180, from Stefan Themerson's surreal comic novel *Bayamus and the Theatre of Semantic Poetry* (1949), "published in the year of my birth," and the second, from Armand Schwerner's "translation" of a fake archaeological find, *The Tablets,* published "in the year of my fiftieth birthday." The first of these nods to the absurdist and intuitive is the rhymed gobbledygook of "*Kardang Garro / Mammul garro* [&c.]" (for which Caddel provides a translation), and the second a scrap of commentary on ritual chant; it might be Caddel's instruction to the reader: "The sound, the proper / Voice for the saying, . . changed by murmur into animal liveliness." Caddel works from notebook jottings, but "before they ever get into the book," he told David Annwn in 1990, "I'm hammering them into a rhythm or a sound which I like. So, from before the start, I'm trying to put a heard element into it."[30] Together those epigraphic quotes invoke a sense of forgotten and lost history, and give voice to those who are, as the first lyric stanza of "Counter" tells us, "living out on contrary margins" where the act of telling marks "a boundary of . . . resistance." The stanza I quoted in full has a double movement: in the direction of sense, an indwelling isolate lament; and in its energizing breathlessness, a turn toward affirmation and play—towards *imagining*. This move is picked up in the following stanza's turn (via the poem's cut-up or collage techniques) to "a compound vision dance." It is a poem which comments upon itself as it goes, and the commentary is one prime of the poem's celebration of complex and sometimes pained awareness, the structure and shape of the poem itself, as the final lyric stanza might be telling us, "deliberate form seeking in fleet foot dance, a signal towards an unknown."

For Caddel, then, uncertainty, is to be celebrated along with and through such undecidabilities as those in the line breaks of "Fantasia":

> to make mistakes
> in a way, once
> in a way,

exploring possibility, fostering surprise, and if the poet's task in composition is to find a way of pulling the notes into a whole, an equally pressing problem is to find a way to make room for echoes and associations to happen, to keep the territory of the poem open, to ease up. So "control is an essential element, even in losing control," as he told Annwn,[31] and poem after poem in *Magpie Words* deploys the juxtaposition of seeming irrelevancies or incompatibilities—frequently, in what I call his quick takes, through the poem's title. What, after all, is exactly the relationship between the title "'*Darknesse and light / divide / the course of time*'" (the italics and quotes are in the title) and the four lines which follow?

> grey coat
> grey eyes
> ellipse of morning
> pebble dash sea

The quotation comes from chapter 5 of Sir Thomas Browne's *Urne-Buriall* and continues: "and oblivion shares with memory a great part even of our living beings."[32] What lifts this juxtaposition, this apparently arbitrary linkage, from being merely a gesture towards opening up the territory? Perhaps nothing—this is an early poem, written in 1973—but the urgency to keep the territory open, to avoid the stifling arrogance of *knowing* that carries closure in its wake, draws thought by risking perplexity. And *memory,* once again, is central. There's a wonderful little poem, the fourth in the "Baltic Coast" sequence, called "Threap"; its title and its dedication to Eric Mottram both a bit of a riddle—how *do* they connect?—until you find, looking it up, that the last lines quote the dictionary. Threap:

> noun, local:
>
> persist in asserting; affirm;
> maintain obstinately or aggressively

and the poem, its untidy edges still suggestive, suddenly but not in the least explicitly voices equivalent affection for Mottram as for the Balts, their stubborn difficult allegiances. Juxtaposition, here deliberate, elsewhere fortuitous, to enlarge scope.

Some time around 1979 John Cage told Kathan Brown and the printers at Crown Point Press when they were tangled and impatient with a technical problem, that "[a]rt's purpose is to sober and quiet the mind so that it is in accord with what happens." When he published it in a mesostic in 1982 Cage added a bit: "The world around it open rather than closed"[33]—the world of untidy edges and intractable materials forcing responsiveness to what is under hand and in the tune—"I am not creating music," Morton Feldman once told a class, "it's already there, and I have this conversation with my material"[34] (157). The great risk of such practice, in which by being enigmatic the poet appears to withhold meaning from the reader, is the risk that he'll lose readers who want safety and certainty, readers who want authors to claim knowledge or understanding the reader presumably lacks, and in the process define the reader's desires or interests in the writer's terms. Caddel wants to neutralize completely that sort of power play or predation in which the writer—like any committee or marketer—tries to control both the reader's response and the matter at hand to achieve a predetermined outcome. It is a sort of intentional planning in which you claim to know what you think before you think it, and has something in common with what I call well-made poems, and Caddel calls "High Street poetry." It leaves nothing to chance.

The last line of "Counter" is "*—thus night—shadow—purple—*"; it is the last line too of the varied refrain of colors which, chanted throughout the poem at more or less regular intervals, serves as a shifting but stabilizing constant as it moves, an irregular rainbow, from white through black to *thus* shadow and its shades. And it is immediately followed, on the facing page, by the grays of "'*Darknesse and light,*'" those words by Sir Thomas Browne I've already quoted, expanding Caddel's even more partial quotation. Browne's complete sentence is worth quoting in full, affording as it does a suggestive commentary on "Counter": "Oblivion shares with memory a great part even of our living beings; we slightly remember our felicities, and the smartest strokes of affliction leave but short smart upon us." Caddel wrote "'*Darknesse and light*'" in 1973, 26 years before he wrote "Counter," and the juxtaposition of these two poems is fortuitous, and perhaps uncannily apt—a consequence of the alphabetical arrangement of the poems. That arrangement, Caddel says in his preface, "affords each of the poems a chance to make its own relationships with readers, and with its neighbors," and he speaks of adopting a "sequencing device" which "brings to light too many examples of synergy and interaction—*sound sense*—between the poems to be dismissed as mere chance" (11): an arbitrary arrangement of "things as they occur, this instant." *Magpie Words,* a note on page 180 says, is "intended . . . for readers rather than scholars." As a Collected Poems it would indeed be a different book, and the course and nature of his writing life would have a wholly different flavor, were the order of the poems, the *same* poems, chronological, because that order would invite us to read the poems as exhibiting the course of the writer's development as a poet—the model is progressive—and because it would cater to the prurient interests of those who like to think of poets in terms of a "career," that career open to assessment; intent on choosing which poem is "better" than which, such readers often fail to read a poem on its own terms, instead wishing it were something else, and were perhaps "more important"—whatever important might mean.

The "sequencing device" is in its abstraction a little disingenuous, certainly a shade mischievous, because it is not strictly true. The poems are not as strictly confined to the alphabetical order which the sequence on the contents page suggests. Here is "Hitting the Vein," one of the texts gathered here, a short prose piece:

> The day I terminated my lightning-fast mustard gas liaison with catholicism was also, "by chance," the first really rainy day of the autumn 1977/78, with its inherent discoveries of torn coats, leaky shoes, and lost slates.
> I became, after this, a firm believer in the workings of chance—a belief which has since been shaken. (137)

But "Hitting the Vein" is not listed on the contents page, instead it is the third of nine poems originally published in *Shelter* (1979), a title that does appear on the contents page, and if, instead of relying on the list of forty-four poems you can find there, you actually count the number of poems in *Magpie Words,* then there's somewhere between a hundred and a hundred-and-eighteen poems, depending how you count, in 163 pages of text. Some of the poems in sequences like "Sweet Cicely," for instance, were first published separately, and some of the eleven amazing variations in "Ground" bear independent titles although none, so far as I know, was published independently of the others—nor should it have been. All this (and more besides) might be a terribly pedantic sort of issue, except that it points first to undecidability regarding some of these texts—is this a separate poem or not?—and second to Caddel's arranging hand: one's response to the poems in *Shelter* as printed in 1979 is quite different from the response to them here, where they appear as a distinct sequence rather than as a collection. But on the other hand, the alphabetical principle brings all six "Rigmaroles," written over 15 years in the order they do *not* follow in *Magpie Words;* they cluster together at about the two-thirds mark of the book, each quite radically differing from the others, all of them—through their shaping of fragment—retrieving grace in what Caddel, following Maurice Scully, acknowledges a murderous time. Powerful music, compelling thought.

There is *work* in Caddel's "workings of chance," but the work is the poet's. From time to time in what I'm calling his Collected Works there are clumps and clusters of poems, presented under a single title, which are true then to the poet's history—the careful and deliberate arrangement of parts, fragments, sequences into more-or-less coherent units ("Against Numerology," for example, or "Ground," or "Underwriter"). But Caddel is careful not to give very much away, and it is finally up to the reader—who can after all figure out for herself that *these* poems apparently linked in sequence can be read independently of one another, and that *these* poems presented independent of one another might very well be linked. "One of the nice things, of course, about poems," he told Annwn, "is that you can rearrange them and put them in different contexts so they can make new friends as it were. There isn't one finite set of them."[35]

The openness of the "set" is crucial; it has a lot to do with why I think people will be reading Caddel fifty and more years from now—not just the wonderful long pieces like "For the Fallen" and "Ground," which are staggering in their skill and inventiveness, desperately moving in their lament and recovery for what is lost, and their celebration of what can be found; anyone with even half an ear, and that made out of tin, will find in them delight. But there are the shorter poems—the scornful comedy of "Flock," the exact thought and accurate narrative of "From Wreay Churchyard," the more obvious music of "Three Reels." And there is the sheer openness of the personal—I would say many of these poems are about family were that word not too abstract. They are about Ann, and Tom, and Lucy Caddel; "the things I love." "I am back in thought," Caddel says at the end of "Fantasia," "in the hills / with scope / to sing / the things I love / as they occur / this instant" (49). That's an interesting list, a statement of poetics. *In thought, to sing*—the music always apparent, always foremost, in tuneful mindful breath—airs, then. Byrd, and Campion; Dowland, and Clare. And the hills? A mark of northern England, perhaps, where Caddel loves to walk, but surely too a mark of the margins and boundaries and heights so many of the poems claim kinship to—another mark of northern England, perhaps. Go contrary, go sing.

Notes

Epigraphs. David Annwn, "[Interview with] Richard Caddel," in Peterjon Skelt, ed., *Prospect into Breath: Interviews with North and South Writers* (Twickenham and Wakefield: North & South, 1991) 89; Richard Caddel, *Writing Rigmaroles,* unpublished paper delivered at the symposium *Language in Time: Temporal Structures of the Text* (Druskininkai: Lithuania, October 1998) and in revised form at the Third Subvoicive Symposium (London, January 1999); John Cage, "Composition in Retrospect," *Etchings 1978–1982* (San Francisco: Crown Point, 1982). This work is one of the source texts for Cage's 1988–1989 Norton Lectures at Harvard, published as *I–VI* (Cambridge, MA: Harvard UP, 1990), where the words I quote appear on p. 427.

1. Basil Bunting, *Basil Bunting on Poetry,* Peter Makin, ed. (Baltimore: Johns Hopkins UP, 1999) 123.

2. Robert Kroetsch, "Listening into Words: 'Again only is it in the thing itself,' " in Frank Davey et al., ed., *Fred Wah: Alley Alley Home Free. Open Letter* 12.2 (Spring 2004): 43.

3. Both published in Sheffield by West House Books.

4. Antonio Tabucchi, *Requiem: A Hallucination,* Margaret Jull Costa, trans. (New York: New Directions, 1994) 76.

5. Tony Flowers, *Quiet Music of Words. Conversations with Richard Caddel* (Sheffield: West House Books, 2002) 28.

6. Caddel, *Writing Rigmaroles.*

7. *Music at the Heart of Thinking* is a serial poem which has engaged Fred Wah since its first installments appeared in the late 1980s; a book with that title was published by Red Deer College Press in 1987.

8. Caddel, *Writing Rigmaroles.*

9. Erin Mouré "Stakes, Poetry, Today," in Davey 32–42.

10. Richard Caddel, *Magpie Words: Selected Poems 1970–2000* (Sheffield: West House Books, 2002) 102. Unless otherwise stated, all quotations from Caddel's poems are from this retrospective collection (cited parenthetically in text).

11. Tony Baker, "Memoir," in "In Memoriam Richard Caddel 13 July 1949–1 April 2003," Peter Quartermain, ed., *Jacket Magazine* 22.

12. Richard Caddel, *Sweet Cicely: New and Selected Poems* (Durham: Taxvs, 1983) 14.

13. Samuel Pepys, *Diary,* Henry B. Wheatley, ed., 3 vols. (London: Bell, 1949) v. 2, 361.

14. Charles Manby Smith, "The Blind Fiddler," *Curiosities of London Life, or, Phases, Physiological and Social, of the Great Metropolis* (London: Cash, 1854) 89.

15. Longstone, "Interview and Information," *Future Music Magazine,* 2001.

16. Most recently, a U.S. reprint of *Uncertain Time* (originally published in England by Shearsman), from William Corbett's Pressed Wafer, in Boston, MA, 2011.

17. For example the bilingual *Psaní v temnotě Writing in the Dark,* translated by Petr Mikeš (Praha: Fra, 2007). A Czech version of *Magpie Words* appeared from the same publisher in 2002 as *Slova Straky.*

18. Baker "Memoir."

19. Caddel, *Writing Rigmaroles*

20. Flowers, *Quiet Music* 26

21. Flowers, *Quiet Music* 21.

22. At the Poetry Conference and Festival for Pauline Butling and Fred Wah at the University of Calgary May 15–18, 2003 (only some of whose papers were printed in Davey, *Alley Alley Home Free,* and at which an earlier version of this essay was read), Marian Penner Bancroft showed her photograph of the Hatzic Rock, an apparent menhir situated between Chilliwack and Vancouver in British Columbia and sacred to the Sto:lo Nation. Unlike longstones, it was not placed by human agency.

23. Richard Caddel, *Uncertain Time* (Newcastle upon Tyne, 1990) 13.

24. Harry Gilonis, "Making a Music Out of Language: Richard Caddel's 'reading' of the Gododdin," *Fragmente* 7 (1997): 103

25. Flowers, *Quiet Music* 21

26. Flowers, *Quiet Music* 28, 33.

27. According to my own count, "everyday" occurs ten times in all in *Magpie Words,* on pp. 45 (twice), 49, 88 (six times), and 114.

28. *Underwriter* was first published by Maquette Press as a pamphlet, in 1998.

29. Kroetsch, "Listening into Words" 44.

30. Annwn, "Richard Caddel," 89.

31. Annwn, "Richard Caddel," 88.

32. Sir Thomas Browne, *Hydriotaphia Urne-Buriall,* in *Selected Writings,* Sir Geoffrey Keynes, ed. (London: Faber, 1968) 152.

33. Kathan Brown, *John Cage: Visual Art: To Sober and Quiet the Mind* (San Francisco: Crown Point, 2000).

34. Morton Feldman, *Give My Regards to Eighth Street: Collected Writings* (Cambridge, MA: Exact Change, 2000) 157.

35. Annwn, "Richard Caddel," 95

"The Tattle of Tongueplay"

Mina Loy's *Love Songs*

> To be in any form, what is that?
>
> —Walt Whitman

> I can see no reason for calling my work poetry except that there is no other category in which to put it.
>
> —Marianne Moore

> At present, most of what we know, or think we know, of women has been found out by men. We have yet to hear what woman will tell of herself, and where can she tell more intimately than in poetry?
>
> —Helen Hoyt

> In a humanistic tradition in which man is the measure of all things, how does an appendage go about telling the story of her life?
>
> —Barbara Johnson

My primary interest is not in social or thematic issues, but in language issues. This puts me at a disadvantage since, like H. D., Lorine Niedecker, Gertrude Stein, and other women writers of almost any century, Mina Loy was, until Roger Conover's careful edition of Loy's selected poems, *The Lost Lunar Baedeker* (1996), ill-served (if served at all) by various editors. It is in any case clear that despite Conover's and Marisa Januzzi's scrupulous work, some of Loy's texts are impossible definitively to fix. Though paying close attention to the text in what follows, I am not going to address problems of textual accuracy, and use the versions Conover established with Januzzi in *The Lost Lunar Baedeker,* or—in the case of "To You"—that in *The Last Lunar Baedeker,*[1] though there is no doubt in my own reading of Loy that the uncertainties attending some of her texts, such as for instance the ambiguity of Loy's handwriting, seem to be something of a happy accident, especially in the first of the *Love Songs.* Does the second line read "Sitting" or "Silting the appraisable"? Does that isolated line near the end of the poem read "There are . . ." or "These are suspect places"?[2] Like Conover and Januzzi, I prefer "silting" and "these," but in neither case is a single reading wholly satisfactory, and each alternative (once one knows about it) hovers palimpsestic beneath the other and informs it. This inadvertent drift toward the text as variorum is wholly in keeping with Loy's writing strategies of enhancing phrasal indeterminacy and syntactic uncertainty; and her text thus refuses completeness in a manner strongly reminiscent of Emily Dickinson's variorum strategies (which Loy could not have known). In her revision and ambiguation (and even perhaps elimination) of phrasal boundaries (through line break, through the avoidance of normalized punctuation) Loy seems to have learned from Gertrude Stein how to achieve what the Canadian poet Fred Wah calls the "para-syntactic," a form of writing which, he observes, "slow[s] the reading down to intense observation."[3] This, surely, is crucial in a poem which seeks to observe closely the ways in which women are complicit in their own economic, psychological, sexual, and social subjugation by men.

I

I take *Love Songs* to be a single work, within which each song is at once a fragment and a whole.[4] It attacks romanticized sexuality as one of the principal means of subjugating women. It explores the damaging myth which creates not love but powerless contempt, and through a variety of strategies, including unresolved ambiguity, approaches knowledge/knowing in an experiential (episodic) rather than a schematized (narrative or linear) way. It understands definition to be imprisonment. As Song 29 puts it, love does not bring "sexual equality," nor even "simple satisfaction"; instead, it brings "own-self distortion." Parodic, comic, angry, scornful, contemptuous, sharp-tongued, occasionally wistful, haughty, ironic, cultivating incohesion and unbalance, *Love Songs* interrogates formally and thematically the dominant male poetic tradition, and seeks to neutralize not only the myths by which women are disempowered, but also the social and psychological definitions of womanhood and the means by which that identity can be expressed.

> Leave off looking to men to find out what you are *not*—seek within yourselves to find out what you *are.*
>
> As conditions are at present you have the choice between *Parasitism, & Prostitution*—or *Negation*"[5]

Dismissing conventional literary discourse and poetic forms because she can find no readily accessible mode of speech for women, Loy relies principally on disruptive syntax and the exercise of wit to reposition herself; she writes with an almost utter disregard for the normative: "I have no idea what English is," she said, "but I am intensely aiming at pure language."

Elizabeth Fox-Genovese has observed that the nineteenth-century representation of separate gendered spheres had important ideological effects, naturalizing women's economic dependence on men, excluding them from the political and public work world, and affording "even privileged women no access to the experience of an authoritative self-hood that for men was embodied in the notions of property, work, and political responsibility."[6] A woman's identity was properly to be found, and of course fulfilled, in the (no doubt joyous) duties and responsibilities of marriage.

Parasitism, prostitution, or negation—or (another way of putting it), Ophelia and Salome. Loy rejects the dichotomy, and refuses too the negative path of sheer denial. She repudiates and violates the formal and thematic conventions for poetic speech by women, and refuses to be defined by a social role, either as glittering ornament (pendant) of passive inspiration (amusement) or as active cultural producer (the Muse). "I was never a poet," she said.[7] A number of readers (Amy Lowell among them) agreed, (erroneously) dismissing *Love Songs* as "lewd and lascivious."[8] After all, poems about erect and comic penises (*Love Songs* 1), about the scrotum as a "skinsack" packed with a "wanton duality" (*Love Songs* 2), and about the sheer *tedium* as well as degradation of fellatio (*Love Songs* 17),[9] are unlikely to meet conventional expectations for poetic speech by women, whether they smoke cigars or not. In denying that she is a poet Loy scrupulously separated her work from both the form and the substance of what in the pervasive social and aesthetic/intellectual context was defined as literary. By turns scornful and hilarious, bitter and exultant, she locates herself on the margins of literary and social discourse in her desire radically to reconstrue gender and the female.

This is not, however, simply a semantic, satiric, explicitly thematic enterprise; it is also—as "To You" (erstwhile prefatory to *Love Songs*) carefully establishes—linguistic.[10] The poem is not at all easily paraphrased, and can I think be read as an early demonstration of Charles Bernstein's textbook-like aphorism that

> [w]riting is not a thin film
> of expendable substitutions that, when reading, falls
> away
> like scales
> to reveal a meaning.[11]

The play of semantic possibilities begins with the title, since we cannot be at all clear whether to read the poem as an address to "You / The city," you the hobnobber and "hybrid-negro," you the group (perhaps all male?), you the reader, or even you the writer's self. As the poem proceeds these possibilities are not resolved. This is partly because subsequent occurrences of the word "you" shift and slide, partly because the poem exploits incongruities of vocabulary (in what sense, for instance, can "impulse" and "unfolding" [line 3] be contraries?); partly because orthographically and notationally it cultivates inconsistency. How many sentences are there in this poem—three? Six? Five? If we follow Ron Silliman's definition of a sentence as everything that appears between periods (after the first), the poem is only three sentences long. But with the exception of the first, each stanza is conventionally a complete grammatical sentence ("Plopping finger / In Stephen's ink / Made you a hybrid-negro") and the poem can be as many as six sentences long (there is a page-break after three lines of the fifth stanza). Playing the conventions of punctuation against those seemingly established by the stanza, the poem exploits line-break and stanza-break to disrupt phrasal and semantic boundaries so that a word, phrase, or even "sentence" detaches itself from a prior sequence to link with a subsequent one. What, for instance, is "Round / The aerial news-kiosk" of lines 6 and 7? Is the "nigger" of line 11 a "nigger . . . Of introspection," or is there only a "deaf-mute / Of introspection"? Is it the "deaf mute / Of introspection" who is "Plopping [his(?)] finger / In Stephen's ink" or is it that "Plopping [your] finger / In Stephen's ink / Made you hybrid-negro"? This sort of syntactic drift makes it impossible to resolve the uncertainty of that "You" in the title as well as in the body of the poem.[12]

So, too, the opening stanza is syntactically challenging, for (even if the sentence extends to the end of stanza 3 where there is a period) from a grammatical point of view it is not a complete sentence, even if (especially if) we read everything after the first line as a sequence of adjectival (subordinate) clauses. It is difficult to find an independent or principal clause in this sentence, since both "wedge" and "bridge" are transitive verbs, here (if not used adjectivally) used intransitively. The net effect of this disruption of convention is to draw our attention to the prepositional activity: wedged *between;* bridged *by;* splintering *of;* egos *round;* hob-nob *with;* mute *of,* and even (though it is not prepositional) kiosk *where.* This is, clearly, a poem of *relation,* and the relation is telling. We are obliged, reading "To You," to pay attention to writing as neither simply representation nor repression but, as Bernstein and others have observed, as the production of meaning.

II

"These fragments have I shored against my ruins," says Eliot in *The Waste Land;* "I store up nights against you," says Loy (*Love Songs* 21), dark and silent. Lacking Eliot's sense of cultural and poetic continuity, in terms of both the tradition and the poem itself, Loy feels the imperatives of poetic *dis*continuity, and deploys lexical and syntactic strategies in order to achieve it. Wit operates throughout.[13]

Lexical. (a) Loy's vocabulary is notable for its reference to body-fluids and to body-parts. There is "mucous-membrane" (1), saliva in "a trickle" (1) "spermatozoa / at the core of Nothing" (9) and "cymophanous sweat" (28). But arms, hearts, eyes, and lips, conventional to love poetry, are not beautified. Lips, if they appear at all, are "promiscuous" (3); eyes are "blind" (30) or "steel" (24); hands carry a "disheartening odor" (11); breath "booms" (12); all, taken together, adding up to a "pubescent consummation" (23); "human insufficiencies" (29) which, added together, sum only a "drivelling humanity" (15). Conventional love poetry, by metaphorizing the body, makes it impossible to be explicit about the body; obliged to metaphorize the world of feeling, it evades male and female sexuality. *Love Songs* sharply distinguishes the biological from the romantic, the physical from the metaphysical. With great skill,

(b) Loy exploits the mixing of vocabularies—especially the clinical or laboratory (scientific) with the colloquial and the conventionally "poetic." This can also be described as a mix of the abstract with the concrete, of the polysyllabic with the monosyllabic, of the Latinate with Anglo-Saxon. This affords irony without detachment, and at the same time (combined with Loy's interesting syntax and punctuation) distances the voice (which is hardly "unified"), while affording both judgment and a sense of the absurd.[14] Such idiosyncrasy (what in another discipline might be called an idiolect) affords *Love Songs,* that is to say, a highly personal voice, and it is difficult to distinguish the voice of the poet from the voice of the poem.

Syntactic. Syntactic strategies operate at both the global and the local level. (a) *Global:* Overall *Love Songs* displays a number of binaries. Speech *breaks in, is loud, driveling, hiccupping, braying brassily;* yet it is also a *silent* harangue. Binaries include, then, *speech/silence;* and also *body/mind; two-ness* as *conjoined/severed; dissonance/resonance; day/night, sun/moon, production/ destruction, birth/death* and so on. These binaries are not resolved, do not cancel each other out, for two reasons. First, though the overall structure of the poem is episodic, one episode does not stand in contrast to its neighbor—the progression is cumulative or agglutinative. Second, though many of the episodes are double-voiced, and can indeed be read in at least two ways (for example, number 13, number 22), the sheer comedy and bawdy hostility of the opening poems (especially 1 and 2) prevent those two voices from neutralizing each other. The poem, and indeed the whole sequence—despite, or perhaps because of, its rage—is finally apositional, and refuses to move toward the sort of conclusion binary oppositions customarily offer. It takes quite seriously Whitman's question "to be in any form, what is that?" and resists the strictures of definition. This is perhaps most apparent at the local level.

(b) *Local:* I've already mentioned syntax at the local level of the line-break, phrase-boundary, and sentence. The subversiveness of Loy's syntax is liberating, for it denies both linearity and hierarchies of the sort found in the conventional English sentence; frequently, what she writes does not "make sense" in ordinary terms, and her language, as Fanny Howe observes of what *she* calls poetic language, "transforms the state of being lost into that of being free, by making judgment on judgment itself. Poetry writes twice, and produces another sound from the ordinary. In this sense it is free out of its longing to escape the cell of syntax."[15] When the sentences *do* "make sense," they frequently rely on the syntactic authority of aphoristic and gnomic utterance. As Carolyn Burke has commented, the use of aphoristic patterns enables Loy to play the radical enclosure of the epigram against and with the radical openness of her larger formal (global) strategies.[16]

The subversiveness of Loy's syntax is most readily apparent in the combination of line-break, punctuation (and its lack), and vocabulary, and is part of Loy's recognition that conventional syntax is unavailable to women—like Stein, and like Nicole Brossard some 60 years later, she felt the need to reinvent the language. Perhaps one reason why readers are only now beginning to pay close attention to *Love Songs,* almost three-quarters of a century after they were written, is our acute awareness of the central *dis*continuity of experience—there has been a shift in our model: "A central aspect of the writing process for women [now]," remarks Fred Wah, "is . . . dissonance and fracture."[17]

III

Dissonance and fracture are both clearly visible in Song 13. In earlier *Love Songs,* phrasal boundaries blurred. Here, the speaker blurs too; we cannot be sure how many voices there are. In its multiplicity of voice, the poem exploits ironic doubleness as a major strategy; it plays the sheer destructiveness of the romantic myth's definition of woman against the speaker's perhaps helpless rejection of all definition as yet another illusion. The poem plays with a series of oppositions, setting them against visible silences, gaps on the page which may on one hand indicate a change of speaker, or on the other, enact what cannot be spoken. Line 2 plays the illusoriness of words and of speech against the silent reality of the gap:

> "I have got to tell you and I can't tell."

The non-verbal, the physical, tells what cannot be told. But the struggle between having to tell and being unable to tell is complicated by the pun in "can't tell," which *can* mean "don't know." Hovering between speech and silence, between knowledge and ignorance, between the nameable and the nameless "something" (which appears nine times in the first 13 lines),[18] and (possibly) between reason and intuition, the tensions between "I" and "you" are amplified rather than resolved. In the central stanza (line 16), when "I" and "you" (hitherto kept spatially at a distance) apparently resolve into "us," the transformation is intolerable, for the opening stanza's list of what is *new* (name, dimension, use, illusion) becomes a list of *very* (jealous, suspicious, conservative, cruel), and the "we" of the following lines (18, 25) separates into the poem's final list, "me you—you—me."

Subject to the male gaze the speaker is caught in a series of contraries and conflicting imperatives which seem actively to seek the dissolution of her identity. Whatever love is, it does not remain inviolate. The tension between desire and the experience of fragmentation which is its companion is reflected in the poem's violent oppositions: push/pull; tell/not tell; shiny/resonant; I must not see/you must not hear; come to me/keep away; only for you/only for me; ambient (surrounding)/in your eyes (containment); please give/Don't. The tension is released, though it does not wholly disappear, by the intrusive exclamation, possibly sardonic, "Oh that's right," which draws back from this multivoiced scene into a single voice. It is very difficult, though, to know quite how to speak that line—almost as though, subject to the male gaze, the voice has lost its own hearing. However we say or hear it, though, it is emphatically and unequivocally a solitary voice. It offers a somewhat confused critique of what has gone before, for through its imperatives and its requests it seeks to hand over control to "you," the irony ("Don't let me understand you   Don't realize me") ambiguated and double-tongued. All of this adds up to a vision of love in which "together" means annihilation of the self yet is illusory, a melding in which, the final line suggests, "me" is absorbed into "you," while "you" nevertheless remains distinct from "me." But that remains suggestion only; in suggesting the possibility of merging identities, this line severely undercuts whatever position the poem might seem to be taking. The technique is very like that in the closing line of Song 1, where "coloured glass" suggests the sheer inadequacy and indeed impossibility of the earlier resolve:

> I must live in my lantern
> Trimming subliminal flicker
> Virginal   to the bellows
> Of Experience
>
>   Coloured glass.

The "I"'s aggressive self-assertion is, finally, only apparent, and remains a gesture. The biological wins out and we do indeed, as Song 26 subsequently tells us, "sidle up / To Nature / That irate pornographist." Small wonder, as Song 33 observes, that protoplasm was raving mad, evolving us.

Such doubleness is parodic. As Linda Hutcheon has observed, parody's "ironic double voicing allows a writer to speak *to* her culture, from *within* that culture, but without being totally recuperated by it. Parody is a weapon against marginalization. It literally works to incorporate that upon which it ironically comments. It can be both inside and outside the dominant discourses whose critique it embodies."[19] If, as I suggested, Loy locates herself on the margins of literary and social discourse in her desire to reconstrue the female, she is in an unenviable situation. For Song 13 enables the kind of doubleness it exhibits in such complex fashion to appear in much simpler and more obvious forms in later songs. Song 22, for instance, is almost nightmarish in its duplicity: split like the word "cleave," it either affirms female dependence upon the male or denies it completely—proclaiming that "without you / I go / Gracelessly / As things go." Grace is a part of the romantic myth of womanhood, an instrument of control. And things? "Green things *grow* / Salads."

Love Songs is deliberately *graceless,* and it enacts its own meanings. Rejecting forward linear movement by circling and regressing (the binaries are dropped, picked up, dropped); rejecting utterly the notion of the well-made poem, *Love Songs* seeks to undermine the notion of privileged content. In refusing to privilege any of the poem's given vocabularies and syntactic patterns it works to neutralize the sense of a unifying central voice. And it rejects the sort of cultural resonance that immediate contemporaries like Eliot cultivate: in contrast to *The Waste Land* or even *Prufrock* this is a sparsely populated poem which seeks severely to control connotation and disempower the aesthetic. The overall effect, then, is of a dismissal of conventional literary discourse and of the customary hierarchies of poetic genres, and it questions (albeit tentatively) the conventional relations between author, world, and text. It rejects, that is to say, that literary discourse whose voice "break[s] on the confines of passion," which rejects the explicitly physical and sexual.

Notes

Epigraphs. Walt Whitman, *Song of Myself* Section 27, line 1; Marianne Moore, quoted by Rachel Blau DuPlessis, "No Moore of the Same," *How(ever)* 4.3 (January 1988): 14; Helen Hoyt, "Retort," *Others* 3.3 (1916); Barbara Johnson, "My Monster / My Self," *Diacritics* 12.2 (Summer 1982): 4.

1. Mina Loy, *The Lost Lunar Baedeker: Poems,* Roger L. Conover, ed. (New York: Farrar Straus Giroux, 1996); *The Last Lunar Baedeker,* Roger L. Conover, ed. (Highlands: Jargon, 1982). These titles hereafter abbreviated *LLB96* and *LLB82* respectively.

2. Conover's admirably lucid discussion of the "complicated textual and editorial history" refers to possible misreadings of Loy's "casual cursive script" and concludes "[m]y decisions should be subject to question, but my reasons should not" (*LLB96* 188–191).

3. For a discussion of Loy's relations with Stein, see Carolyn Burke, "Without Commas: Gertrude Stein and Mina Loy," *Poetics Journal* 4 (1984): 43–52, though my emphasis, conclusions, and approach differ somewhat from hers; and Fred Wah, "Which at first seems to be a going back for origins: Notes on a reading of some American women writers," *A Mazing Space: Writing Canadian Women Writing,* S. Neuman and S. Kamboureli, eds. (Edmonton: Longspoon/NeWest, 1986) 376.

4. In "Grandma's Story," her remarkable and I think ground-breaking exploration of "the bond between women and word," Trinh T. Minh-ha suggests that all stories transmitted woman to woman are at once a fragment and a whole, "a whole within a whole" (*Woman Native Other: Writing Postcoloniality and Feminism* [Bloomington: Indiana UP, 1989]). Loy's poetic practice in *Love Songs* would confirm this insight.

5. Mina Loy, "Feminist Manifesto," *LLB96* 154 (typographic emphases not reproduced here).

6. Elizabeth Fox Genovese, "Placing Women's History in History," *New Left Review* 133 (May-June 1982): 24.

7. Conover, "Introduction," *LLB82* xv.

8. I take "lewd and lascivious" from Carolyn Burke, who uses the phrase twice in "The New Poetry and the New Woman: Mina Loy," *Coming to Light: American Women Poets in the Twentieth Century,* Diane Wood Middlebrook and Marilyn Yalom, eds. (Ann Arbor: U of Michigan P, 1985): 37–57. Burke reports that Lowell found the first issue of *Others* (in which some of *Love Songs* first appeared) deeply offensive.

9. Song 17 can equally plausibly be read, I think, as a poem about giving birth; Loy seems determined, in her exploration of meaning, to relinquish much of its control to the reader. Characteristically, the poems in *Love Songs* invite (as I suggest later

in this essay) at least two and possibly more interpretations, usually but not always contrary. "Truth does not make sense," Trinh has observed in another context, "It exceeds measure." (Trinh, "Grandma's Story" 150).

10. Text in *LLB82;* for discussion of its connection to "Love Songs" see *LLB96* 191.

11. Charles Bernstein, "Artifice of Absorption," *A Poetics* (Cambridge: Harvard UP, 1992) 86–87.

12. The play of syntactic drift seems to operate along lines similar to the transegmental drift familiar to linguists; by the second half of this century its manifestation and exploitation in *apo koinou* (ambiguation and resonance through line breaks) had been quite extensively explored by William Carlos Williams, Louis Zukofsky, and a host of others, and is perhaps no longer so startling as it was when Loy was writing this poem. Her sheer inventiveness of resource is easy to overlook.

13. There is, surely, no need to point out or document the sheer range of Loy's wit. But the opening of poem 3 is irresistible:

> We might have coupled
> In the bedridden monopoly of a moment

where "bedridden" not only carries the weight of suggested confinement, the invalidism thus carried over to the bed-*riding* suggested by the "coupled" (which never took place), but also hints at the printing term, to *put to bed* (go to press, be printed), which points towards the poem's close, where "We might have given birth to a butterfly / With the daily news / Printed in blood on its wings."

14. Loy skillfully deploys Latinate and abstract diction to resist the colloquial, so that (for example) when in Song 13 we come to "terrific Nirvana" the principal effect is terror not delight.

15. Fanny Howe, "The Contemporary Logos," *Code of Signals: Recent Writings in Poetics,* Michael Palmer, ed. (Berkeley: North Atlantic Books/*Io* 30, 1983) 54.

16. Carolyn Burke comments that "Loy's formal principle, the aphorism, typically calls attention to itself through its radical enclosure" ("Without Commas" 46). It is worth noting that Loy's syntax in *Love Songs* is quite unlike that of *The Waste Land:* Eliot's sentences are fairly conventional, syntactically speaking.

17. Wah, "Which at First" 376.

18. Word counts: "I" 3, "me" 8, "my" 1; "you" 6, "your" 1; "us" 2, "we" 1.

19. Linda Hutcheon, "'Shape Shifters': Canadian Women Novelists and the Challenge to Tradition," *A Mazing Space* 226.

"Conversation with One's Peers"

George Oppen and Some Women Writers

My title comes from a letter George Oppen wrote to the English poet Charles Tomlinson in 1963: "I have come to believe again, perhaps in more rather than less despair, that the only possible hope is in the conversation with one's peers."[1] In the following pages I sketch the situation of women writing in the 1960s and possibly the 1970s, and Oppen's bearing toward them. Oppen, in his considerable struggles for an adequate form and language, found that he had a great deal in common with a number of women writers, had news for them, and quite possibly got news from them. His position with regard to language and many of his writing strategies are closely akin to those of quite a few feminist women writers. It is tempting, but certainly misleading, to suggest that Oppen occupied and wrote from a feminist position. We now tend to take for granted what Oppen had to struggle to realize.

Pretty well from the time he started writing again in 1958, Oppen paid a great deal of attention to women writers, reading their work, encouraging them, corresponding with them.[2] Kathleen Fraser said that hearing Oppen read in 1967 "cut through everything"; he "spoke to some level of gravity that was new," providing "modesty, severity, and close scrutiny, in contrast to the flash and dazzle of any number of stylistic 'performances' by various N.Y. based poets."[3] Oppen had a considerable (but not always benign) effect on the writing lives of quite a number of women in the 1960s and 1970s, and his work has certainly not been without influence on a subsequent generation of women. Preparing this paper, I wrote to a number of women poets, and received a quite surprising as well as generous range of responses. What follows partly draws on what some of them wrote to me, and so I thank, now, for their promptness and thoughtfulness, Norma Cole, Jane Cooper, Beverly Dahlen, Rachel Blau DuPlessis, Kathleen Fraser, Barbara Guest, Susan Howe, Frances Jaffer, Denise Levertov, Maureen Owen, Naomi Replanski, Joan Retallack, Adrienne Rich, Diane Wakoski, and Rosmarie Waldrop. The diversity of these poets and their responses leads me to formulate my question in two parts:

(1) What sort of news did Oppen have, for so many women writers? and
(2) Why did he *notice* them, why, in the 1960s and later, would he be drawn to pay close attention to their work?

These are not simple questions if only because Oppen's relations with women are divided and complex. Reading his work pretty extensively and intensively over a period of three or four weeks before setting pen to paper I found that I probably would have liked George Oppen (or rather, the unit George-and-Mary) if we'd ever met; indeed I'm pretty sure of that. He sounds like a smashing person, and he's an astonishingly wonderful poet. But it would be easy, paying attention and tribute to what Sharon Olds calls "that feminist side of George,"[4] to sentimentalize or idealize him; it would be equally easy, too, to demonize him—and that, not simply because he seems to have enjoyed the company of younger long-leggy women. Among his papers at San Diego there's a fragmentary draft of what might be a letter—I have no idea whether it was ever sent, nor do I know when he wrote it, or who to: "Among the things I don't want to say—out of old friendship—is this: if we did NOT undertake the 'Space Program' we would cease to be anything we have meant by 'human' ((all the women I can remember speaking of the space program have been opposed to it—Secretly, at those moments, I regard the women as sub human———I do, I do."[5]

Well. I'm not sure I'm going to even *try* to unpack that quite astonishing statement, though I do think it needs unpacking. I do want to get at some of the complexity of his relations with women and his attitudes toward gender, so I'm going to start by reading a couple of Oppen's poems. They trouble me—and it was that troubling quality, indeed, which led me to write to a couple of dozen women writers when I was casting around for my topic.

THE ZULU GIRL

Her breasts
Naked, the soft
Small hollow in the flesh
ear the arm pit, the tendons
Presenting the gentle breasts
So boldly, tipped

With her intimate
Nerves

That touched, would touch her
Deeply—she stands
In the wild grasses.[6]

Sharon Olds, interested in "the place women have in his work," says of this poem that she was "moved by the way [Oppen] identified with [the Zulu girl] *from within,* as a desirer."[7] But I don't see it. Whose desire, hers? or his? and for what? The adjectives, after that first "Naked," pretty clearly propose a male gaze: "*soft* / *small* hollow"; "*gentle* breasts"; "*intimate* Nerves"; "*wild* grasses"—and there's an almost prurient quality about that final adverb: "her intimate / Nerves / That touched, would touch her / *deeply.*" The title identifies the Zulu girl as a piece of exotica, and there's a curiously possessive attention in this desirous regard for this Othered female, viewed from the outside—her Othered culture, her Othered race. Oppen insisted, famously and repeatedly, that one write from one's own experience. But the experience registered here, surely, is that of seeing a picture in the *National Geographic,* not seeing an actual Zulu girl. It's an oddity, an uncharacteristic instance of Oppen's spectatorism, Oppen as tourist.

But on reflection, I wonder how uncharacteristic it is. Here's another poem, one I like very much (I'm not sure how to voice it, say it, especially the unobtrusively splendid syntax of the penultimate sentence):

THE HILLS

That this is I,
Not mine, which wakes
To where the present
Sun pours in the present, to the air perhaps
Of love and of
Conviction.

    As to know
Who we shall be. I knew it then.
You getting in
The old car sat down close
So close I turned and saw your eyes a woman's
Eyes. The patent
Latches on the windows

And the long hills whoever else's
Also ours.[8]

The play of tenses and the line breaks are crucial in this poem: "you getting in, the old car sat down close"? or "you getting in the old car, [you] sat down close"—both readings at once, of course, the car shifting with her weight as she gets in, the inanimate registering her presence. The poem is really quite wonderful, opening as it does with that lovely deictic play of the first two words, "*that* this," the really quite baffling syntax of the first two lines—"that this is I, / Not mine," and the pun of upper case "I" and e-y-e "Eye." That pun may only occur to us, perhaps, in the middle of the second stanza, though we are invited to awaken to it as it "wakes" in the second line: "that this is I, / not mine, which wakes / To where the present / . . . ." Who's looking here? whose eye / I? There's the shift in time, too, that nicely complicates the poem, that *then* of line 8 anticipated perhaps in the repeat of those two *present*s which may themselves pun *gift*. The whole poem registers and celebrates the shift from *I* and *your* to *we* and *ours*—a shift around which gendered identity in the poem turns; it almost relinquishes gender. The sheer unexpected difficulty of assigning any kind of antecedence to that appositional phrase "not mine" in line 2 ("that this is I, / not mine,") obliges us, I think, to consider the possibility of uncertainty among a possible multiplicity of *I*'s, an uncertainty and fluidity of identity which stabilizes in that final *ours*, and the poem works at least in part because "the words," as Oppen once asked of them in poems, "move with almost equal weight on every word."[9] In so far as they do so, perhaps, they depart from ordinary speech—this is a hard poem to say.

Perhaps that equality of emphasis, the weight then on *woman's*, is why I'm a little troubled, disturbed, not wholly at ease, with "I turned and saw your eyes a woman's / Eyes" in that lovely sentence of the second stanza. Actually, though, I'm not quite sure exactly *what* I think about it, *how* I feel about it. That shift from *your* eyes to a *woman's* eyes, from the immediacy of the personal, individuated *you* to the generalized, essentialized, and perhaps even stereotyped *woman*, Other, disturbs me. But then, perhaps it's supposed to. After all, the poem is, as Oppen said in a letter in 1959 soon after he wrote it, a poem "of our meeting, Mary and I." It's a love poem, and like many love poems "The Hills" sounds gender difference: there's a frisson, a little shock of sexual recognition in that generic "*woman.*" In that 1959 letter Oppen called his meeting with Mary, that recognition and discovery of *us*, "the first victory in my life over the stone," and spoke of his "hatred of the 'Stone universe.'"[10] "The Hills," then, testifies that the meeting with Mary was a victory in the long and hard struggle we each of us face—what in another poem[11]

Oppen called the human "undertaking"—to feel a kindred sense of companionship, to build community, to share—to *feel* one's own numerousness. "I report emotion, I speak only of emotion," he wrote in his working papers,[12] declaring human feeling as stop and buttress against "the idiot stone. The universe—it should excuse me, but I don't like it."[13]

But that idiot stone the universe is itself a little tricky: on one hand it is, as he said in a poem, "the mystery . . . that . . . we stand on,"[14] beyond our control, beyond, most of the time, our perception. So Oppen would praise William Bronk, in whose poetry "the stone revealing itself is magic and absolutely conclusive."[15] Conclusive? Because in revealing itself to us, it enables us to feel with surety the fact of our existence. And magic? Because in revealing itself to humankind in poems, in language, in words, the stone—"the atom we are made of" and which "we didn't make"[16]—abates and allays the ubiquitous and almost desperate hunger we have for "being numerous." But there is also a social, political, and institutional landscape and world of things, as inert and resistant and mysterious to human perception and agency as is the idiot stone, and an extension of it. "It is not a feminine culture, it is very hard for women. Terribly, terribly hard," he told Andy Meyer in 1969 or so.[17] The stone universe consists too of "all we have made of the universe by looking at it,"[18] and includes, then, "the enslavement of women [which] has been an agony to me."[19] But if that is the case, how can he even for a moment "regard the women as sub human"?

In part my difficulties with "The Hills" arise because I'm talking about the poem in 1996 and Oppen wrote it in around 1959—a lot has happened in feminist politics and thought in those 40 years. In part, too, my difficulties arise because Oppen (born in 1908), when struggling with the political question in the 1930s did not see it as being at all specifically a matter of gender. And wherever his political sympathies lay, he was nevertheless a child of his generation. "He felt very guilty towards the women in his family," Mary Oppen told Dennis Young on 2 July 1987, "because for his younger sister, for his niece Andy, for our daughter, for me, *he* was the man, he was the male, he was *the* one. That's a terrific responsibility, and he felt it very much. His older sister too, but she died. And he was the *one* male for all these women. That was a tremendous responsibility. They had other men in their lives, but it never mattered. It had been his father, and George just inherited that position. The one man who they really could trust and love and accept."[20] Gender difference; gender roles; gender identities.

There's a distinctly patriarchal side to George Oppen, and I'd *guess* that it flavored his relations with Mary. It's not that he sees women as helpless so much as he sees them as, well, dependent, perhaps weaker than men, certainly softer, gentler. There's a side of him that associates the feminine with the decorative, with "flowers, flowering, and . . . alternatives to male competitiveness," and in a 1966 letter, discussing the weakness of Imagism, he speaks of "feminine self-love." Discussing Sappho's "feminine distance" (which I take to mean something like difference, Otherness) the same year, he suggests *feminine* means "something like 'domestic,' " and about three years later he asked Andy Meyer, "What is the feminine? The love of standing still, of hugging to oneself, of containing?"[21] Woman as domestic and *practical,* nesting. There's an odd comment at the end of his essay "The Mind's Own Place," in which he obliquely takes Denise Levertov to task for writing overtly political poetry. "The poet's business is not to use verse as an advanced form of rhetoric," he says in the closing paragraph, "nor to seek to give political statements the aura of eternal truth." And then he offers the sardonic comment (this is early in 1962) that:

> we have seen peace treaties before; we know what they are. This one will be, if we get it, if we survive, like those before it, a cynical and brutal division of the world between two great powers. Everyone knows what must be in that document: the language of both sides has been euphemistic but clear. A free hand in Eastern Europe to Russia: to the United States in Western Europe and in this continent and some other places. And the hope that China will not soon acquire a bomb. And where is the poet who will write that she opened her front door, having sent the children to school, and felt the fresh authentic air in her face and wanted—*that*?[22]

It's an odd example. Oppen is asserting that the important things in life are not the larger political issues and the machinations of politicians but the everyday, the minutiae of the ordinary—*there* no doubt we might agree with Oppen.[23] But the assumption behind the example seems to be that woman's place is in the home, looking after the children and no doubt acting as support-system for her husband.

Oppen subscribed to the orthodoxy of his time, which maintained that women would not give their lives over to anything as abstract and of no immediate practical use as an *idea,* and he saw this, I think, as a kind of salvation. Frances Jaffer says that after she published "a small feminist, but fairly mainstream book of poems" in 1977 she said to Oppen

> "I don't know how to continue. I can't seem to write in the old way and I don't have any idea what to do next; I'm really blocked."

He thought for a while and answered, "The trouble with women poets is you don't read enough philosophy."

"But I don't like philosophy. I can't stand all those systems."

"I don't read philosophy for the systems," he said. "I read for the language."[24]

I think Oppen may even have thought (or perhaps it's more accurate to say that he probably wanted to think) that women *could* not give their lives over to an abstraction, that they are *constitutionally* incapable of loyalty to an abstraction. There is some such strength of feeling, at any rate, in his fierce and even bitter disagreement with Levertov, who in his view had given her intelligence, her passion, and her poetry over to an abstract and therefore empty ideology. He saw a "poem which begins with an idea," as essentially turning its back on itself, because "a poem is itself a process of thought, a means of thought,"[25] the poet, as Zukofsky put it, "thinking with things as they exist."[26] Determined that the poem not state or present a position arrived at before writing the poem, he distrusted abstractions, loathed the transcendent ideal, and saw all political ideologies as lies. Instead, he favoured the immediate, the object directly before the senses, unmediated relationships, unmediated language, unmediated experience: "I choose to BELIEVE IN THE NATURAL CONSCIOUSNESS, I SEE WHAT THE DEER SEE," he wrote in his working papers, and added: "the desire NOT TO is the desire to be alone in the fear of equality."[27]

All this may account in part, perhaps, for his noticing women writers, paying attention to them. But I think actually he was puzzled by them, and indeed puzzled by woman generally. Certainly he was intensely curious about them, almost as if they were a foreign or alien species. "Women? women? women are like everyone else except men," he told Rachel Blau DuPlessis in 1966, "God help you. God help us all." And seven years later, sometime in 1973, appealed to Andy Meyer: "I want so very much to hear about women; the men are insane."[28] But what did he hear? What did he pay attention to? Patriarchal he may have been, at least in part, but Oppen was nevertheless very strongly a feminist: in his working papers he called "Women's liberation the most dramatic and the most to be loved of all the political 'movements,' "[29] and in 1965 called "good" Carol Bergé's poem in Diane Wakoski's magazine *Hardware Poets Occasional Software* ("Dream issue"). The poem begins:

I piss on you
in your bed
in your navel

where you lie
not dreaming
because I say
you must not dream[30]

He sought out Diane Wakoski (not she him) because he liked her poetry. What news did he find there? "I believe that George liked my poetry," Wakoski says in a letter, "because it represented something that might be called a female spirit. . . . he liked the fact that I was bald and bold about my interest in sex, my passionate search for a man to love me and offer me sexual fulfillment. That all my poems were about it."[31] But for Kathleen Fraser it was a slightly different story. In a letter she talks about a George Oppen, and I quote, "who may have been 'right' but was always wanting me to cut out most of the poem and to stop writing about 'female material' (love affairs, motherhood, etc.). I simply had to stop showing him my poems because I didn't want to ruin our friendship."[32] He wrote to her in 1972:

> I have to say this bluntly: to be told of the men, and the men, and the men: we can NOT accept this from women poets any more, we can NOT
>
> For the love of God, for the love of God (the phrase halfway between swearing and religious exhortation) for the love of God come UP into the world
>
> . . . or if "men" then *start* from the assumption that we know now, having tried, that the monogamous couple will not solve the problems of society, the whole problem and structure of society[33]

One interesting thing about Oppen's comments to Fraser is his impatient insistence that she explore larger political themes—that she adopt, in her poetry, an ideological motif, that she explore overtly social and "feminist" themes. Yet his hostility towards Levertov's poetry is largely a matter of her having done that, having explored larger political themes, adopted an ideological motif. When he asks Fraser to "come UP into the world" he's asking her to move toward abstraction, towards a more general and presumably universal critique through her language—to have, then, a plan for the poem. Yet in his working papers time and again he talks of his own writing as an *in*ward and *down*ward movement: "Not only to say, but to be IN IT   Each word is a stance, each word also a question never answered," he once wrote, and exhorted himself "To go *down,* to go *into.*"[34] He seems, indeed, explicitly and constantly to have associated downward and inward movement with the specifically human:

SOUND GOES IN: Sight goes out.
One is human: the other is miracle[35]

The movement outward may be a miracle, but it is a movement toward the idiot stone.

Now the difficulty about the idiot stone is that, while revealing itself, the atom that we are made of is "magic and absolutely conclusive," and that as the world we made, social, political, and institutional—the ideological world—it is repressive and inhibiting. The ideological world prevents our seeing, works against the stone revealing itself. The central task of Oppen's poetry is indeed—though he rejected the term—redemptive: his poems almost without exception disclose his impossible desire to be free of all ideology, to disclose unmediated experience, unmediated relationships, in an unmediated language. "There are things for each of us around which meaning gathers," he wrote Frederic Will in 1967: "The mission is to hold them, and to be able to keep them in his mind, to try again and again to find the word, the syntax, the cadence of unfolding—I don't mean to promise redemption of course. A matter of being able to say what one is and where one is. And what matters."[36] And to say it, dare I say, "purely"?

Perhaps I'm being rather simplistic, but with Fraser and Wakoski we have two writers (Fraser especially) who are politicizing the personal, bringing the directly personal, their own sexuality and gender, into the poem and thus into the politics of feminism. Interested and supportive though he may have been, for Oppen it was not, it seems, either quite appropriate or quite enough—the poet of the 1930s faced with the politics of the 1960s. In autumn 1962, after seeing a movie of Euripides *Electra,* he spoke of "the importance of a culture as against the simpler relations and simpler emotions of father and child and mother and child."[37] The simpler relations and simpler emotions: it is clear that the larger social implications of human action preoccupied Oppen throughout his writing and indeed working life. He wants larger issues, more complex feelings, drawn into the poem. And this is, of course, a very tall order, for it raises yet again the whole problem of abstraction. It is a big jump from the perception of oneself as singular— or even of oneself as *us* as in the case of George and Mary—to the perception of being numerous, the perception of generalities. "You see the separate waves but somehow there is the *sea,* just as you see people and somehow there is, or could be found, *humanity,*" he told Larry Dembo when he was talking about "The Party on Shipboard" (*Discrete Series* 1934): "one does have to know a wave is just a wave; one doesn't experience 'the sea.' . . . the sea as a whole . . . I don't accept it unless it is also a perception . . . unless one actually experiences the fact of the weight and solidity and unity of the sea. . . . , I *know* there is such a thing as 'the sea,' the whole. But the poem doesn't manage to see it, and it records the poet's—my own—inability to see it. So that it leads directly to what I've told you about my giving up poetry."[38] Somehow the sexual and the personal doesn't quite cut it, any more than it would cut it in the politics of the 1930s.

As I've already said, Oppen was a child of his generation, a poet of the 1930s, and he was deeply suspicious of the poem as a vehicle of direct personal expression: his own poems are themselves curiously impersonal—reading them I do not get any particular sense of George Oppen the person at all. A poem like "Night Scene" (*Collected Poems* 118) may indeed risk the sentimental, but in its bald recounting of simple narrative it almost completely avoids the judgmental, and at no point does he allow his own or Mary's feelings to intrude.[39] Oppen does not elaborate his social identity for us, and he's in two minds about these women writers he sought out and strongly encouraged, whose work he is a shade reluctantly drawn to. So why, exactly, *was* he drawn to the particular writers he was drawn to? The answer to that question is closely intertwined with the question of what sort of news he had for women writers, and I think I've already sketched some of the answer.

Talking with Dembo about his poem "The Undertaking in New Jersey" (*New Collected Poems* 63), Oppen was surprisingly inarticulate, stuttering and stumbling his way toward the somewhat inadequate conclusion that the "undertaking" of the poem's title is "to make a community." Here is the poem:

THE UNDERTAKING IN NEW JERSEY

Beyond the Hudson's
Unimportant water lapping
In the dark against the city's shores
Are the small towns, remnants
Of forge and coal yard. The bird's voice in their streets
May not mean much: a bird the age of a child chirping
At curbs and curb gratings,
At barber shops and townsmen
Born of girls—
Of girls! Girls gave birth . . . But the interiors
Are the women's: curtained,
Lit, the fabric
To which the men return. Surely they imagine
Some task beyond the window glass
And the fabrics as if an eventual brother

In the fields were nourished by all this in country
Torn by the trucks where towns
And the flat boards of homes
Visibly move at sunrise and the trees
Carry quickly into daylight the excited birds.

In his account Oppen is quite clear that he is, in that poem, looking at a world in which men and women lead separate *perceptual* lives, and that the difference between male and female perception is a social construction:

> I don't think the poem lends itself to paraphrase too easily. And then all the many contradictions in this which I've sort of touched on in other spots; these were just girls who had the babies, and that this is a woman's house; they were just kids who got pregnant, produced a baby. And out of that came this whole elaboration of the curtains and the men down to this—I forget how it went. The men come home and enter this woman's world, and must, to live, to live in anything, to live in a purpose at all. And yet it's really very alien to them. The men come home from their jobs with other things they could describe with maybe a touch of dissatisfaction, but which lead nowhere. And do we imagine? And the sparrows, again, they're just the raw . . . they can be treated just as plain objects. The sparrows just sit on the street because it's there.[40]

The problem of gendered perceptual worlds is a feminist problem, and is one with which Oppen himself felt great kinship. He's drawn towards women writers of a younger generation than his own because like them he's been sidelined, exiled, and is marginal. When Kathleen Fraser wrote to him after (for the first time) hearing him read, he replied: "It is painful to be isolated, not to say amputated, from the preceding generation. . . . We experienced it too—we were one of those generations. Most markedly, we were among the early explorers—or rather settlers in that condition."[41] But that condition is not the conventional modernist one of "*make it new*"; we are all familiar enough with the canon to know that, and Oppen is voicing his own sense of separation: he sees his as the only post-Poundian generation to be completely separate from both its forebears and its contemporaries. He told John Crawford in 1973 that *Discrete Series* "was avant garde alright Primarily because I could not have expressed what I felt in the old forms," and in 1965 had said to David Antin that

> David [Ignatow] as well as I—And Reznikoff, and Williams, and other long-lived persons, arrived on the scene when obviously the way to

> write, the manner that defined poetry, was the manner of Sara Teasdale or the John Hall Wheelock or something called Joseph Auslander or etc. etc. We did not—none of [us] did—agree. Nor to the obvious modernity of the Eberharts, the Shapiros and the other greatest poets of their time, nor to Dylan Thomas and and and Our error was clear to almost everyone—
>
> One avoids that swamp by no prescience, but simply by asking oneself what one does know and what one doesn't know, what really is important and what is not— Important in one's life.[42]

It's hard to tell from the working papers, because few if any are dated, but in them there's a recurrent image of his own writing situation, and I suspect it recurs pretty well throughout his writing career. Certainly the thought and passion is central to Oppen's poetic:

> If a man—or a woman of course . . .—goes rowing in the park, tho he may row as well as anyone who ever lived, tho he may row so well that he seems to be ice-skating, waltzing round and round the lake to the strains of the Blue Danube—still, he cannot row around and around that lake forever. But suppose he sets sail across a sea which, so far as he knows has never been crossed. . . . He too may turn back after a while, but if he does it can only be a failure of nerve. He will be tempted to turn back, but he will also be tempted not to. And he will not be tempted to continue only by the hope of approval. He will *want* to keep going, if only his nerve does not fail, even tho he has only his bare and anxious self in the boat.
>
> Like the poet, if he becomes distracted by the desire to display his virtue, his grace, his anything at all—he will not get there. Because what he has to do is slug it out. A voyage in the open sea—unlike a row in the park—is no joke. It is not virtuous. If he makes the trip, that's his own affair, and in his heart he knows it.[43]

It's not surprising, then, to hear him speak dismissively of "Sandburg, etc: they accepted the language as they found it, and were carried into sentimentality, having no where else to go."[44]

The language.

There's something awfully grim and even puritanical about Oppen's repeated and urgent insistences. The beleaguered poet, not heroic, but enduring in the struggle for clear vision. "I speak only of emotion," he said, "Of which the most powerful is the emotion of conviction."[45] And hence

> . . . I need time to think
> to feel again the presence of the world
>
> the power to originate lies not in aesthetic man (the
> exercise of "taste") but in ontologic man;
> man as he confronts the world.[46]

I don't think it's gendered, that statement, but it sure is hungry in its moral earnestness. In its intensity it is reminiscent of the fervour of religious revivalisms in earlier stages of American or British religious history—Thomas Hooker, say, Richard Baxter, or even Jonathan Edwards—but it's a desire to *originate,* while confronting the world. So that when Oppen says he wants "to see what the deer see," opposing a "natural" to a cultured or "aesthetic" consciousness, he not only proposes that the poet cut out all the crap of inherited thought and custom, presupposition and social obligation, but recognizes that the activity is essentially solitary. He seeks a kind of primeval nakedness and solitude which he carefully, I think, distinguishes from isolation.

Oppen is quite explicit: "the desire NOT TO [see what the deer see] is the desire to be alone in the fear of equality"—and he adds: "I am not discontented."[47] The kind of vision Oppen is here proposing then, is from an intellectual and social view at least completely non-hierarchical. It does not hide its fear of equality in the righteousness of power, nor is it afraid to confess its ignorance and helplessness and turn to others: "Being democratic," he dogmatically reminded June Oppen Degnan in 1959, "has got to be absolutely non-dogmatic, a-political, unsystematic: whereas system, dogmatism and all the rest is found tolerable in Yeats Pound Eliot."[48] Seven years later he told her that "the search for power is the attempt to *hide* the world from oneself; it is fatal."[49] It's surely no accident that the working paper entry immediately following his comment about seeing what the deer see moves into plurality:

> I see what the grass would see
> if it had eyes

("We are members of each other," he told Denise Levertov in 1963).[50] And it's equally no accident that, as the copyright page of *Collected Poems* tells us, "In *Of Being Numerous,* phrases, comments, cadences of speech occur, in some instances without quotation marks, which are derived from friends." Rachel Blau DuPlessis has observed, that "circulation of the poem to various friends and some of the provocative comments that resulted, created some of the conditions which allowed Oppen to complete the poem."[51] It's surely apt, then—and here I complete Frances Jaffer's story about reading philosophy for the language—that "I became excited by Heraclitus and Parmenides, and wrote the first poem (a feminist conversation with George's poem quoting "If all the world went up in smoke") in my next collection, *Alternate Endings,* which began to approach the kind of poems I had been hoping to write." Oppen's benign influence. The conversation. The collaborative work. The writer venturing forth, reaching out from her own language to the language of another. The writer unpossessive of his or her own language, his or her words. This is the world of *How(ever), (f)lip, 6ix, Poetics Journal,* and *Raddle Moon.*

It is a commonplace of feminist thought that our language habits are—like much else—gendered, and gendered male. See what the deer see and you cannot accept the language as you find it, for it has a history (if it has a history at all) and a meaning alien to your own, utterly divorced from your experience. We may all share with Adrienne Rich a dream of a common language, but for Oppen that is even more difficult to attain than a sense of the numerous, and twice as unlikely. It's "impossible to use a word without finally wondering what one means by it," Oppen reflected in his working papers. "I would find that I mean nothing, that everything remained precisely as it was without the word, or else that I am naming absolute implausibilities, which are moreover the worst of nightmares."[52] He told Serge Fauchereau that "the question is not of the meaning of a specific word, but of restoring *words* to meaning   as, I do not think one could speak of restoring language to *its* meaning, but to meaning."[53]

What then, do we do when we use words? when we write a poem? what are words for? And, indeed, how can we write at all? The necessity to reinvent the language has been a recurrent necessity in English writing during the last few centuries, and it was particularly acute and ubiquitous in the last forty years—witness the fortunes not only of feminist but of postcolonialist and philosophic thought, if nothing else. When the Quebecoise poet Nicole Brossard asks, "How do I exist in a language that doesn't want me to exist, or makes me exist as a fiction, as *la femme*?"[54] she reminds us, in her rage and anguish, of the power of words, and of the necessity to divorce ourselves from them. Rosmarie Waldrop has said that "One thing I know: his 'When the man writing is frightened by a word, that's when he's getting started' is the single most important statement on poetics that I know."[55] That fear, I should add, is not just a fear of the political power of the word, of course, but of its power epistemologically as well as ontologically to mislead—of the word's sheer opacity. "I was given to quote once, in a work of my own," says

Beverly Dahlen, a line from Oppen's poem "Route": "Words cannot be wholly transparent. And that is the 'heartlessness' of words"—and she adds: "Their otherness, one might say. Their stoniness."[56]

It may be, as Oppen firmly believed throughout his life, that "the universe is not an abstraction, it cannot be abstracted from anything, it exists of itself in a pure state."[57] But it is equally clear that it is also unknowable. Language fills us with doubt, it uncertains the world as it uncertains the writer. So how write? and—much more pressing—*what* write? "One revises a line," wrote Oppen, "one alters a word,   then one revises the punctuation, and then one alters the line division—after altering the line, one restores the original punctuation. . . . In all that, who tells you what is right? Who is there? Who taught Reznikoff, or Bronk, or Naomi [Replansky]??   who was there?"[58] If you desire to see what the deer see, then clearly every poem is a new beginning, every poem is a new search for an adequate form; earlier poems, earlier forms, by their very existence exhibit ideological taint. Writing, Oppen noted, one can "feel oneself at the very beginning of language."[59] An exercise of honesty and a struggle for clarity, writing the poem is a struggle with and courtship of the unsayable, and it begins, as Oppen said thinking does, with "silence—the simple awareness of the world and oneself in it."[60] For the poem (and I quote Oppen yet again) "is not speech. Something else: the poem enters the room. Revise, revise, it is a search for what one meant, what one means - - The change of a syllable, and - - - - - -. we have thought our way into what we wanted to speak of.   Revision to find what you meant."[61] The voice of Oppen's poems is the voice of coming-to-speech, that moment on the threshold of speech where syntax as we have been taught it is thrown over as we come to words, as words come to us. The politics is in the syntax. As we move to utterance, the mind and the body cast for and negotiate possibilities, override if only momentarily the rhetoric of socially differentiated understanding, with nothing quite adequate to the exact event, nothing ever exactly sayable. Bob Grenier, in his well-known 1971 essay "On Speech," put it this way: "what now I want, at least, is the word way back in the head that is the thought or feeling forming out the 'vast' silence/noise of consciousness, experiencing world *all the time* . . . I want writing what *is* thought/where feeling is/*words are born*."[62] Where words are born. Perhaps, at this point, Oppen joins women in *his* sub-humanity: stuttering, stammering, hesitant disjointed and even inarticulate freshets of words, phrases, lines, syntax, silences. It is, certainly, a place of great vulnerability, and great trust. It calls for exact and scrupulous honesty. It is, I think, the central feature of the news he had for some women writers.

Notes

1. George Oppen letter to Charles Tomlinson, 5 May 1963 (*Selected Letters,* Rachel Blau DuPlessis, ed. [Durham: Duke UP, 1990] 83). This notion of conversation seems to have occupied Oppen for some time in the early 1960s—it appears twice in a letter he wrote in January 1962 to June Oppen Degnan: "I mean to be part of a conversation among honest people" and "I mean to be part of a discussion among honest people . . . without inventing imaginary geometries" (*Selected Letters* 55, 56). The notion also occurs in almost identical phrasing ("I mean to become part of a conversation") in his working papers ("'Meaning Is to Be Here': A Selection from the Daybook," Cynthia Anderson, ed., *Conjunctions* 10 [1987]: 189). A number of women writers embrace the notion that reading and writing poetry is perhaps more an act of conversation than of engaging in (male) literary tradition.

2. In the 1930s, faced with the rise of fascism and the desperate conditions of the Depression, the Oppens became increasingly involved in political activism and stopped writing poetry altogether, after the Second World Wear living in Mexico. He returned to the United States in 1958.

3. Kathleen Fraser, "Notes toward a letter to Peter Quartermain," personal communication, 19 August 1994.

4. Sharon Olds, "George and Mary Oppen: Poetry and Friendship," *Ironwood* 13.2 (Fall 1985): 76.

5. "The Anthropologist of Myself: A Selection from Working Papers," Rachel Blau DuPlessis, ed. *Sulfur* 26 (Spring 1990): 151.

6. George Oppen, *New Collected Poems,* Michael Davidson, ed. (New York: New Directions, 2002) 148.

7. Olds, "George and Mary Oppen" 75–76.

8. Oppen, *New Collected Poems* 75.

9. "Selections from George Oppen's 'Daybook,'" ed. Dennis Young, *Iowa Review* 18.3 (Fall 1988): 13.

10. Oppen's comments on the poem, and on his meeting with Mary, come from a 1959 letter to Julian Zimet, in which he quotes a slightly different (and considerably less interesting) version of "The Hills" (*Selected Letters* 33).

11. Oppen, "The Undertaking in New Jersey," *Collected Poems* 42.

12. "Anthropologist of Myself" 146. In a letter to June Oppen Degnan on 27 September 1963, he wrote of a specific sentence that "I don't know the meaning of any one of these words, unless possibly the word 'we.'" "Letters to June Oppen Degnan," *Ironwood* 26 (1985): 224.

13. Letter to Julian Zimet, late April or May 1959 (*Selected Letters,* 33).

14. "An Adequate Vision: A George Oppen Daybook," Michael Davidson, ed., *Ironwood* 26 (1985): 11.

15. Letter to William Bronk, 2 September 1964 (*Selected Letters* 104).

16. Letter to Julian Zimet, late April or May 1959 (*Selected Letters* 29).

17. Letter to Andy [i.e., Diane] Meyer 1969? (*Selected Letters* 185).

18. Letter to Julian Zimet, late April or May 1959 (*Selected Letters* 29).

19. "Selections from 'Daybook,'" 15.

20. Dennis Young, "Interview with Mary Oppen," *Iowa Review* 18.3 (Fall 1988): 44.

21. Flowers: letter to George Johnston, late 1969-early 1970 (*Selected Letters*, 206); self-love: letter to Serge Fauchereau, 14 October 1966, ("Three Oppen Letters with a Note," Serge Fauchereau, ed., *Ironwood* 5 [1975]: 84); domestic: letter to John Crawford Summer 1966 (*Selected Letters*, 137–138); What is the feminine: letter to Diane Meyer 1969? (*Selected Letters* 185).

22. "The Mind's Own Place," *Kulchur* 10 (Summer 1963): 8.

23. On more than one occasion Oppen recorded his great admiration for Levertov's "Matins," for instance, and her delineation of the "authentic." "[R]ead sometime Denise Levertov's *Matins*, in The Jacob's Ladder," he wrote to Rachel Blau DuPlessis in 1965. "The speckled egg that we must break—- if we would be nourished. A most wonderful of speckled eggs that I stole from her—with acknowledgement—in Mayan Ground." (*Selected Letters*, 392–3 n.20).

24. Frances Jaffer, letter to Peter Quartermain, 16 November 1966. The "small feminist" collection was *Any Time Now* (Emeryville: Effie's Press, 1977). The story does not end where I end it. Jaffer continues:

"I said 'Then maybe I could read the Pre-Socratics. Their systems are lost and fragmented. And they are so ancient that in them one might find traces of the matriarchal religions.'"

25. Letter to Rachel Blau DuPlessis, 16 August 1965, *Selected Letters*, 388n21.

26. Louis Zukofsky, *Prepositions +: The Collected Critical Essays*, Mark Scroggins, ed. (Hanover: U of New England/Wesleyan UP, 2000) 12.

27. "The Philosophy of the Astonished (Selections from Working Papers)," Rachel Blau DuPlessis, ed., *Sulfur* 27 (Fall 1990): 211.

28. Letter to Rachel Blau DuPlessis, 25 August 1966, "Letters to Rachel Blau DuPlessis." *Ironwood* 24 (Fall 1984): 128; "Simone Weil & Women: An Exchange (with Andy Meyer) and Its Aftermath," *Ironwood* 26 (1985): 177.

29. "Selections from 'Daybook'" 15.

30. "I think the poem is good; and Carol Bergé's also." Letter to Diane Wakoski, February-March 1965, *Selected Letters*, 387n2, where DuPlessis quotes Bergé's text.

31. Diane Wakoski, letter to Peter Quartermain, 28 October 1996.

32. Kathleen Fraser, "Notes toward a letter to Peter Quartermain," 19 August 1994.

33. George Oppen, letter to Kathleen Fraser, dated fall 1972 by Fraser. Original in the possession of Kathleen Fraser.

34. "'Meaning Is to Be Here'" 203.

35. "The Anthropologist of Myself" 149, "'Meaning Is to Be Here'" 203, 202.

36. Letter to Frederic Will (after 22 July 1967), *Selected Letters* 161.

37. Letter to Ethel Schwabacher (late fall 1962), *Selected Letters* 72.

38. L. S. Dembo, "Oppen on His Poems: A Discussion," *George Oppen: Man and Poet*, Burton Hatlen, ed. (Orono: National Poetry Foundation, 1981), 201–202.

39. Here's the poem, first published in *This In Which* (1965) (*New Collected Poems* 137):

NIGHT SCENE

The drunken man
On an old pier
In the Hudson River,

Tightening his throat, thrust his chin
Forward and the light
Caught his raised face,
His eyes still blind with drink . . .

Said, to my wife
And to me—
He must have been saying

Again—

Good bye Momma,
Good bye Poppa

On an old pier.

40. Dembo "Oppen on His Poems" 208.

41. Letter to Kathleen Fraser and Jack Marshall (November 1965). Original in the possession of Kathleen Fraser.

42. Letter to John Crawford after 23 January 1973; to David Antin October 1965; *Selected Letters* 254, 120.

43. "The Circumstances: A Selection from George Oppen's Uncollected Writing," Rachel Blau DuPlessis, ed., *Sulfur* 25 (Fall 1989): 12–13.

44. "Selections from 'Daybook'" 13.

45. "Anthropologist" 146.

46. "Anthropologist" 148.

47. "The Philosophy of the Astonished" 211.

48. Letter to June Oppen Degnan, before 9 Feb 1959, *Selected Letters* 22.

49. Letter to June Oppen Degnan, after 5 August 1967, *Selected Letters* 165.

50. Letter to Denise Levertov, after 13 April 1963, *Selected Letters,* 81.

51. *Selected Letters* 391n3.

52. "An Adequate Vision: A George Oppen Daybook," Michael Davidson, ed., *Ironwood* 26 (1985): 7.

53. Letter of 25 July 1966, "Three Oppen Letters" 83.

54. Nicole Brossard at The New Poetics Colloquium, Vancouver, 23 August 1985.

55. Letter to Peter Quartermain, 14 October 1996. Waldrop slightly misquotes Oppen, who wrote (in a letter to Rachel Blau DuPlessis, 21 October 1965) "When the man writing is frightened by a word, he may have started," *Selected Letters* 123.

56. Letter to Peter Quartermain, 2 November 1996. The line from Oppen is from *Collected Poems* 186.

57. Letter to John Crawford, September 1965, *Selected Letters* 120.

58. "The Circumstances" 14.

59. "The Philosophy of the Astonished" 212.

60. "Selections from George Oppen's 'Daybook.'" 13.

61. "Meaning Is to Be Here" 198.

62. Robert Grenier, "On Speech," *This* 1.1 (Winter 1971): (unpaged); also in Ron Silliman, ed., *In the American Tree* (Orono: Maine: National Poetry Foundation, 1986) 496–497.

Momently

The Politics of the Poem, a Note on Robert Creeley

> I can no more avoid political concerns than I can avoid the fact that it's raining outside.
>
> —Robert Creeley, 1965

In February 1962 Robert Creeley gave a landmark reading in Vancouver. It consisted largely of poems from *For Love*, published two months later in April. The audience had in its number the students in Warren Tallman's year-long undergraduate course *Approaches to Poetry*, which in its second semester focussed largely on Don Allen's anthology *The New American Poetry 1945–1960*. The reception Creeley got was completely beyond his experience, the audience listened with such close attention, spell-bound and appreciative. He told Fred Wah, who later became a friend, and who was there, that it was a terrific boost to his confidence at a time when he was particularly unsure of himself.[1]

In September 1962 Robert Creeley and I both started teaching at the University of British Columbia, me with a renewable tenure-track appointment as assistant professor, him with a one-year appointment at the lowly rank of lecturer. He got that job perhaps *partly* as a result of that reading, and certainly as a result of Warren Tallman's unceasing efforts on his behalf in an English department largely devoted to the traditional canon. Basically, he was hired to teach English composition to first-year students in a course whose syllabus was fixed and inflexible—and to do so for a pretty low wage (I was paid almost twice as much as him). But he was given an undergraduate creative writing course in poetry for upper division students—perhaps because *For Love* had recently been published and *The Island* was forthcoming.[2] Strongly devoted to hierarchy and its trappings of power, the English department was not an especially friendly place, and Creeley himself was somewhat sidelined by the intense politicking as his new colleagues teaching creative writing struggled to break away from a department firmly ruled by an unsympathetic head and senior committee who held office for life. That was a battle which could not, in the very nature of things, concern Creeley, any more than Creeley's personal welfare could concern the powers running the English department.

Creeley's year in Vancouver was by no means miserable, but it certainly could have been better. Warren and Ellen Tallman were an important lifeline, and Creeley's poetry-writing course was a life-saver, the students were so amazingly committed. I asked Fred Wah *Who took it?* and he said "We all did"; that would mean, among others, the whole *Tish* group: George Bowering, Frank Davey, Gladys Hindmarch, Lionel Kearns, Daphne Marlatt, and Fred Wah, all of whom have since gained considerable reputations as writers. Daphne Marlatt told me Creeley's course, focusing on how to question, how to think, how to pay attention, was "very much an eye-opening experience, an *ear*-opening experience,"[3] it had a profound effect upon her life as a writer. When Creeley left Vancouver at the end of the school year, to take up a teaching post at the University of New Mexico, Fred Wah followed, to work on an M.A.; he was Creeley's teaching assistant there. During his year in Vancouver, Creeley was instrumental and indispensable in the organization of the Vancouver Poetry Conference, held in the summer of 1963—a credit course arranged by Creeley and Warren Tallman through the University's Extra-Sessional Studies Department. In addition to Creeley, the faculty included Robert Duncan, Allen Ginsberg, Denise Levertov, and Charles Olson. That Creeley had an influence on Canadian writing—and especially poetry—is beyond question; it also looks as though his Canadian experience had its effect upon him, and for the rest of his life he maintained constant contact with writers and writing in Vancouver through correspondence, readings, and fairly regular visits. He had many Canadian friends.

For Creeley, that year in Vancouver was marked by a sharp division between the public and the personal: he held a place in an institution totally indifferent to his personal identity as an individual and essentially indifferent to or suspicious of his writing. Institutionally, outside his course in writing poetry he could find no Common Place—as he says of the American president: "It isn't that I can't be in the same room with him, but I can't find a place to be the way that he presumes the world to be, or thinks of the world as a place to act."[4] Creeley made lifelong friends in Vancouver, but the institution, if it noticed his leaving, probably breathed a small sigh of relief.

That split runs through much of his work. There's a short Creeley poem I've cherished and recited to myself at odd more-or-less patriotic moments for quite a few years, ever since I heard Creeley read it. Two lines, two words: "Oh. / Canada." It sounds like the opening of the Canadian national anthem. But it's not, of course—not quite: the "O" of "O Canada" lacks the disappointed shrug signaled by that added "h." Creeley's two words have a nice political edge. But they don't exactly make a political poem as we seem customarily to think of such. Is it a critique? Does it offend my patriotic Canadian self? Or does it simply raise a chuckle? There are many ways to say those words—exhilarated or despondent, awestruck or scornful, heartbroken or mirthful. And, in the light of that brief history I gave, those two lines take on, perhaps, a subtlety and complexity they otherwise lack, and the weight and significance of that opening "Oh" remains indeterminate. I'm interested in that undecidability, which reflects—or rather, enacts, *performs*—that split Creeley spoke of regarding the president, that split between the institutional (call it) and the personal; the public, and the private; the general, and the individual. That cusp of undecidability, of indeterminacy, that gap, is itself a Common Place, a common ground: a site in which writer and reader meet in *shared* activity. At the same time, *both* lines, "Oh. / Canada," neatly characterize the position Canada seems to hold and play both in people's minds and (at least until recently) in international affairs.

The poem really does seem pretty characteristic of a lot of Creeley's work. It sounds just like something in *Pieces*, but it's a little too indeterminate, a little too open to be political. Whatever ideology it reflects is certainly up for grabs, and it has nothing whatsoever to do with party politics or current topical public issues. That is to say, it's like most of Creeley's actual political poems, some of which I'll discuss. But unfortunately, Creeley didn't write it, at least not that I've been able to find. So far as I can tell, *I* wrote it, in my wishful memory. It seems to be *my* poem!

Thinking about Robert Creeley as a political poet, and about his political poems, is a problem. I mean, where *are* they? And *what* are they? In conversation, essays, and interviews he frequently talked of political issues, attacked corruption, chicanery, political malfeasance, and the machinations of power, and in his fiction he examined and anatomized the power struggles, gendered and otherwise, of domestic and ordinary life. "It's impossible," Creeley told Linda Wagner in about 1965, "It's impossible that a man should be indifferent to what qualifies him in the world. That is, my ability to live and make a living and secure the possibility of family for myself—this is political. Its *polis* is the fact of living together in some common place and time, as an organization of people" (*Contexts* 82). A poem like "Some Afternoon" may indeed, as Peter Middleton has suggested, be "one of Creeley's most powerful political poems,"[5] but it does not directly address immediately current political issues, and such issues do not appear in the poetry. In 1978 he told William Spanos that "during the Vietnam war I wanted insistently to write something specifically involved with that political horror."[6] But there are no such poems. "It just didn't work," he said, and there are no poems arising from his

1959 experience in Guatemala, to say nothing of his time in Burma and India. Where are the poems of protest about El Salvador or Nicaragua, about Rosa Parks, about the assassination of Martin Luther King, about Oliver North? So far as I can see the only explicitly anti-war poems Creeley wrote—"Help!" and "War"—appear in *On Earth,* published in 2006. There's only a handful of poems overtly addressing current political and social issues, and only one that I can see—"News of the World," in *So There*—has the kind of direct and overt address, the naming of names, the political topicality, that mark the sort of intervention into current events that we associate with "political poems." Why did Creeley write so very few? What sort of political poems *did* he write? And what is a political poem anyway? How can the poet meet and/or discharge what social and political responsibilities and duties difficult times call forth? How might the poem, as Martha Nussbaum asks, reconcile the workings of the public sphere with the workings of the personal life and the private imagination? How can it contribute to "moral and political life"?[7] There is, historically, a long and alert tradition of poets, playwrights, novelists again and again persisting in writing about topical *public* matters. Creeley avoids them—partly because they stale-date so quickly. Talking to Charles Tomlinson about E. E. Cummings, he said that "once people were willing to admit typography could be variable and could have a useful effect the particular value was lost," and quite astonishingly said it was "like suffrage, once women were given the vote. I have a difficult time feeling much involvement with people who fought for suffrage because, I mean, now we have it, so to speak" (*Contexts* 19). How acute Duncan was to say, "You're not interested in history, are you?" (*Contexts* 156).

But he *did* write topical poems. He *did* write one about Canada. It's a mild joke, a bagatelle, a bit of mischief, and it *is* in *Pieces:*

CANADA

"The maple leaf forever"
"in 1867—"
"Inspired the world
to say—"

(*Collected Poems* 415)

The first line is the title of a candidate for a new Canadian National Anthem; the second, the date of Canadian Confederation (its centenary celebrated so extravagantly with Expo 67).[8] "It's a quote," Creeley told an interviewer in 1971: the "grand proposals" of a Canadian patriotic song "heard on the radio . . . . gave me the poem. I just like the way it went together" (*Contexts* 203). His comment may be a little disingenuous, since the poem ends so abruptly in the world's unimpressed silence. It's mild wit invites us to read it ironically and comically. We do not have to recognize its topicality to get the mockery. But it's not exactly a political poem.

So what, for Creeley, might *be* a political poem? By the time we read "Canada" in *Pieces*, we've already read his poem "America"—it comes just three pages earlier. It starts with an ironic gesture towards Whitman, and whatever it is, it's not exactly comic. What irony there might be after the opening line is certainly downplayed, and the speaker is not at all amused. "America" is by no means the same as "Canada":

AMERICA

America, you ode for reality!
Give back the people you took.

Let the sun shine again
on the four corners of the world

you thought of first but do not
own, or keep like a convenience.

People are your own word, you
invented that locus and term.

Here, you said and say, is
where we are. Give back

what we are, these people you made,
us, and nowhere but you to be.

(*Collected Poems* 412)

Here we see the speaker separating himself (the poet) and (by extension and vocabulary) the reader from a labelled entity *(America)* which has itself brought about that alienation. *Us,* separate and distinct from *you.* But who—or what—exactly is the *you* of this poem? "America"? Not, surely, the whole continent, nor even North America. The United States, presumably, but not the several fifty-one states of the Union. The nation, perhaps? Or the state? Treating "us" as property, subservient to its convenience, turning *us* into subjects. But who, exactly, is the *us*? Well, the poem says we are the *people,* but it also tells us that *people* is an abstraction invented by *you,* America. America the political entity, a power divorced from the real, America an *idea,* itself (in the poem) an abstraction, with institutional power. America as a *political* idea, an abstraction which in its power mistakes its idea of the world and everything in it for the physical human world and every thing in it. Like the "people," an abstraction without particulars, a creature of mind divorced from body, turning the world of *here* into *nowhere,* turning *itself* into nowhere in a pornography of want. And thus turning the Common Place into No Place.[9]

Might *this* be a political poem? Perhaps, but not if that means a poem "which has politics for its content," a poem which sees politics in terms of current events, partisan politics, the kind of poem Robin Blaser once called "an opinionated sponge."[10] "America" is not a spur to action, it doesn't address a specific political or social issue, and it's not an attack—or if it is, its target isn't easy to see. It is not a poem in which content is all, in which "message" is paramount—the curious syntax of the final sentence negates that possibility. So do those recurrent sites of decision, the line breaks, the registry of the ear demanding attention, demanding thought. Fred Wah has said that "if any poet's spent his life on the line it's Creeley."[11] The line weighs the personal against the grand abstraction, each line break opening up possibilities to be explored or denied as the eye and ear moves to the start of the next line. The sheer precision of attention, the focus, is—especially in the context of *this* poem—political. The poem demands attention, and it demands *thought;* in doing so it calls to our attention what in 1978 Creeley called "the awful success of the process of objectivity and abstraction so that the mind seems to have almost no consciousness of the body it lives in, even when it's preoccupied with that."[12] As we read the last line it becomes possible to see that the whole poem derives from that word "for" in the opening line. "America" is not an ode dedicated *to* reality, nor even an ode in which reality sings, an ode *of* it; the America it addresses is instead a grand political abstraction, a mental creature only, a substitute *for* reality.

The whole poem grows out of that opening line. So how did that word "for" get there in the first place? Perhaps it was a mistake? Perhaps not. But this poem was not, surely, written according to plan. On February 3 1969, that is to say just over a year after he wrote "America"[13] meditating and "wondering rather insistently on what one is 'doing' here"—writing *A Day Book*—Creeley found himself writing this: "Whether errors, as meaning to write *Echoes* become *Whether,* as the finger meant to strike the E key, hits the W—and the thought moves on to include it, to use it in the thought, and so on."[14] The thought moves, to include the "mistake," to incorporate it into the work (as narrated in, for example, the mildly amused account and analysis of muddling "teeth" and "teach" in *Mabel: A Story* [*Prose* 282]). This is very different from his writing habits of a couple of years earlier, in 1963, when working on the typewriter (as he told Allen Ginsberg): "If I'm writing and I make a mistake, I take the paper out and copy it down to that point, correct the mistake, and then throw the paper away. In other words, I have a great difficulty writing on the paper" (*Contexts* 35). Incorporating the error into the writing ensures (perhaps) that the poem is error free. But, as Creeley himself said, "It's an awfully precarious situation to be in, because you can obliterate everything in one instant. You've got to be utterly awake to recognize what is happening, and to be responsible for all the things you must do before you can even recognize what their full significance is" (*Contexts* 26): "I am not anticipating any content before it occurs. At the same time, I'm trying to recognize, or rather, I'm awfully bewildered by confusions between certain terms—the states of consciousness—e.g. the difference between recognition, understanding, realization, knowing. I'm trying to describe a state in which one primarily feels what is happening as a fit balance. . . . You're not intentionally putting it there, but you're recognizing the feeling of its occurring there" (*Contexts* 34–35). "America" is not an instance of the poet sitting down deliberately to write a poem on an already chosen and even defined topic (which is what political poems do)—in that it's perfectly representative of a great deal of Creeley's work. "How do I know what I'm going to say before I've said it," he asks in "A Day Book" (*Prose* 279)—thinking *with* the poem, he cannot anticipate the content.[15] If he's trying to avoid the sorts of predeterminations that accompany any intention to write *about* a given topic, then the *fitness* of that "balance" will only arise if the poem faithfully registers the characteristic movements of the poet's mind, no interference of the will: "the moment the will enters for me it gets really muddy and difficult" ("Talking" 42). Not, then, what you want to say, but what you find yourself saying. What you *find yourself* saying: "The point is," Creeley said in his *Autobiography*, "there isn't any point, more than what being human can make."[16]

But if the point is that there isn't any point, then it's rather hard to write conventional political poems, or even political poems of the sort Creeley himself seems to have in mind when he speaks of them. "America," whatever else it does, does not bring Creeley's ideological commitments to the forefront of our attention the way familiar and explicitly political poems do. "An old, mad, blind, despised, and dying King," inveighed Shelley's lyric political catalogue in 1819,

> Princes, the dregs of their dull race, who flow
> Through public scorn,—mud from a muddy spring;[17]

Shelley's sonnet, "England in 1819," is rhetorical; it deploys standard strategies of rhetorical speech. It may not name names, but its targets are specific, they would be instantly identifiable to his and Leigh Hunt's readers.[18] The poem addresses an audience which shares, if not his convictions, his knowledge.

Political poems by Creeley's contemporaries, Duncan, say, or Levertov, Blaser, Ginsberg, or Olson, reveal what Creeley called "a very direct involvement with contemporary political events" (*Contexts* 82). They leave you in no doubt about how to respond. Here's Blaser's troubled and angry meditative voice:

> here, plagues galore weave among us—aids, racism, homophobia, displacement and poverty, *christianism* with its political plans, the Vatican sending out "advisory letters" to the Bishops that it's okay to discriminate against gays in jobs, housing, and professions—wacky—and the murder of Dr. David Gunn, "justi-fication," they say, "as a pro-life casualty"—I see his sad, sad son listening—none of this in *god-lore's* hands—[19]

If we have forgotten (or never knew) why David Gunn was shot down, the poem reminds us, just as it invokes current political slogans and labels: pro-life, homophobia, racism. Like Creeley's, this is carefully weighed and felt language—you cannot lightly pass over the implications of that "*christianism* with its political plans"—but its mix of abstract and the concrete is not the language of Creeley's "America."

Duncan does something similar in "The Multiversity, *Passages 21*," but his rhetoric is inescapable, overtly oratorical and scornful, and equally explicit in its detail:

> here: Kerr (behind him, heads of the Bank of
> America
>   the Tribune
>   heads of usury, heads of war)
>
>   the worm's   mouthpiece   spreads
>   what it wishes   its own
>
>   false news:

The vocabulary is savagely over the top as he talks of

> Chancellor Strong,   the dragon claw
>   biting his bowels, his bile

raging against the lawful demand
for right reason.[20]

This is the rhetoric of demagoguery, of rabble-rousing, as much a call to action as the soon-to-follow "Up Rising, *Passages 25*"—one of the great political invectives of the turbulent 1960s and beyond. Creeley called these poems by Duncan "very abrupt and highly articulate attacks upon modern political contexts, that is, literally on Johnson and the administration; also upon the circumstance at the University of California in Berkeley and the Free Speech Movement" [1965] (*Contexts* 82). And, one might add, the rhetoric of the poem is at base discursive—it rests on an *argument.*

There's an *overt* political thread running through much of Duncan's work in *Bending the Bow* and indeed later, and recurrent in Blaser's through to the present. But not in Creeley. In this respect, Creeley is closer to the political mode of the young Wordsworth than he is to the demon-driven Shelley. In 1801 Wordsworth sent Charles James Fox a copy of *Lyrical Ballads* to draw Fox's attention to their *political* burden; the accompanying letter abhorred the grand abstractions of political economists, and instead rehearsed particulars: "By the spreading of manufactures through every part of the country, by the heavy taxes upon postage, by workhouses, houses of industry, and the invention of soup shops etc., superadded to the increasing disproportion between the price of labor and that of the necessaries of life, the bonds of domestic feeling among the poor . . . have been weakened, and in innumerable instances entirely destroyed."[21] The political burden of *Lyrical Ballads* is indeed unobtrusive, and there is no evidence that Fox heeded Wordsworth's letter. T. S. Eliot suggested that "without this preamble Mr Fox could hardly be expected to make head or tail of the Idiot Boy or the sailor's parrot."[22] It is surely true that to ignore what Eliot called Wordsworth's "public spirit" and "social passions" is to misunderstand and misread such ballads as "Goody Blake and Harry Gill." Similarly, it is easy to misread Creeley's emphasis on the personal, his emphasis and focus on the immediate, the particular, and the apparently trivial as somehow registering a disconnect with the larger public world. In 1978 Creeley praised Wordsworth's "*factual* power . . . in making articulate feelings that are extraordinarily human . . . *senses* of how physically one's in the world. Extra ordinary" ("Talking" 63; emphasis added).

For Creeley was by no measure politically inert, "having been taught politics by the Y[oung] C[ommunist] L[eague] while still in college" (*Contexts* 181), and having worked for the Henry Wallace party in the 1948 election, to say nothing of his opposition to the Vietnam war, which he called "an outrage of human beings . . . literally against life itself" (*Contexts* 183). He held draft cards and read for the anti-war group known as Draft Resistance. But he wrote no poems directly addressing the war. "It's almost," he said in 1970, "as if I've given so damn much to that idiot war I'm damned if I'm going to give it my experience of words" *(Contexts 194).* Too, he was active in his opposition to the first George Bush's war, tirelessly urging resistance over the internet, and Michael Boughn told me about "meeting Bob in Montreal in 1969 when I was hanging out with Robin [Blaser], and his articulate agony over being unable to write a political poem, his feeling that others didn't understand his dilemma."[23] That was the year Creeley told an interviewer "I've not been able to write directly to a purpose of political involvement" (*Contexts* 182–183); what he said a couple of sentences before that suggests one source of his dilemma: "I don't see that art and politics, or that order of present experience involved with the post-political, should all be kept separate. I don't see how they can be. *One can't, perhaps, entirely respect an art committed to propagandizing or to a use of life not clearly initiated in its own activity.* But when men and women are outraged by political malfeasance, it's hardly likely that their art will not make that quite clear" (*Contexts* 182; emphasis added). The italicized sentence states in a nutshell the problems raised by poems given "directly to a purpose of political involvement," and it needs a little unpacking. "A *use* of life not clearly initiated in its own activity."[24] Calculated use, appropriating and converting something to your *own* ends—such as making money or consolidating personal power—is a monstrous abuse of reason, for such overruling of individual diversity and interest is a betrayal of the common trust on which the social contract rests. Falsehood, deception, inescapably distorts and ultimately destroys what Creeley calls the Common Place, the shared. That indeed *is* political.

But the work should not be "*committed* to propagandizing"—such work, he had said in 1965, "distorts and beguiles and coerces by means of language" (*Contexts* 84)—he called it "criminal distortion on the part of those who make use of it" (*Contexts* 84). Propaganda is inescapably falsehood. That's a moral issue, and the moral quickly moves over into the political. So, in its attack on "language subverted to the meager" the poem "America" attacks the linguistic abuse and manipulation of power, the diminution of a life of feeling and thought into the empty closures of abstraction. Hence his early and lifelong distrust of "a symbol which in effect exhausts its references as opposed to a sign or mark of something which constantly renews its reference" (*Contexts* 15). Such renewal of reference, such openness, comes from a life "clearly initiated in its own activity," from the poem which, in Creeley's words, "might be . . . primarily the fact of its own activity" (*Collected Essays* 490). The writing must generate itself, not be driven by thesis.

Despite all this, there are, pretty well throughout Creeley's writing life, poems with a marked political edge. Towards the end of "Citizen," for instance, Creeley mildly exhorts the reader:

>   Why
>
> not clean up the world.
>   You need it, I
> need it—more than
>   either one of us can get.
>
> (*Collected Poems* 413)

The last line's pun on "get" undercuts any possible political urgency as it answers the opening question. "Citizen," from the late '60s, is no more likely to spur one to action than are these lines, from "Myself" written some ten years later, on 31 January 1977[25] and collected in *So There: Poems 1976–1983*):

> I want, if older,
> still to know
> why, human, men
> and women are
>
> so torn, so lost,
> why hopes cannot
> find better world
> than this.[26]

This poem, a lament for the loss of hope as one grows into disillusion, at its close quotes Shelley's incomplete and apparently despairing final major work, "The Triumph of Life": the Men of Power, as described by Rousseau's ghost, "vanquished," as Donald Reiman put it, by "their own recalcitrant souls,"[27] Shelley's lines relineated:

> Taught them not this—to know themselves; their might
> Could not repress the mutiny within,
> And for the morn of truth they feigned, deep night
>
> Caught them ere evening.[28]

"Myself" is hardly a political poem; disillusioned but not despairing, Creeley's eye, though it takes in the outward world, is turned inward, the dream faint, possibly inert, but still there, and the spaced periods at the end of the poem leave matters open. The lines from Shelley invite us to assess our own world and its future possibility, but they also call our attention to the speaker's and one's own ("myself's") position in that world as the poem quietly voices its perturbation. But it's by-and-large panoramic, and the politics non-specific.

It's a problem of intention. In 1974, as he neared the completion of his *Dante Études,* Robert Duncan said in an interview that no given line or phrase of a poem could contain any "prediction of what's going to go on ahead of itself";[29] the task in writing is to avoid imposing goals upon the work. Creeley, though perhaps not as deliberative as Duncan's comment suggests, is much the same: "I wanted to write something specifically involved" with Vietnam. "It just didn't work. The moment will enters for me it gets really muddy and difficult" ("Talking" 42). "A poem . . . cannot be . . . subjugated to some intention," he told the *New American Review* in 1969 (*Contexts* 177): "The primary occasion in writing is a situation I've never been able to design, even when I've much wanted to" (179). "As soon as I plan to do it," he said, "I've all but stopped it. I don't know how I am going to get past that" (110). So his refusal to contribute to a book of poems responding to Kennedy's assassination was more than a simple refusal to write on the topical. He *said* he refused because a poem, written to order, could only be "making capital so to speak of an event that was much more profound in its implications than this kind of use of it would frankly admit" (*Contexts* 83). But how can you know what you think until you think it? How can you know what you'll say before you say it? "What I have written I knew little of until I had written it." (*Collected Essays* 504).

But writing a political poem—a poem addressing current political, human, *lived* public crises, poems addressing the nature, use and especially misuse of power—drew Creeley again and again. Making the poem up as he goes along is largely responsible for the poem's shape, for the movement of language and thought as the poem proceeds. There is, for example, "Guatemala," which Creeley wrote on 27 February 1977 in the same notebook as "Myself" but about three weeks later (*Boundary 2* 125–126):

GUATEMALA

When I heard
the story
in the company—

of the priest strung up
by his thumbs,
while his humble young

woman servant was raped,
and his moneys taken
I was impressed,

and told my wife
all of it. Later
my sources explained to her,

the verbs and the noun,
in Spanish, meant,
the priest had lost

his gold. No one
was with him more
than his wanting.

It's a curiously revealing little poem; it starts, promising a personal narrative, but the title almost inevitably determines a set of stock responses to the second stanza's "the priest strung up by his thumbs" and the rape of "his humble young woman servant." No matter how horrific this may be, this is cliché stuff, the familiar material of newspaper reports, the title suggesting this is the sort of thing you can expect to read about Guatemala, and it immediately brings to mind the lawlessness of a country in which a robbery is not simply a robbery—the money appears almost as an afterthought—it's a priest, after all, that got strung up—that's the primary fact of the story, and that fact alone, in the familiar territory of gossip and news, evokes the brutality of secular and political violence in Guatemala and our propensity to associate it with Latin American rebels or dictators, our propensity unconsciously to heed propaganda, our propensity as more-or-less comfortably distant observers to be comfortably shocked. But the poem shifts focus from the socially and perhaps politically significant event to the more-or-less rueful discovery, through the agency of the wife to whom he transmitted the shocking tale, that he had got it wrong, he had *mis*-heard. The fact that what "I heard" is *not* what "I" was told throws into doubt the final curious judgment, an implied judgment as speculative and hence uncertain as the story we just read was mistaken. But what sticks in the reader's mind? The linguistic-translation problem towards which the poem moves? The priest's worldly desire and even greed? The violence of Guatemalan life? The speaker's relations with his wife?

"Guatemala" is finally unsatisfactory, it ends so scattered, and Creeley did not collect it. But the movement, the shape of the poem, is pretty representative of Creeley's political poems, in its shift from a more-or-less general sketch inviting political and social judgment to the personal. Frequently (but not in this case) when the poem looks as though it's going to move toward judgment, it shies away from it, withdraws, shifts, *connects* to the personal. Here's "After Lorca"; it's an early poem, written in about September 1952):[30]

AFTER LORCA

The church is a business, and the rich
are the business men.
When they pull on the bells, the
poor come piling in and when a poor man dies, he has a wooden
cross, they rush through the ceremony.

But when a rich man dies, they
drag out the Sacrament
and a golden Cross, and go *doucement, doucement*
to the cemetery.

And the poor love it
and think it's crazy.

(*Collected Poems* 121)

The first stanzas look like an attack on the hypocrisy of the church, its treatment of the rich, presumably the ruling class, and its scornful disdain for the poor. As Robert von Hallberg observes, they "nicely elaborate the sort of class analysis common in political verse and oratory."[31] The discursive movement of the first nine lines is broken by the slightly sonnet-like reversal of the last two, the poem moving through the long prosy fourth line toward and through the stately *doucement, doucement* pacing of the second stanza. The ceremonial pace of that stanza is abruptly broken in the last two lines, the slight redundancy of the apostrophe *S* bringing the voice of the poem to the *personal*—the poem avoids the formal construction "they think *it* crazy." Von Hallberg suggests that in these lines "systems analysis and good humor supplant politics" and "the social relationships . . . fall within the province of manners," but these lines pull the poem away from the social and political world—the outer world—to the speaker's mild abstracted wonder—the inner world, and the speaker's bemusement reveals his outsider status at the same time as it exhibits his distrust of the conventional pieties. In pulling away from the implied thesis of the opening lines, the poem relaxes the will to power, the poet relinquishes any claim that the poem might be *his*, his property, *possessing* the reader's thought.[32] Creeley's very good at invoking what he called "a total social organism" (*Contexts* 23)—the moral and political judgment the opening lines invite is a luxury only afforded the onlooker. It is the outsider who would like to construct an argument, but the argument has nothing to do with actual human circumstance; the fact that "the poor love it" is beyond the reach of discursive understanding. As Creeley put it in his *Autobiography,* "in some curious way, I cannot finally believe anything I *think,* only feeling can survive there."[33] Actual human circumstance, how people actually live, is not a matter for the conduct of reason; we do not behave "reasonably."

In 1968 Creeley told two interviewers from *Road Apple Review* that the writing of *Words* opened up "the possibility of *scribbling,* of writing for the immediacy of the pleasure without having to pay attention to some final mode of significance" (*Contexts* 42). "Words /" one poem in *Pieces* says (*Collected Poems* 408), "are / pleasure. / All / words." And elsewhere:

I figure

if I eat so much,
I get so fat.

If I don't eat so much
I don't get so fat—

so,
so.

(*Collected Poems* 431)

The sheer inconsequentiality of that, its play with the word *so,* is thoroughly representative of the territory opened up in *Pieces* (1969) and its immediate predecessor *Words* (1967).

Those two books mark a turning point in Creeley's poetry; thereafter, he said again and again, echoing Williams, writing is *fun:* the sheer pleasure of it, its necessity, its demand for attention, its playfulness, its intensity. So deep. He was, he said, "*given*" to it. Not, then, that it was given to *him.* A necessity, then. So deeply engrained was that necessity and pleasure, that—as Bunting said of later Zukofsky[34]—sometimes he writes poems that don't seem to be about anything at all, like that astonishing wonderful little poem in *Pieces:* (written 18 November 1967)[35]

—it
 it—

(*Collected Poems* 391)[36]

If there is any subject matter at all, it is there simply as something to hang the words on, to get the words moving on the page and in the air, singing to the eye, ear, and mind. Or rather, the words themselves, *their* purpose, the indeterminacy of the utterance, the *value* in that silence, the shifts as the mind moves into and through the activity of those two lines— it's a play along the line of expectation which Creeley may have learned from Williams and Zukofsky—and the almost palindromic symmetries, *are* the subject-matter, the substance, even as they severely undermine and even disqualify the very notion of subject-matter itself. "There is never," Creeley said in a lecture he gave ten months before he wrote that poem, "there is never a 'subject' *about* which one constructs an activity called 'poetry' " (*Collected Essays* 504).

"The *line* is, after all, the *measure* of the man writing, his term, peculiarly, as he writes, weighing, in the silence to follow, the particular word sense, necessary to his own apprehension of the melody, the tune—that he *hears*, to write" (*Collected Essays* 163). That little poem "—it / it—" really does not seem to be "about" anything at all. It is an uncompromising language act, a pronoun, repeated, which in its context entirely lacks any referent. The English poet Peter Riley has spoken contemptuously of politics as a "safe haven" in which to hide from "the terror of free-roaming thought"[37]—in which case this poem is deeply subversive. The subversiveness comes in the first place from its sheer unparaphrasability—you can't possibly figure out what was going on in the poet's mind when he penned these words, save in the most general and speculative way. Yet our apprehension of the poem depends on our own "apprehension of the . . . tune," our own *particular,* detailed, and precise mental activity—or (if you prefer) our grammatical and syntactical activity—that, too, is subversive.

Creeley once said, "I don't speak for a generality of people" (*Contexts* 20) but that is not strictly true, for in its engagement with the reader, in kindling the reader as writer, the poem becomes a site for shared thought and activity, a Common Place. "Poetry," said Creeley, "seems to be written momently—that is, it occupies a moment of time. There is, curiously, no time in writing a poem. I seem to be given to work in some intense moment of whatever possibility" (*Contexts* 105). There is an inconsequentiality about this poem's extreme move to the personal, a move not unlike that in such poems as "America", "After Lorca," or "The Times" (in *Places*). It poises the power of the individual and the personal against the public and institutional; free-roaming thought against the predictable and comfortable. "After Lorca" and "America" move from conventional pieties to acute or rueful personal observation; bring the general *up* to the particular, the public sphere *up* to the personal. The movement is frequently from the outer to the inner, and usually takes the shape of a more-or-less abrupt reversal, as the poem sets up a series of expectations which are then frustrated, and the poem brings us to the concrete. "The Times," a poem from around 1990, follows this pattern with some subtlety:

THE TIMES

If they had something
to worry about these
people wouldn't sit there
thinking about what

doesn't even exist they
would take each day as it
comes and thank their
lucky stars they had

enough to eat it says here
it reflects the hopeless
times make what isn't
the case all that is.[38]

The anti-war poem "War" (in *On Earth*) does so with fairly heavy irony. It looks as though Creeley's mind habitually, or rather, characteristically, works through what is almost a play of thesis-antithesis—a subtle or occasionally an obvious reversal, usually late in the poem, where the thought turns itself on its ear. That little poem "—it / it—" is rather like the poem "Canada" in that it leaves you there hanging, expectant; it engages the reader in an immediacy of apprehension and thought. It's life-affirming.

"Language," said Creeley, "is a political act" (*Contexts* 83).

Notes

Epigraph. Robert Creeley, *Contexts of Poetry: Interviews 1961–1971* (Bolinas: Four Seasons, 1973) 82. Hereafter cited in-text as *Contexts.*

1. In "The Dishonest Mailmen" (in *For Love*) written about ten years earlier, Creeley voiced his doubts about his work and its lack of readers, talking of "the poem supreme, addressed to / emptiness—this is the courage / necessary" (Robert Creeley, *The Collected Poems 1945–1975* [Berkeley: U of California P, 1982] 123). Hereafter cited in-text as *Collected Poems.* Creeley wrote the poem in 1952 or 1953 (Mary Novik, *Robert Creeley: An Inventory, 1945–1970* [Kent, OH: Kent State UP, 1973] 85 [item 485]). Hereafter cited in-text as Novik.

2. *For Love* was published on 9 April 1962; *The Island* on 13 September 1963.

3. Conversation, 3 September 2006.

4. Robert Creeley, "Some Senses of the Commonplace," in Tom Clark, *Robert Creeley and the Genius of the Common Place* (New York: New Directions, 1993) 90.

5. Peter Middleton said this in a paper he delivered on 13 October 2006 at the Robert Creeley Conference, "On Words." At the same conference, Michael Davidson similarly nominated "Anger"—see " 'The repeated insistence': Creeley's Rage," (*Form, Power, and Person in Creeley's Life and Work,* Stephen Fredman and Steve McCaffery, ed. [Iowa City: U of Iowa P, 2010, 69–88]. Middleton's words reported here do not appear in the published version of his paper). Creeley wrote several such poems of great power.

6. William V. Spanos, "Talking with Robert Creeley," in *Robert Creeley: A Gathering,* William V. Spanos, ed., *Boundary 2,* 6.3/7.1 (Spring/Fall 1978): 42.Hereafter cited as "Talking." The entire "Special Issue" is hereafter cited as *Boundary 2.*

7. Martha Nussbaum, *Poetic Justice: The Literary Imagination and Public Life* (Boston: Beacon, 1995) 3.

8. The typescript is dated January 25, 1968 (Novik, 107 [item 724]).

9. As Creeley put it elsewhere, "it has no resonance, there's no one there. . . . It doesn't have any body. So that there's no knowledge of *any* order. . . . It's utterly vacant" ("Some Senses of the Commonplace" 114).

10. Robin Blaser, "Particles," in Miriam Nichols, ed., *The Fire: Collected Essays of Robin Blaser,* Miriam Nichols, ed. (Berkeley: U of California P, 2006) 13.

11. Fred Wah, with Brian Kim Stefans, correspondence, *PhillyTalks* 7 (Nov 2nd, 1998): 17.

12. Spanos, "Talking," 40. Creeley's remark gibes nicely with Blaser's remarks, on a poem by Nerval, which "point to the responsibility of the poet for the experience of power as it is seen and felt in the world . . . held in image, not a tractful of wisdom, but a reality created, held by image and sound" ("The Fire," *The Fire* 11).

13. "America" is dated 25 January 1968 (Novik 106 [item 719]).

14. Robert Creeley, *The Collected Prose* (Berkeley: U of California P, 1988) 298. Hereafter cited in-text as *Prose.*

15. "As living," Creeley says in *Autobiography* (in Clark, *Robert Creeley* 126), "each moment seemed to me utterly impossible to anticipate."

16. *Robert Creeley* Clark 140. This is closely tied to Creeley's often-repeated insistence that "*Here* is where one seems to be" (*Contexts* 186). As a poem in *Windows* (1990) puts it, "isn't the human // just that echoing, resonant edge / of what it knows it knows, / takes heart in remembering / only the good times, yet // can't forget whatever it was" (*The Collected Poems 1975–2005* [Berkeley: U of California P, 2006] 304).

17. Percy Bysshe Shelley, *The Complete Poetical Works,* Thomas Hutchinson, ed. (London: Oxford UP, 1943) 574.

18. Had Leigh Hunt published it, that is, in the *Examiner.* It was first published in 1839, by Mary Shelley.

19. Robin Blaser. "Image-Nation 24 ('oh, pshaw,' " *The Holy Forest: Collected Poems,* Miriam Nichols, ed. (Berkeley: U of California P, 2006) 388.

20. Robert Duncan, *Bending the Bow* (New York: New Directions, 1968) 70.

21. William Wordsworth, *The Letters of William and Dorothy Wordsworth: The Early Years, 1787–1805*, 2nd ed., Ernest de Selincourt, ed., rev. Chester L. Shaver (Oxford: Clarendon, 1967) 312–313.

22. T. S. Eliot, *The Use of Poetry and the Use of Criticism* (London: Faber, 1933) 73.

23. Personal e-mail, 10 October 2006.

24. So, too, writing: "I first felt a poem to be what might exist in words," Creeley wrote in 1965, "as primarily the fact of its own activity. . . . I wanted the poem itself to exist and that could never be possible as long as some subject significantly elsewhere was involved" (*Collected Essays* [Berkeley: U of California P, 1980] 490).

25. A facsimile of the first notebook (dated) draft of the poem is in *Boundary 2* (120–121).

26. Creely, *Collected Poems 1975–2005* 95.

27. Donald H. Reiman, *Shelley's "The Triumph of Life": A Critical Study* (Urbana: U of Illinois P, 1965) 43.

28. Shelley, *Complete Poetical Works* 512. Creeley observes of "And for the morn / of truth they feigned . . ." that "Somehow the human apprehension and/or determination and/or recognition hadn't managed to come to the common place, almost, one wants to say, with respect to the fact that it was a commonplace—that it was no longer strange, original, and new; that it was trite, trivial, and hackneyed" ("Some Senses of the Commonplace" 105).

29. Howard Mesch, "Robert Duncan's Interview," *Unmuzzled Ox* 4.2 (1976): 94.

30. Novik dates the poem "by September 9, 1952" (*Inventory* 85, item 483).

31. Robert Von Hallberg, "Robert Creeley and the Pleasures of System," *Robert Creeley's Life and Work: A Sense of Increment*, John Wilson, ed. (Ann Arbor: U of Michigan P, 1987) 201.

32. I am grateful to Miriam Nichols for this point (e-mail, 20 September 2006). "It is in that loosening of the grip on the thesis," she wrote, "that one finds also the relaxing of the will to power—this latter the trap of most political writing . . . [where] the poem is no longer open, no longer common. It becomes the property of the poet."

33. Creely, *Autobiography* 142 (emphasis added).

34. "Zukofsky gets stronger and stronger, particularly in short pieces, that don't seem to be about anything," Basil Bunting, letter to Ezra Pound, 10 April 1958, in the American Literature Collection, Beinecke Rare Book and Manuscript Library, Yale University.

35. Creeley gave his lecture, "I'm given to write poems," in Berlin in January 1967 (*Collected Essays* 496); the poem is dated in Novik (*Inventory* 105, item 706).

36. Written in a "very small" notebook—"the smallest and the first" such, where it reads

This size page forces the
damn speciously gnomic
sans need for same -
  —it
   it— (*Contexts* 43)

37. Riley is perhaps over-simplifying a little when he says, "Poetry is created in the space which evades politics," since by his own account poetry in engaging "free-roaming thought" cannot possibly escape the political. See Peter Riley, *Spitewinter Provocations: An Interview on the Condition of Poetry* (London: Reality Studios Occasional Papers 4, 1986).

38. Robert Creeley, *Places,* paintings by Susan Barnes (Buffalo: Shuffaloff, 1990) np.

Syllable as Music

Lyn Hejinian's *Writing Is an Aid to Memory*

> In their debauch of easy magnificence—for it has become more difficult to avoid than to achieve the over-rich—English poets have hazed over sharp outlines . . . [and thrown] a hampering haze of glory [over English verse]: their vowel-successions, their alliterations, have been too commonly splendiferous, until verbal splendor has lost its virtue in English: and when, as recently, they tried to restore it by the use of contrast, they frequently fail because they will not devote sufficient care and labor to anything much below the sublime; because they do not understand that cacophony is at least as intricate an art as harmony; because they despise or patronize jazz and other popular music.
>
> —Basil Bunting, c. 1933

Musicating language—making language into music—composing, that is to say, poems. I'm going to talk about Lyn Hejinian, and I begin with two quotations. The first is from John Dryden (1687):

> From Harmony, from heav'nly Harmony
> 　　This universal frame began.
> 　When Nature underneath a heap
> 　　Of jarring Atomes lay,
> 　And cou'd not heave her Head,
> The tuneful Voice was heard from high,
> 　　Arise ye more than dead.
> Then cold, and hot, and moist, and dry,
> In order to their stations leap,
> 　　And MUSICK's power obey.
> From Harmony, from heav'nly Harmony
> 　　This universal Frame began:
> 　　From Harmony to Harmony
> Through all the compass of the Notes it ran,
> The Diapason closing full in Man.

I shall return to this later, but let it serve, now, as a gesture toward traditional notions of the music of poetry. Music and poetry may be twins, Basil Bunting reminds us, "but they're not identical twins."[1] My second quotation runs counter to Dryden; it is from Gertrude Stein (1928): "Music is nondescript."[2] Language cannot possibly be mistaken for music, Stein reminds us, and poetry is of course *not* music. Words are words. Music is beyond words, nondescript because not to be described. *Nondescript:* "of no particular kind, odd, unclassifiable," says the *New Century Cyclopedia;* "neither one thing nor another," says the *Oxford English Dictionary.*[3] Stein's uncertainty about music is very much to my point, for in their antiphony to Dryden's, her words extend the reach of music beyond the play of sound, into the patterning and play of apperception, syntax, image, thought.

In 1951, Pierre Boulez told John Cage in a letter that " 'composing' amounts to arranging sound phenomena along two co-ordinates: duration and pitch. We are thus freed from all melody, all harmony, and all counterpoint. . . . All these (essentially modal and tonal) notions . . . disappear."[4] I take Boulez to be representative of the Stein side of the Dryden-Stein equation, and take to heart Hejinian's enjoinder that "Words . . . simply can't help but give onto ideas," as well as her reminder that "Music in poetry is completely different from music in music."[5] I take "musicating" analogously, to mean giving the arrangement of words something of the qualities of the arrangement of sounds as music: "speech, language, utterance, tongue moved for a time to sound."[6]

This is of course far too simple. Traditional notions of the music of poetry, Hejinian reminds us, tend to equate the musical in poetry with aestheticized surfaces, with the "beauty" afforded by rhyme, meter, assonance, and so forth—but the music of verse is not a matter of the mellifluousness of the writing, it is a structural matter. The sounds of music are not the sounds of language, but the orders of music may well be the orders of poetry.[7]

Apologists for the New Formalism[8] equate metrical language with "melodiousness"; Robert Richman claims (through his anthology) that "after two decades of obscure, linguistically flat poetry," metrical language "is clearly the best means for poets to come to terms with their experience now."[9] The persistent association of rhymed metrical verse with accessibility, meaning, "splendor, beauty, and upliftment" is an enduring undercurrent in literary history.[10] In a very interesting book, *Missing Measures: Modern Poetry and the Revolt against Meter* (published in 1990), Timothy Steele says that "Though the modernists abandoned meter out of a genuine wish to renovate verse and reconnect it to a real world and a real audience, the effect to a great extent has been to deprive poetry of resources that enable it to examine human experience appealingly, distinctively, and meaningfully."[11] Ideologically speaking, Steele is the direct descendant of the poet Robert Hillyer, who threw

James Laughlin out of his poetry class at Harvard in 1934 for mentioning Eliot's name,[12] and of Stanton A. Coblentz, who (putting Steele's argument a lot more bluntly) in 1951 complained that on the basis of modern verse "one could not read that man had any feelings deeper than a cockroach."[13] Such notions of the poem elevate rhyme and meter to the status of "laws," and identify poetry as essentially and transparently expressive and communicative, and the poem as a vehicle of the paraphrastic. Hejinian will be bound by no such dogma, yet her work is astonishingly dense in aural effects—assonance, consonantal repeat and echo, vowel leading, and silence.

Between August 1976 and September 1984 Lyn Hejinian printed and published first at monthly and then at bi-monthly intervals a series of poetry pamphlets, fifty in all, under the imprint of Tuumba Press. By the middle of 1978, which is to say, when *Writing Is an Aid to Memory* was published,[14] the series was clearly identifiable with language poetry, publishing Bruce Andrews, Charles Bernstein, Bob Perelman, Ron Silliman, and Barrett Watten among others: writers who give the New New Formalists nightmares. *Writing Is an Aid to Memory* consists of 42 numbered sections ranging in length from 3 lines (sections 6, 15, 20, 24, 31) to 151 (section 2), observing a strict formality imposed by line-indentations arbitrarily determined by the alphabetical position of each line's initial letter. Hejinian's prospectus for the second series of Tuumba pamphlets, issued some time in 1977 (contemporary, that is to say, with the poem before us), has a prefatory note: "Though we publish the new and avant-garde in literature, we do so in an old tradition. Our faith in the literary arts is passionate, so is our love for them. We hope that others feel likewise and would take pleasure in becoming a Sponsor, a Patron, or a Friend of Tuumba Press."[15] Though Hejinian's work is not musical in the conventional sense of mellifluousness, it deliberate exploits phonetic, semantic and lexical elements for the sake of aural and other patterns.

I

Hejinian has cautioned against "confounding the 'musical' in poetry with aestheticized surfaces, or with 'beauty'" because "sound values in poetry are intrinsically linguistic, not musical."[16] Yet in *My Life,* a book Hejinian was in the process of revising as she wrote those words, there is the really quite fine vowel-leading that closes the twenty-first (unnumbered) section of that work—and I take vowel-leading to be one "musicating" device harking back to an older tradition: "What can those birds be saying. That day there was wind but no air, because we were inland."[17] These two sentences echo the opening of the 19th section: "Those birds are saying, over and over, this tree, my branch, my field of seeds, my herd of worms."

But it would be a grave mistake to limit the musical qualities of poetry or language to the noises it makes. Noise is only *one* kind of rhyme. One structural device in *My Life* is the recurrence of syntactic patterns: "A does B"; "An X is a Y which Z." Another is simple formulaic repetition of fragment, phrase, clause, sentence: "As for we who 'love to be astonished,' X is Y." It is difficult to see such devices as "intrinsically linguistic, not musical," if by that we are to understand the linguistic and the musical to be incompatible. But formulaic repetition of this sort seems to me to fall under the category of "musicating" structure rather than "language," especially if, following Pierre Boulez, we think we must "go through an entire work in order to become aware of its form; that form is no longer architecturized, but is *woven;* said otherwise, there is no distributive hierarchy in the organization of 'sections' . . . , but there are successive distributions in the course of which the various constituting elements assume larger or smaller functional importance."[18] Local clarities, that is to say, and attentions and hierarchies, furthering the work. There is neither time nor space, here, to follow up in detail the structural implications of Boulez' words I just quoted; that they apply also on the level of the syllable will, I hope, become clear as I proceed. But it is worth looking briefly at section 6 of *Writing Is an Aid to Memory:*

> you must show yourself to catch
> to be amused, to equate the man, to
> shoot his autobiographical work

Remarkably open-ended, these three lines invite us into a hermeneutic act at the same time as they resist interpretation and paraphrase. A finite verb followed by four infinitives: The first line, with its imperative, finite, and reflexive verb *(you must show yourself)* looks a bit like a thesis statement: you must show yourself [in order] *to catch*—presumably, to catch *the man.* But in what sense catch? as in fishing? as in marriage? as in catching his essence? The subsequent verbs suggest other ways to catch: *to be amused, to equate, to shoot*—the progression is modal. *To catch:* transitive; against which is posed the intransitive and syntactically quasi-reflexive *to be amused,* semantically passive where *to catch* is semantically active. *To equate* is a further progression, transitive, followed by adjective + noun *(the man);* syntactically equative but semantically essive (i.e. to do with being), it in turn is followed by *to shoot,* transitive, semantically aggressive (?), followed by a *possessive* pronoun + adjective + noun. Transitive, intransitive, equative: these are all ways of dealing with the world. You become aware of these variations because of the repeated syntactic structure, and—like music—it is a structure with resonance; the repeated infinitives create overtones in the reader's head. Is this a "musicating"? I think so, but it is mainly, I think, a musicating of structure.

"What presses as a question upon writing now," Hejinian said in 1979, about a year after *Writing Is an Aid to Memory* was published, "(when it comes to talk of structures, for example, or systems) is how to *arrange* words, or word groups, rather than how to choose them. How to lay them there, or, rather, string them—the only simultaneity available now being a kind of potent neutrality—susceptibility, or piling *up on* words (as opposed to the Elizabethan cumulative techniques, which amount to a (lovely to me) piling *on of* words."[19] Writing as arrangement. In "What can those birds be saying. That day there was wind but no air, because we were inland" there is, surely, evidence of vowels working as agents of discovery in the compositional process, vowels in arrangement. Vowel-leading, repetition, recurrence, weaving: these are not, in Hejinian's hands, a matter of aestheticizing the surface, but of furthering the work. Which is to say, adapting Bernstein, that the writing—and therefore its musicating—constitutes experience, for experience "is a property" of language.[20] Such experience—and the musicating, therefore—takes place at all levels of the language: semantic, phonetic, and lexemic. And we should not forget that language—and hence a great deal (if not all) of our experience—is a social construct, an "exchange" with "the world." Musication at times involves exophoric (extra-textual) gesture.

II

Hejinian wrote in 1979 about "putting things together in such a way as to enable them to coincide, [in] an attempt (by analogy with music's chord) at *suggesting* (since that is all one can do) *simultaneity,* hoping for inherence, haphazard, happy chance" (emphasis added). The aleatory, then, has its part to play in the accomplishment of a writing which, in Hejinian's words, "is scored for meaning but independent of my own physique or psychology."[21] Two elements, then: simultaneity, and the aleatory. Chance, I suspect, operates on the syllabic level. For if we set polyphony and scoring for more than one instrument to one side, simultaneity is achieved in music by two means: the chord (playing more than one note at once), and repetition—which through echo evokes memory, the ghost or shadow invoking presence. *Writing Is an Aid to Memory* is dense and rich in both.

Hejinian's preface to *Writing Is An aid to Memory*[22] is a statement about the possibility and nature of meaning, and teaches us by demonstration how to read the fragments which make up the poem and make up our knowledge of the world. "Knowledge is part of the whole," says the third sentence, coming as it does on the heels of the second sentence's violation of ordinary grammar and syntax, and what we read in this page and a half of prose is liberally provided with bits and pieces of words which invite us, on rereading if not on first reading, to fragment words into puns, partialities, and temporary closures. Thus we learn to read words as doubles: "Memory is the girth, or again," says the sixth sentence, the press of this strange syntax leading us to read "Memory is . . . a gain." Such punning is a device which empowers the reader in the composition and discovery of meaning, and it is—as a form of transegmental drift—a musical device which recurs in the poem itself. Lines 13 and 14 of section 2 of the poem read:

> time is somehow glamorous as well
> a gray sea although it is the Pacific (10)

The proximity of that "gray sea" (repeating as it does the "gray sea" at the end of line 6) permits "as well" to read "a swell." Again, resonances and overtones. Music.

In the preface we find "*vities,*" "*vative,*" and "*mentary,*" an apparent fragmenting to which we may respond in a variety of ways. What is interesting in terms of musication, however, is the play they provoke between the absence and the production of meaning: this is a crucial element in *Writing Is an Aid to Memory.* Much of the poem's energy comes from the contrast between our (cultural?) habit of discerning the syntactically, semantically, or orthographically unconventional as fragmentary, in some sense incomplete or incorrect, and the poem's own clear declaration that nothing has been omitted. Left as they are, that is to say, "*vities,*" "*vative,*" and "*mentary*" are semantically unyielding—in which case, as Steve McCaffery comments,[23] their quality lies not in their recoverability to ordinary meaning but in their resistance to it, and in their force as a negative adjacence to terms that do yield a meaning. We are thus enjoined to read them as indeterminate and *resistant,* semantically, and thus to read them materially, much as we may read/hear music. Punctuating the text, such islands of resistance at their very least play a structural role. But (so deeply are we accustomed to focusing on the meaning) we may also recognize these words as a form of fragmenting by omission, in which case we find ourselves committed to the production of meaning by the provision of a prefix. But which one? Cavities, nativities, or proclivities? Conservative, derivative, or preservative? Commentary, elementary, or supplementary? Or whatever.[24] Some words in the poem, like "*pand*" in section 2 (13), seem to invite the addition of both prefix and/or suffix (expand or pander). Sometimes Hejinian combines the fragmenting of words into transegmental drift with fragmenting by omission, as in the case of the quite complex sequence in section 4 (14) "*yon door for which shape,*" which offers (among other choices) the word "beyond" as well as "yonder." And the possible archaism of "*yon*" enables a further sort of response, too, perhaps "literary" or "aesthetic," a kind of self-conscious prettification gesturing "beyond" the text and at the same time undermining its own exophoric prettification. It's a risky business, this poem.

Not without irony, section 4 tells us (15) that

> a syllable is a suggestion
>   is the beginning of an inclusion.

Some syllables are a suggestion in a slightly different way, for we cannot tell whether they are complete or not; they can be seen to omit nothing. In such words, the dual strategies and responses, the absence of meaning, the production of meaning, come together in a simultaneity of response. "*Vative,*" for instance, in the preface, could possibly stand alone, unfragmented, a modified "vatic." In inviting such duality of response it is closely related to what is possibly the single most prevalent syllable of the poem, as visible in its clear exclusion as in its overt use: the "*ness*" at the start of the poem:

> apple is shot nod
>   ness seen know it around saying

where "ness" could as easily be a complete word (it means promontory or cape) as it could a fragment, and it suggests to us, of course, the meaning of ness as a suffix itself. "Words . . . simply can't help but give onto ideas," in this case the idea of essence. Finally, not all of the fragmentary words in *Writing Is an Aid to Memory* permit multiplicity, but remain uncompromising, like "*zontal.*" Yet even here, where we are tempted to read the word as a term presented before the understanding, positivized by semantic construction into "horizontal," we are inescapably faced with the resistant materiality of the word.

Such strategies have a double effect. In the first place they enact, on the level of the syllable, what I take to be the theme of the poem—"the message remains undelivered" for "knowledge is part of the whole." In the second, they profoundly ambiguate the poem by on one hand making us distrust the completeness of the words we do see as complete, whilst on the other they encourage us to provide our own substitutions and omissions—creating, once again, resonances, overtones. So, for example, the context in section 5 permits us to read "flexible thoughts starts shine" as "flexible thoughts stars shine" (8).[25] Hejinian, that is to say, encourages us to *mis*read her text, and thus encourages us to agree that "abridgement is foolish." As section 7 of the poem puts it,

> substitute inventing music of a series
> of changes very little understood

This is a music of metonymies. And the metonymies afford the strategies of chance.

This sort of strategy occurs not only on the level of the syllable, but also on that of the sentence. Such strategy not only has its "musicating" effect, it also amplifies and even "explains" the poem's title; it does so in several ways. Thus Hejinian has taken a cliché, proverb, popular saying, and in distorting it (usually by substitution, but sometimes by omission) implicitly invites the reader to correct it. Thus in section 2 (lines 19–20) we read

> compare beats of the dime were wishes
> so the classic clink of feet. (10)

If wishes were horses then beggars would ride; brother, can you spare a dime? Later in the same section it recurs (lines 141–2)

> a wish is sufficient that teaches me this
> lagger imagine a full morning. (13)

and that *lagger* came out of that earlier *absent* beggar. In this sort of dual allusion—to the Great Depression of the early 1930s, and to conventional folk wisdom— the poem works exophorically, evoking material exterior to the text, cultural knowledge. This is one kind of memory Hejinian's poem encourages. But it also requires another—a close and careful attention to the poem itself, so that the act of recognition can occur, 120 lines later on. Described this way, Hejinian's poem begins to seem remarkably conventional; clearly, it sites itself within a tradition.

There is another form of this strategy, and this brings me back to the opening lines. The first word of the poem is "apple." The first word of section 8 is "potato," which is of course in French a kind of apple (*pomme de terre*). Now one way of reading the first five words of *Writing Is an Aid to Memory,* "apple is shot nod / ness," is to understand that "apple" (noun) is, as a term, shot (ruined, inadequate, has outlived its use) as a register of the essence or identity (ness) of things. That word "potato" at the beginning of section 8 is evidence of noun as fragmentary. "Something spills," says the preface; "abridgement is foolish."

In 1989, some ten years after *Writing Is An aid to Memory* was written, Hejinian observed that "in comparison to metaphor, which is based on similarity, and in which meanings are conserved and transferred from one thing to something said to be like it, the metonymic world is unstable. While metonymy maintains the intactness and discreteness of its particulars, its paratactic perspective gives it multiple vanishing points." Metonymic thinking, she continued, "moves more rapidly and less predictably than metaphors permit—but the metonym is not metaphor's opposite. Metonymy moves restlessly, through an associative network, in which associations are compressed rather then elaborated. . . . Metonymy, even while it condenses thought processes, may at the same time serve as a generative and even a dispersive force."[26] Gertrude Stein, whose writing seems in important ways to point towards Hejinian's, hated nouns for their sheer inadequacy: "A noun is a name of anything, why after a thing is named write about it. A name is adequate, or it is not. If it is adequate then why go on calling it, if it is not then calling it by its name is no good."[27] "Knowledge is part of the whole, as hope is, from which love seeks to contrast knowledge with separation, and certainty with the temporal" (preface [5]). The poem demands of the reader a close and careful attention to the poem itself, so that the act of recognition can occur, nine pages later on.

Such activities are essential to Hejinian's musicating strategies; they empower the reader in much the same way as a musical score empowers the performer: a continuing series of minute and strategic decisions affecting the structure of the whole. Permission to misread is crucial to the poem, for it is not misreading at all. One recurrence that runs through *Writing Is an Aid to Memory* is the line, usually but not always made up of monosyllables, which reads like a list. Each is a miniature lyric catalogue; my own favorite is "sit cat has stop wrap" in the truly wonderful ninth section, but there are plenty of others: "dump hind light sprint" in section 2 (12); "rosy soda bishop" in section 8 (17); "zoo love slide where rides in a tub," also in section 8 (17). So too, from time to time in the poem, there are consonantal shifts and plays (e.g., fortress/forest), or even semi-anagrams; as well as vocabulary- and syntax-repeats.[28] In cases like these, more obviously than elsewhere in the poem, it is the sound that is foregrounded, consonantal and vowel play generating the words. Sound potentiates substitution and "correction," generates multiplicity of meaning and resistance to meaning, invites and at the same time inhibits semantic production. Recurrence, that is to say, whether semantic, lexical, or phonetic (material), is a *weaving:* "form is no longer architecturized," Pierre Boulez said of serial music, "but is *woven;* said otherwise, there is no distributive hierarchy in the organization." Similarly, Hejinian: "Any coincidence is a relationship, puts a line out or takes one in. There is always a relationship as soon as there is a coincidence. I am thinking here now more of taking lines in, or 'taking it all in,' than of any putting out."[29] This too is a music. It is a form of musical "chording" which bops the poem along in its scat/cat music. And it seems to work metonymically. Thus in section 32 of this poem through which cats endlessly play, we find "grammar a copy cate" (43), the "dupli" thus suppressed but intri- and imbri-cate, quite forcefully implied as well (catered). But when in section 25 we read the line "slate rove boat" (35), the only word which seems to be indubitably "complete" is the last, "boat"; the boundaries of the words strain and slip in a potential reach outside the poem as well as the section, limited in their range only by the memory. "The meaning of a word in its place," Hejinian said in a talk she gave in April 1983, "derives both from the word's lateral reach, its contacts with its neighbors in a statement, and from its reach through and out of the text into the outer world, the matrix of its contemporary and historical reference."[30] "Memory," says section 21, "is a trick of coincidence / which overturned has invisibly legible / use" (31).

The forms of simultaneity, then, do two things: they undermine a linear clarity of meaning, a thread of discourse, which might otherwise be possible/discernible in this writing; and they prevent what Hejinian calls "a lopping off," opening up a plurality of semantic fields and of paralinguistic (and hence musical?) "events." Simultaneity and musicality thus act out what Hejinian has explained in the preface: "I am always conscious of the disquieting runs of life slipping by, that the message remains undelivered, opposed to me. Memory cannot, though the future return, and proffer raw conclusions. . . . Abridgement is foolish, like a lopping off among miracles." The poem declares, through its music, that fragments and uncertainty are the best we can have though not all that we hope for. It teaches us to cultivate memory and at the same time to recognize its gaps, its tentativeness, its incompleteness. Language is a form of memory, and in this poem is what Hejinian calls "an operation of connection."[31] "more parted, pasted dog up" says a line in section 7 of the poem (16); "when someone tells me that they don't understand what my poem . . . *means,* I can respond by saying, Well, what does any one of Bach's *Brandenburg Concerti* . . . *mean,* and this may give that someone a momentary insight into reading."[32] "Structure," Charles Bernstein has commented, "can't be separated from the decisions made within it."[33] "Even in poetry," Hejinian wrote in her first published book, "honesty is more important than felicity."[34]

III

Where does this leave us? Let me close with some quotations. The first is Ezra Pound, talking about the music of poetry: "you begin with the yeowl and the bark, and you develop into the dance and into music, and into music with words, and finally into words with a vague adumbration of music, words suggestive of music, or words in a rhythm that preserves some accurate trait of the emotive impression, or of the sheer character of the fostering or parental emotion."[35] These words put Pound on the Dryden side of the Dryden-Stein equation, see poetry as a repository of "wisdom" as well as "beauty," for so I read the "fostering or parental." And on the Stein side there is Jackson Mac Low: "It was such a relief to stop making artworks carry that burden of 'expression'! To let them become themselves, watch them grow & take shape without one's pushing & shoving them around too much, was & is a great pleasure."[36] Avoiding the conventionally harmonious and melodic, but far from denying beauty and hope, *Writing Is an aid to Memory* claims beauty through the music of its language—and that music is also an *active* music of thought and of accord. But it refuses to write paradise, for paradise is not of *this* world ("Honesty is more important than felicity"). It empowers the text and the reader and the world by exhibiting magnanimity toward them. "I would like to discover a line that is scored for meaning but independent of my own physique or psychology," Hejinian told Andrew Schelling, "and perhaps eventually such a line will be best determined by sound values. But those won't be music."[37] I suspect that misreading is impossible.

Notes

Epigraph. Basil Bunting, "The Lion and the Lizard," *Three Essays,* Richard Caddel, ed. (Durham: Basil Bunting Poetry Centre, 1994) 30, 28, 31.

1. *Basil Bunting on Poetry,* Peter Makin, ed. (Baltimore: Johns Hopkins UP, 1999) 160.

2. John Dryden, "A Song for St. Cecilia's Day, 1687," *The Works of John Dryden: Poems 1685–1692,* Earl Miner, ed. (Berkeley: U of California P, 1969) v.3, 201; Gertrude Stein, "Sentences and Paragraphs," *How to Write* (Barton, NY: Something Else, 1973) 30.

3. Entries for *nondescript, The Century Dictionary and Cyclopedia.* 10 vols. (New York: Century, 1902); *Oxford English Dictionary* (Oxford: Oxford UP, 1933).

4. Pierre Boulez, Letter to John Cage, "The System Exposed," *Orientations: Collected Writings,* Jean-Jacques Nattiez, ed.; trans. Martin Cooper (London: Faber and Faber, 1986) 141. Quoted by Charles Olson in a letter to Cid Corman, 13 June 1952, Boulez' letter was originally published in "4 Musicians at Work," *Trans/formation: Arts, Communication, Environment* 1.3 (1952): 170; George Evans, ed., *Charles Olson & Cid Corman: Complete Correspondence: 1950–1964* (Orono: National Poetry Foundation, 1987) v. 1, 272; see also Charles Olson, *Letters for Origin 1950–1955,* Albert Glover, ed. (London: Cape Goliard, 1969) 103.

5. Hejinian, "Smatter," *L=A=N=G=U=A=G=E* 8 (June 1979): 18; "Lyn Hejinian/Andrew Schelling: An Exchange," *Jimmy and Lucy's House of "K"* 6 (May 1986): 8.

6. Louis Zukofsky, *Bottom: On Shakespeare* (Austin: Ark P, 1963) 369.

7. It is of course true, as Steve McCaffery reminds me (in a letter, 27 February 1992), that the orders of language may also, when we consider song, be the orders of music, if in those orders we include (and how can we not) the relation of music/song to vocality: pitch, stress, ictus, duration. In a sense, then, many of the sounds of music *are* the sounds of language; what is important here is to note simply that such sounds are most emphatically *not* to be thought of in terms of harmony and the mellifluous, any more than the poetic image is to be thought of as being merely pictorial.

8. The term is James E. Breslin's, to distinguish a later generation of writers from the New Formalists (Merrill, Merwin, Rich, Wilbur) in "American Poetry: 1945 to the Present," *Columbia Literary History of the United States,* Emory Elliott, ed. (New York: Columbia UP, 1988) 1081.

9. Robert Richman, introduction to *The Direction of Poetry* (Boston: Houghton Mifflin, 1988) xii, xxi, quoted by Joseph Conte, *Unending Design: The Forms of Postmodern Poetry* (Ithaca: Cornell UP, 1991) 270, 271. Similar claims for the musicality of rhyme and meter are implicit in Philip Dacey and David Jauss, ed., *Strong Measures: Contemporary American Poetry in Traditional Forms,* with a foreword by Richard Wilbur (New York: Harper & Row, 1988).

10. Stanton A. Coblentz, *New Poetic Lamps and Old: An Analysis of the New Movement in Poetry* (Mill Valley: Wings, 1951) 47.

11. Timothy Steele, *Missing Measures: Modern Poetry and the Revolt against Meter* (Fayetteville: U of Arkansas P, 1990) 15.

12. Laughlin recorded that when he was an undergraduate at Harvard in 1934 "You couldn't mention Pound's or Eliot's name in [Robert] Hillyer's class or you'd be sent out of the room." "James Laughlin Interviewed by Robert Dana," *American Poetry Review* 10.6 (November–December 1981): 20.

13. Coblentz, *New Poetic Lamps* 71. Though he would reject the claim as too simplistic, Steele quite clearly considers meter to be the *only* means of achieving musicality in poetry. That the adoption of "free verse" constitutes a total abandonment of "nearly three millenia" (26) of musical practice in poetry is the polemical base upon

which *Missing Measures* rests: "our ability to organize thought and speech into measure is one of the most precious endowments of the human race. To throw this away would be a tragedy" (24).

14. *Writing Is an Aid to Memory* (Great Barrington: Figures, 1978). This book is unpaginated; in my parenthetical documentation which follows I take the recto of the double title page as page 1.

15. Lyn Hejinian, flier announcing *Tuumba* Second Series, numbers 11–16 (Berkeley: Tuumba, 1977).

16. "An Exchange" 9.

17. Hejinian, *My Life* (Los Angeles: Sun & Moon 1987) 57–58.

18. Pierre Boulez, *Notes of an Apprenticeship,* Paul Thévenin, ed., trans. Herbert Weinstock (New York: Knopf, 1968) 210.

19. Hejinian, "Smatter" 17.

20. Bernstein, "Semblance," *Content's Dream: Essays 1975–1984* (Los Angeles: Sun & Moon, 1986) 35.

21. "An Exchange" 8.

22. Reprinted in *The Language of Inquiry* (Berkeley: U of California P, 2000) 23–24.

23. "Why can't we propose these terms," McCaffery asks in his letter of 27 February, "as paralinguistic 'events' that foreground the material resistance of the sign (within the sign's endorsed context) against which the reader experiences the absence of meaning."

24. Some further examples, more-or-less at random: *porated, scription, coo, limb, brating, covery, pensated* (all from section 2); *guage, straction, ception, tory, ysis, cerns* (all from section 5); *object able* which might or might not resolve into *objectionable(ness)* (section 4). Other patterns include *light off of abstraction* where *of* is an *abstraction* of *off;* the nice little complication of "*I recommenced the horse forth nothing whole all / this*" in section 5, which plays with *henceforth* and thereby with fragmented wholeness.

25. Other examples: *bread,* which we might well read as *bred,* in section 2. Among other sequences to be mentioned are two: complete lines repeating the same vowel, as in "And a tight find of firelight under I smile"; and plays with line constraints, where the return to the left margin is the return to the alphabet's initial *a,* or where we read an echo of those constraints in a line which begins *I know* (with its "ghost" *j* falling between that *I* and *k*); *a cheap* and *a clock* (ghost *b*); and the mischievous variants, like *a blink* (no ghost at all), echoing an earlier *a link;* all in section 2.

26. Hejinian, "Strangeness," *The Language of Inquiry* 148, 149.

27. Gertrude Stein, *Lectures in America* (New York: Random House, 1935) 209–10.

28. Other examples: *leaning learning; happy hobby* (horse), both in section 2.

29. Hejinian, "Smatter" 17.

30. "The Rejection of Closure," *Language of Inquiry* 50. Hejinian gave the talk on 17 April 1983.

31. Hejinian, "Smatter" 18.

32. "An Exchange" 8. This, Hejinian adds, "does not mean that my poem is by definition musical" (9).

33. Charles Bernstein, "Semblance" 38.

34. *A Thought Is the Bride of What Thinking* (Willits: Tuumba, 1976) 4. This book is unpaginated; in numbering pages I take the title-page as page (1). The text differs considerably from that in *Language of Inquiry* 11.

35. Ezra Pound, "The Serious Artist," *Literary Essays,* T. S. Eliot, ed. (London: Faber and Faber, 1954) 51.

36. Jackson Mac Low, "Museletter," *L=A=N=G=U=A=G=E* 2 (April 1978): 26; *The L=A=N=G=U=A=G=E Book,* Bruce Andrews and Charles Bernstein, eds. (Carbondale: Southern Illinois UP, 1984) 26.

37. "An Exchange" 8–9.

McCaffery's Diptych

The Black Debt

A sentence makes not it told but it hold. A hold is where they put things.
—Gertrude Stein *How to Write*

The epigraph to Steve McCaffery's *The Black Debt* gives fair warning to the reader. It is Samuel Johnson, quoting Horace's *Ars Poetica* and adding a Latin tag apparently his own. He is instructing the Rev. Dr. Maxwell about James Macpherson's *Fingal, An Ancient Epic Poem in Six Books* (published 1762): "In vain shall we look for the *lucidus ordo,* where there is neither end or object, design or moral, *nec certa recurrit imago.*" Johnson's words are apt indeed, and they stand in playful relation to McCaffery's text, since the charges levelled against Macpherson's work might equally be aimed at McCaffery's. Johnson is complaining about a poem of dubious stature, citing Horace's insistence on clarity of order as one authority for demonstrating that *Fingal* is not only no poem at all but also a forgery, and Ossian (the epic's putative author) an invention, a non-existent person. In Johnson's view (but not in his words) "Ossian" is a signifier without a signified. McCaffery, using Johnson's criticism as epigraph, implicitly claims that his poem will be as unsettling to the reader of current verse, habituated to seek end, object, design, moral, and an overall coherence and unity to the experience of reading poetry, as was Macpherson's unfamiliar and disruptive territory to Johnson. The claim is justified. *The Black Debt* is a direct assault upon conventional reading habits, and a number of people will no doubt think it no poem at all. It is quite unlike any other in the English language that I can think of; it is a brilliant and intricate *tour de force* which demands the sort of scrupulous and sustained attention all difficult, good poems do. It is also, I should add, very funny, even hilarious, in its assiduous courtship of Johnson's censure. And it is puzzling.

Here, for instance, are the opening words of "Lag," the first of *The Black Debt*'s two sections (the second is called "An Effect of Cellophane"). I do not reproduce the layout or the poem's appearance on the page—the whole book, with justified margins, is set in 18-point type: "SENTENCE NOT SEN-

TENCE, A RED envelope, the rain stood up, the prolonged cosseting or a silhouette the customer knows, dead drunks arriving at a gate, these enormous movements of soap intact and called a breakdown on the road, winterthorn but a floating crow in flight, as secondary systems round the kitchen, a list of old socks" (11). Aside from the occasional apostrophe/possessive and upper-case initial, the only punctuation in "Lag" is the comma, and its 108 pages make one long paragraph without a break. It begins "sentence not sentence" and ends "Nature not Nietzsche," (119)—that is, with a comma. Sentence not sentence indeed, neither end nor object. Johnson's complaint seems pretty straightforward in its application, even (especially) if we read "object" as a term of grammar. As McCaffery prints the epigraph, Johnson's Latin tag *nec certa recurrit imago* sounds a bit like the sort of observation freshman students of English learn to make, that the imagery is not consistent. This is a charge that certainly seems to apply to the apparent disorderliness of the poem. Turn to Maxwell's account from which the epigraph comes, however, and the charge behind Johnson's tag shifts, in a nice ironic reversal that McCaffery surely echoes by various means throughout his own text. By taking it out of context, McCaffery has apparently reversed Johnson's meaning. In context, it seems (at least to the cursory view) to contradict itself. Here it is in full, as it appears in Boswell's *Life of Johnson* (December 1770, *aetat* 61). Maxwell is reporting to Boswell: "The poem of Fingal, he said, was a mere unconnected rhapsody, a tiresome repetition of the same images. 'In vain shall we look for the *lucidus ordo,* where there is neither end or object, design or moral, *nec certa recurrit imago.*' "—nor any fixed (settled, definite, probable, unambiguous) image returns, says the Latin. If *Fingal*'s imagery is too consistent, too repetitious, then Johnson's Latin cannot mean what it did at first sight or removed from context. Johnson's *recurrit* probably means returns to the memory—once you've finished the poem, that is—and in using *imago* Johnson has in mind something like a unified overall structure, something along the lines of an overarching and transcendent "object, design, or moral."

Though it is still a matter of some dispute, Johnson's estimate of Ossian and the Finn poems is mistaken. The lament that Macpherson (or someone else) did not scrupulously (or even at all) record the oral tradition, the ballads and tales from which he drew, is not infrequent. What is remarkable to my mind about *The Black Debt* is that it is so constructed as deservedly to draw Johnson's ire while at the same time, in an act of great mischief, meeting Johnson's criteria for the good poem. Both sections of *The Black Debt,* which as McCaffery claims "stage a mutual interrogation and an interdependent challenge" (McCaffery's statement printed on the back cover), are packed with Johnson's "mere repetition of the same images," especially if we read *image* as *device* rather than *likeness;* one meaning of *mere,* it is worth recalling, is "pure, unqualified, utter," or "in the fullest sense." Printed as prose (cross-generic, then, or at any rate challenging our notions of genre and indeed of discourse), the apparent chaos and disruption, nonsense and childish play of *The Black Debt* are simply the means by which the work achieves unity, coherence, and indeed purpose, while at the very same time—and thus by the very same means—calling those qualities into question. A work which in central ways seeks to refute the ethical, it is nevertheless a work of moral stringency.

Thus, the opening of "Lag," *sentence not sentence,* contains its own reversals. Is it a self-contradiction (and hence "false"), or a description of the comma-filled but period-less work it introduces (and hence "true")? If it's a pun, is it jokey? Ironic? "Poetic"? Intense? Is it telling us we're going to get sententiousness without (grammatical) sentence? Or the reverse, perhaps, since we do find perfectly clear and grammatically orthodox "sentences" later on, marked off by commas. But then we find quite a bit of sententiousness later on too, like the absurd reversal of the cliché, "news is the poetry that stays poetry" (110), or even the somewhat enigmatic "this text is made to move beyond its words" (64)—a statement that the work seems designed to refute. Some of that sententiousness, indeed, occurs in sentence fragments like "the possibility that grammar masks a military practice" (102). Perhaps *sentence not sentence* is then some sort of (clearly unsatisfactory because not at all clear) instruction to the reader, an authorial voice telling us what to expect—but the phrase *a red envelope,* immediately following, undermines that notion since it becomes almost impossible to synthesize the two phrases into a single coherent "meaning," thereby completely neutralizing our ability to read these fragments as sentences. (By the time we reach the bottom of the first page we have a lively sense indeed of the phrase as occupying a place somewhere between word and sentence.) Whatever else the opening phrase does, it alerts us to the possibility of pun—a conjecture confirmed by the *red envelope.* Here the pun is aural, where the first was visual, and the next phrase, *the rain stood up,* encourages us to suspect that pun is going to be ubiquitous in this writing, and points to the nonsensical. After all, rain doesn't stand up, it falls down. And if we respond to idiomatic usage, *stood up* embodies, like many idiomatic constructions, contradictory meanings: either the rain lasted, or it stayed away. The first time we get a bit of writing that makes grammatical sense (in that it stands as an independent clause and *could* be written as an ordinary sentence), it resists description, its meaning undecidable.

The reader, that is to say, is at first thrown into a quizzical stance by an inability to "understand" any given individual phrase, and then by a failure to synthesize sequences of phrases into a coherent unit. The reading process gives rise to a series of unanswerable questions: is this "true"? Does this refer to something? What does this mean? Does this "make sense"? We are driven to pay attention both to the sheer separateness of each phrase from its companions and to the (usually inaccessible) link between them. No single reading strategy works. Reading the opening phrases, the eye starts to cast hurriedly through the writing, scanning it like a list. So we get caught up short when we reach *dead drunks arriving at a gate,* partly because of the pun between *dead* and the metaphorical *dead drunk* (our awareness of the pun triggered by the plural *drunks*), but mainly because of the consequent incongruity of the sheer inertness of *dead* and the sheer activity of *arriving.* There are, then, extremely isolated local instances of meaning which serve vividly to separate phrases one from another, yet give the reader working through this text something to hold on to. Those moments of comparative lucidity come up like oases on the desert horizon, only to prove mirage—for the lucidity of one statement does not match the lucidity of the next, which may "make sense" in a different way; the relief it offers is short-lived. Johnson's "mere unconnected rhapsody" indeed!

So, after the eye has hurried over an intervening clause "about" *enormous movements of soap,* another pun catches us up: *winterthorn but floating crow in flight.* This pun is syntactic: does that *but* signify limitation (of the kind used in definition) or contrast? The text has moved into a new kind of ambiguity, untranslatability, pun, for we cannot decide what sort of phrase or cluster this might be, nor sort out what the relationship is between its parts, *winterthorn* and *a crow in flight,* X and Y. *Sentence not sentence* is, after all, pretty clear syntactically, and can be described *X is not Y.* Here however the sentence can be rescribed as both *X is not Y* and *X is (an instance of) Y.* While the mind ponders, moreover, the eye has moved on to *as secondary systems round the kitchen,* and we break the reading, reanalyze (could *round* be a verb?). No wonder this section of the poem is called "Lag." The eye speeds on as the mind labors to catch up, in a series of persistent but not necessarily regular double takes. Parts of speech slide around in this writing, transformed by their fluid grammatical context. Possible meanings and possible contexts shift again and again, from one segment to the next as well as within segments.

No single reading strategy works because the kind of link between each phrase and the reader alters from phrase to phrase, and as we move from phrase to phrase we face incompatible discourses. It is not simply that we cannot find a way to make sense of the sequence *a red envelope* and *the rain stood up,* but that each of those phrases behaves in a particular (and different) syntactic and referential way, and indeed seems to belong in a kind of discourse whose presuppositions do not match those of its neighbors. Because each phrase is on a different wavelength, it is impossible to assign an authorial source to the words we read. "Lag" rapidly dislocates not only the reader but also our sense of the writer as an author whose principal activity, occupying an identifiable "position," is to control the production of meaning, gain the reader's assent to propositions, engage through language a social, political, economic, aesthetic (etc.) activity or "theme" which resides outside the text. Indeed, we cannot even discern that "Lag" is a text about writing, for very few of the phrases constituting it can be read as self-referential. So radical is the instability of this text that the reader is caught up both in an intense awareness of the segmented nature of language and by its refusal to identify itself as utterance. As McCaffery said in March 1991 at a reading in Tucson, the heterogeneity of language never presents itself to understanding and is only experienced through the necessary sacrifice of conceptual conviction. That heterogeneity, as manifest in "Lag," demands that the reader attend what Lyotard calls the differend, the links between the segments: "a differend would be a case of conflict, between (at least) two parties, that cannot be equitably resolved for lack of a rule of judgment applicable to both arguments. One side's legitimacy does not imply the other's lack of legitimacy. However, applying a single rule of judgment to both in order to settle their differend . . . would wrong (at least) one of them (and both of them if neither side admits this rule). . . . A wrong results from the fact that the rules of genre discourse by which one judges are not those of the judged genre or genres of discourse."[1] Our inability to mediate between phrases leaves us on the threshold of meaning, the event of coming to mean.

Yet "Lag" is not babble, nor is it formless. As Marjorie Perloff has remarked of *The Black Debt,* phrasings repeat, providing a compendium of grammatical and syntactic forms and modes ranging from simple negations (which, after the initial *sentence not sentence,* thereafter reappear as puns like *get up at eight o'clock not get a potato clock* [45]); definitions; noun phrases; simple declarative sentences; "when" clauses; "as" clauses; statements of discrimination which, because the second term is regularly missing, gesture ineffectually outside the text; corny puns (*it's a butcher not Athens owns the aisles of grease* [23]), some of them cross-linguistic (*in due course two parts* [27]); palindromes (*pull up if I pull up* [43]); anagrams (*conservative not vice versa* [22]); lists of names; and lists of numbers. All of these recur at more-or-less regular intervals, and several other devices are scattered more sporadically throughout the text: parodies of slogans, headlines, titles of magazine articles, billboards; statements of range (*baritones to booze* [109]) and of ratio (as X is to Y); statements that can be taken as (perhaps mistaken or deliberately misleading) commentary on this text (*the intention is always to thwart design* [28]) or on politics, or on science, or on almost anything else. There are substitution strategies (*the goat that failed* . . . [117]), and there are clusters of technical vocabulary too—some sections of the text play with mathematical terms, others with philosophy, and so on. Some readers might well find these constitute Johnson's "tiresome repetition of the same images," of course. But recurring like rhymes to stabilize the text, these devices are not formal only, and McCaffery breaks their repetition. As *The Black Debt* proceeds they acquire *as devices* both a strategic and more importantly a semantic function.

Chiming repetition throughout the poem, sometimes with an almost incantatory quality, these now divert the mind from the semantic and lexical blockages of the text and give relief, sometimes comic, sometimes not. Referentiality ceases to be a goal, and redundancy becomes a rhythm in the text. In a strange inversion of normal reading practices, semantically inert lists of numbers draw the reader's attention; we notice the lexical and semantic features of the words before our eyes less and less as we seek the next anagram or palindrome, and hoping the while that we have not let one slip by we scurry through the text anticipating the next pun; we know we can rest at any comma, for the comma is an agent of semantic and formal separation; we look for covert rhymes and sound echoes, for they are more meaningful in their physicality than the (translatable) text they have informed. *Share not Cher* (76—the pun is wicked, gesturing outside the text as it does) is the most overt sort of sound play, of course, but "Lag" also uses rhyme and consonantal cluster (*chewn patties barely* [14]), formulaic echoes of pop culture, and so on. Frequently, what looks like consonantal play turns out to be an anagram, as in *kleptomaniacs task policeman* (86)—which offers the sort of truism good anagrams often do, and which once again gestures outside the text while at the same time cancelling the gesture, locating the attention firmly within it. Reading *The Black Debt* we attend what McCaffery on the back cover calls "the materiality of reading as a first order physical encounter"—an experience, he hopes, brought into play too by the book's large type.

This push towards semantic inertia indeed makes "negotiation of the lines" (McCaffery, on the back cover) "a highly visceral experience" by playing against and with our deeply ingrained demand that what we read make consistent and articulated sense. One function of the poem's length is to fill with surprises the semantically neutral, to rid the poem, by a curious reversal of our customary reading habits, of its apparent inertia. As a (grammatical) rule, for instance, the comma is used to stabilize a sentence by punctuating it "to indicate" (I quote the *Century* dictionary) "the smallest interruptions in the continuity of grammatical construction, the marking of which contributes to clearness." McCaffery's comma radically breaks the text by showing how discontinuous the (grammatical, semantic, lexical, referential) construction is—the whole of "Lag" can be described as one continuous self-interruption. But, as with other devices, McCaffery plays his repetitions with great variety and ingenuity, and the mind, following the eye through the comma into the next phrase, sometimes discovers to its great surprise that there is indeed a coherent link operating in this text. That such a move comes as a surprise is, I need hardly add, another instance of "Lag" enacting its title. *a monarch is a butterfly, a king is not a crab* (29), for example, breaks the "rule," indeed breaks more than one: A variation on the *sentence not sentence* pattern, it also gestures exophorically toward a referential world outside the text, the comma between the two phrases acting pivotally to rotate the meaning. At this point in the text, then, the comma has a crucial semantic function, encouraging synthesis of meaning. For the space of one phrase the reader shifts into having thoughts *about* language, in which words stand for something else and become a transparent window that seeks to deny its own existence through an act of self-effacement. The whole of *The Black Debt* is an assault on what McCaffery has neatly labeled the "fenestrational necessity, a mandate to linguistic transparency through which all beings and events [are] forced to pass."[2] The alternative is for the writing (and the reading, therefore) to promote (again, McCaffery's words) "forms based upon object presence: the pleasure of graphic or phonic imprint, for instance, their value as sheer linguistic stimuli."[3] To seek, that is to say, immediacy of experience/effect in reading/writing, rather than point through the words to a destination outside the text.

Consequently, "Lag" and "An Effect of Cellophane" both play in more or less complex ways with the dynamics of reference and the nature of "understanding" as a postponement of presence. The sequence *Did Hannah say as Hannah did, tautology, a way of frightening by fear* (34) plays with the reader by providing a little island of coherence. The shock of recognizing the six-word question about Hannah) as a palindrome undermines the dictionary/referential function of *tautology*, yet *tautology* in turn enjoins us to attend to semantic features where we had, startled, attended the orthographic, and we vacillate between the phenomenal immediacy of the text and the more comfortable commentary upon it. We thus recognize that commentary of this sort is only possible by subordinating immediacy through retreating from the text itself into thoughts about it—from the page to the head might be one way of putting it. It is no accident, then, that the next phrase, a tautology itself, should use *fear* as its example.

Akin to explaining jokes, writing about "Lag" like this risks tedium, as does the text itself in its exploration of unsatisfactory and trivializing procedures. But the essential feature of this section of *The Black Debt* is its sheer wit. In one infrequently recurring sequence a non-existent signifier is followed by a non-existent signified, as in *a French gerund meaning beauty spot, the decals on the handlebars between each currant bush* (28), though the formulaic *an X meaning Y* does not always produce the expected next step. Later on page 28 we read *an anglo saxon diphthong meaning communism, we meet today and organize tomorrow, a steward draws tea,* links generated, surely, by associative means. But the steward, once he has arrived (presumably through shop-stewards organizing meetings?), fulfils another function in this text by being the first half of an anagrammatic phrase (by which the meetings are seen to have been about tea-breaks?). That this sort of play occurs with increasing frequency as the text goes on may be a corollary of our learning to notice it as we learn to read it. "Lag" bristles with potential (and often silly or absurd or satiric) significations, but the only ones that move beyond empty gesture are those that return the reader to the materiality of the text: anagrams, palindromes, patterns of sound, and the like.

This sort of gestural polysemousness, in which we can read a phrase generated by apparently arbitrary means as "true," is but one aspect of a drifting phenomenon that pervades the whole text and is its most characteristic feature. It is also a major source of the poem's great resourcefulness, ebullience, and energy. Meredith Quartermain has observed of the *X not Y* sequences like *surplus not surplice* (13) that "they insist that the reader stop and substitute a term or a phrase for the one already given. There is a lag or gap while this occurs. Paradoxically what flows into the gap is the meshing of the two terms or phrases into one polysemous unit, not a total replacement where one term obliterates another. Thus for a moment anyway . . . the surplice is surplus."[4] The combination hovers in the reader's consciousness. Which is why *share not Cher* is such a wicked pun. This sort of cross-fertilization or drift (I am leery of the sexual metaphor here) gradually, as "Lag" proceeds, begins to wipe out semantic and lexical distinctions. The semantically inert list of numbers acquires ambiguity (is *forty three* one number or two?) but the lexically meaningful becomes referentially inert, as in *grass to de Maupassant* (70), which puns not only *mow* but also *to grass* (to tell tales); this is witty but agreeable nonsense. A sequence like *did Hannah say as Hannah did, tautology, a way of frightening by fear,* we learn as we read, shows us that tautology is a special case of palindrome, and that palindrome is a special case of anagram.

By the time we are halfway through "Lag" we begin to see that a palindrome is a special case of anagram is a special case of *X not Y* is a special case of consonant cluster is a special case of rhyme is a special case of definition is a special case of premise is a special case of inversion is a special case of. . . . There is no discernible difference between palindrome and nonsense, or between nonsense and sense, and what sense there is is therefore something we make, and make by means as arbitrary as any that we have encountered in the words of "Lag." The reader produces local pockets of meaning which (McCaffery's words) "as semantic eruptions or events . . . do not accumulate into aggregated masses."[5] The only aggregated mass in "Lag" is the cumulated and repeated experience of lag, of hermeneutic delay, of time. But it is a *linguistic* accumulation and experience.

We cannot read through "Lag" toward something like a "conclusion" any more than we can determine the "actual" meaning of any given phrase. The comma so partitions and orders the spatiality and sequence of the text that it eliminates the need for specialized competence to relate the sign on the page, the glyph, to some prior text while at the same time it gestures toward that possibility, that "Lag" is an open, highly developed, rich and subtle text that welcomes the reader in. Through its insistent imperative to semantic and syntactic reanalysis it investigates and plays on our linguistic experience and perception of time, and thus stands in marked and even radical contrast to "An Effect of Cellophane," the section that follows. "An Effect of Cellophane" also investigates and plays on our linguistic experience and perception of space and three-dimensionality, but it rushes forward in nine unnumbered unpunctuated sections at almost breakneck pace. Here are the opening lines: "INTERVENE AND BE MASTERED the blank snow sails for its mark the valences inconstant discard add to those whose theme takes on the fold and blends exposing rifts as they can play preventing any being simply opening to make closed liberties agglomerate the lateral moves the ones the proper meanings hold once more the rarest of suspense projected as extinction the contingency remaining for grammarians" (123). The sheer breathlessness results in part from the narrative impetus provided by so many active verbs in the present tense, partly from the reader's sheer inability to voice this writing intelligibly, since the phrase-boundaries are so extremely indeterminate. The forward pull of the syntax prevents you from dwelling on the details of either the syntax or the vocabulary. Except for the recurrent and strictly limited vocabulary drawn from several semantic fields, there is nothing so to stabilize the text that we can predict what might come next or even remember what just happened. The vocabulary revolves around birds (especially swans), keyboards (especially clavichords), weapons (especially knives and bullets), dance, dreams, and travel, and non-etymological linkages abound—swan and cygnet are related to cipher signet and sign, plumes and plumage to pens and thus to ink and writing. As a result no word is what it seems to be, playing as it does upon other recurrences of words more-or-less arbitrarily connected with it. Words like *fold, loop,* and *trigger* recur through the text, and the effect of cellophane is enacted in a prose which is all brilliant, coruscating, shifting surface through which we catch glimpses of not-quite determinate objects. "An Effect of Cellophane" is impossible to describe; there are loops and branches, plays and cross-references, puns and sonic plays, syntactic uncertainties and indecipherable glosses, all interlocking in an astonishing subtle interplay which demands extraordinary attention and concentration. At each reading a different vocabulary seems to take the forefront of one's attention, a different object seems to be struggling to declare itself through the cellophane surface—trigger, detonation, set off, shields, break, for instance, on one reading; lines, charts, sphere, page, margin, edge, balance, on another. Meanwhile the writing remains utterly impenetrable, utterly resistant to the reader's attempts to get inside. In his note on the cover McCaffery suggests some of the intractable possibilities this writing might point to, what it might be "about": "a dying swan? a trip through France by train? a nameless subject writing? the muted description of a murder or torture? an elaborate system of wordplays? an abducted dancer . . . ?" But it is none of these. The words we are reading constitute in their multiple suggestiveness the back end of each other. What we glimpse through the cellophane—if we glimpse anything at all—is simply the cellophane on the other side, reflecting surface. McCaffery's model is the Klein worm, a special case of Möbius strip and Klein bottle beloved of topologists, three dimensions but one surface.

"An Effect of Cellophane" is utterly tantalizing to read because it has many of the characteristics of narrative yet is clearly not a story, from phrase to phrase or even word to word, acquiring, then losing, semantic meaning. Principally, however, by playing with the notion of transparency in language, it undoes memory, that essential ingredient for narrative and indeed for virtually all forms of discourse. The reading eye sails over the text on the crest of the now, the sheer immediacy of the word appearing in its moment. It throws us *out of* time. And just as "Lag" in its way prevented us from subordinating one phrase to another in an attempt to break the paratactic field the phrases made, so here we cannot hierarchize the words or phrases; we cannot even pin them down, and the text thus engages the reader in the risk of unmeaning. That the text before us is at least in part a set of variations on a vocabulary drawn from Derrida's long meditation on Mallarmé's *Mimique*[6] provides no clue to supplement that given us by the title. This writing, as Jacques Attali observed of certain kinds of music, calls into question the distinction between worker and consumer, between doing and destroying; it calls into question a fundamental division of roles in which usage is defined by a code.[7]

In neither portion of *The Black Debt* can meaning be stockpiled. We can decipher neither text, and their mutual interplay once we have finished reading the book cannot be stated any more than the interplays in *sentence not sentence* can be stated, any more than the great variety of links between phrases in "Lag" can be stated. It seems, finally, to operate in the gap between the spatial and the temporal, but to attempt such a statement affords only a serious distortion of the text, for such an attempt is, finally, what Louis Zukofsky used to call predatory, an attempt at possession, and it suggests as corollary that the text has predatory intentions toward the reader. But the text does not define the reader as the recipient of a message, and it does not provide the reader with a sense that there is an identifiable and indeed recoverable origin for the words. The writing undoes the archaeological notion of authorship, and we know as little about McCaffery when we have finished *The Black Debt* as we did before we started. The writing equally undoes the notion that there is anything out there beyond the text called "language," to which and through which we can turn in a desperate attempt for meaning which somehow can be "communicated" and "shared."

One accomplishment of this astonishing poem is that the text is complete, entirely self-sufficient; it demolishes the expressive-communicative model. Texts which await decipherment are partial—imperfect in the terms of *The Black Debt*—precisely because the reader can (as the writer did) look outside the text for authority which properly can only be found within it. *The Black Debt,* then, makes an essentially radical proposition. It dismantles truth as exterior to the signifying practice and yet forces the reader to an experience *in* language rather than to a representation *by* it, and thus at the same time it refuses the notion of a finished reading. Refusing a line of mastery, subverting with great ingenuity the notion of the written word as a source of "knowledge," *The Black Debt* in its exploration of the epistemological and social power of language flattens not only our customary notions of the poem, but also the distinctions between reading and writing, both of which dissolve before the opacity of language itself. Reference is no longer promissory, for the words are themselves the referents. Or, as McCaffery might phrase it, reference enters the very flow of language to become immanent in the very thing it structures. Though McCaffery himself would reject the claim, it is in this that the poem shows its moral stringency, for it refuses utterly to move outside itself. It resists, that is to say, taking a "position," but moves rather to demolish the very possibility of positions. In a more recent work, McCaffery transforms a statement whose sentiments he might approve of: "The history which bears and determines us has the form of a war rather than that of language: relations of power not relations of meaning."[8] Such utterance—indeed all utterance—denies heterogeneity.

Notes

The Black Debt (London, Ontario: Nightwood, 1989). All references to this book appear in parentheses following the quotations. I owe much to both Marjorie Perloff, *Radical Artifice: Writing Poetry in the Age of Media* (Chicago: Chicago UP, 1992) 104–111, and to Meredith Quartermain's review of *The Black Debt*, "Mirrored Interior," *West Coast Line* 5 (Fall 1991): 130–134. Though we differ in sundry particulars and their discussions take a somewhat different approach from my own, both are indispensable reading for anyone interested in McCaffery. I have also benefitted from conversations with Steve McCaffery who kindly provided me with copies of unpublished and hard-to-find work.

Epigraph. Gertrude Stein, "Sentences and Paragraphs," *How to Write* (West Glover, VT: Something Else P, 1973) 29.

1. Jean-François Lyotard, *The Differend: Phrases in Dispute*, trans. George Van Den Abbeele (Minneapolis: U of Minnesota P, 1988) xi.
2. "And Who remembers Bobby Sands?" Steve McCaffery, *North of Intention: Critical Writings 1973–1986* (New York: Roof; Toronto: Nightwood, 1986) 39.
3. Steve McCaffery, "Intraview," *The L=A=N=G=U=A=G=E Book*, Bruce Andrews and Charles Bernstein, eds. (Carbondale: Southern Illinois UP, 1984) 189.
4. Quartermain, "Mirrored Interior" 133.
5. McCaffery, "Language Writing," *North of Intention* 149.
6. Jacques Derrida, *Dissemination*, trans. Barbara Johnson (Chicago: Chicago UP, 1981), especially "The Double Session" and "Dissemination."
7. Jacques Attali, *Noise: The Political Economy of Music*, trans. Brian Massumi (Minneapolis: U of Minnesota P, 1985) 135.
8. Steve McCaffery, "Gnote," *Hot Bird Mfg* 1.7 (January 1991).

"Getting Ready to Have Been Frightened"

How I Read Bruce Andrews

> Consider the facts, if you know what I mean.
>
> —P. G. Wodehouse

Anticipating what Steve McCaffery calls "the possibility that grammar masks a military practice," Wittgenstein observed that "Grammatical conventions cannot be justified by describing what is represented: any such description already presupposes the grammatical rules."[1] In "Gnote" (1991), McCaffery demolishes and reconstitutes in formal and witty visual play the statement "The history which bears and determines us has the form of a war rather than that of a language: relations of power not relations of meaning,"[2] a sounding very close to the poetics of Bruce Andrews. If the many poets known as Language writers have anything at all in common besides their extraordinary wit it is probably their insistence on meaning (and hence the poem) as an exploring of relations produced by the reader; such an assertion of the autonomy of reading assaults the instrumental uses of language, and firmly locates the poem in a political and social arena.

In 1987 Bruce Andrews observed that "the expository is hideous."[3] It is so precisely because the expository act, claiming knowledge and/or understanding the reader presumably lacks, defines the reader's desires or interests in the writer's terms. The political and the institutional, demanding discursive, narratized and explanatory modes of language as they do, conventionally subordinate both reader and matter to the writer in the interests of hierarchized social and political powers. The sheer instrumentality of expository writing makes for difficulties, especially in a literary tradition in which the poem includes its own instruction manual; a crucial problem in late twentieth-century poetics has been how to teach the reader how to read without hierarchizing the author-reader relationship. If reading is the *production* of meaning, how can you tell the reader what to do without preempting, usurping, the reader's means of production?

Political and institutionalized modes of language are to be avoided since they erect discursive or narrative scaffoldings which alienate the reader from the physical immediacy of language as experience. They point to a translatable and referential content by asserting the primacy of a hierarchized ideological/political frame. Yet at the same time meaning, no matter how or where produced, is by its very nature social (hence political), as are the acts of writing and reading; one cannot avoid the political and institutional by apparently transcending the temporal, thereby inviting the reader to contemplate the poem as an aesthetic object which turns its back on the ideological frame.

Thus preserving the independence of the reader from the writer's authority and control is an acute formal problem. In an interview important to an understanding of Andrews's project, Marjorie Perloff sketched it in another way by asking: "If language is . . . denied its 'transparency,' how will 'social dialogue' take place?"[4] How can the poem expose the methodologies of political and institutional constraints and the assumptions underlying them when in order to be intelligible to its readers it perforce follows those methodologies? It is acutely difficult to teach the reader to read if the poem can include its own instruction manual only through demonstration, and no reading of a poem can claim authority beyond itself.

Faced with this problem, Andrews has from his earliest writings been extraordinarily resourceful, through a variety of means radically recontextualizing more-or-less familiar utterance to incapacitate conventional ideological and poetic frameworks. Thus the complete text of one early poem is the phrase "lost & found"[5]—a perfectly intelligible and unambiguous statement when printed on or beside a door, but radically ambiguated if printed by itself on a page. Printed as a poem it suggests the title of a melodramatic nineteenth-century novel, or the caption to a sentimental painting. It suggests too what happens to the meaning as we try to figure the meaning out, wittily presenting us with a commentary on its own poetic technique. On a door "lost & found" is a label, a name which signifies a function. When the environment is changed to a page the signifier loses its signified, puzzling the reader. In 1977 Steve McCaffery suggested that this sort of recontextualization and similar activity "serves to return language elements to their primary meanings"—whatever those might be.[6] Language so treated is no longer instrumental. Nor is it communicative; it is, rather, language for its own sake. Such writing denies the personal (authorial) voice, presents a radical relocation of context, and repudiates readily accessible ideological frameworks which enable the words to "make sense."

Characteristic of a great deal of Language writing, "lost & found" is part of a sequence which, providing its own (shifting) framework as it progresses, gives a sharply political dimension to Andrews's detachment of the signifier from the signified. The polyvalency and polysemy at the heart of his work demand that the reader produce her or his own reading procedures and meanings, while at the same time invoking and thus holding up for inspection the larger social, political, and economic frame within which they operate and by which they are customarily defined. Andrews's poems walk a very fine line indeed, hovering on the edge of the expository in order to deny it, bordering unintelligibility in order to force meaning, and through the opacity of language enfranchising the physical body of the reader as a linguistic and especially in the later work as a social presence.

Like most of the first generation of Language writers—such as Bernstein, Harryman, McCaffery, Perelman, Silliman, Watten—Andrews was a teenager and then at college during the Vietnam War, a circumstance which points to the political element in his writing.[7] The ten turbulent years before the U.S. withdrawal from Vietnam in 1975 saw an increasing manipulation of language by politicians and by the military: the doublespeak in which the "pacification" of an area meant the slaughter of all its inhabitants.

Andrews was born in Chicago on 1 April 1948, spent three years (1965–68) as a social science major at Johns Hopkins University, and then earned his master's degree there after spending the summer of 1968 in Paris (he was there on 1 June). After a year out, he did his Ph.D. in political science at Harvard, in 1975 taking up an appointment which he still holds at Fordham University in the Bronx. Andrews began writing in 1969, and the poems I want to look at mostly come from his years as a graduate student at Harvard, where his studies "kept constantly in mind some general matters which are far from standard toolkit items for young poets—power & violence, prescriptions for law & order & deviance & reproduction within a landscape of institutions."[8] Andrews's graduate studies centered on imperial foreign policy—France in Indo China, and then (in Andrews's words) "the immediacies of U.S. anticommunist aggression in Vietnam during the years of its escalation, from 1965 on."[9] The period at Harvard and the years immediately after make an astonishingly productive apprenticeship: his four pamphlets published in 1973 seem to be the tip of an iceberg, since books published later were also written during those years.[10] The early work is notable for its exuberant wit and delight in language as well as for its resourcefulness in a kind of writing which arose, as Andrews put it, from "an enthusiastic response to 'avant garde' tendencies in other arts."[11] From the very beginning, Andrews's work constitutes a challenge to received or institutionalized means of adequating utterance and proposition, explaining and justifying meaning, discovering value. In its investigation of meaning it has from the very beginning a marked political and social dimension. The work gathered in *Getting Ready To Have Been Frightened* (1988) suggests something of the formal range and technical variety of Andrews's work, and clearly anticipates such more overtly political and assaultive work of the 80s as "I Guess Work the Time Up," collected in *Give Em Enough Rope* (1987).[12] The later work explores the ways in which every aspect of language is exteriorized, is framed socially and politically, and in which every relationship between reader and writer is circumscribed. All of Andrews's texts seek to demonstrate the nature of such circumscription by inviting the reader to participate as equal in the act of writing: "Explanation embeds itself in the writing itself."[13] The primary motive in the writing is transformative, though as Andrews's own pessimism about the outcome of his project increases, the invitation to the reader becomes increasingly confrontational. Some think it offensive, and refuse to read.

I

The sequence "Getting Ready To Have Been Frightened" is a fairly extensive re-ordering and reworking (with additional material) of a set of poems Andrews published in his first book, *Edge,* in 1973, where it was called "Getting Ready To Be Frightened," a title which survives in the poem in another transformation, punctuated, "Getting ready, to be frightened" (81). The title-change is worth noting. *Getting ready to have been frightened:* future perfect: preparing for the time when what has not yet happened has happened, and what has happened is an instant of time impossible to get ready for, or not needing preparation, for the fright is over. The title, with or without its variants, performs a terrible pun, by enacting a tense situation. It warns us that we're in a difficult if not impossible situation—pleasant? Unpleasant? Promising? Threatening?

"Getting Ready To Have Been Frightened" consists largely of odd little scraps of social language, virtually isolated on the page, surrounded by space, by visible and aural silence: "lost & found," for example, "with me," or "spooning out the bird"— their nonsensicalness opened up for delight and consideration. Each page consists of three short poems separated by a short rule, followed by up to seven lines of writing with justified margins (looking more or less like prose) marked off with a rule which runs the full width of the page. It is possible to read across the pages (recto to verso) instead of down each in turn, and it is not entirely clear that each short rule marks the end of one poem and the beginning of another. There's a lot of verbal play: visual

All I want
All I want
Hollywood
Hollywood

---

all over you

---

my daughter
every spurious minute

Night moves of unnatural science Wasp to wasp At all Divinely legitimate Whatever whichever it playoffs Anyhow, percussive to a fault Gives aerial oral over went done did ever you have Fealty That fealty Believers impresses doubts lightly, imposed noun own figurine atop back seat recedes

"Getting Ready to Have Been Frightened"

and aural puns, phonemic play, lexical transformation: "accept/except." It has something in common with joke- and puzzle-books, and like them actively resists the expository.

Removed as they seem to have been from any interpretive frame, these lines and phrases look and sound like public speech, colloquialisms, bits of popular songs, clichés from ordinary social speech or social one-upmanship, boasting to one's peers; scraps of language which once, in a context from which they seem to have been removed, were no doubt perfectly clear. They are samples of the sort of language we use instrumentally to gain some end, and they gesture toward a prior history. The opening poem on this page is clearly a *lie:* how could the fakery and glitz of Hollywood (if that is what

"Hollywood" means) possibly be all *anyone* wants? How can we possibly know *all* of what we want? The four lines gesture towards social comment because they do not take for granted the apparatus of reference; in the process they demonstrate that "social," as Andrews once remarked, "means unnatural, or constructed."[14] The humor is perhaps a shade sardonic. The one-liner immediately following echoes the language of popular songs that the first poem gestured towards: "all over you." Ruled off in the middle of the page as it is, this is downright funny, at least if you've got a mind like mine, which instantly thinks of puke even at the same time as it thinks of the sorts of speech (and song) situations in which this phrase occurs. What, after all, *can* be "all over you"—skin? air? roof? lover? Rendering the conventional language-situation absurd, the humor empties the signifier.[15]

Such decontextualization points to the essential inaccuracy and even literal meaninglessness of the colloquial, of common usage, and reminds us that there is no such thing as "literal" meaning. Such activity assaults, undoes, the suspension of disbelief endemic to institutionalized language (literary, legal, instrumental) and in the process reminds us that all language is an act of faith. It is context which makes the suspension of disbelief at all possible; that context is primarily social-political. Andrews's recontextualization of ordinary language offers a critique of both context and suspension of disbelief by suggesting that primary meaning (whatever it may be, if there is such a thing) is itself questionable and up for grabs, for (re-) definition.

In foregrounding the multivalency and polysemousness of words and phrases, these verbal scraps draw us to the non-semantic aspects of language. Undermining and challenging the semantic, they remind us (through the sheer exercise of sorting for possible meanings) of the necessity, in instrumental speech, to keep the terms clear ("pacification" is not an acceptable synonym for slaughter). These opening two poems offer an archaeology of the contemporary, an archaeology of language which reveals the metaphoric base of (all?) utterance: words can do no more than gesture, yet are *physical*. And like other archaeologies, these pages are layered into strata: a series of ruled lines which both separate and link the bits of language. The strata problematize the text, since they suggest or even encourage us to read across the two pages, top level then second level and so on, rather than in the conventional top-to-bottom mode. Such topological features—especially when extended and enlarged in *Film Noir* and in some of *Love Songs*—enjoin us to read improvisationally, and thus take responsibility ourselves for the meaning. In so far as they are *non*sensical, they gesture too toward the criteria and procedures by which we make sense, pointing to the *exteriority* of sense to the text, the exteriority of the signified to the signifier.[16]

But this writing is not simply done at random; there's an editorial and even a compositional process at work in these pages; choices are being made. As Andrews puts it, "self-governing is not free-floating."[17] "Hollywood" is equivalent to "all I want" not only in its more-or-less meaninglessness, but also quantitatively, durationally; the rhyme and time of those four lines manifest the poem as *body,* physical. So too does the *look* of the poem on the page, the three (syllables and) words of the opening lines squeezing down into the unbroken type of "Hollywood," a funnel. The poem works, however, not simply through repetitive patterning, but through the juxtaposition of two separate but nevertheless related echolalic phonemic clusters, the second of which (Hollywood) is a name, a Proper Noun. The next poem, "all over you" picks up on the "all/oll" of the first, but it is a different sort of poem for it is an isolated phrase. And the third poem on the page—"my daughter / every spurious minute"—uses a somewhat different technique which nevertheless draws on features of the opening two. Although it seems to revert to the juxtapositional pattern (seen in the line-breaks) of "all I want", the insertion of "spurious" offers a critique: what, after all, is being spurious here? The "minute"? The notion of "daughter"? Or the possessiveness expressed in "my"? Which is to say, "spurious" severely disqualifies the attitudes implicit in the sort of utterance the first line makes through a simple (?) act of substitution: we are more used to a context in which someone might say (equally falsely, surely) "My daughter, every wonderful minute." Is it worth remarking that this pair of lines *lacks* what "all I want" had, a proper noun, where we might expect one (the daughter's Name)? Whether or no, that word "spurious," as carefully placed as the hinge word in any short poem by William Carlos Williams, offers a critique of conventional familial pride and its social extensions; it shows us how tenuous is the base on which such pride rests, and how indeterminate the social functions of such utterance.

All this is to make heavy weather of what is after all pretty obvious (like the joke-book, the poem actively resists the expository). What needs emphasizing is that these clusters of words demand the reader's activity; the poems insist on the hermeneutic act whilst at the same time they withhold too much for that act to be satisfactorily completed. By calling into question the notion of completion in reading and in language they force us, through the sheer impossibility of attaining certainty of meaning, to locate meaning in the very act of reading itself, in the play between possible signification and concrete referentiality. They deny, then, conventional or institutionalized habits which locate the more or less visible world of meaning as exterior to the text, attainable through a decoding exercise based on a communicative model of discourse and poetry. "Context," observes Andrews, "robs words of their contingencies and encourages them to operate as transparencies."[18]

This opacity of Andrews's language is emphasized by the physical layout of the page. What exactly is it that we are looking at on these opening pages? Is this eight poems? Six? An inter-connected sequence? A single work? It's hard to sort out. Do the ruled lines divide a two-page spread into three (four?) paired poems? The sheer visual appearance is ambiguous because it conforms to no convention that we can recognize, though the long rule clearly separates off (rules out?) the foot of each page from what goes on above. But what is this stuff at the bottom of each page: Leftovers? Detritus from the processes of composition seen on the page above? Alternative or abandoned materials of the sort we have more or less got used to from reading the poems of Emily Dickinson? Footnotes? They are hardly commentary, not even in the sense that Williams's explanations in *Kora in Hell* are commentary. They look like a sediment precipitated from words held in solution higher up the page. Visually dense, physically more obtrusive (something of the look of a precipitate), syntactically complex and semantically more textured (is "divinely legitimate" descriptive or imperative?), the bottom lines of each page layer the text (like footnotes), though their plenitude of syntactic forms and instabilities provide visual solidity and hence stability to each page. They laminate the words on the page *and* their effects. They are colloidal, another poem radically different perhaps from what is above, but certainly not like the similarly layered writing in McCaffery's *Panopticon.*[19] They remind us of the sheer physical (non-lexical) qualities of the words, and at the same time actively encourage topological (and therefore improvisational) reading.

II

Topological readings take a variety of structures. The uppercase letters of *Love Songs* "No 73" for instance are so arranged that we are strongly tempted to complete them into the two words, "little flag." Neither is spelled out on the page as a word, however; indeed there seems to be no consistent rule by which those words can "properly" be deduced. The poem itself is difficult to describe: it may or may not consist of twenty lines; we may or may not read the text horizontally. Since some of the "lines" slope uphill, we are in fact tempted to read the letters in non-lexical clusters as well as in words, and to see words where "in fact" there are none.

That "in fact," invoking as it does a set of criteria and habits external to the text, is extremely problematic. The practice of gesturing toward what lies

NO 73

I T L

L G

I T

F A

L A

L I T L

F L G

L T E

I T L

L A G

L I T E

F L G

F L A

I T L E

L I T

F A G

L T E

I T L

Love Songs "No 73"

outside the text and at the same time making its appropriation manifestly impossible takes a variety of topological forms, each following (and initiating) a careful strategy demanding as much of the reader as of the writer. As Steve McCaffery observes, "with reader writing writer listens."[20] The ways in which a writer might listen to a reader can be glimpsed in the sequencing of words and the topological structure of a passage in *Film Noir,* where distinct clusters of words (not, then, to be read horizontally) unevenly mingle with other groups which seem to drift and curve across and down the page, wavering to uneasy rest in a group of five words scattered in large type across the foot of the page.[21]

Reading (and no doubt the writing) is improvisatory. The first four words on the page, an arc in the top left corner, are "taunts oral hustle cradle"—potentially a narrative reminiscent of Gertrude Stein's one-liner "A Petticoat": "A white light, a disgrace, an ink spot, a rosy charm."[22] Those four words are followed, next line right margin, by "Druid?" in large and small caps. Is this, then, a new age incantation? An echo of Doughty's epic *The Dawn in Britain*? As a query "Druid?" radically transforms and dismantles whatever narrative scaffolding we might have thought there was. This semantic and modal shift is echoed by the visual fluidity of the page as a whole, a fluidity tentatively stabilized by the upper-case words at its foot. But the predominant impression is of space, of white paper, of gaps, uncertainty, and incompletion.

In sequence, these words don't look very much like a sentence, though "hustle" could (like "cradle") be a verb in this rather weird syntax, and one sorts for possible relationships. The layout discourages a semantic and/or lexical reading and invites us to read graphically rather than literately: the *look* of the page is important. But these are, after all, words, and if we read them aloud they begin (one might say) to make sound sense. There's a play of eye and ear: the *au* of *taunts* is the same (vowel-) sound as the *o* of *oral;* the *al* of *oral* (drifting to schwa, long drifting to short) is the same (vowel-) sound as the *le* of *hustle,* which word exhibits in *its* two syllables the same drift to schwa, long drifting to short, that was in *oral.* So we look for and perhaps have found a pattern—which is repeated in *cradle,* though there is noticeable consonantal shift from *stle* to *dle* (recalling that *d* is voiced *t*). One might also notice that three of the four words so far discussed are six letters long—and the *next* word, *Druid?,* is lengthened to six by the added query.

But how did *Druid* arise? *L* and *r* are liquids (and in some languages, such as Cantonese and Mandarin, aren't differentiated): the sequence *cradle* to *Druid* is a variation of the sequence so far, in that the final syllable has become initial. One might also notice, however, that the *r-d / l-d* sequence is

TAUNTS

ORAL

HUSTLE

CRADLE

DRUID?

HINGES

RIDE

LAVA

XEROX

BADGES

TATTLE

SHILL

FEEBLE

MY PICKININNY

NATIONAL

TOXIC

EAR-DRUMS

LULL

TINT ECLAIR

PRAT

SPIRE

MUCUS

HOLOGRAPH

INDIGENT

PURE

HAY

Film Noir

preserved in consonantal order, in a manner reminiscent (especially if this sort of thing continues) of Welsh *cynganned*d. The drift to schwa is less pronounced, but the long-short shift is preserved (albeit in the space of a diphthong). Perhaps the next variation will be from this sort of diphthong to one in a monosyllabic word.

But no. The next word is *hinges*. So the pattern is basically two-syllable words, long-short? And damn! the next word is *ride*, lined up with *hinges* (thus making with that word a kind of hinge?), its single syllable satisfying the earlier guess while maintaining consonance/consonants, and quantitatively approximating *hinges*. This is not, indeed, a predictable pattern. *Lava* moves us back to two syllables, but (like *ride*) is only four letters. And the next word *Xerox*, patterning *druid* but unpunctuated, is Greek for dry, so it has a semantic/lexical/associational connection to *lava* as well as to the *dr(y)* of *druid*. Patterns of repetition and variation, transforms and breaks. In 1973 Andrews talked about referential meaning as "the part that draws the reader away from the words themselves";[23] rules have a similar effect, which is why as soon as we think we've got a handle on the rules/procedures, they change. Zukofsky plays that game a lot.

That bit of *Film Noir*, like *Love Songs* "No 73," operates on the tension between absence and presence, desire and accomplishment, by tempting us to find "completion" outside the text, in our own reading habits. It thus invokes the *reader as context* for the utterance, and in part forces us to create or recreate *our own* intentions in the act of reading. In Andrews's words, it moves "towards an active contextualizing of Production, in the Other, in *you*."[24] But "Love Song No 29,"[25] which ends with an apparently random sprinkling of grouped letters on the page (moving away from the more-or-less-coherent recognizable words of its opening), does much the same thing by quite different means. We tend to cluster these more or less unpronounceable groups of letters in curves. The eye makes choices before the mind starts sorting or even discerning possible meanings: with the eye coming to rest twice on *mms* for instance, the choices include repeats and thus encourage a simultaneity of multiple readings. It is impossible to read this text linearly if only because we cannot assign any hierarchical order of any sort to this writing: each bit seems sovereign, yet has no claim over any other bit in its group. Hence, though it sporadically gestures toward the semantic, the text actively discourages the reader from assigning lexical meanings. In 1973, the year he wrote this poem, Andrews wrote that "Most of my stuff is based on fragmentation and the qualities of words other than (along with) their meaning. The words aren't related at the center but by their edges (connotation, etc)—like the interrelated pieces of a non-representational ceramic sculpture."[26] This par-

vy
pn

oea

ao

isy
bx

oonern

et

hoa
mino
mms

rbn
fl
yf

oc

The close of *Love Songs* "No 29"

ticular text almost completely disempowers conventional reading capacity, interpretation, and skill, yet it has semantic residue: there are, tantalizingly, ghosts of words, of language; none of the singular bits on the page is singular in its possible meaning. What is dominant in this passage is the feeling of absence: *absence made present,* therefore. This is a curious enactment reminiscent of that in "All I want," where the ghost of an ideological framework by means of which we make sense could not be eliminated.

What these poems disempower is control, both readerly and authorial. No interpretive frame, no overarching ideological shelter, can be enlisted to provide us with a meaning. But the work is not merely fragmentary; what we experience is language in its opacity, and what we discover is that to look for lexical association is to retreat from the text, from the language, into someplace other. It is not that there is no meaning, but there is too much, and it is beyond our control. The close of "Love Song No 29" demonstrates what Andrews called for in an essay on Barthes: "the yearning singularity of the phonemes bursting off the page, tape, or lips." It calls forth the *reader's* desire, and it is thus empowering as well as disempowering: "reading becomes the

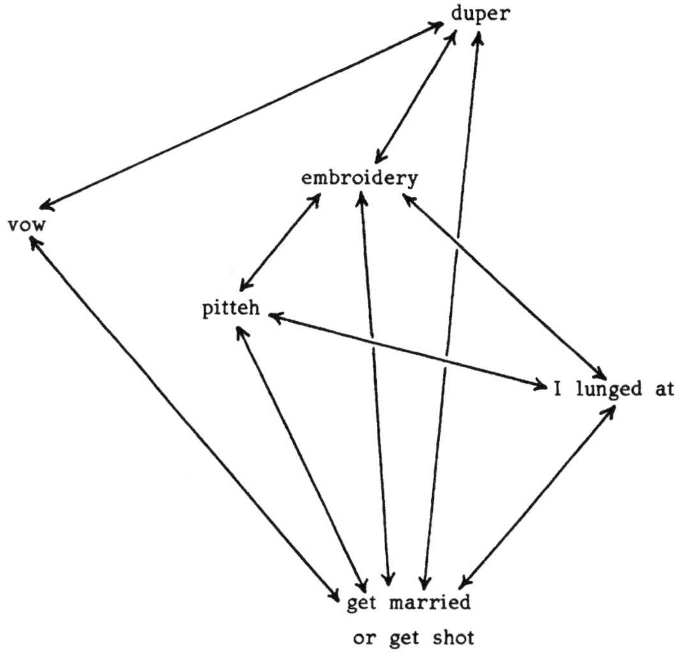

Love Songs "No 63"

first *production,* rather than consumption—not a relay of an author's vain transcriptions of a representational content."[27] Forcing the reader's improvisation, it moves to the limits of meaning.

Such an abandonment of intelligibility is also an abandonment in any meaningful sense of the poetic line, a convention assaulted and exploited in *Love Songs* "No 63", which combines the topological poem with the linear to set up a field of possibility. Double-ended arrows link (and separate) the words and phrases of the poem, which on its facing pages looks like a pair of geometric figures. Like other poems in *Love Songs,* it is a performance piece, though it can equally be read as a written work. Andrews explains in his note to the poem: "As a written work, the connected words & phrases are simply parts of a pattern which expresses the entire spectrum between & including the two words along a variety of axes (signification, sound texture, etc.). As a score, the connections are cues for performers to have at their disposal any word, gesture, phoneme or sound suggested on these spectrums. Simultaneous action or tape for two performers. . . . Spectrums which are not notated by arrowed lines between words can also be used, . . . for example 'dungeon' [a word not printed on the page] between 'duper' & 'I lunged at.' " Elsewhere in *Love Songs* Andrews describes "the entire spectrum" as "grammatical relations, texture, denotation, sound, association, etc.," and talks of a poem's "field of possibility" in terms of "order, pitch, pacing, volume, etc."[28]

Love Songs "No. 63" does two things. First, it points the reader to what Lyn Hejinian calls "a hopefully uninhibited extension of any of several possible language-thought operations."[29] Second, it severely disrupts the ways in which lines regulate or control meaning by parodying the poetic line graphically: where traditionally poetry suppresses the multiplicity of connections between words, these lines enhance them, and by emphasizing the graphic qualities of writing they emphasize the sheer physicality of words—what Julia Kristeva calls the *genotexte*.[30] "I don't try to give up the *feel* of words," Andrews wrote in *Edge*, "or treat them as just clumps of sound. The *individual* words have meanings and possible associations. It's just that these meanings and connotations aren't yoked together and aimed *outside the poem* at a single externally applied meaning for a poem as a whole (a tightly knit network of references). The way words fit into a sentence (or a line of thought) doesn't grab me as much as how they relate to the space and silence around them. I like the edges, discreteness, fragments, collision."[31] Those double-ended arrows make the reading and writing both endless and goalless. No set of Coles Notes is going to help us through this writing, which actively resists making the reader feel comfortable; it refuses to comfort the reader. If you stack *Love Songs* up against the great Western tradition of love poetry it reads as an assault on the Liberal Arts.

III

That assault is not, however, simply upon comfort, or upon the sense of direction and identity which the liberal arts tradition institutionally claims to afford. As an assault on conventional poetic technique Andrews's poem seeks to renew the physical and experiential grounds on which the great traditional themes are founded, by disqualifying not only the means of making sense but the very notion of sense as exterior to the experience. "Texts," Andrews wrote in 1977, "are themselves *signifieds,* not mere signifiers. TEXT . . . requires no hermeneusis for it is itself one—of itself."[32] The array of Andrews's technical resource is formidable, and the work draws upon the (literary) tradition it seeks to undo: the reader who is unaware of or has not thought about the function of the line in poetry, for instance, is unlikely to spot what's going on in the poems I've discussed, and the poems all emphatically declare that they are to be read as poems—that is, as made things which themselves make the reader make.

In the writing, choices which produce effects (plural) are carefully being made. It is part of the design of an Andrews poem that it have what Steve McCaffery neatly calls "permanent centralities of gap";[33] we should not be able to reconstruct the series of choices made because the more successful we are at making such a reconstruction the less successful will the poem be. The poem, as we read it, renders whatever interpretive strategy we adopt useless, forcing us to abandon any attempt to integrate what we read into a larger whole—we abandon, that is to say, any attempt to "make sense" of it all.

Vowels (1976) exploits a series of semantic and syntactic strategies specifically designed to be self-defeating, in order that the work be its own hermeneusis. Demanding of the reader a variety of reading-strategies familiar to the tradition in which Shakespeare's works were edited, this sequence of 22 poems demonstrates through practice the ways in which such strategies—and the canonical assumptions underlying them—constitute a misreading of text and a retreat from the actualities of language. The reader is thus led to reject institutionalized notions of the definitive, and exteriorized definitions of the real. Here is the opening poem:

> avoid doing extra when you have. it will
> swell up. have all of it faltered to see it
> changing. changing. changing your mind later
> the sooner or better will make it exact, exacting.
> so consider how graceful, carefully, all the ones
> how many you do and how you would possibly want them.
> giddily. once is the worst. you prosper.[34]

This is modal play: the whole design of the opening sentence emphasizes the imperative; the second is indicative, with a marked exuberant as well as predictive tone; the imperative of the third modulates into a descriptive participial sentence fragment which in turn modulates (changing changing changing) into a declarative and then imperative sentence. Meaning is thus seen here as modal rather than as referential, and the poem as an assault on referentiality.

Yet there is, especially in the opening sentence, an implicit invitation to put together a paraphrasable meaning. The syntactic-modal combination strongly encourages us to read the sentences as making sense only to discover that they do not, because they are either tautological or downright self-contradictory. Andrews, that is to say, manipulates us into unacceptable (nonsensical) interpretations. The "have" at the end of the first sentence is extremely problematic, and enjoins a re-reading. If we read it as an auxiliary (thereby understanding *when you have done so*) the sentence is virtually nonsensical, since there is nothing to avoid when you have avoided already. This reading, which the adverbial *when* strongly encourages (by signing time, and thus inviting us to read *have* as an expression of verb-tense), emphasizes the sentence's ungrammatical quality. Such ungrammaticalness invites us (if we do not reject the sentence out of hand) to read it grammatically—or rather, to heed the grammatical play. Viewed lexically/semantically, and as expressing an imperative, the sentence offers the reader three by no means mutually exclusive reading strategies, each of which involves a play of transitive against intransitive readings of the verbs, and each (but especially the first two) has a long and respectable history in the scholarly editing of texts.

1. Interpolation/"restoration": This "straightens out" the grammar:

> [You [one][&c.] must] avoid doing extra [things][work][&c.] when you have [to][no need to][done enough][&c.].

On first reading, "avoid doing extra" tends to read *extra* as an adjective, simply because the imperative *avoid* invited us to read *doing* transitively, leading us thereby to expect a noun. The adjectival *extra* immediately encourages us to expect a noun-phrase to follow, but instead we get an adverbial clause *when you have*—which we can either reject (hence the interpolation), or transform into a noun-clause to which it is unfortunately extremely difficult to assign intelligible meaning (à la Gertrude Stein). What, after all, could an *extra when-you-have* be? Having thus read "doing" transitively, providing "[things]" or the like to satisfy the syntax the adjectival *extra* demands, we have so limited the possibilities the sentence offers that we are obliged similarly to read *have* transitively, providing *[to]* or the like. The addition of *[to]* converts *have* to *must,* making the sentence nonsensical. One immediate recourse is then to read the whole poem that way, and dismiss it.

Alternatively, *extra* might lead us to expect an adverbial construction rather than a noun-phrase, as in *avoid doing extra well,* which might then lead either to a further adverbial construction modifying *have,* providing *[already finished],* or to a participial phrase *[passed the course]* or the like. The adverbial construction *doing extra well* is interesting in that as a colloquialism it gestures toward the intransitive aspect of *doing* (see strategy 3, below), though the sentence might then more conventionally and grammatically have read *avoid extra doing,* transforming *doing* into a noun-gerund. This yields, as "translated" meaning:

> avoid extra doing when you have [X]—done enough?

but the sheer idiomatic awkwardness to the ear of "avoid extra doing"—adverb before participle—strongly (to my mind, completely) discourages this reading.

A major difficulty with such a strategy arises with the next sentence, for if we read

> You must avoid doing extra work when you have no need to

then although we get the perfectly acceptable *It will / swell—it* being *work*—we also get the problematic *it will swell UP,* which problematizes the text all over again—a process compounded by the remainder of line 2:

> have all of it faltered to see it.

We are then left with the prospect of recognizing that (at the very least) this poem plays with pronoun antecedence, and we begin to approach strategy 3 below. Alternatively, we dismiss the whole work as "meaningless," because we cannot summarize or encapsulate the meaning in an alternative form subsumed under the formula "this is what the poem says." Interpolation, that is to say, is inadequate as a reading strategy because it attempts to take control of the work, not to take pleasure in it, and fails.[35] Interpolation/"restoration" is thus a self-defeating strategy whose very self-defeating processes reveal to the reader the poem's assault on the kind of meaning the processes themselves attempt to elicit.

2. *Substitution:* usually but not necessarily of an intransitive for a transitive verb at the end.

> avoid doing extra when you can [or want, &c.].

This invokes the colloquialism *doing extra* without any difficulty, but has the severe disadvantage of rewriting the text without first paying attention to what the "actual words" of the text are. It suffers from the same shortcomings as strategy 1.

3. "*Constitutive*": This is "to explain—by doing—how sense makes sense."[36]

> avoid doing extra when you have.

Reflection, or reference to a good dictionary, reminds us that *have* also means possess or own, and like *doing* is not exclusively transitive: each has an intransitive mode. *Doing* intransitively means acting, conducting oneself, arranging or managing (how shall we do for food?), succeeding (doing well or ill), and so on (as well as How do you do?); *have* intransitively means to complete (as in *to have done*, a meaning which conspicuously signs tense); there is also the Elizabethan "Have with you." Reflection also reminds us that *extra* can be used as a noun as well as adjective and adverb—the Mock Turtle quizzes Alice about "doing extras" in *Alice in Wonderland* (Chapter 9). *Doing extra* is a common colloquialism, and a variety of possible readings of the first sentence emerges, including the implied *done enough.*

The point I'm trying to make is that we have to *resist* the sentence's encouragement to read *extra* as adjective—this writing is crammed with blandishments to be resisted—and the second sentence encourages that resistance, for the *it* can then refer to

a) *doing extra* or to
b) *avoiding doing extra*

Each of these possibilities might be said to swell up, especially if one *has* (i.e., owns, did, avoided, managed) and the meanings proliferate (*swell up* means "bloat"?)—or rather, the ways in which we make meanings proliferate, and we perhaps engage in a more-or-less-desperate faltering process to keep track (paradoxically) of *all* of it. The faltering is a species of altering, and the third line's repetition of *changing* serves not only as a commentary on what we are doing reading these words but also suggests to us that there is more than one way in which meaning is to be generated here—the rules, that is to say (if there were any) have changed. Certainly we cannot summarize paraphrase or translate. The meaning of the passage is the activity of coming to meaning, of the reader making it mean, discovering possible meanings, noticing relationships. Non-lexical and non-semantic elements contribute: the vowel-consonantal echoes in *faltered* and *all of it,* perhaps the mild quarrel between the eye and ear in the *oi* of *avoid* and *doing,* and even the complex play of line breaks (the enjambment progressively spilling further and further over into the next line), encourage us to notice generative and filtration/alteration procedures in the writing—as does the quite remarkable play on *w,* declared in *doing,* and the vowel-sequence *ill ell all.* In this poem which draws on a variety of traditional prosodic techniques, the words take on a strong *physical* presence.

The pleasure arising from the text is that of seeing *having* as a form of *doing* (and vice versa), of seeing *avoid* as a kind of *doing* (and vice versa), and so on. To read the poem thus is to read the internal movements and their transformations in the writing, and to delight in them. The great weaknesses of interpolation and substitution as reading strategies is that this sort of pleasure is not available to them, and their sheer inadequacy reading *Vowels* forces a constitutive reading, as a result of which not only this text but *all* texts are seen, finally, as indeterminate. Interpolation and substitution seek to make sense within the confines of a larger social, political, ideological system; they gesture toward and appeal to a realm outside the text and find their authentication not in the language but in the social/political world; as Andrews puts it, they seek to make sense through "framing the privacies of language against some larger organization of signifieds—or the conditions by which those signifieds get organized." It is a "social method."[37] They seek to make sense through pointing toward "a destination," in McCaffery's words, "outside of the graphic, phenomenal immediacy of the physical text presented."[38] Pre-*sent*ed. *Pres*ented. The poem manifests and indeed enacts a world in which, in Andrews's words, there is "nothing to save, invest, accumulate, secure or amortize. not knowing where it comes from or where it's going. to no longer subordinate this present to some future project or classically meaningful *telos,* nor to assimilate value to itself by assimilating the Past, delayed into monuments, to the Present."[39] Later in the same essay he calls for "an intoxicated futurism (as presentism)" which, working through ludic play and flatly denying interpretation, refuses "to integrate into larger wholes which are machines of control." It is an intransitive world, then, a world of gratuitous act, act without use.[40]

IV

Overwhelming in its insistence on "presentations of the present, not representations of tense,"[41] brutal in its consonantal plosiveness and abrupt imperative phrasing, Andrews's overtly political, confrontational, and in some eyes thoroughly offensive work of the 1980s carefully and deliberately exploits the techniques he developed and refined in the apprentice years of the early 1970s. A harsh and indeed terrifying critique of institutionalized language, thought and practice, a poem like "I Guess Work the Time Up" savages the instrumentality of a hierarchic control which exploits (in Sally Silvers's words) the body as "public and formed by social relations."[42] A savage diagnosis and enactment of alienation, the poem is a bludgeon which nevertheless celebrates the intransitive and the inutile, the body and the mind, and views the victims of murdered (dissociated) language with a sharp sense of loss.

"I Guess Work the Time Up" resembles what one of its lines calls "a kind of teenage trash compacter." The title puns catchphrases and idioms: guesswork; getting worked up emotionally; working something up to gain mastery over it; time's up; work-time (versus play time); and so on. Thus presenting in miniature the complexities and shifts running word by word and phrase by phrase through the poem, the title relies on found language, public and private speech intermingled; control and the loss of control—a series of activities neatly embodied in the abrupt and grim opening split: "Apart / meant."

"I Guess Work the Time Up" is a very frightening poem, filled as it is with the detritus of social, political, and commercial language: State Department papers, newspaper advertisements, hard rock and rap records, book reviews, political economy. This "semiotic rubble" salvaged from one sign-system after another (the observation is Barrett Watten's),[43] the language of use and of ideological manipulation, is the language of control, for it is the language of definition and of promise. "*These* thighs promist install a bathroom" ("all I want / all I want"). A found language of consumer gluttony and appetite and disappointment and multimedia confusion which in creating desires thwarts them in what Charles Bernstein has called "the congealed / syntax of forced instrumentation."[44] It is above all the language of absence, and hence the language of control is also the language of desire. It promises liberation and play but it enthralls and limits, by declaring the boundaries of legitimized content and consent. Hence the poem, recontextualizing this language, reveals the essential inaccuracy and the literal meaninglessness of the institutionalized cliché—the cliché of advertising, of government, of conduct, the cliché which defines and indeed appropriates desire by laying out an illusion of presence in a world which prizes use above felicity.[45] The poem, with its blockages, its non-sequiturs, its very turbulence of sound and syntax matched by the horrific self-contradictions and denials its propositions make, is itself felicitous. The uneasy pleasure it affords demonstrates, as no expository writing could, how the users of this language are also its victims, precisely because language is what they USE: "Use value is an abstraction. It is an abstraction of the *system of needs* cloaked in the false evidence of a concrete destination and purpose, an intrinsic finality of goods and products. It is just like the abstraction of social labor, which is the basis for the logic of equivalence (exchange value), hiding beneath the 'innate' value of commodities."[46] Language entraps its user.

"Words divide, lines unite."[47] The phrases of the poem are held in tension; the lines draw them together, their sense forces them apart. With its astonishing play of consonants, with its choreographed phrases and fragments which resist linear "sense" (a term which implies linked connectedness not, perhaps, unlike that announced by the arrowed lines of *Love Songs* "No. 63"), the poem is utterly untranslatable but instantly recognizable. The intense play of coherence against incoherence, of the linear against the non-linear, of the "out there" as speech against the "in here" of the reader. All this contributes to an opacity of the text which is immediate in its sheer physicality and untranslatability; the language of absence is here made present, directly to be experienced, and the overall effect is of the world gesturing toward the poem, rather than the poem toward the world. The world is in the work, says Barrett Watten, or it is nowhere. But work here is verb, not noun; it is reading, and it is play; writing works to un-control itself and so to discontrol meaning.

The poem, then, empowers the voicing of desire—whether direct or blocked. Voicing the physical and the present in order to demonstrate the sheer inadequacy of desire as socially and institutionally defined, the poem founds desire in the body, bypassing the socially constructed self in favor of the uncontrollable, irrational, apparently arbitrary physicality of the reader's own voice, eye, breath, necessarily bludgeoning a way through the illusion which, founded on absence, determines and rules. "Language as discourse & ideology . . . gives us . . . fakery, . . . makes us already non-sovereign. subjects are fixed by name, by image, by idea in such a suprapersonal system, such interpellation by a social body."[48] By confounding the act of writing with the act of reading, the poem forces the reader to produce meaning. And in doing this, it locates Andrews quite squarely within a long tradition: Wordsworth spoke in "Tintern Abbey" of a world that we half perceive and half create; Whitman in *Specimen Days* of leaving the reader to do his or her part. Andrews has said that "meaning is constituting itself only in relationship to other meanings, and the text is not producing meanings from scratch. It's only working—through readers—on other texts, on other kinds of constructions, other kinds of operating arrangements. And it is *transformative.* It has this social material that it's working with. And that material . . . regulates this giddy flux of signifiers."[49] Hence, constitutive reading makes all texts indeterminate. The resulting compositional problem is acute, for the writing *must* give the reader control of meaning in the sense that it gives the reader choices over which the writer has relinquished control. To do less is to view the reader instrumentally, and to invite the reader so to view the writer. The expository is indeed horrendous. "Writing must look toward a radically transformed society that would provide the code (and the ideal communications system, and counter-communication system) needed to fully comprehend it. *Utopia.* Take nothing for granted, leave nothing intact, move outside, heterogenize, wake up the patient from stupefaction, desocialize the ego (so that eventually we might be resocialized)."[50] Charles Bernstein has said that it is possible to read anything poetically; in an early draft of "Hegel's Eyes" Steve McCaffery has performed a tour-de-force poetic reading of the Toronto telephone book.[51] A corollary, of course, is that it is just as possible to read anything *non*-poetically, looking for the meaning which can be neatly encapsulated and passed on as a form of wisdom (another mechanism of control)—or, finding none, to dismiss what is read as sheer gobbledygook. It is essential: these poems must *not* make sense. The difficulty and absurdity of that sentence is itself a measure of our social and communal need. Andrews's poet has a redemptive function, to transform the reader into the poet, making the office of poet supererogatory. Utopia. Where to read is to write, and everyone reads poetically.

Notes

Epigraph. P. G. Wodehouse, "Indian Summer of an Uncle," *Very Good, Jeeves!* (Harmondsworth: Penguin Books, 1959) 207.

1. Steve McCaffery, *The Black Debt* (Toronto: Nightwood, 1989), 102; Ludwig Wittgenstein, *Philosophical Remarks* (New York: Harper & Row, 1975), 9.

2. Steve McCaffery, "Gnote," *Hot Bird Mfg* 1.7 (January 1991). *Hot Bird Mfg* is edited in New York by Ray DiPalma.

3. Bruce Andrews, "Be Careful Now," *Paradise & Method: Poetics & Praxis* (Evanston: Northwestern UP, 1996) 127.

4. Bruce Andrews with Marjorie Perloff, "Interview Project Interview," *Paradise & Method* 75.

5. *Getting Ready To Have Been Frightened* (New York: Roof, 1988) 76. The poem first appeared in the sequence "Getting Ready to Be Frightened," *Edge* (Washington, D.C.: Some of Us Press, 1973) 6–11; revised and enlarged as "Getting Ready To Have Been Frightened," *Roof* 8 (Winter 1978): n.p.; collected in *Getting Ready To Have Been Frightened,* which reprints "Vowels," "Film Noir," "Praxis," "Getting Ready To Have Been Frightened," and "Plex." Reference to these poems appears parenthetically in my text.

6. Steve McCaffery, "The Death of the Subject: The Implications of Counter-Communication in Recent Language-Centered Writing," *Open Letter* 3rd series, 7 (Summer 1977): 73.

7. The two most conspicuous exceptions, Ray DiPalma and Lyn Hejinian, were born in 1943 and 1941 respectively.

8. Andrews with Perloff, "Interview" 78.

9. Andrews with Perloff, "Interview" 79.

10. Most of the early work has been collected in *Wobbling* (New York: Roof, 1981), *Getting Ready To Have Been Frightened* (1988), and *Executive Summary* (Elmwood: Potes & Poets, 1991). Books written during Andrews's student years are *Edge* (1973); *A Capella* (East Lansing, MI: *Ghostdance* 17, 1973); *Appalachia* (Pellet Press, 1973) n.p.; *Corona* (Providence: Burning Deck, 1973); *Vowels* (New York: O Press, 1976); *Film Noir* (Providence: Burning Deck, 1978) and *Love Songs* (Baltimore: Pod, 1982). *Praxis* (Berkeley: Tuumba, 1978) was written in 1976.

11. Andrews with Perloff 78.

12. Andrews, "I Guess Work the Time Up," *Give Em Enough Rope* (Los Angeles: Sun & Moon, 1987) 7–31.

13. Andrews, "Poetry as Explanation, Poetry as Praxis," *The Politics of Poetic Form: Poetry and Public Policy,* Charles Bernstein, ed. (New York: Roof, 1990) 24.

14. Andrews, "Total Equals What: Poetics and Praxis," *Paradise & Method* 41.

15. Bob Perelman attempts similar effects, but by different means: for example "the sea / is all under / the water" ("Oceanography," *In The American Tree,* Ron Silliman, ed. Orono, ME: National Poetry Foundation, 1986, 74) utters what is semantically false (if all the sea is under the water, then it has no surface; if the sea is all there is under the water, then either there are no fish, plants, and so forth, or the sea is its own bed).

16. Sense is the legitimation of utterance, as Wordsworth well knew; sending Charles James Fox the 1801 *Lyrical Ballads* to demonstrate the evils of enclosures and of industrial manufacture was a risky act, since the language of the *Lyrical Ballads* was itself an assault on the hegemonic modes of meaning it sought to undo.

17. Andrews, "Lines Linear How to Mean," *The Line in Postmodern Poetry,* Robert Frank and Henry Sayre, eds. (Urbana: U of Illinois P, 1988) 178.

18. Andrews with Perloff, "Interview" 80.

19. Steve McCaffery, *Panopticon* (Toronto: Blewointmentpress, 1984).

20. McCaffery, *Black Debt* 71.

21. Andrews, "Film Noir," *Getting Ready* 36. With its splendid typographic design by Rosmarie Waldrop of Burning Deck, *Film Noir* shows every evidence of having been written with the (printed) page as compositional unit. This gives rise at times to an unevenness of effect which may or may not be deliberate.

22. Gertrude Stein, "Tender Buttons," *The Selected Writings of Gertrude Stein,* Carl Van Vechten, ed. (New York: Modern Library, 1946) 471.

23. Andrews, "Dear . . .", *Edge* 12. My thanks to Steve McCaffery for the gift.

24. "Be Careful Now" 128 (Andrews's italics).

25. The organization of *Love Songs* is seemingly arbitrary and the titles, which are all by number, vary: the book opens with "Love Song No 163"; "Song No 163" is near the end. The overall structure, that is to say, defies conventional titling and sequence.

26. Andrews, "Dear . . ." 12.

27. Andrews, "Code Words," *Paradise & Method* 191

28. Andrews, Notes to *Love Songs* No 93 and to No 114.

29. Lyn Hejinian, "Hard Hearts." *Poetics Journal* 2 (September 1982): 44.

30. The graphic pun here is an extension—though for quite different ends—of the pun in Mallarmé's "*Las de l'amer repos ou me paresse offense,*" where he uses a *line* of verse to figure a line of blue figuring a lake, painted on a vase, bounding the bare porcelain:

> Une ligne d'azur mince et pale serait
> Un lac, parmi le ciel de porcelaine nue.

Stéphane Mallarmé, *The Poems,* trans. K. Bosley (Harmondsworth: Penguin, 1977) 80. (I'm grateful to Harry Gilonis for suggesting this comparison.)

31. "Dear . . ." 12 (Andrews's italics).

32. Andrews, "Text and Context" *Paradise & Method* 10–11.

33. McCaffery, *Black Debt* 70.

34. Andrews, *Getting Ready* 6.

35. My thanks to Meredith Quartermain for this formulation.

36. Andrews, "Be Careful Now" 125. "Constitutive" is Andrews's term for this strategy ("Text and Context," 9), which McCaffery calls "decipherment." It stands in marked contrast to the first two, which McCaffery calls "augment" and "complete" ("The Death of the Subject" 64.) Augmentation and completion attempt to view language instrumentally. Andrews's essay first appeared along with McCaffery's in *Open Letter* 3rd series, 7 (Summer 1977).

37. Andrews, "Total Equals What" 42.

38. McCaffery, "The Death of the Subject" 65.

39. Andrews, "Be Careful Now" 126.

40. Andrews's insistence on an intransitive world matched by an intransitive text which "breaks down" into language is, despite severe differences, strongly reminiscent of David Jones's notion of the poem and of art as the gratuitous and intransitive act. Jones quite fully explains and explores this notion in the preface to *The Anathemata* (1951), and especially in "Art and Sacrament" (1955)—at the end of which Jones invites the reader to consider "what was done on Maundy Thursday by Good Friday's victim . . . : 'He placed himself in the order of signs' " (*Epoch and Artist: Selected Writings*, Harman Grisewood, ed. [London: Faber, 1959] 179).

41. Andrews, "Text and Context" 10.

42. Sally Silvers, "Lack of Entrepreneurial Thrift," *O.ars* (1986): 203.

43. Barrett Watten, "The World in the Work: Toward a Psychology of Form," *Total Syntax* (Carbondale: Southern Illinois UP, 1985) 159–160.

44. Charles Bernstein, "Part Quake," *Islets/Irritations* (New York: Jordan Davies, 1983) 99.

45. I adopt "felicity" from the usage in Marilyn French, *Beyond Power: On Women, Man and Morals* (New York: Simon and Schuster, 1985).

46. Jean Baudrillard, *For a Critique of the Political Economy of the Sign*, trans. Charles Levin (St. Louis: Telos, 1981) 131.

47. Andrews, "Lines Linear" 177.

48. Andrews, "Be Careful Now" 131.

49. Andrews, "Total Equals What" 36.

50. Andrews, "Code Words" 192 (Andrews's italics).

51. Charles Bernstein, "Artifice of Absorption," *A Poetics* (Cambridge: Harvard UP, 1992) 9; Steve McCaffery, "Hegel's Eyes" performed at the New Poetics Colloquium, Vancouver, August 1985 (a work not be confused with the poem "Hegel's Eyes" published in McCaffery's *Theory of Sediment* (Vancouver: Talonbooks, 1991) 9-46.

Paradise as Praxis

Bruce Andrews's *Lip Service*

> She had once accused [her husband, Guy Pringle,] of considering her feelings less than those of anyone else with whom they came into contact. Surprised, he had said: "But you are myself. I don't need to consider your feelings."
>
> —Olivia Manning

> If there is to be a "we," it is not one tyrannized into supposed consensus but one founded on interaction.
>
> —Robert Sheppard

In what follows I draw quite extensively on two essays by Andrews: the title essay of *Paradise & Method,* in which he discusses the compositional principles and procedures of his nearly 400-page poem *Lip Service,* and his major but largely neglected essay on sexuality in writing, "Be Careful Now You Know Sugar Melts in Water," first published in *Temblor* in 1987.[1] *Lip Service* is a line-by-line re-working and "near-translation" of Dante's *Paradiso.* A number of readers have found especially the early sections of the poem to be extremely offensive, and it is certainly true that the experience of reading Andrews's poem is remarkably unlike the experience of reading Dante's. The following brief extract, from the seventh part of the sixth section, "Mars," reworks part of Dante's sixteenth canto.

> To get more joy out of sex, specify male or female—
> keep away from clothes, airbrush your vanity
> obstinately persistent & oblivious to circumstances,
> oooh oooh oooh, *besame mucho*
> delay pride's quake enhances
> pubic esplanade.
> Explosive smudge that silk
> overthrows straight seeking empties with stamina
> I yet squander—foresworn careful, saboteurishly culling
> a sexual diversion for the noontime meal
> but then he said my vagina was too big, taking coke with freon.
> Ovum aura sordid chaise—I like disturbed

don't hatch married women are always martyrs in a hurry:
                                        I don't feel selfish about this, this is
                                        something coming together between us—
                                        exasperating deporting eroticism as decision;
I took a shit in the bed . . . dream abruptly ends.
          Oh spring attacking cushion reference—
                                        poutless ardor, winter iron spoiler
                                        barb buy warmth on margin
preferring the mud to the fist, become nobody
lye sent us, sully refrigeration open to her
then, her—her repeat the frost
                                          superb!— (195)

All those voices, with the uncertain and shifting phrasal boundaries, the disjointed syntax. And the wit, the humor, the puns. These are all highly problematic: Why do we laugh (if we do), and what at, exactly? The uncertainties of phrasal boundaries profoundly disorient the reader—and what of the pronouns? The "you" and the "I" encountered so often in this poem are who? The self? Men? Women? Can we differentiate with any certainty?

George Oppen once said that "the 'plain sense' of the poem is the paradise of meaning."[2] But his remark leaves open, of course, the question what exactly "plain sense" might be. What, especially, might the "plain sense" of this poem be, and—which is much more to my purpose here—what is the connection between this poem, in its hellish vision of a world in which the word "love" scarcely appears at all[3] and in which *no one* is beloved, and Paradise, specifically Dante's *Paradiso*? *Lip Service* is an extremely problematic text. Not least among the problems is that of intelligibility—"plain sense"; closely connected to it is the problem of voice. Overall, like the work collected in *Give Em Enough Rope* (1987) and *I Don't Have Any Paper So Shut Up (or, Social Romanticism)* (1992), there is a truculent in-your-face quality to *Lip Service,* which draws on many voices to sound its disposition. The poem *contests* the protocols of readership.

If *Lip Service* is, like Dante's *Paradiso,* a portrayal of the Beloved, then that portrayal of the Beloved is pretty horrific. One reason why the *Paradiso* informs and models this text is because—in Andrews's words—his own poem seeks to map and contest "*sense* in a particular present (of 'late capitalism') where sexuality figures so prominently in a near-totalizing machine of social discourse" ("Be Careful" 125), and to this end his poem "reverberates with the romance and utopia-saturated materials" ("Paradise" 251) of Dante's poem. The portrayal of the Beloved in *Lip Service* runs savagely counter to the myth of women and sexuality purveyed in the market place and the entertainment industry (to say nothing of the *Paradiso*), yet at the same time it clearly reflects it: by and large, women in this poem—and especially in the first five sections—are, like women in advertisements, unreflective and largely uncritical creatures whose major interests and passions revolve around cosmetics, breast implants, sexual performance, and social standing; vain, manipulative, inconstant, they seem by and large to participate more or less willingly in a life which is, by any standards, undesirable and indeed dehumanized—as the poem proceeds, its title comes among other things to suggest joyless oral sex. This paradise is a Hell in which women are more or less willingly complicit in their own damnation. It is a world of "hot / narcissism" (186) in which "falsies exult" (194); it is a world of "mimetic emptiness" (71) in which women are as scornful of their own bodies as they are callous toward the men they exploit but are dependent on, whom they despise and contemn. The explicit sexual language, the events referred to ("I took a shit in the bed"), are horrible.[4]

So horrible, in fact, that we tend to overlook other aspects of this text. If we read the predominant voice in the poem as female, then we are obliged to recognize three things. First, that many of these utterances suggest the extent to which the speaker is caught up in a system not of her own devising, and is in fact as much a victim as an exploiter of the system. Second, that on occasion the speaker is remarkably self-aware of her condition and position, and sees no escape from it save through sardonic and grimly comic, often sexually suggestive or even explicit, expression: "I traded my brain / for legwarmers"(58); "I find that having a personal life / just keeps me home more" (95); "nice guys are finished first" (103)—these women have intelligence and wit: "think me ostensible, I need a good social personality / because I don't have any ideas?" (58); "If I'd been a ranch—which is often /—they'd have named me Bar Nothing" (194). This is very much the language of satire: "I traded my looks for my health—bad bargain" (60); "M[en] use intimacy to get sex; W[omen] use sex to get intimacy" (128). And third, that quite often the voice is not necessarily female: on occasion it is male, quite often it is indeed completely indeterminate. Who is it that says "today Joan of Arc would get thorazine" (60), "what you call reflection / I call constipation" (54), or " 'there are no rules' means 'women get hurt bad' " (87)? Sometimes the speaker might well be an authorial third-person omniscient and genderless narrator commenting ironically on what we've just read, or simply giving us, in neutral voice, the "facts." Who, after all, tells us that "the most popular in all cosmetic surgery is breast-size increase" (92), or reflects that "poverty becomes more & more a women's issue" (103)? Overall, the world portrayed in this version of Dante's *Paradiso* is joylessly bereft of the personal, and the poem is astonishingly difficult to take, except in short doses, because it is almost unrelievedly so very disturbing. Indeed, Andrews himself has said "*I'm* upset by that material. That material makes *me* very nervous, it's very unsettling because it's about this social machinery which is horrifying. . . . I have a horrific response to what I write, myself."[5] It is a vision and version of Hell, and it is not exclusively gendered female—as the poem proceeds we discern that men too are trapped in and victims of this world they seem to have made; they are, perhaps, their own creatures. As Ezra Pound whispers in a suffocated scream in Robin Blaser's poem on Dante, "Here is hell. Here."[6] How, then, can we glimpse Paradise? That is the task of the poem.

Drawing on materials he began generating in 1986, and written from 1989 to 1992, *Lip Service* is divided into what Andrews calls ten "planets" corresponding to the ten "bodies" of the *Paradiso,* and each is divided into ten parts: Earth, Moon, Mercury, Venus, Sun, Mars, Jupiter, Saturn, Fixed Stars, and Primum Mobile. The complete poem is in two large sections, the five "planets" of part 1 corresponding with Dante's cantos 1–13, and the five of part 2—"a little less critical & more optimistic" than part 1 ("Paradise" 252)—corresponding with cantos 14–33. In "Paradise and Method" (252–254) Andrews maintains that he is using "thematic cues" from Dante as well as "resonances" between his own materials, topics, imagery, and sound-patterns and those found in Singleton's edition of Dante,[7] including "cognates or so-called 'false-friend' relations with the Italian," as well as punctuation and paragraphing based "strictly on Dante's punctuation & tercet structure."[8] In "Paradise and Method," written when he was about two-thirds of the way through writing *Lip Service,* Andrews outlines the great intricacy of its structure. In writing the poem he superimposed the detailed thematic outline of *Tips for Totalizers,* a projected book on poetics, not only onto the overall organization of the complete work, but also in "increasingly detailed" form onto the "internal organization" of each of its one-hundred parts, "sometimes" using the three-part breakdown of that poetics project "even to organize a fifty- or one-hundred word paragraph." The intricacy, that is to say, echoes something of the intricacy of Dante's poem, and provided him with a set of technical difficulties to work with and against.

The materials for the poem, and the compositional procedures, are another source of the poem's great and even manic energy. For several years Andrews has generated materials for his poetry by recording phrases, words, and scraps of sentences, usually though not always fragmentary samples of speech and discourse, on small cards, one to twenty words each. They might be what he overhears on the street or in the bus, on radio or television; they might be what he reads, in academic journals, government publications, billboards, newspapers. He files these (in chronological order) at the end of every day, and when he started the preliminary work on *Lip Service,* he sorted the thousands of cards he'd gathered during 1986, 1987, and 1988 into some sort of thematic coherence. What is worth noting here is that all these words are public utterance, overheard or read: *none* of these words or phrases is Andrews's own. Sorting them as he is up to three years after they were recorded, each has lost its original context, and comes from a now unidentifiable source and voice. It is very much to Andrews's purpose that voice—presumably the origin of any given word or phrase—be uncertain and multiple and hence unstable: it's almost impossible, reading *Lip Service,* to decide where any given voice comes from, who might be speaking. Gender blurs. It is equally to Andrews's purpose that these are all extracts from *utterance,* from discourse in the public rather than the private or personal domain—this is *public speech,* public language, at varying removes from the personal. It is worth reminding ourselves here that our identity, our sense of who we are, our sense especially but not only of gender, comes very largely from the language in which we live and by which we are surrounded: we do not easily *choose* how to behave as men and as women: we are defined by the institutions and practices that govern our social and linguistic lives. As Andrews was sorting his cards, one theme he pursued was what he calls "Existential action—issues about mediation & subjectivity and relations" ("Paradise" 251)—the major thematic focus of *Lip Service.*

Reading the poem is a bit like listening in on the powder-room of a somewhat sleazy night club in the down-market end of town on a big night out, the sort of conversation, peppered with smutty jokes, obscenity, and scorn for human tenderness and individuality, with boastfulness and derision about sexual performance and the human body, more traditionally or conventionally associated with men in country club locker rooms than with woman as customarily viewed in public discourse, as sexual object or as Beloved. The language of the poem reads like a detritus of social, political, and commercial language in a world of "hype" (53). Trade names abound (Kotex, Breck, Lanvin, Camay, Hallmark), as do phrases from a variety of sources both overheard or read—above all from personal conversation in a world suspicious of the personal and vulnerable, suspicious of feeling and passion. It is composed of what Barrett Watten fittingly calls a "semiotic rubble,"[9] salvaged from one sign-system after another. This suggests two things: first, that whatever desires these speakers might be giving voice to in this world of consumer gluttony, appetite, disappointment, multimedia confusion, and (that remarkably astonishing word) cupidity, those desires are not their own, but originate in a series of manipulations—the social fabrication of a desire which the Self rejects—all too often, in this text, the sexual stimulation of the body to produce unwelcome desire—what Charles Bernstein has called "the congealed / syntax of forced instrumentation."[10] Thwarting and frustrating interior life, then, and undermining—or at least re-scripting—one's sense of one's own identity by at the very least blurring the distinction between inner and outer, personal and public, individual and social volition.

At the same time, this semiotic rubble (and this is my second point) is in a highly disrupted, discontinuous, and even incoherent (yet still offensive) language and syntax. Nothing in this text, if we take it item by item, phrase by phrase, line by line, is stable, yet overall it is thematically clear and horrific: an upside-down world where vanity and self-regard are ever-fixed, and love is flimsy in its caprice: an inversion of the mutable and immutable. Venus (or whatever) the poem may be, but nevertheless sublunary throughout. The mixing of vocabularies and discourses is extreme, and the unassignability of voice, moment to moment, unsettle the understanding as the pronouns shift.

How do we make sense, and what sort, of lines like "Oh spring attacking cushion reference rest—" (195) or the radical shift of voice with the two words "*it* burns" in the sequence "a burning phallus for modern times, / pronoun burns—*it* burns—faithless freshness" (194). Those shifts, those difficulties, undermine what stability the text might seem to possess, demolish and dissipate any sense we might have of unity of voice, and as a consequence work to disperse any concept we might have of coherent and stable individual human identity. Because the poem so often implicitly invites the reader to put together a paraphrasable meaning (what we might think of as "plain sense")—for there are clear islands of lucidity, of clarity, in this text—the poem forces the reader both to construct possible meanings and to see how that construction itself is determined by larger social and historical forces outside the reader's control as much as it is by one's own psychic volition.

The aim of the poem is to enable its readers to become, as Andrews has suggested, "less of an exile in our own words—the words we read by writing" ("Poetry as Praxis" 58) by undoing the language of control and ideological manipulation. The first task of the poem is to undo the power of the sign which promises liberation and play but actually enthralls and limits; to undo the boundaries of legitimized content and consent, to undo the sign and address how reference works in language—by drawing on the institutionalized cliché, of the word, of public and private language, of advertising, of government-speak, of conduct, the language which defines and indeed appropriates desire by laying out an illusion of presence in a world which prizes use and efficiency above felicity. The poem, with its blockages, its non-sequiturs, its very turbulence of sound and syntax matched by the horrific self-contradictions and denials its propositions make, is itself felicitous. The uneasy pleasure it affords demonstrates, as no expository writing could, how the users of this language are also its victims.

The second task of the poem is to address the larger context of language: how meaning arises in a social context, in the whole framework of a discourse whose assumptions are so pervasively distributed throughout our culture that we cannot easily identify them or escape from them, so deeply embedded that they are the blind spot of our vision. If Andrews's theme is that late capitalism thus constructs women (and indeed men) in public as well as private discourse, then it is essential to his project that the language in the poem be not his own, but *found,* and that the poem undermine, indeed, through demonstration, any delusion we might have that our words are, in this particular moment of history, our own. If Andrews's project is to succeed, then the complete undermining of language and discourse effected by the poem will lead to the reader's rediscovery of meaning through the construction of a meaning or rather series of meanings which can then, indeed, lead to a re-inhabitation of language, a realm or discourse in which we can dwell, and find and found our lives. "Paradise," Andrews has said, is "a total repertoire of possibilities" ("Paradise" 268). So too is language, when we live *in* it. The aim of the poem is to make such a repertoire available. *A total repertoire:* "Paradise," which is also "Infinity" ("Paradise" 259), is outside the confines of any tight system, and the poem, by laying bare the device, seeks to undo an established order which "in sewing itself up into permanent stability sews us and our meanings up inside it" ("Poetry as Praxis" 58). *Lip Service,* then, is a Utopian project, in which reading is a form of writing, in which the difficult practice of reading, of choosing among an increasing plethora of possible meanings and holding them all at once, is a praxis of Paradise. There is no suggestion—in Dante or in Andrews—that Paradise is an easy place or condition, either to reach or to maintain.

Andrews is not the only so-called Language Poet to draw on and rework Dante in a quest for a poetic mode which will bring to an end our exiled condition in language, bring readers home again: one section of Ron Silliman's long serial project *The Alphabet,* for example, is called *Paradise;* Lyn Hejinian has in her critical writing come back again and again to the nature and possibility of achieving paradise through and in writing, language; one finds it a recurrent theme in the work of Susan Howe and Rosmarie Waldrop. It may very well be that such interrogations of Paradise derive, in their more or less immediate ancestry, from Ezra Pound's famous conclusion in *The Cantos,* "*le paradis n'est pas artificiel.*" Pound was pointing, first, to the futility of believing that we have any life other than this one, and second to the actual possibility of the individual achieving, however momentarily, a sense of paradise. Moments of coherence are unstable and transitory, but they are in Pound's view nevertheless paradisal and actual; if they manifest the transcendent, that transcendence is secular and earthbound.

More recent writers have emphasized that the achievement of Paradise, however fleeting, is also *linguistic.* What is important to realize about the Language poets in this narrative is that in their investigation of Paradise and its possibility of potentiality, they are deeply suspicious of those moments of coherence, and it is very much a part of Andrews's project in *Lip Service* to *undo,* to destabilize, the authority and unity of signs, to undo any security there might be in the referentiality of words. It is a part of his project, that is to say, to negate the "plain sense" of the poem, to undo George Oppen's "paradise of meaning." Hence the extreme problematics of the poem.

For Andrews such problematics are inextricable from the problem of Love, and of the nature and identity of the Beloved. Love, after all, impels speech and is a making possible, which is why Guy Pringle's words quoted as epigraph to this essay are so monstrous. Love cannot freeze the multiple subjectivity of the Other into uniformity and stasis. The identity of the Beloved—though inevitably perceived through and thus structured by the Lover's own eyes and desire—must be always autonomous, independent, Other. And inevitably it will be concealed if not withheld, so that the Lover and the Beloved may live in what Andrews calls an "erotic mutuality of self and other" ("Be Careful" 125), recognizing a You, the Outside of *this* experience.

If love is a *making possible,* that is to say, then it resists definition and *refuses* possession: the Beloved is always a YOU, a not-me, and it is multiplex. By the same token the world is equally a "you"—that is to say, a not-me or a not-us—for it has its own ardors and desires, its own possibilities struggling for recognition. The Beloved extends beyond the individual, and is an extension of the individual, an extension of the personal, and takes a multiplicity of forms. The Beloved is Language, Language is the Beloved; the word; words; always beyond the writer's and reader's control, always skirting and pressing the edge of the writer's desire. Language, the realm of possibles; "a total repertoire of possibilities." Paradise, and the language of the poem. Hence the poem's apparent *in*coherence: for the writer Andrews must not control the *reader* Andrews, nor by that token any other reader. The reader, like the language, is the Beloved, and therefore MUST remain "an Other, an Outside which is a not-us" ("Paradise" 251), autonomous, independent, Other.[11] The reader, too, then, takes part in, shares, this "erotic mutuality of self and other."

For things to be otherwise—for the poem to be an exercise in "communication" where the reader comes to share the thoughts and experiences, the desires and needs and conclusions, of the writer—for the poem to be, shall we say, wholly intelligible, is to engage another sort of Utopianism altogether, the dream of tyranny. The poem which seeks to persuade the reader, to hand over a "meaning" in the sense of a paraphrasable digest which can be separated out, cashed in at the end of the reading in exchange for the knowledge-claim that "this is what the poem means," is a closure of the possible, an imprisoning of desire in the interests of achieving "perfect communication." It assumes that we all come to see exactly the same things in exactly the same ways, that we assume an identity and uniformity of "reality" and "perception." The aim of such communication is to eliminate difference and to standardize desire, to catch us all up in the same web of pre-existent established order. Such communication is, indeed, the closure and elimination of desire by construing identity in terms of an achieved and uniform meaning: a form of possession in which the Beloved—Language, the Reader—is absorbed into, bound into, the Lover—the writer. In such a case we see the Disappearance of the Beloved, and the Disappearance of the Reader, who becomes a chimerical fantasy, inaccessible in her or his own identity and reality, destroyed. Or all too delusionally accessible as the Lover's Mirror. "*Language,*" Philippe Sollers astutely observes, "*turns upon and possesses he who believed he possessed it but in fact was only one of its signs.*"[12]

Lip Service is thus an attack on so-called "romantic" love, that alluring and seductive face of brutal sexism, because "romantic" love seeks to destroy the Beloved by Possession: the reader shall be subject to the writer, the subject obedient to the Author, the material of the poem utterly subservient to its Creator and User. Hence Andrews's poem is indeed what at the Kootenay School of Writing he called a "mad-dog attack" on antifeminist practice, upon institutionalized notions of the feminine, upon institutions. It undoes Romance. If the women in the poem seem dehumanized, then the poem assaults too the notions of "human" and "humanized" which lie behind that judgment, and which produced their "dehumanized" "nature" in the first place. The poem thus shifts the ground of meaning from what perhaps can best be called a series of cultural imperatives to the very act of reading itself. Value is thus shifted from artifact to process: the voices, the play in and of language, the dialogue with the poem taking place in the reader's consciousness, all move toward some sort of cognition and recognition of meaning which cannot be separated from the decisions made within the writing/reading.

"Paradise," says Andrews, "is translated as Love and as Language" ("Paradise" 258). Language, "an Other or an Outside which is both a not-us and a not-yet" ("Paradise" 259); language as a complex and difficult ongoing activity (a PRAXIS), most readily to be identified as "a total repertoire of possibilities": that which is to be realized, that is to say, only as a plural of potentialities, a promise or rather promises which can never come to completion or fulfillment but shift, change, illuminate, suffuse. Paradise, then, is the experience of potential, a perpetual opening up of perhaps ineluctable possibilities, fostering and furthering. It is a making possible, and the Language of Paradise—the language of the poem—is by necessity *in*coherent. Paradise is, in this view of things, a rage for *dis*order, though a disorder of a very specific kind. Hell may be *here,* but in its difficulties so might Paradise. The essential problem of Paradise is a problem of method. Whether *Lip Service,* with its tortured and torturing difficulties, succeeds in its aims is after all necessarily up to the reader, for the task of the poem has been regrounded, outside the poet.

Notes

Epigraph. Olivia Manning, *Friends and Heroes,* in *The Balkan Trilogy* (London: Mandarin, 1990) 765; Robert Sheppard, "British Poetry and Its Discontents," *Cultural Revolution? The Challenge of the Arts in the 1960s,* Bart Moore-Gilbert and John Seed, eds. (London: Routledge, 1992) 170.

1. Bruce Andrews, *Lip Service* (Toronto: Coach House Books, 2001); *Paradise & Method: Poetics and Praxis* (Evanston, IL: Northwestern UP, 1996); "Be Careful Now You Know Sugar Melts in Water" is on pp. 125–133; "Paradise & Method: A Transcript" on 251–270. Later in this essay I refer to Andrews's "Poetry as Explanation, Poetry as Praxis," which is on 49–71. All further references to these essays are documented parenthetically in my text by short title.

2. George Oppen, "The Philosophy of the Astonished (Selections from Working Papers)," Rachel Blau DuPlessis, ed., *Sulfur* 27 (Fall 1990): 212.

3. "Love" first makes its appearance in the eighth part of the second section, "Moon," reworking a section of *Paradiso* Canto 5: "no sapphire can make of your love a seductress" (54), while the opening of the third section, "Mercury" (*Paradiso* Canto 6), talks of "love's winterization" (72).

4. My summary somewhat distorts Andrews's text, which in part 2 reflects much less jaundiced views.

5. Bruce Andrews, talk and discussion at the Kootenay School of Writing, Vancouver, 18 May 1990. My thanks to the Kootenay School of Writing for the loan of a tape-recording of this event.

6. Robin Blaser, "Great Companion: Dante Alighiere," *The Holy Forest: Collected Poems,* Miriam Nichols, ed. (Berkeley: U of California P, 2006) 456.

7. Dante Alighieri, *The Divine Comedy*, trans. with commentary Charles S. Singleton, Bollingen Series LXXX, Princeton UP, 1970–1975.

8. But I have not correlated Andrews's text with Dante's, and do not discuss it here.

9. Barrett Watten, "The World in the Work: Toward a Psychology of Form," *Total Syntax* (Carbondale: Southern Illinois UP, 1985) 159–160.

10. Charles Bernstein, "Part Quake," *Islets/Irritations* (New York: Jordan Davies, 1983) 99.

11. This does not necessarily, of course, imply "separation." At the Kootenay School of Writing in 1990 Andrews talked of the drive in his writing to investigate "the seducing aspects of identity creation, stemming from quite pervasive social conditions" and spoke of "trying to lay out some way of mapping, of implicating, the social conditions which are constitutive of identity across the board."

12. Philippe Sollers, *Writing and the Experience of Limits*, David Hayman, ed., trans. Philip Barnard with David Hayman (New York: Columbia UP, 1983) 33. I am grateful to Robin Blaser for this reference.

Undoing the Book

This chapter seeks to raise problems rather than to solve them. It is directed at two general questions about bibliography: What is it, and What good is it? Though I propose to raise both, my primary concern is with deliberate challenges to the art of bibliography understood as the study of the book as material object. I'm interested in the exploitation of meaningful systems-violations in the production of the written and printed word.

The central passionate desire of the bibliographic enterprise, surely, is through complex acts of critical and physiological description to stabilize the text and its provenance (including authorship—however we define that term—and the means of production), and by extension therefore to stabilize the visible and the invisible, the material and the immaterial world, by rendering it subject to description and thus to control—as painlessly as possible, one might say, to absorb the work into the culture. Like all systems of control, bibliography is subject to opposition. It is, like science, economics, psychology, and metaphysics, a fiction. It is not any the less useful or useable for that, and like other fictions it has its characteristic forms.

Like other fictions, too, it has in the last twenty or more years suffered challenges, importantly but by no means exclusively from critical theorists. If the critical theorist asks what it is to read or to write, surely the challenge now is *What is it to bibliograph?* What exactly *are* we doing when we describe a text as a material object? This may or may not be related to Stanley Fish's famous question *Is there a text in this class?* But it does have, surely, a more than peripheral connection to the confusion of text and world, image and text, in popular culture and the media—books, after all, are also the media, or one of them. It is no longer clear, that is to say, what a book is—or, if it is, then whether *books* are what bibliography is all about. For we are in a world, as Jerome McGann recently observed, that is "saying farewell to the book as we know it."[1] But what, after all, is a book?

There is, first, the *power* of the book as an intellectual construct, as an authority. If it's in a book it must be what? "True"? Right? Carefully wrought? "Good"? Worthy our attention? Of value, at any rate—and we still believe *that,* surely, in the face of apparent evidence to the contrary cluttering up the supermarket and drugstore shelves. But what authority is it? What authority does it have? Historically, we seem to have associated the power of the printed word with "authenticity," and the office of the bibliographer has been to certify origins, to attest the genuine, and to distinguish the true from the counterfeit.

"Space is a swarming in the eyes, and Time a singing in the ears," says John Shade, a modern poet, as quoted by an invented philosopher ("Martin Gardiner") in *The Ambidextrous Universe,* page 165.[2] So says Ivan Veen, meditating on Time and Space, and we read *his* words in a book called *Ada or Ardor,* a novel whose subtitle nicely mingles fact and fiction by calling itself *A Family Chronicle.* But the invented "Martin Gardiner" (whose name sounds suspiciously close to the Martin Gardner who set puzzles in *Scientific American*) is misquoting his source: in their original published version Shade's lines read

> Space is a swarming in the eyes; and time,
> A singing in the ears.[3]

But John Shade is himself an invention, straying into *Ada*'s pages from another fiction by Vladimir Nabokov *(Pale Fire).* So we have a fiction in which an invented philosopher in his imaginary book misquotes lines (lines 215–216) from a real poem (canto 2) by an invented poet in a real book which itself turns out to be an invented fiction by a writer who published his earliest books in Russian under the invented name V. Sirin but who as author of this book claims *really* to be Vladimir Vladimirovich Nabokov. No wonder the aim of Bibliography is to stabilize the world. A persistent theme of Nabokov's fiction is (as Simon Karlinsky puts it) that "life may be converted into art by turning a given project or course of action into a creative act";[4] a persistent pleasure Nabokov's fiction affords is the continued rhyme between his fictional-world-as-real and the real-world-as-fiction. No wonder the aim of Bibliography is to stabilize the world! By and large an archaeological enterprise seeking to establish as well as preserve a sense of authentic origins for the written (published) work, bibliography is but one of the many fictions by which we seek to discipline the world in which we live when it is increasingly difficult to do so. The challenge now facing bibliography is that it seems no longer adequate, or even perhaps relevant, to the invented lives most of us willy-nilly lead: the challenge for the bibliographer is to describe his or her own fiction in the course of telling the bibliographic story. New elements have entered this narrative.

Now, high-school and freshman-English texts talk of fiction in terms of headings: Character, Plot, Setting, Style, Theme. A bibliographic parody might run: Author, Title, Place, Publisher, Date—these are the initial terms, at any rate, which we teach the acolyte. The modern bibliographic narrative relies on notions of authority and reliability, of fact and of value, closely tied to its origins in the early history of printing, and in these terms is by and large ill-equipped to deal with a view of the world as multiple, polyvalent, and shifting.[5] In its devotion to balance, stability, prediction, and hence above all to the sort of clarity which comes with *completeness,* the bibliographic narrative is engaged in the Promethean task of bringing order to the world, and its text follows an essentially diachronic model; it is sequentially chronological, couching its tale and presenting its facts as features of a discourse whose special terms constitute a significant vocabulary: manuscript, primary text, original, proof, first edition, copy text, impression, signature, etc., etc. The major shift facing the bibliographer, the describer and historian of the book as material object, is that the customary bibliographic story is being deliberately undone by both writers and publishers, who subvert the diachronic time-bound model of the bibliographic narrative. Technology, too, of course, in the shape of desk-top and electronic publishing is playing its part in rescripting or even dismantling the customary bibliographic plot, whether by accident or by design, so that even the very materiality of the book is now in question. Increasingly, we read texts which defy description, and works which disguise and indeed renounce origin.

In her meticulous bibliography of Guy Davenport's work Joan St.C. Crane distinguishes two states of the first edition, second issue, of *Trois Caprices* (1982). The title panel of the first state is "17 to 19 mm from the top edge measured at the spine"; that of the second state "approximately 2mm shorter."[6] Crane's bibliographic description is a model of investigation and clarity. But how can you even achieve an accurate detailed description of the sort of books produced by say Rebis Press, whose *Half Off* (stories by Mimi Pond) has nylon net endpapers and shower-cap binding? "Like many Rebis books, this one is difficult to describe, but memorable to see, read, and touch," proclaimed the publisher in a promotional flyer.[7] You might well have to demolish the book in order to describe it, which immediately confounds the bibliographic purpose of authenticating as genuine the fetishized book as art-object.

But in looking at the unclassifiable and even indescribable (as material object) book I do not in fact have in mind the book as *objet-d'art,* but the book or periodical which is produced with more down-market objectives: the literary-critical journal, the little magazine, the book designed to be read rather than the book designed to be admired and cherished as object. If we are interested in tracing the chronology of publication or the frequency of reprint, the plan of a magazine like Barry Alpert's *Vort* (1972–c. 1975) poses problems, since Alpert proposed to reprint early issues on demand. Later in that same decade Coach House Press in Toronto produced a series of "Manuscript Editions" which, and I quote from the prospectus (issued in about 1977), "are computer line-printer copies of works in progress—long poems, poetry collections, etc. They are run off and bound up as orders are received at the press. The compositional date and number of the particular draft is clearly marked and as the manuscript is revised by the author these revisions are fed into the computer and the compositional date and draft number altered accordingly. It is our hope with these editions to allow readers and writers more access to each other during the compositional process."[8] Thus the "first draft" of Fred Wah, *Breathin My Name with a Sigh* (a book whose third draft was eventually published by Talonbooks in Vancouver [in October 1981]), appeared in January 1978 (with the second in January 1979), but Eli Mandel's *Mary Midnight* (announced in the second draft of Wah) is identified simply as "new draft." I have a copy of George Bowering's *Uncle Louis* (1980) which is neither bound, nor precisely dated, but which nevertheless is clearly a computer dot-matrix print-out and claims to be a Manuscript Edition. I do not know if it is possible to order an earlier draft of a subsequently published book, but without access to an authenticated "original" computer printout it would be difficult if not impossible to determine the exact status and even provenance of the text so produced. Perhaps such publications might be said accidentally to subvert the notion of book.

Alternatively, there are magazines like *Open Space* (San Francisco, 1964–1965), edited by Stan Persky,[9] with its fifteen irregularly numbered issues; like *Curtains,* a loose leaf magazine edited by Paul Buck in 1970s England, which changed its name every issue (*Bald Curtain; Curtain le prochain step,* and so forth); and like *Aspen: The Magazine in a Box,* of which volume 1 number 2 (1966) contains records, pamphlets, folders with cards in them, and single printed sheets. There is mischief here, of course, as there is perhaps in the Vancouver magazine *Yuth,*[10] whose six issues (1993–1999) bear neither a date nor an editorial name and address; as there is mischief too in an English little magazine which appeared irregularly but with no date of issue in the early 1990s, whose title and editorial address appears to change each time it comes out, which may or may not be for sale (if you can ever find a copy), and whose editor may or may not be Talbot Rothwell, or Tony Baker, or Ken Edwards.[11] Such bibliographic intransigence can perhaps be ascribed to political or mischievous rather than aesthetic or philosophic motives, as can the cataloguing dilemma posed by Michael McClure's book of poems, published in 1966, with a typographical oddity as its title: • (usually catalogued as *[Black Dot]*).

Other works, however, are perhaps best described as programmatic in their subversion. Witness the two panels of Steve McCaffery's *Carnival* (1973, 1975), a book of typewriter art which is also a poem, and which has to be demolished in order to be read. They consist of 20 pages (in the first panel) and 21 (in the second), the pages' top edge stapled; each panel was accompanied by an instruction card with a miniature of the assembled work; the first panel has an errata sheet. The instructions for the first panel read: "In order to destroy this book please tear each page carefully along the perforation. The panel is assembled by laying out pages in a square of four."[12] The final assemblage is presumably framed and hung. There's a long history in this century of publishers, editors, and writers deliberately violating bibliographic decorum, or indifferent to it. When the English poet Thomas A. Clarke (who runs Moschatel Press) carefully sews a single sheet of paper, a poem printed on one side only, between stiff card covers, do we call this a book? How many pages are there in Raymond Queneau's *Cent Mille Milliards de Poèmes* (1961), in which the pages have been cut evenly into horizontal strips, each strip bearing one line of a poem? What is the title of Steve McCaffery's 1987 book, *Evoba—Above Backwards,* or (as a note on the cover seems obliged to tell us) *Vubba?*[13] There are countless little magazines like *King Ida's Watch Chain, Hanging Loose,* and *Orange Bear Reader* that consist of a packet or envelope or box of loose sheets of different sizes which may or may not have had a table of contents which sometimes gets lost. There seems to be a tradition of such folio publications among fine art magazines, like *Art Now* (published in the 1970s), and Wallace Berman's *Semina* (1960s). The model for such publications might well be Marcel Duchamp's *Boîte Verte:* (1934), 93 documents relating to *La Mariée mise à nu par ces célibataires, même* (some dated, some not, but all from the period 1911–1915), boxed but with no inventory, in no particular order and itself, therefore (though issued in a deluxe edition of only twenty copies), a bibliographic nightmare which had to wait until 1986 to be adequately described by Ecke Bonk.[14] There have in the last fifty years been countless books like Robert Grenier's *Sentences* (1978), Michael McClure's

Poem Cards (1966), or bpNichol's *Still Water* (1970).[15] These books, simply a bunch of loose sheets with perhaps only one word on each placed in a box or, like decks of cards with writing on them to be shuffled at will, in their deliberate violations of book-making protocols resist and even undo the idea of completeness. They thus—like Allen Fisher's later *Place* and *Gravity as a Consequence of Shape* (works of a quite different order)—argue not only against the text as a totality, but also against the notion that even the "culture" can complete the text (since the text undergoes constant recontextualization and rescription), and thus show kinship with work like that of Olson and Pound, which I have elsewhere called variorum texts.[16] The bibliographic enterprise, by implication, is yet another version of Enlightenment, Romantic, and Encyclopedist anxiety over missing the total. Obliged to settle for what it sees as the partial and the incomplete, it fails to recognize the partiality of its own encyclopedic impulse.

"I detest the world" says the English poet Peter Riley in his poem "What Is":

> I detest the world
> as it is known. I couldn't
>
> Get out of that quick enough. The world
> as it is seen
>
> Is my bed forever.
> Be there too.[17]

As a general rule, however, works like those I've enumerated undermine the bibliographic act piecemeal, by challenging our notion of title, pagination, edition, or even the provenance of the text. Peter Riley's poem, and indeed *Reader,* the book from which it comes, points in a more radical direction. The major challenge to bibliography arises from the current practices of the indeterminate text, for the indeterminate text necessarily enjoins a concomitant indeterminacy of the book. Here we move into a consideration of the book *as* politics—the deliberate attempt to undermine the notion of book. I want to look briefly at three examples, each of which seeks to undo a particular sort of knowledge—of what is to be known, and what it is to know.

1. If we include books, pamphlets, drawings, paintings, videos, music, and taped readings, the English poet and painter Allen Fisher (some of his work is in the Tate Gallery) has published over seventy works since 1966, all of them interlinked as part of an overall as yet undefined and possibly indefinable project, each at the same time independent, the large project itself divided into a series of what he calls "processual" works. "I do not base my pro-

posals on a belief structure—nor upon certainty of any substance," he has said. "On the contrary I expect a multiple virtuality which cannot be stabilized or made definitive."[18] His work is extremely unstable, defying bibliographic description as it defies formal description. One of his books, *Bavuska or the Rub: The Rubber or Greta's Bust* (1969) consists, the title page tells us, of "random selections from Allen Fisher's simultaneous novels";[19] those selections (otherwise unpublished so far as I know) are titled *Busk 1, Ava,* and *Busk 2,* and the texts appear to be interchangeable. His first major project to be published and apparently completed is the extensive work *Place,* but it is extremely difficult to sort out. A note in the final volume (*Unpolished Mirrors* [1985 printing]) identifies nine volumes covering books I through V,[20] but the text omits some forty pages of "works which moved out from *Unpolished Mirrors,*" notes, and "tentative work" which "would be out of tone with this edition." Fisher distinguishes between the "serial" (1979?) and the "collated" (1981) editions of the poem, whose text in any case overlaps with other texts. One version of *Unpolished Mirrors* (1979? 1981?) carried the notation "being *place book II* informed by *place book V.*" A note in the second printing (1976) of *Place I-XXXVII* remarks that publication of the work is "not expected before 1980, that is after its abandonment" and calls itself a "*preview* of Book I being the main parts of the First Movement" (my emphasis). Interleaved in this edition however are parts of another work "Lakes," in which is interleaved a portion of Place XXXII, a section which itself "appears elsewhere" as *Blood Bone Brain* (prefatory note, unpaged). But in 1980 Fisher published *Hooks place 32 being taken out of place;* it prints work not found in the 32nd section of Place Book I and seems indeed to have been written *after* that book was published. *Place* Book I, meanwhile, itself weaves back and forth, some pages being parts of the second, fifth, and eleventh sections of *Place* at the same time. A long note at the end of *Unpolished Mirrors Serial H* (the final section, perhaps, of *Place*) offers the reader advice on how to read the book, in the form of six versions of "a map of approaches." The fourth approach, "considered void," consists of "simply reading *place* through from page one in book one to the last page in *Becoming,* or in *Unpolished Mirrors,* dropping out 'cut-in' material like *Grampians, Lakes, Eclipse, William Rufus* or *Birds Locked In The Roof* en route" (99). So far as I know, *William Rufus* has yet to be published. The note adds that one purpose of the "cut-ins" was "to ensure breakage of chronologic or developmental apparency offered in works of process; as well as to suggest to the reader a different set of simultaneous activities that were impinging on and leading from *Place*" (99)—to read any "set," section, or book as an entity, Fisher says, "misreads the work" (100). More recent work shows more complex overlapping, interference, and interweaving, since *Stepping Out* seems simultaneously to be a part of both *Gravity as a Consequence of Shape* and of his long gloss on Bach and optics, *The Art of Flight.* Overall, Fisher's writing presents itself as an immense synchronic seriality, and its method of publication seems designed to present the work as not subject to the constraints of linear time.[21] "A multiple virtuality which cannot be stabilised" indeed, his is a text without bounds.

2. My second instance of a writer deliberately undermining the notion of book is Susan Howe, who in 1989 published a book-length poem with a title long familiar to bibliographers and historians of the book: *A Bibliography of the King's Book; or Eikon Basilike* (Providence: Paradigm, 1989). The book is not paginated and, as Kent Lewis has shown, it stringently resists all attempts to standardize its text: 16 pages into the book, after such preliminaries as the half-title and an *inaccurate* bibliography of books "Also by Susan Howe," after five pages of prose text and a poem, we get the copyright notice.[22] And *then* we get the full title page. The prose introduction and poem, foregrounded as they are among the preliminaries, disrupt the publication proceedings, the work and its frame blending into such continuity (or pervaded by insistent discontinuity) that even the detachable dust-jacket becomes (or does it?) part of the text. The poem thus problematizes bibliographic identification and description of the book's parts, destabilizing the boundary line between text and bibliographic matter and rendering the conventional bibliographic narrative an irrelevant fiction and the book even dissolves conventional distinctions between author, printer, and publisher, since the design of the dust-jacket, presumably the work of Rosmarie Waldrop who set the cover and title-page, seems an integral part of the poem.[23] The margins of the book are blurred, and title, layout, and physical substance of the book all further the plurality of the text itself, which ambiguates authority and authorship. "A First didn't write it," says one line of this strangely collaborative poem, filled as it is with multiplicities and contradictions. It calls into question the very notion of "corrupt" text, and even quite possibly entices the reader into making *authorial* intervention.

3. My third instance is a book in its own way as cheeky and subversively mischievous as any book about sex by Madonna falling to pieces the moment you open it. It is William Gibson's *Agrippa.* Originally priced at $1,500.00 (later at $2,000.00) the book was an electronic text illustrated with "etchings." It is a poem roughly 1800 words long, the text apparently approved by Gibson himself, and was designed to self-destruct automatically by encrypting itself as it was read, apparently by means of an encryption process possibly hacked from an unnamed U.S. government agency, perhaps the CIA or the FBI. It could, then, only be read once, and was, of course, a hacker's dream.

The text of "*AGRIPPA (A Book of The Dead)* Text by William Gibson. Etchings by Dennis Ashbaugh © 1992 Kevin Begos Publishing All Rights Reserved Hacked & Cracked by Templar, Rosehammer & Pseudophred" is available on the net as an electronic archive: text, etchings, essays, and sundry papers.[24]

In the hacked text as downloadable in 1992 from Compuserve it was virtually impossible to tell where the introduction by Templar ends and Gibson's text begins. The reader cannot tell where these lines belong:

> I hesitated
> before untying the bow
> that bound this book together.

Second, the text so downloaded was possibly and even probably corrupt: section numbering is inconsistent (section IV lacks a period), and a line towards the end of section V, "moving as though contours of hot iron," is surely in error, for its context demands that it read "moving as through contours of hot iron." These somewhat trivial points indicate several interesting features of the electronic text, not least of which is one's inability, faced with "Templar's" version of Gibson's text, to verify the authenticity and hence accuracy of that text; closely allied to this (in 1992) was the impossibility of describing the text at all, except as hard copy. No reader could produce the text itself, for "the text itself" had no material existence that one could personally detect; and one was led to wonder whether the "etchings" ever had an actual material existence. Readers were (and still are) obliged to rely on a machine which (one trusts) would decode impulse into text. The text, that is to say, exists (like the etchings) outside the range of the sensorium.

That we nowadays understand this observation to apply to all texts is only part of my point, for an electronic text like Gibson's *Agrippa* constitutes a radical change in our relations with the literary text, whether we are authors or readers. This is a new kind of book indeed, which can only be read through the mediation of the machine. As Barrett Watten described it in 1988: "text is entered on a keyboard into a small memory bank and is displayed on a video field. Once this is done, the text is transferred to a magnetic disc which in turn causes the text to be produced. The text here is being treated as a material mass as a whole—it is not broken down into keystrokes signifying direct action through the machine."[25] This means not only that the operator of the machine is obliged to go into the machine (via keyboard, VDT, software, etc.) in order to discern the text, but that the operator of the machine can "go into the machine in order to straighten things out" *only* by means of the language of the machine, a language that the operator usually cannot read. This process changes the very workings of the machine itself and hence the very nature of the text. As Watten puts it (later on the same page), "he can deform, replace, or eradicate letters altogether," but we must once again remember that in the world of the sensorium these letters have only an invisible, directly indiscernible and hence indefinite or even equivocal existence. Under this scheme of things Alice B. Toklas—or Gertrude Stein herself, of course!—reading through the drafts of Stein's *Stanzas in Meditation,* could effect a global Search and Replace, eliminating all instances of "may" and substituting "can," with only nine keystrokes, without actually reading the text.[26]

Bibliographers, I believe, will be hard pressed to meet the challenge of such apparently authorless work unless and until they recognize the partiality that lies at the core of their own desire for complete and definitive authority. We need a more flexible fiction.

Notes

1. Jerome J. McGann, *Black Riders: The Visible Language of Modernism* (Princeton: Princeton UP, 1993) xiii.

2. Vladimir Nabokov, *Ada or Ardor: A Family Chronicle* (New York: McGraw-Hill, 1969) 542.

3. Vladimir Nabokov, *Pale Fire: A Novel* (New York: Putnam's, 1962) 40.

4. Simon Karlinsky, "Nabokov," *Columbia Dictionary of Modern European Literature,* J-A. Bédé, ed. (New York: Columbia UP, 1980) 557.

5. There are of course exceptions to that "by and large"; one need only think, for example, of the Tudor and later English practice of circulating verse in manuscript, with its concomitant bibliographic complexities.

6. Joan Crane, *Guy Davenport: A Descriptive Bibliography 1947–1995* (Haverford: Green Shade, 1996) 48–49.

7. *New Books & A 1981 Checklist* (Berkeley: Rebis Press, 1981).

8. The final sentence quoted suggests that Manuscript Editions are the immediate antecedent of the now defunct e-mail journal *Swift Current,* which encouraged readers to respond to and if need be amend texts so published. The final typescript page of the Second Draft of Fred Wah, *Breathin' My Name with a Sigh* (January 1978) repeats this statement and lists "some Manuscript Editions currently or soon available." All are poetry unless otherwise specified:

Frank Davey. *The War Poems.* 3rd Draft
Gerry Gilbert. *The '79 Spring Tour of the Canadas.* 1st Draft.
Liz Lochhead. *The Grimm Sisters.* 1st Draft.
Eli Mandel. *Mary Midnight.* Drama, an Oratory. new draft.
bpNichol. *The Martyrology Book V, Chain 8.* 2nd Draft.

D. Ann Taylor. *The Patty ReHearst Story.* Drama. 1st Draft.
Fred Wah. *Breathin' My Name with a Sigh.* 2nd Draft.

9. So far as I know, there were fourteen issues of *Open Space* as follows: 0 (January 30 1964), declaring itself a "prospectus" but in fact a complete issue of the magazine; 1; "Valentine" issue; 2, 3, 4 "White Hope"; 4 "Taurus"; 5; 6; 7; 8; 9; 10 "Setting to the Blues His Foolish Hopes"; 11 "The Penguin Book of Modern American Verse edited by Donald M. Allen" (a ghost title); and 12. Not all issues were dated, and the final issue seems to have been issued in 1965.

10. *Yuth* is a xeroxed satirical literary magazine, edited and indeed written and composed by Michele Fogal and Karen Stankunas, undergraduates at the University of British Columbia. Copies were produced at cost on demand.

11. The only two issues (so far as I know) are *Language Issue* and *Solicited Material*—both appeared in 1992 or 1993. I am indebted to Harry Gilonis for informed speculation regarding the editorship.

12. Steve McCaffery, *Carnival the First Panel: 1967–70* (Toronto: Coach House, 1973).

13. Steve McCaffery, *Evoba: The Investigations Meditations 1976–78* (Toronto: Coach House, 1987).

14. Ecke Bonk, *Marcel Duchamp: The Box in a Valise de ou par Marcel Duchamp ou Rrose Sélavy, Inventory of an Edition,* trans. David Britt (New York: Rizzoli, 1989).

15. A lineal descendant might be David Bromige's *Tight Corners & What's Around Them (being the brief & endless adventures of some pronouns in the sentences of 1972–1973): Prose and Poems* (Los Angeles: Black Sparrow Press, 1974). The text is derived from note cards which, though originally in flexible order, are here constrained by the bound codex.

16. Peter Quartermain, *Disjunctive Poetics: From Gertrude Stein and Louis Zukofsky to Susan Howe* (New York: Cambridge UP, 1992) 63–65.

17. Peter Riley, *Reader* (London: 1992) n.p.

18. Qtd. in Ken Edwards, "Bloom in the Plain Acoustic: Allen Fisher: Stepping Out," *Fragmente* 5 (1993): 72

19. Allen Fisher, *Bavuska, or the rub; the rubber or Greta's bust: the rubble/rubato/rubbing/rubbish/rubicund/rubric: random selections/from Allen Fisher's simultaneous novels* (London: Big Venus, 1969).

20. Place Book I place I–XXXVII appeared (with omissions) in 1974 with a complex index mapping the interleaving repeats and shuffles of the text, and was reprinted in 1976 with revisions. Book II, which is to say parts 38, 39, and 40, was split and recombined in a variety of ways. Part 38 appeared in note form as *Unpolished Mirrors* (1977) which also included a portion of Book V; part 39 appeared as *Eros: Father: Pattern* (1977); part 40 was "taken out of place together with parts of place 32" and published in part as a section of another work, *Convergences,* published in part combined with bits of part 32, the preface being published separately as *Hooks* (1980) with additional material (and the index); Book III, *Stane,* covers places 45–81; Books IIII and V appeared in 1978 as *Becoming,* which omits the "place" numbers

from the text. Other works of somewhat indistinct but actual relationship to *Place* are *Fire-place* (published with *Hearth-work* by Pierre Joris as *Fire-Work* [1977]), *Splashed Ponds (leading from Unpolished Mirrors)* (1979), *Docking* (leading into part of *Stane*), and *William Rufus* (which Fisher listed in December 1978 as "in progress"). *Stane,* Book III, is also the second movement; Book Two comprises the second movement. Place 32, which is itself part of Book I, is preface to place 40, which is in turn the close of both Book Two and of the third movement. Here is a partial (since a complete one is stridently resisted in the work itself) bibliography of Fisher's *Place:*

Becoming, Place Books IIII and V (London: Aloes, 1978).
Convergences, in place, of the play, stage eight; place 40 (London: Spanner, 1978).
Docking; which led to parts of place 66 shown in that work and here (Bishop's Stortford: Great Works, 1978).
Eros: Father: Pattern; place 39 (Warehorne, Near Ashford, Kent: Secret Books, 1980).
"Fire-place; being the full version of place 76/50 & 78," with Pierre Joris, "Hearth-work," *Fire-works,* (Hebden Bridge, West Yorkshire: Hatch Books, 1977.)
Hooks; being those parts of place 32, 'taken out of place' from Book II to act as an opening into 'Convergences, in place, of the play', place 40 (Baltimore: Pod Books, 1980).
Pit Stop, which led out of Grampians interweaving place 74 published as follows:
  Played Against Drum Beats (Cambridge: Perfect Bound)
  Enclosed Delight (Hebden Bridge, West Yorkshire: Curtains)
  Cleopatra's Sonority (Hebden Bridge, West Yorkshire: Curtains)
  Gripping the Rail (Newcastle upon Tyne: Pig, 1976).
Place typescript drafted 22.4.73 comprising most of book I place one to thirty-seven First Movement (London: Aloes, 1974).
Place Book I drafted 22.4.73 comprising most of Book I place one to thirty-seven (Carboro, NC: Truck Books, 1976).
Prologue and Intonation to the Vespers of the Revolution: Unpolished Mirrors Serial G (London: Spanner, 1981).
Splashed Ponds: Unpolished Mirrors Serial F (London: Spanner, 1981).
Stane, drafted 31.12.75 comprising most of place Book III place forty-five to eightyone Second Movement (London: Aloes Books, 1977).
Stepping Out (Durham: Pig, 1989).
Unpolished Mirrors Serial H (London: Spanner, 1981).
Unpolished Mirrors "Collated form" (London: Spanner, 1981).
Unpolished Mirrors (London: Reality Studios, 1985).

In 2005, about 12 years after I wrote this essay, Reality Street Editions (in Hastings, East Sussex, UK) published *Place,* a "complete text" of "the major constituent books": *Place Book 1, Becoming, Stane, Eros:Father:Pattern,* and *Unpolished Mirrors.* The book includes a brief "Introduction," a list of "Resources," and a partial list of Fisher's publications. A note on the back cover says that *Place* "has never received definitive, single-covers publication, though it is partly written in such a way as to defy that possibility" and identifies the book as "probably as close to that definitive edition as you are likely to get."

21. "Not subject to" is not the same as "free of." But Fisher is building a temporally variable text, in that he refuses to correlate the sequential position of the poem with its temporal. That is to say, parts written early in the serial may refer structurally backwards to parts as yet unwritten and even unplanned.

22. The list omits *Cabbage Gardens* (Fathom P, 1979) and *The Liberties* (Guilford, CT: Loon, 1980), and includes a ghost title, *Scattering as Behavior Toward Risk,* as forthcoming from Wesleyan University Press. This work appeared as a section of Howe's *Singularities* (Hanover and London: UP of New England for Wesleyan UP, 1990).

23. As Lewis points out, such ambiguation extends even to the binding: the spine bears the title "a bibliography of the king's book; or, eikon basilike"—a variation of the front cover and half title, which omits the semicolon, and of the full title, which mixes upper and lower case and omits the punctuation: "A Bibliography of The King's Book or Eikon Basilike". See Kent Lewis, "Susan Howe's Poetics of the Bibliography," *West Coast Line* 10 (27.1) (Spring 1993): 118–127.

24. Agrippa.english.ucsb.edu/. Last accessed 28 June 2011.

25. Barrett Watten, *Conduit* (San Francisco: Gaz, 1988) 34.

26. For the sake of illustration I am oversimplifying the complex history of Stein's text, though it is clear that (for whatever reason) Toklas did indeed, as Ulla Dydo thoroughly documents, substitute alternatives for many of the "m-words" like *may* and *May,* and Stein accepted some of her substitutions (see Ulla Dydo, "How to Read Gertrude Stein: The Manuscript of 'Stanzas in Meditation,'" *Text: Transactions of the Society for Textual Scholarship* 1 (1981): 271–303; and "Stanzas in Meditation: The Other Autobiography," *Chicago Review* 35.2 (Winter 1985): 4–20.

Poetic Fact

> The Cantos meaning is The Cantos: in spite of all the complexities they deal with. Restituting love and hate to a chain of poetic fact they have for instance devoted the duration of one canto to Confucius.
>
> —Louis Zukofsky

Those two sentences have intrigued me for some time, they raise so many fundamental questions regarding the nature of poetry. Limitations of space make it difficult to consider here in any detail either what Zukofsky calls a *chain* of poetic fact or what he might mean by that difficult word *restituting.* Those two words provoke consideration of complex and large assumptions, about reading and the nature of writing and thinking, which underlie the apparently straightforward notion that Zukofsky sidesteps, that of a "poetic fact," a term which rests on similarly complex and largely unformulated assumptions about what we call the aesthetic. Robert Creeley gestured briefly toward it when he remarked to Linda Wagner in about 1964 that a "fact in a poem is very distinct from that fact in conversation."[1] He seems to have had in mind ways in which our understanding of a fact is inflected by what he calls the "*mode* of address" (conversation or poem). Our response in that mode is reciprocally inflected by the fact itself.

William Carlos Williams indirectly sketched a fuller sense of a poetic fact in book 5 of *Paterson,* in his responses to Mike Wallace's hostile questions about the "fashionable grocery list" in his poem "Two Pendants for the Ears." Answering Wallace's question "Is it poetry?" Williams said of the list that "[r]hythmically, it's organized as a sample of the American idiom. It has as much originality as jazz. If you say '2 partridges, 2 mallard ducks, a Dungeness crab'—if you treat that rhythmically, ignoring the practical sense it forms a jagged pattern. It is, to my mind, poetry. . . . Anything is good material for poetry." Wallace's response (whether genuine or not), is bafflement: "aren't we supposed to understand it? . . . shouldn't a word mean something when you see it?"[2] His position is not simply that a shopping list is not a poem, but that certain kinds of fact in the world—in this case a shopping list—by their very nature *cannot* be facts in a poem, because they are "in fact" a shopping list.[3] In pursuing his point, Wallace has ripped the eight lines of shopping list from their context—a poem that is over 250 lines long (255 to be precise) about Williams's mother as she lay dying. That shopping list is one of several disturbances in the poem; that disturbance itself is a fact in the poem.[4] It may or may not be a "poetic" fact.

When Wallace asks, "Shouldn't a word mean something when you see it?" he is not, of course, saying that the words "2 partridges" are meaningless—they mean, of course, "two partridges." But he wants them to mean more than that, he wants words in poems to say more than one thing at once. Poems should gesture beyond themselves, beyond their lexical meaning, carry the reader (in transport) some place else, out-of-the-ordinary and preferably transcendent. Poems, that is, should say something suggestive and profound, should be invested with let's call it large meanings, be beautiful, and even perhaps a little difficult—a kind of elaborate lie which needs to be decoded. In homing in on the meaning, all Wallace can see is one *kind* of meaning (and indeed he seeks *one* meaning), and he wants that meaning to be *more:* he wants the resonance of image, metaphor, and symbol, all tending to a single end, unitive. But Williams, who in his poetry generally resists the conventions of connotative device, is interested in sound, homes in on the prosody, on line-breaks—he follows the play of one context with or against another, the patterning of speech and rhythm; he's interested in the sound as well as the sense and the syntax as they all work together to constitute the multipart experience that reading the poem is. The poem patters on, patterning, tracking Williams's interest in juxtapositions, here of lists and speech and the fact of Elena dying—he's into the play of different voices and discourses. So Williams rebukes Wallace for just "listening to the sense, the common sense of what it says." For Wallace, words are transparent, not opaque, little windows through which we see the visible world of things. But poems offer another kind of meaning, another *means*—Creeley's mode. Williams is metonymic.

One might say that the "fashionable shopping list" that so troubled Wallace is a poetic fact, in the sense that a fact in a poem is there because it is part of what makes a poem a poem, and that it exists for the sake of the poem. But such a formulation is tautological, substituting words for words, and leaves open the question of what makes a fact "poetic," what constitutes a poetic fact.

I

As word and as concept, "fact" is notoriously slippery, it slides so readily off the tongue or pen. The "common sense" Williams referred to makes assumptions which do not easily stand up to examination. In 1935, when Henrik Fleck published his astonishing and revolutionary study of syphilis, *Genesis and Development of a Scientific Fact,* one person when he heard the title asked "How can such a book be? A fact is a fact. It has neither genesis or development"[5]—an observation that rests on the assumption, which Fleck questions, that scientific facts are flat, impartial, neutral, objective. Wallace, talking to Williams, knows that poetry is not prose and poems are not shopping lists: for him, facts are self-evidently and even perhaps axiomatically true; in all cases the categories, and the taxonomy that defines them, hold firm. Hence colloquial usage, that is to say social custom, can safely assert that grass and trees are "green," a claim that is demonstrably—and hence "in fact"—false.

But the slight irony of that "in fact" in my previous sentence, points to a central and inescapable fluidity and uncertainty about "fact" both as word and concept. A fact can be demonstrated, but it cannot be argued. Arguments about facts, that is to say, only occur when the evidence is seen as inadequate, irrelevant, or unfounded—and over time, as its foundation changes, the verity of a fact, and indeed its nature, decays. The fact ceases to be axiomatic, and is questioned. It requires proof. The word *fact* comes from *factum,* Latin for *deed, act, exploit,* something *done;* hence it carries a strong residue from the verb. It's closely related to the French *fait: do, make, pass.* A fact is also, in Middle English, a *feat* (deed, fact). A fact is a deed, a doing, something that has been done. It is something *made.* And we use facts to settle arguments, we appeal to facts in order to establish the truth of something.[6] The syntax of that observation might suggest that facts exist on their own account, but on reflection it is clear, first, that facts are remembered, or even noticed, when they confirm something under dispute, or disrupt a framework of understanding, challenging the order of things; and second, that "an isolated fact" is a nonsense. "There are no self-sustained facts, floating in a nonentity," observed Alfred North Whitehead. "Every proposition proposing a fact must, in its complete analysis, propose the general character of a universe required for that fact."[7] There has to be agreement, not only that a fact is *worth* remembering (a value judgment) but indeed that a fact is a fact at all—a consensual agreement heavily dependent upon a fairly wide cultural context. A "pure" fact, could there be such a thing, would be inert, unchanging, finally and definitively beyond debate.

Wallace's argument with Williams is not in this respect unlike an argument between an astronomer who assumes on the basis of contemporary data that the universe is approximately thirteen billion years old, and a literalist reader of the Bible who on the basis of Archbishop Usher's calculations accepts that the planet Earth was created by God in October 4004 BC.[8] Such a fact, indeed any fact, is thus a feature of a given discourse, and is dependent upon it.

This is not as simple a matter as my examples suggest, for the terms of a given discourse may be so widely used as to be culture-wide, to all intents and purposes universal, invisible because unconsciously held—and of course unquestioned. In 1543 Andreas Vesalius (1514–1564)—"the father of human anatomy"—published *On the Fabric of the Human Body,* an atlas of human anatomy, in seven volumes.[9] Startlingly original, the work is the outcome of literally hundreds of dissections—he refused to rely on earlier anatomical drawings—and it changed European knowledge of human anatomy forever: it revolutionized medical education in the West; it led to the hands-on training in anatomy of future doctors, and became the basis of medical art and illustration for generations. It's a standard text, and it had a long life as a reference book and teaching tool. It was frequently republished, summarized, revised; the illustrations were often redrawn and copied from Vesalius's woodcuts, the redrawn versions maintaining whatever in the original was erroneous. The engravings in a 1642 edition of Nicholas Fontanus's *Librorum Andreas Vesalius de humani corporis fabrica epitome* are beautifully clear—indeed exemplary—as those in a *vade mecum* should be, since they claim to represent fact, and are in a handbook-guidebook to human anatomy. The engraving of human female reproductive organs, specifically the ovaries, uterus, and vagina, is to a modern eye most notable not for its disproportions and misplaced parts (which may have pragmatic or pedagogical justification), but for its strong resemblance to engravings of *male* genitalia, penis and testicles inverted: a cylindrical vagina (the labia resembling a foreskin) pendant from a uterus which closely resembles a pair of testicles sheathed in a (vaguely heart-shaped) scrotum.[10] Fontanus's commentary, following Vesalius, asks, "How does the seed enter the woman during ejaculation if the womb is so tightly closed that not even a needle can enter through it, according to Hippocrates, Book 5, aphorisms 51 and 54?" and answers: "Through a branch leading from the ejaculatory tract entering the cervix of the uterus, as this illustration shows." That "branch," clearly labeled as that "through which the woman becomes impregnated by the seed ejaculated at the time of intercourse," does not exist. The close visual correlation, in the engraving, of the shapes of male external and female internal genitalia, possibly stimulated (if that is the right word) by the linguistic parallel of sword and sheath, suggest that from the very start Vesalius-Fontanus assume a fundamental similarity between male and female genitalia—an assumption inherited from the ancient world, from classical texts, from the work of Hippocrates and Galen. One might conclude that Vesalius-Fontanus see what they expect to see, and even what they want to see, so caught up are they in the mind-set of their contemporaries, in contemporary theories of the human body—especially the male human body—and its place in the natural order of things. What their drawings present is something like a fiction. Clearly, the path from dissection to pictorial representation is extremely complicated, and prone to error.[11]

The diagrams in modern school and college textbooks are overtly schematic, and make no attempt to show what any particular internal organ looks like; laying no claim to representation the way a drawing from Vesalius does, they do, like Vesalius's atlas, claim to present *fact*. The green and black diagram of figure "9.31. Reproductive tract of human female, anterior view," in the second edition of Keeton's *Biological Science* (1972),[12] in schematic form identifies only ovaries, oviducts, uterus, cervix, and vagina, but in contrast to Vesalius the diagram has been emphatically feminized—genderized—in a middle-to-late twentieth-century style.[13] The overall shape is strongly suggestive of a curvaceous and laterally symmetrical female torso. The oviducts and ovaries reach out in hovering curves like graceful shoulders bearing arms or even wings, horizontally stretched to each side; the apparent rib cage of that torso is furnished with slight bulges suggestive of breasts, but anatomically speaking the suggestion offers an absurd deformity, since the entire diagram is a very simplified cartoon demonstration of the internal arrangement of the female body below the waist; below that putative rib-cage the torso pinches at its waist (the cervix) and curves out voluptuously at hips which in their fleshy outline shelter a vagina large enough to house a pair of very robust twins. Presenting a highly abstract version of the anatomy shared by all (normal) women, in its tidiness and uniformity the drawing offers an idealized version of the "natural" or "real" thing. Actually the work of a female artist, in its reflection of social and cultural values it seems to have been designed to attract and please the male gaze. The net overall effect, in both Vesalius/Fontanus and Keeton, prizing symmetry as they do, is to aestheticize as well as to tidy up the unruly messiness of the human body; to aestheticize, that is to say, the "facts."

A fact thus recorded in the textbook or field guide is a disturbance, a disruption, a discontinuity of the actual physical world. It distorts the world as experienced. In his interview with Wallace, Williams (like many poets and artists) wants to lift the sealed surface of fact, expose the rupture; Wallace prefers (if he even notices its existence) to paper over the disruption at the heart of "fact"; he resists the new, the unusual, the unconventional. Such disturbances, a stylization, normalization, and concomitant idealization of the intense variety of the (imperfect) physical world, have a very long history indeed; and are not confined to handbooks of human anatomy. Inflected by social and political assumptions and practices, they shape observation and thought, they shape textbooks, handbooks, and field guides—primary instruments for the transmission of knowledge, authoritative sources of essential information.

The digitalis in the poisonous foxglove has for centuries been known as an important remedy for heart disease. Yet the herbals which have survived from say the twelfth century are frequently filled with unrecognizable figures and incomprehensible vocabulary.[14] Historically, there are three great herbals, by Theophrastus, by Dioscorides, and by Apuleius Platonicus ("Pseudo-Apuleius"); all three were standard international authorities and were in circulation for hundreds of years. Theophrastus, born in about 370 BC, was Aristotle's son-in-law and successor; his was the first systematic attempt we know of in Europe to organize the knowledge of plants. Dioscorides compiled his great medical herb catalogue, *De Materia Medica* in the first century CE—Nero was Emperor of Rome—and Apuleius drew on Dioscorides when he put his *Herbarium* together two or three hundred years later. *De Materia Medica* is a handbook and field guide to medicinal plants, and it was used as standard text and reference book for about a thousand years. An identification drawing in a manuscript of about 1120 from Bury St Edmunds (MS. Bodley 130), a Latin version, identifies the plant as a "foxes glove," but with its four blooms drooping from stems radiating from a central stem and three buds branching from the tip it's quite clear that the artist has either never seen and surely didn't step outdoors simply to look at one, or has got the name completely wrong.[15]

Once compiled and illustrated, these three herbals were copied from hand to hand, translated, and circulated widely. Manuscripts of *De Materia Medica* exist in Greek, Latin, Anglo-Saxon, Italian, Arabic, Persian, and Hebrew. In its many versions, it was a standard handbook and reference book for well over fifteen hundred years; it was used as a sourcebook even as recently as 1934. Yet, though they often tell us a great deal about the culture in which they were produced, such reference books are as a rule almost useless for identifying plants. They claim to be factual, but many drawings—like those of *artemisia* (wormwood) in MS.Sloane 1975 (in the British Library) are highly stylized or woven into the text as highly decorative elements in elaborately designed pages. Some plant names are gobbledygook; some drawings—of Centaury, for example, or of houseleek—are anecdotally embellished with symbols arising from myths about the plant, and show nothing of the plant at all. The mandrake frequently appears as a human figure with leaves growing from its head, or shows men being bitten by mad dogs attached by rope to an indeterminate-looking plant.[16] The text in such herbals is, to a modern eye and mind, totally unhelpful, for the kind of knowledge they refer to is no longer relevant or useful and is of interest perhaps only to the historian of ideas or an old-fashioned antiquarian. In some instances the material circumstances under which a manuscript was produced, the means of production, determined its accuracy or error. Thus drawings of the asphodel, common in Mediterranean countries but not growing in northern Europe and Britain, are frequently the work of artists who have never seen the plant and who copied from other drawings perhaps by artists equally innocent of first-hand knowledge, and embellished to invoke a larger cultural or social significance.

Never having seen the plant, the artist copies a picture from another manuscript, itself no doubt a copy—or invents it from a verbal description. Evidently the general neglect of the medical aspect of the herbals by modern students and readers is more than a little due to the extreme difficulty and in many cases impossibility of accurate plant-identification even in printed herbals. Like Keeton's schematic cartoon of the "reproductive tract of human female" with *its* unstated assumptions about gender and the normal, many of the drawings in herbals draw on such collectively held ideals as cosmic harmony and interconnectedness. The "facts" they offer are, as Fleck observes of all facts, "not objectively given, but collectively created" (157), a social construct.

In his *Enquiry into Plants* (c. 370) BC, Theophrastus saw plants as animals who had their feet in the air and their mouths in the ground. He thought this was a fact; the modern reader might view it as simply a different way of describing plant life. It doesn't exactly match our own view of what we call the "natural," but it makes its own wonderful sense—it's quite magical—and, if you let it, if you move it into your felt imagination, it transforms the way you see the world, how you think of it, no matter how briefly. And it becomes possible, if you feel something of that magic, if you can let go of your own presuppositions about the world and what makes things true or false, your presuppositions of what's real and what's delusion, if you look beyond the cultural and philosophical presuppositions and ideas of the world, of what "nature" is, of the relations of the visible to the invisible, the seen to the unseen, and your identity and individuality in the cosmos, then it is possible to glimpse something of the mind-set where Theophrastus is coming from. The break with one's own common sense is a break with one's syntax, logic, and sense; such a break makes the irreparable gap between the syntax of the world and the syntax of our observation, thought, and understanding—the syntax of ordinary discourse—visible.

Theophrastus's notion, to borrow Whitehead's words, is not "capable of being understood apart from interpretation as an element in a system." As an "immediate brute fact" (Whitehead's term) it calls forth, it "*requires* its metaphysical interpretation as an item, in a world with some systematic relation to it."[17] That systematic relation shifts the grounds of our perception by engaging the imagination; it changes the *fact* of the world. It might, then, be a poetic fact, for poems, in their break with ordinary syntax, offer, indeed create, a dwelling (in all senses of "dwell"), and demand of their reader an *imaginative* response.

II

Theophrastus's notion points to one kind of poetic fact—the sort which people vaguely gesture toward when they say of something "Oh isn't that poetic!" One might think of it as a poetic fact which resides in some sense beyond or outside a poem in that it transcends ordinary language and ordinary discourse. This kind of "poetic" is very complex and more than a little baffling. It breaks through the crust of accepted fact and its discourse and *obliges* you to re-think and re-imagine the world. Another kind of poetic fact is most easily described as a fact within the poem—it's a matter of technique, perhaps, or at the very least is simply a feature of poetic discourse. We can start with that notion, at any rate. It may be, for instance, that when Zukofsky said Pound's *Cantos* "restitute love and hate to a chain of poetic fact," he meant that we should not mistake whatever the *Cantos* say about love and hate for what Pound personally or politically has to say about these things *in the world.*[18]

This is one of the great vexed questions, of course, for it is a question of meaning and intent, deeply entangled with the question of the truth-value of poetry, and it's an especially and famously vexed question in the case of Ezra Pound. Meaning is a very tricky matter indeed, and discussions of meaning tend to get confused because of the slipperiness of that word. On one hand it signifies intention ("I mean to change my habits") and on the other it means signification or understanding ("I don't know what that means"). Meaning and intention are inextricably intertwined: what I mean is not necessarily what you think I mean. That's, um, a fact. Meanings change—that's another fact.

Here's a passage from Canto 76—one of the Pisan Cantos, written with a typewriter on a desk in the commandant's office while Pound was awaiting trial for treason, imprisoned at the Military Detention Center at Pisa; written when the only book Pound was allowed to see was a simple college dictionary in that office.

"c'mon, small fry," sd/the smaller black lad
  to the larger.
"Just playin'" ante mortem no scortum
(that's progress, me yr' ' ' se/call it progress/)

(Canto 76 p. 455)[19]

That last line is very puzzling, and it brings me to a topic central to this somewhat perplexed rumination on the nature of poetic fact: punctuation.

Just what is going on in the typographic disturbance in that line? What sort of typewriter was Pound using? What was the keyboard like? Was the single-quote apostrophe where the asterisk used to be? On some keyboards, the apostrophe is above the figure 8, on others the asterisk. Did he mean to type three asterisks? Don Wellman suggested to me, when I asked, that in Pound's more customary orthography it might have been an apostrophe followed by two asterisks indicating missing letters; the line would then (perhaps) read "yr' **se" for "yr' arse," "establishing a large slur for the purposes of intonation."[20] Accidental or purposeful, the punctuation is surely inventive, and the typographic disturbance surely echoes, wittingly or not, the kind of disturbance this Canto plays, especially in this passage's concern with the fate of two black soldiers waiting under sentence of death in the cages next to Pound's at Pisa.

What I'm saying here, of course, has no obvious relevance to the nature of "poetic fact," but let me link it up. Robert Duncan was fond of telling the story of Ezra Pound some time in about 1930 buying an Italian typewriter and the keyboard was different: there's a forward-slash mark (/) where the period used to be on his old one. Half-way through typing a Canto to send to Harriet Monroe's magazine *Poetry* Pound noticed that where his original had contained periods, his clean copy had a forward-slash, like this:

With respect to his motives (Madison writing) I acknowledged
I had been much puzzled to divine any natural ones
without looking deeper into human nature
than I was willing to do.

(in re/Mr Robert Smith)

So critical of the state of that country
moneyed men I imagine are glad to place their money abroad.
Mr Adams could borrow there for us.

from Canto 31 (1931) p. 154

A couple of Cantos later he did it again, in Canto 33:

Rogier (minister) told me that this government (Brussels) had
been intending to introduce such a law but found itself (re/
child labour not limited to 12 hours per day) always blocked
by the jealous uneasiness that met any law tampering with
the absolute freedom of labour.

Lord H. de Walden from Brussels. 1862

from Canto 33 (1931), p. 162

Duncan said that Pound, instead of correcting the mistake the way ordinary people do, read the fact of that slant-bar as a message from the poem and instead rewrote the poem to incorporate the change as a necessity. *If so,* then that forward slash becomes a poetic fact, for it registers an intent not the poet's. I really don't know whether the story is true—Duncan had seen Pound's manuscripts at Yale and I haven't—but if you track the forward slash as Pound uses it throughout the *Cantos* you see that Duncan's story is true in its essentials. In Pound's hands the forward slash starts out as a fact in the poem, and soon becomes a *factor,* an *agency,* in the poem—that is to say, it becomes a poetic fact.

Pound uses the forward slash well over 200 times in the course of the *Cantos*—but I'll try to sketch its development. At first, he uses it simply to mark "re" as an abbreviation (this is a habitual idiom as we see from his letters etc.), and throughout the *Cantos,* after Canto 31, he uses the slash to mark abbreviations, *wd/ shd/ cd/ gt/ yr/ sd/ recd/ etc/* and the like, *Ld/* [as in Lord Byron]; *natr/* [nature]; *Ct/* [Count]; *op/* [opinion] and so forth.[21] Among other things, that slash comes to mark pronunciation as well as abbreviation—in some Cantos we get the word *said,* for instance, spelled out in full in one line, and abbreviated with a slash in another—*sd* is a much shorter sound, *cd* shorter than *could,* and so on. But Pound doesn't stop there; by the time he gets to Canto 35 ([1934] p. 175), we get:

foot like a flowery branch. That
Venice be *luogo do contratto* may we
say the place where the deal is made

and the profits
most assuredly from the pocket
of the last man who buys / exempt from customs
be food stuffs and nothing else so exempted
9 per cent in, and 9 out, for the upkeep of "The Dominant"
and De Gama (Vasco) a great inconvenience in fact the
worst news that there could be but:
Can Portugal keep it up?

from Canto 35 (1934), p. 175

Here he's using the slash like an opening parenthesis, marking an explanatory interruption. That's a shift in the syntax of the sentence as well as a shift of attention, focus, and sense—it invites you to shift gears, or change key. Later, in one of the *Pisan Cantos* (Canto 77, ten or more years later), he uses it much more precisely, to mark a closing parenthesis: he marks the opening of the parenthesis with an elision mark—but here it's two periods in a row, not the conventional three, close-set:

Von Tirpitz said to his daughter..as we have elsewhere
recorded / he said: beware of their charm

from Canto 77, p. 464

And it seems, here as elsewhere, to mark a rhythmic shift, a change in pace, or a pause, but also quite possibly a shift in tone. That's especially clear in an earlier Canto (#46 [1936]); this is the second of the usury cantos:

19 Years on this case/first case. I have set down part of
The Evidence. Part/commune sepulchrum
Aurum est commune sepulchrum. Usura, commune sepulchrura.
helandros kai heleptolis kai helarxe.
Hic Geryon est. Hic hyperusura.

FIVE million youths without jobs
FOUR million adult illiterates
15 million 'vocational misfits', that is with small chance for jobs
NINE million persons annual, injured in preventable industrial
accidents
One hundred thousand violent crimes. The Eunited States ov
America
3rd year of the reign of F. Roosevelt, signed F. Delano, his uncle.

CASE for the prosecution. That is one case, minor case
in the series/Eunited States of America, a.d. 1935
England a worse case, France under a foetor of regents.
from Canto 46 (1936), pp. 234-235

It's quite clear he's exploring the potential of the slash as a punctuation mark, exploring its ability to mark something ordinary punctuation can't. In Pound's hands the forward-slash is a remarkably versatile device to mark grammatical and syntactic shifts as the thought moves, as reference broadens, as the attention shifts. The poem—the voice of the poem—is changing gears, and the forward slash is a signal to that effect. I must emphasize that we don't necessarily know in any given instance what exactly that forward-slash is doing, we certainly don't know in advance—we have to wait and see, work it out—and I think that's true for Pound as well, writing the poem. The forward-slash is a poetic fact; it is a disturbance in the poem, and like all such disturbances it tells us to sit up and pay attention. And the disturbance can be quite complex—in this instance, just to take the second through fifth lines in this quotation:

The Evidence.   Part/ commune sepulchrum
Aurum est commune sepulchrum. Usura, commune
sepulchra.
Helandros   kai heleptolis   kai helarxe.
Hic Geryon est. Hic hyperusura.

A mix of languages: English to Latin to Greek (transliterated so we know the noise it makes), back to Latin. "The Evidence. Part / Gold is a common sepulchre. Usury a common sepulchre. destroyer of men   destroyer of cities   destroyer of governments. Here is Geryon. Here hyperusury."[22]

At first sight, the final forward-slash in the extract from Canto 46 looks pretty straightforward:

in the series/ Eunited States of America, a.d. 1935

If anything, it seems to be acting as a colon or some other fairly conventional punctuation, such as a closing parenthesis (in this case opened up by the comma in the previous line)—"a minor case in the series:"—but it's also a command and reminder to the reader, a *sit-up-and-pay-attention!* device, drawing your attention to the repeated corny pun in "Eunited States of America"—a sort of *eeuw* sound of disgust perhaps? More likely the *Eun* of

Eunuch, the emasculated United States, and certainly a pun across from the Greek, prefix *eu-*, "done well."[23]

It's not that Pound gives the forward-slash a new turn every time he uses it; much of the time it simply marks an abbreviation of some sort. But just as you're getting used to it, here it comes again, signalling something else. Sometimes it's at the end of a line all by itself, sometimes with a period right after (as happens, for example, in Canto 53). Sometimes—quite often, actually—it appears mid-line, perhaps marking an interruption, or the end of one, but always, so far as I can tell, in this position marking a shift in the sound and/or pacing, perhaps a shift we haven't come across before:

> who played the spinet on Johnnie Bach's birthday
> do not exaggerate/ he at least plays on some such instrument
> and learned to pick out several tunes European)
>
> *from* Canto 59, p. 326

What do we make of that "do not exaggerate"? Is he addressing himself, addressing the *writing*? It *is* an imperative, and it looks as though the *line break* after "birthday" registers or signals a shift in syntax and voice; whoever is being addressed here it is not the same as whoever is addressed in the previous line (unless by any chance he was talking to himself there too?) and the forward slash that comes right after registers another shift, a self-correction brought about by that brief imperative. The forward slash here is a pause, it marks the end of an aside, and the aside—though it may be a disturbance of the sentence—does not, hmmm, interrupt the main thread of thought. How could you conventionally punctuate this? It strikes me that Pound is deploying the forward slash in ways he could not have foreseen back when he bought that typewriter and typed Canto 31.

So, like Pound attending to detail, we come to see the forward slash, sometimes doing two things at once, like marking an abbreviation and opening an aside:

> bound by no laws made by Parliament
> since our ancestors came here
> Bill of Rights
> wished to hear in Congress at large
> law of natr/ Brit. constitution
> trade of Empire cd/ be under parliament
> Mr Rutledge of S. Carolina said:
>
> *from* Canto 65, p. 364

The forward slash of that "cd/ be" breaking the crust of habit yet again, as it signals a slight pause and so shifts emphasis (could *be*) in a phrase usually almost slurred together (could-be). Pound is recounting the history of the First Continental Congress in 1774. In Canto 65 there are three in a row:

> Sir Edward Coke, who being in King's displeasure,
> was removed from his place by writ of the King
> reciting that whereas etc///...appointed to desist from...
> timid jurors and judges who held during pleasure
> never failed to second views of the Crown
>
> *from* Canto 66, p. 385

It looks to me that the forward slash here indicates one set of elision marks, and the three periods mark another, and surely it conveys something of his own—and our—irritation and impatience with boring and intractable but necessary source materials. It's a pretty complex set of moves, I think, rhythmically, tonally, syntactically, the bored impatient voice moving on but despite itself lingering.

And lastly, this, the closing lines of Canto 83:

> but if Senator Edwards cd/ speak
> and have his tropes stay in the memory 40 years, 60 years?
> in short / the descent
> has not been of advantage either
>   to the Senate or to "society"
>   or to the people
>   The States have passed thru a
>   dam'd supercilious era
> Down, Derry-down /
>   Oh let an old man rest.
>
> *from* Canto 83, p. 536

Look at the variety of notation, no space before the forward slash in line 1—clearly, then, marking *cd* as an abbreviation, but by now we're so used to it marking a brief pause as well that it marks emphasis, as in the previous example. But the space either side of the slash in lines 3 and 9 surely marks a breath pause, a more apparent shift in intonation. And then there's the line-breaks, how they work. Not all in the same way by any means.

Pound's use of the forward slash is especially frequent and varied in the *Pisan Cantos,* which were written under great urgency. In the cage at the

DTC at Pisa, Pound really did not know whether the next morning would be his last, whether tomorrow morning he'd be facing a firing squad. He has no access to any books (save a simple college dictionary in the commandant's office)—he's driven, perhaps for the first time in his life, to rely on his own resources, and the only resource he has is memory. The writing has a desperate urgency about it; the *Pisan Cantos* are astonishing organized feats of memory, feats of organized memory, and his use of the forward dash carries some of that urgency. It is a factor in the writing, an energizing and generative resource.

III

I've spent so much time on this for two reasons:

First, because one conviction lying behind twentieth-century poetry (and before, for that matter) is that poetry is speech. That's one of the assumptions behind Pound's use of the forward slash. One of the assumptions which underlie the growth and development of what used to be called free verse is that the poem, on the page, must register the movement of the voice and breath. So notation—how to get that voice on the page so that the reader can reproduce it accurately, so that the reader can get the voicing right—is a problem that haunts poet after poet.[24]

Second, because punctuation—in Pound's use of the forward slash and indeed in his practice generally—is a poetic fact. He revolutionized the punctuation of poetry in English. I don't think this was a deliberate act, done with full intent—he didn't start out determined to do that—I think it came about simply because he bought a new typewriter. It's a kind of accident.[25] He freed poetic notation from the strict confines of conventional grammar and orthography, from such ridiculous rules as the one which says "a clause introduced by the word 'that' is not preceded by a comma, whereas a clause introduced by the word 'which' is." Louis Zukofsky said that such rules and their makers "exist entirely in that frozen realm without crisis that Dante called the 'secondary speech.' In poetry," Zukofsky observed, "one can sing without stopping and without commas of the redundant commonplace action of the species."[26]

With the forward slash Pound invented a system of notation for the poem and extended notational possibility—he opened the floodgates. There's Charles Olson, for example, and William Carlos Williams. Olson used the forward slash as early as 1945 in a poem addressed to Pound—where it works much as it does in Cantos 35 and 46. He extended Pound's revolution of punctuation very early in his writing career, most notably and characteristically perhaps in his habitual use of parentheses—it's very hard to open a page of *The Maximus Poems* without finding an opening parenthesis that never closes but instead moves into yet another opening parenthesis. And Williams—who said that he "discovered" triadic stepped verse as he wrote book 2 of *Paterson*—found the spaced period an enormous resource. He explored it over about twenty years, in the process varying the size not only of the space, but of the period itself—in some poems it's actually a small bullet.[27] As Williams uses it in his last poems, the spaced period is a notation for the voice and breath, but it doesn't just mark a breath-pause or a rhythmic pause, it's not *simply* a brief silence in the sound and rhythm of the poem. It is agency. It *loads* the silence, freights it, the thought held in suspension before—when the period arrives—it's brought to a conclusion. The spaced period at one and the same time suspends the end of the sentence, delays it, while at the same time it marks it, signals it, and we hold in abeyance the purport of that sentence until the period comes along to close it (and the voice) off. It marks, then, the sort of down-shift in intonation that we use in speech to signal the conclusion of a sentence, but at the same time—especially when it occurs mid-line—while bringing the sentence to a close opening up a small anticipation in the very process of delaying-and-then-fulfilling that small completion; it effects a continuation of attention. Robert Duncan called the suspended period "A beat syncopating the time at rest; as if there were a stress in silence, . . .so that words are freed, having bounds out of bound" (*Bending the Bow* ix), liberating the words into more than one syntax.

The spaced period is clearly an example of what I'm calling a poetic fact.

When I started my little cruise through Pound's use of the forward slash, I said that Pound, instead of correcting his typing error the way ordinary people do, read the fact of that mistake—the forward slash—as a message from the poem. That forward slash was, then, a mistake, a typing error. But instead of changing his typing habits by adapting them to his new keyboard, Pound refigured the punctuation and notation conventions of his poem. And as he worked his way through the *Cantos,* he adopted that mistake, adapted it, transformed it so that it was no longer a mistake but instead one of the necessities of the poem. He learned from it. It's not so much that he was teaching himself how to read the forward slash as he worked through the *Cantos,* as that *it* was teaching *him;* the typewriter was teaching him. That forward-slash was a poetic fact, as a poetic fact it was *generative*—it led Pound somewhere. The *poem* led Pound somewhere.

I want to say two things here:

1. "Writing is first a search in obedience." That's Robert Duncan.[28] I think it's a cardinal principle.
2. *Poems* don't make mistakes. Of course, poets might, and do. Jack Spicer was insistent that the poet's task is to stop interfering with the poem, poets *must* let the poem do its own work.

This means that you can't, in writing the poem, say "Oh no, I'm not letting that word go there, that's not what I want at all, I want the poem to say so-and-so." But the word's right there, now, down on the page, you've got to deal with that fact—that is, after all, a fact—and in any case who do you think you are to think you know what you want? You have to abandon your own intent—if what you intend is that the poem *say* something—and discover what the writing intends, let it declare its own meaning, what the poem means. Keats called this process "negative capability." You have to start *thinking with the poem.* The poem is an instrument of thought—not what you think *about,* but what you think *with.* If you permit the poem to be obedient to the history of its own composition—and that is actually a very difficult thing to do—then writing is truly a process of discovery, and the process of writing the poem becomes part of the poem's subject-matter, part of the poem's business.

Notes

Epigraph. Louis Zukofsky, "'Recencies" in Poetry," *An "Objectivists" Anthology* (Le Beausset, Var: To, 1932), 24. Reprinted in *Prepositions +: The Collected Essays,* Mark Scroggins, ed. (Hanover and London: Wesleyan UP 2000), 214.

1. Robert Creeley, *Contexts of Poetry: Interviews 1961–1971* (Bolinas: Four Seasons, 1973) 75.

2. William Carlos Williams, *Paterson,* Christopher MacGowan, ed. (New York: New Directions, 1992) 222. The interview first appeared in the New York *Post* (18 October 1957) with the header "Mike Wallace Asks William Carlos Williams Is Poetry a Dead Duck?" Curiously, the word "fact" does not appear in this exchange.

3. Williams had already complicated the issue when in book 1 of *Paterson* he said "No ideas but / in the facts" (*Paterson* 27).

4. "Two Pendants: For the Ears" *Collected Poems,* vol. 2 *1939–1962,* Christopher MacGowan, ed. (New York: New Directions, 1991) 201–215; the "shopping list" is on 208–209. Elena Hoheb Williams died on 7 October 1949.

5. Quoted by Thomas Kuhn, "Foreword," Henrik Fleck, *Genesis and Development of a Scientific Fact* (Chicago: Chicago UP, 1979) viii.

6. It's by no means irrelevant to notice here the etymology of *thing,* another word

derived from a kind of doing (more specifically, of *deciding*)—in this case (in Old English) a meeting or assembly, especially a deliberative or judicial court.

7. Alfred North Whitehead, *Process & Reality: An Essay in Cosmology* (New York: Macmillan, 1929) 14

8. In 1650 Archbishop Usher (1581–1656) published his calculations of the age of the universe. Not everyone agreed with him: John Lightfoot, in a work published 1642–1644, calculated it as 3929 BC; Bede had much earlier said 3952 BC; Scaliger 3949 BC. But different versions of the Old Testament vary in their report of how long after Creation was the Flood: Samaritan Pentateuch, 1307 years; Hebrew, 1656 years; Ethiopian, 2262 years.

9. Andreas Vesalius, *De Humani Corporis Fabrica (On the Fabric of the Human Body)* (1543, 1555), 7 vols. On the basis of this work he became personal physician to the emperor Charles V. A sampling of volume 1, which illustrates the human skeleton, is available online at http://archive.nlm.nih.gov/proj/ttp/flash/vesalius/vesalius.html (last accessed 6/28/2012); a fully annotated English translation of all seven volumes, including facsimiles, is in progress at Northwestern University; volume 1 is available at http://vesalius.northwestern.edu/ (last accessed 6/28/2012).

10. *Librorum Andreas Vesalius de humani corporis fabrica epitome,* Nicholas Fontanus, ed. (Amsterdam, 1642). Reproduced in Fleck, *Genesis* 34; the commentary from which I quote is in Fleck 33.

11. Discussed in some detail by Fleck, and also by Mary Poovey, *A History of the Modern Fact: Problems of Knowledge in the Sciences of Wealth and Society* (Chicago: U of Chicago P, 1998).

12. William T. Keeton, *Biological Science,* 2nd ed., illustrated Paula DiSanto Bensadoun (New York: Norton, 1972) 307. Like many of its kind, this successful college textbook (6th edition 1996, by James Gould) has through various editions been in print for well over 40 years.

13. In a prefatory note, Keeton says that the drawings are designed to "help the student toward a more vivid and realistic conception of organisms and their parts and a readier grasp of processes and inter-relationships" (xiii).

14. Much of this and the following account of herbals draws on Wilfrid Blunt and Sandra Raphael, *The Illustrated Herbal* (London and New York: Thames & Hudson/Metropolitan Museum of Art, 1979). From among the many such studies and surveys, I draw also on Frank J. Anderson, *An Illustrated History of the Herbals* (New York: Columbia UP, 1977); Minta Collins, *Medieval Herbals: The Illustrative Tradition* (London: British Library, 2000); Anna Pavord, *The Naming of Names: The Search for Order in the World of Plants* (London: Bloomsbury, 2005); and for printed herbals, Agnes Richardson Arber, *Herbals: Their Origin and Evolution 1470–1670,* 2nd ed. (Cambridge: Cambridge UP, 1938).

15. For an illustration, see Blunt, 38. MS. Bodley 130 is available on microfilm from the Bodleian library; an English version, complete with reproductions, was published for members of the Roxburghe Club as *The Herbal of Apuleius Barbarus from the early*

twelfth-century manuscript formerly in the Abbey of Bury St. Edmunds (Oxford: Oxford UP, 1925).

16. According to legend, the mandrake screams when pulled out of the ground and will kill the harvester; one way to avoid this fate is to tie it to a dog and have it pull it out of the ground. This makes the dog mad; its bite will then make men mad.

17. Whitehead, *Process & Reality* 18 (emphasis added).

18. As Robert Duncan put it in an essay on Zukofsky, "The truth of a poem was the truth of what was felt in the course of the poem, not the truth of a proposition in whatever political or religious persuasion outside the poem. The particulars of the poem were in process." "As Testimony: Reading Zukofsky These Forty Years," *A Selected Prose,* Robert J. Bertholf, ed., (New York: New Directions, 1995) 143.

19. Page references, cited in text, are to the New Directions one-volume edition of *The Cantos* (New York: 1972), which includes Canto 120.

20. Or, more likely, a slash followed by two asterisks. I have to thank Don Wellman for these suggestions, following my query, on the Buffalo Poetics list, 20 June 2006.

21. He also uses the slash conventionally, as for example to indicate fractions (e.g., p 364, Canto 65) or in the English notation for a shilling in Canto 62 (p. 341) where he feels the need to explain it (presumably in case the reader expects it to mean something else): "ten head 40 acres at 3/ (shillings) per acre."

22. In classical (Greek and Roman) mythology, Geryon is a winged three-headed/three-bodied monster killed by Herakles (Hercules); in Dante's *Inferno* Geryon is the guardian of the eighth circle of Hell and the symbol of fraud; he has the face of a just man and a forked tail. In Dante he is also a symbol of usury, and of violence against nature and against art.

23. Thanks to Daphne Marlatt for pointing this out.

24. For example, Louis Zukofsky: "Typography . . . if print and the arrangement of it will help tell how the voice should sound." ("An Objective," *Prepositions* + 17).

25. An accident of the sort Creeley later explored in *A Day Book* (New York: Scribner's, 1972) n.p., where he records one such discovery: "Whether errors, as meaning to write *Echoes* become *Whether,* as the finger meant to strike the E key, hits the W—and the thought moves on to include it, to use it in the thought, and so on." Duncan, I might add, was insistent on the centrality of accident in his work pretty well throughout his writing life.

26. Zukofsky, "Poetry," *Prepositions* + 10.

27. Robert Duncan picked up the spaced period from Williams, and exploited it in his poetry, notably in the hand-drawn poems of *A Book of Resemblances* (New Haven: Wenning, 1966) and *Fragments of a Disorderd Devotion* (San Francisco: privately published, 1952), where sometimes the spaced period is almost the same size as the x-height of a letter.

28. Robert Duncan, "The Structure of Rime I," *The Opening of the Field* (New York: Grove, 1960) 12.

Sound Reading

> So I go to these readings and that old singsong starts in—half rapt, half-assed—Thank God for the shining exceptions, the formed intensities.
>
> —David Bromige

> Strength of vocables: to bind.
>
> —Edmond Jabès

I want to consider in general terms the vexing question of whether it is possible to read a poem aloud badly—and of course, its corollary, whether (and under what conditions) it might be possible to read a poem aloud well. On the face of it this looks pretty absurd, since we've all been to lifeless readings of leaden parlor-poetry, or have walked out of mumbled (or shouted) performances by drunken readers more attentive to their friends in the audience than to the inept words they are attempting to read.[1] If, as Charles Bernstein suggested in a slightly different context, "a poetic *reading* can be given to any piece of writing" (his emphasis),[2] then, plainly, so can an *un*poetic. Clearly, the question of what "poetic" and "unpoetic" might mean is crucial, though it remains unstated throughout my discussion, partly because of its great complexity. It is deeply intertwined with the notion of readerly competence, and that notion is under scrutiny, implicitly more often than explicitly, pretty well throughout what follows.

I shall not explicitly consider obviously "bad" readings of the kind I've mentioned at all, though it seems to me that the terms *good* and *bad* are notoriously up for grabs, and a moment's reflection will suggest that readings of this sort are perhaps most appropriately to be considered as primarily social rather than "aesthetic" or "literary" occasions. And I want to simplify my discussion by excluding from detailed consideration such (possibly lesser) extremes of apparent readerly incompetence as those of first-year university English courses and the like, where (sometimes) an embarrassed youngster reads aloud to her or his more or less inattentive peers a poem s/he's never seen before. It may be that such a performance, with its social ineptitudes and attendant miseries, does not constitute a "reading" at all, for it is frequently hesitant and confused, marked by stumblings, mispronunciations, stutterings, and mumblings—or it is delivered at breakneck pace and metronomic regularity, with scarcely a pause for breath and scarcely any inflection whatsoever. But anyone who has heard John Cage reading "Mureau," with its attendant inaudibilities and sudden clarities (as the poem moves into and out of various articulations), or has heard Tom Raworth's mercurial gallop through a poem like the highly political *Survival* will perhaps suspend judgment.[3] Raworth said after his 1991 reading of part of that sequence in Vancouver that he takes the poems at speed because that's the only way he can get through them to make sense to the ear and voice; read slowly with the eye, certainly, they present an almost baffling opacity which seems designed to defeat any attempt at intelligible inflected expressive voicing as speech.

For the moment, however, it is convenient to think of these as special cases, though we should caution ourselves, too, that the sort of reading that is learned in high school and university English courses is also a special case. Or rather, a series of special cases, since it is plain to everyone who has undergone the process that reading practices and performances vary widely from teacher to teacher and room to room as teachers privilege their expert reading. It is equally evident, though, that experienced readers have learned to take the poem slowly and/or repeatedly, paying attention to each word as it combines with others into the sentence, heeding each word as it unfolds to the ear, balancing the play of speech patterns with or against prosodic patterns, following the syntax as the resonances of the work draw forth. What I'm saying, I need hardly add, makes it pretty clear that what I have in mind are more or less conventional poems, not necessarily rhyming or metrical, but certainly recognizable as poems by pretty well any reader, written within a clearly identifiable and familiar poetic tradition. Such poems as a rule have a long history of interpretation, and enjoy what can be loosely referred to as canonical status.

Poetry readings, of course, take place in a great variety of conditions, and the contingencies attendant upon the occasion affect the reading performance itself. It is one thing to hear a text for the first time (and be obliged to cultivate your aural memory), and another to be able to follow that text with the eye (because you bought the poet's new book as you came into the reading). Texts which are familiar to the audience might well be heard in a more critical frame than would texts which are completely new to the hearers, perhaps because the recital of a familiar poem, as well as the reading occasion itself, affords a kind of comfort food for the spirit. This certainly seems to have been the case at Dylan Thomas's lucrative public readings in the 1950s, though unquestionably the cult of his personality also helped pack the crowded halls, as did his slight Welsh lilt which lent the music of his recitation an exotic air. And it is true that, once you've heard Thomas reading, his

Welsh voice flavors the sound of all of his poems. His readings were very much a Public Occasion; they enjoyed a ceremonial and even ritual status. That flavor leaches over into some of his recordings (notably his readings of Shakespeare and Webster).[4] As a public reader, Thomas was enormously influential, setting a standard for mellifluous expressiveness which could famously lull the hearer along on the wings of poesy, and it is instructive to compare his readings with those of his chief disciple and imitator, Theodore Marcuse.[5]

Marcuse, a professional actor, emphasized the expressive while keeping an eye (if that is the right word) on the mellifluous, and it is hard indeed to see why his readings were at all popular. His performances of Keats and Shelley (to crowded performance halls) are blatantly virtuoso. It is extremely difficult to describe his performance of Keats's "Ode to a Nightingale" at all: the drawn-out vowels and the highly nasalized consonants of the opening, lingering especially (I think for as long as a second) on the mbn of "numbness," presage what is to come: exaggerated and dramatic expressiveness. Marcuse's articulation of "Fade far away and quite forget," for instance, is to my ear more appropriate to a performance of King Lear's most histrionic speeches: a somewhat high-pitched diminuendo through the first three of those words, so that by the time he reaches the word "away" his voice has faded to the lower limit of audibility; it is followed by a quite rapidly rising crescendo which climaxes in the last syllable (almost a shout) of "forget." To put it bluntly, Marcuse's reading is tediously funny (I cannot even attempt a description of his performance of Shelley's "Ode to the West Wind"). His reading is, I think, almost unhearable, and affords this listener at least little instruction and some unintended pleasure. As a virtuoso performance it draws our attention to the performer and his skilled range of voice and expression rather than to the poem—in this, I think, it is representative of many actors' readings, as well as of readings by imitators of Thomas's luxuriant style. Thomas's own style, however, has a long tradition: "There is a *chaunt* in the recitation both of Coleridge and Wordsworth," William Hazlitt recorded in 1823, "which acts as a spell upon the hearer, and disarms the judgment."[6] But fashions of reading change.

Another difficulty is much more perplexing. When Marcuse lingers on a syllable, or prolongs a consonant, our ear is so caught up in the sound itself (an almost two-second sibilant, for instance) that we tend to lose the syntax and the sense. We lose track of what presumably the reading is all about: the narrative/discursive thrust which this reading of Keats's "Ode" is presumably trying to bring forth. Such apparent inconsistency should not be dismissed out of hand, however, as symptomatic of "badness." In the first place, for me to do so is to claim that my own historically flavored response is exempt from historical contingency: fashions of reading and recital indeed do change, sometimes quite rapidly. In the second, to anyone familiar with them, Marcuse might well seem a forerunner, however unwitting, of the pataphysical performances of The Four Horsemen or the sound-poetry of bill bissett, just as he might equally perhaps be seen as an unconscious follower of Hugo Ball or Velimir Khlebnikov. Similar effects are achieved, on occasion, by readers with a strong ("foreign") accent; hearing them, we find ourselves responding to the non-syntactic and non-semantic qualities of the language, and even on rare occasions feeling as though we have stepped outside it and are viewing it as a foreign tongue.

This might suggest that a poem, then, would best be read in the dialect of its maker. But Wordsworth's Cumberland dialect rhymed *water* with *chatter, July* with *duly,* and according to Hazlitt he talked "with a mixture of clear gushing accents in his voice, a deep guttural intonation, and a strong tincture of the northern *burr,* like the crust on wine" (118). Class-prejudice to one side, what would an audience expecting the *koiné* make of him, puzzling out the words. Audience expectation (and for that matter, I suppose, audience "competence") does to some extent determine the success and the nature of a performance. Marcuse and Thomas both read in a more or less standard *koiné* unlikely to offend the ear—Marcuse, cis-atlantic American; Thomas, educated Anglo-Welsh—and this in turn might suggest that a poem might best be read in the dialect of its audience. That's a very tall order, though, for a public reading. Most of us manage our vowels with consistency and precision (or so we suppose), but each of us manages them differently, and if we move into an unfamiliar dialect region we may find (as a result of our listening) that our vowels begin to slide all over the place. The instabilities and inconstancies of pronunciation vexed Spenser and Harvey in their correspondence, and the sound of the vowel slides as it dopplers through time. "I compose by the tone-leading of vowels," Robert Duncan wrote; "the vowels are notes of a scale, in which breaths move, but these soundings of spirit upon which the form of the poem depends are not constant. They are the least lasting sounds in our language; even in my lifetime, the sound of my vowels alters. There is no strict vowel standard."[7] How, then, read well? Dialect; inflection of sentence pattern: the perplexing variables. Markers of class, of economic and educational status, and of race. To insist on—or even expect—any sort of uniformity is to privilege one reading community over another, and make the sort of reading we learn in high school and university English courses the universal, transcendent case, rather than the special case it actually is.

Douglas Oliver has suggested that poems, where there is an "absolute agreement" between different readers in a given dialect group about "the semantic, emotional and syntactical interpretation," have "an ineffable 'neutral' tune" which is "fairly standard across many performances."[8] I find this somewhat imponderable, since (as Oliver's "absolute" recognizes) it boils down to a reading group of one; plainly no such "agreement" is possible, and the hypothesized tune is, as Oliver says, "unattainable" (x). This is partly because, as Deleuze and Guattari have famously pointed out, "there exists no ideal 'competent' speaker-hearer of language, any more than there exists a homogenous linguistic community."[9] But it also has to do with the nature of sound itself. Tape recordings have confirmed the intuition that no two readings of a poem are ever exactly the same; sound is the least constant part of the poem, the least durable, and possibly the most elusive. The visual habit of print has taught even professional readers to ignore by-and-large the momentary nature of close hearing, caught in the instant as it is, and to forget that each time we read the poem it sounds itself differently in that voice we all (except perhaps those of us born deaf) have in our heads.[10]

But the more any of us reads a given poem, silently or aloud, the more established becomes an inward notional neutral tune which persists from reading to reading, familiar but elusive in its fine detail. There is a wide and inevitable disparity between how we hear the poem when we read it silently, and how we sound it, saying it aloud; the poem performed in the head is an imagined poem in the world of sound. This may be why, when we voice the poem, we can never match what we breathe to what we think we heard. The inner speaking we hear as we read is not the voice we hear when we outwardly speak, and the noises we make when we read a poem aloud are never the noises we think the poem makes. But the difference between our internal reading and our oral performance will vary from poem to poem, and also from occasion to occasion. Maybe the variation has to do with the familiarity of the poem, the fixity of our interpretation, or the frequency of our performance.

The difficulty in voicing the poem, though it has something to do with our understanding of the work, may also have to do with a kind of tentative polyvocality, a simultaneity of possible tones and interpretations, possible (at least in a gestural sort of way) inside the head but impossible of public performance—a kind of undecidable music or tune. The eye moves so much faster than even the inward voice and ear that by the time we begin inwardly to "hear" a speech-segment we've already considered a number of alternative voicings in light of what is to come. Some poets deliberately surprise the mind by exploiting undecidability of voice, as in the Janus-headed "near" of:

the whole pageantry

of the year was
awake tingling
near

the edge of the sea[11]

That "near" is an odd sort of voiced non-committal crux in the unorthodox syntax and sound of Williams's poem. Temporal in relation to the words before it, and spatial in relation to those following, "near" obliges the reader of the poem radically to rebalance the rhythm- and intonation-pattern the sentence seems to demand: the voice necessarily flattens out into a curious and unanticipated music.

But the rhythm is a problem. Since Williams's poem is unpunctuated and the syntax rather unorthodox, some readers provide their own punctuation to clarify their voicing of the poem. The poem seems in such cases to resolve into three or four sentences, but their boundaries are undecidable, and a variety of punctuations is possible. Sentence breaks affect intonation: they are usually signalled by a falling pitch. For ease of discussion, I write the poem out as prose: "According to Brueghel, when Icarus fell it was spring. A farmer was ploughing his field, the whole pageantry of the year was awake, tingling. Near the edge of the sea, concerned with itself, sweating in the sun that melted the wings' wax, unsignificantly, off the coast, there was a splash quite unnoticed. This was Icarus drowning." An obvious alternative is to open the poem with a principal clause introducing a lyric catalogue: "According to Brueghel, when Icarus fell it was spring: a farmer." Clauses introducing a list usually signal the start of that list by rising in pitch—a voicing, then, in complete contrast to the closing fall of an opening sentence.

Punctuation has a strong rhetorical function. By reducing the range of voicing possibilities it makes this subtle and complex poem (despite the interesting syntax of the third putative sentence) pretty banal; it decides what Williams left undecidable, porous, and fluid, and it fixes a narrative meaning. In the process it tells the voice what to do, how to intone. When we look at the poem as Williams wrote it, without punctuation, we see that it is actually unvoiceable in any completely satisfactory way: the polyvocality, the simultaneity of possible tones, rhythms, and interpretations, is available only to the inner ear, and cannot be spoken. One might therefore conclude that it is impossible to read this poem well aloud. Certainly, it cannot be voiced as "ordinary" speech.

It may be that Williams's poem presents such difficulties because there is not a long history of its interpretation, and because it has not been absorbed into the culture the way well-established canonical works have. It may even be that in 300 or 400 years' time a tradition may have grown of repunctuating and modernizing twentieth-century texts along the lines accorded the texts of Wyatt or of Shakespeare. In Shakespeare's case, editorial practice has over the past three centuries focussed upon deciding what Shakespeare (or his printers) left undecidable (and, perhaps, well-nigh unvoiceable). The third quatrain (lines 9–12) of Sonnet 129, "Th' expence of Spirit in a waste of shame" (and especially its final two lines), is a famous instance of what I am calling voiced non-committal crux:

Made In pursut and in possession so,
Had, hauing, and in quest, to haue extreame,
A blisse in proofe and proud and very wo,
Before a ioy proposd behind a dreame,
[version of 1609]

Editors since Lintott in 1709[12] have assiduously recast and repunctuated this text, in most cases agreeing with Booth's 1977 version, which is as follows:

Mad in pursuit, and in possession so,
Had, having, and in quest to have, extreme,
A bliss in proof, and proved, a very woe,
Before, a joy proposed, behind, a dreame.[13]

The impulse behind this editorial activity is akin to that behind the late twentieth-century practice of tape-recording poets reading their own poems: to provide an authoritative and authentic register of the poem's sound—how it *should* be said in order to keep the meaning straight. Such practice congeals an interpretation and defines a voicing which, as Laura Riding and Robert Graves argued, severely limits available responses to the poem, in effect closing it down.[14] It is arguable, perhaps, that *all* readings of the repunctuated Sonnet 129 are "bad," and that *no* "good" reading of the 1609 version is possible. Whether or no, the punctuated version of line 12 (the last line quoted) completely forfeits the tenuous polyvocality of the 1609 version and establishes an orthodoxy which necessarily determines the criteria by which to determine the quality of a reading.

Not all canonical poems, however, have suffered this fate. Donne's first Holy Sonnet offers a much more complex instance of voiced non-committal crux, because the poem has a long history of canonical recognition and interpretation, and because we know what we do of the circumstances of its author and its composition. "Misvoicings," though possible, are dismissed as eccentric, unimportant, and "bad." The crux is in the opening line, indeed in the first four words:

> Thou hast made me, And shall thy worke decay?
> Repaire me now, for now mine end doth haste,
> I runne to death, and death meets me as fast,
> And all my pleasures are like yesterday;
> I dare not move my dimme eyes any way,
> Despaire behind, and death before doth cast
> Such terrour, and my feeble breath doth waste
> By sinne in it, which it t'wards hell doth weigh;
> Onely thou art above, and when towards thee
> By thy leave I can looke, I rise againe
> But our old subtle foe so tempteth me,
> That not one houre my selfe I can sustaine;
> Thy Grace may wing me to prevent his art,
> And thou like Adamant draw mine iron heart.

What's interesting about this poem is its emphatic vehemence, which Donne achieves through a high count of monosyllables, dense consonant clusters (especially but not only in the opening line), a prosodic variety which ranges from the iambic almost-doggerel jingle of line 4 to the paired apparent anapaests opening line 10, and his characteristic measure of adjacent strong stresses (speech stress overriding the perhaps anticipated weak syllable characteristic of strict iambic pattern). The poem's strict control of pace, indeed, emphasizes the quantitative rather than the accentual elements of the sound and draws us to pay attention to the duration of the syllable as much as (if not more than) to the stress. Consequently, we tend to process the utterance one word at a time rather than in our more habitual speech-clusters.

The first four words, "Thou hast made me," set the whole poem up. How they are said determines how the rest of the first line shall be said—it's a matter of tone—and how the first line is said determines our understanding (the meaning) of the whole poem. Meaning, after all, determines tone; tone determines quantity; quantity is (usually, in English) a function of stress. When I was a schoolboy we used to bait our teachers by saying "good morning" sexily, angrily, comically, obsequiously, scornfully, and so on; everyone knows how to pack the most trite expression with strong and malapropos feeling.

Change the stress, and you change the quantity; change the quantity and you change the tone; change the tone and you change the meaning.

So how voice those first four words? My own rather conventional and orthodox ear bids me to take them slowly, delivering them with more or less equal duration but by no means in a monotone. This severely slows down a line which is already slowed by the density of its consonant clusters *(st/m; d/m; ll/th; k/d),* and almost completely overrides what iambic imperative the line seems at first glance to have, yielding a sound which is very close indeed to one word at a time (I italicize the long syllables):

Thou hast made me, And *shall thy worke* de*cay*?

I'm talking duration here, rather than accent, though clearly there is a relationship between the two, and I must add right away that I'm not at all sure that I can satisfactorily *say* the poem this way, it gets too rodomontade (I'm not at all sure that I can sound this poem in any other way either). But my inward ear—what Don Wellman once called "a speaking within hearing"[15]—tells me this is how the line should sound; those first four words are a voiced noncommittal crux. This is not simply because of the poem's curiously *meditative* vehemence, but because almost any other distribution of durational (quantitative) stress radically alters the speaker's attitude toward "Thou," and quite possibly eliminates the meditative note altogether. Put primary stress on "Thou" and "thy" and the speaker might be blackmailing the Lord—I'm not sure Donne is incapable of such an attitude, but the unorthodoxy or inappropriateness of such a reading gives me pause. So does that of other readings, distributions of stress and duration, which by turns make the speaker snivelling and whining, truculent, self-regarding, or scornful, and my difficulties arise from what I know of the circumstances of the poem's author and its composition.

My assumption here is not that my ear is "correct," or even that it's a representative index of any heard emotional register other than my own; my voicing of this poem is quite possibly very eccentric. The semiotics of tone in ordinary and even in highly structured formal speech is notoriously uncertain: the fearful voice can be heard as resentful; the shy but friendly as aloof and ironic. Weeping is sometimes mistaken for laughter.[16] Donne's poem and its various readings demonstrate in a quite obvious and dramatic way that tone is a matter of quantity is a matter of meaning, and confirm—were confirmation necessary—that there can be no ideal "competent" hearer of language any more than there can be such a speaker; to some extent each of us speaks a foreign tongue. Some, more foreign than others, perhaps. Students, inexperienced readers coming across the poem in a footnoted textbook in a classroom setting, have much to contend with: "knowing" that they had better understand the poem "correctly" they find themselves confronted with their ignorance, and bullied by it. It affects the way they say the poem. Teachers, (presumably) experienced readers, bring to the poem their knowledge of the canon, of Donne's place in it, and of other of Donne's poems. They find themselves confronted with their knowledge, and possibly bullied by *it*. It affects the way they say the poem.

It would be an exaggeration to say that Donne's (or even perhaps any) poem needs to be protected from the reader's knowledge, but the modernist practice of "make it new" led some poets to court an unpredictability designed to undermine the presuppositions and expectations that accompany any experienced reader's knowledge of poetry generally. Yet they almost invariably sought to control the sound. William Carlos Williams, pretty well throughout his career, sought a notation-system which would adequately register the sound of the poem as he heard it; he was at one stage strongly attracted by Sidney Lanier's notions of musical notation, and for much of the time (but especially in the 1920s and 30s) tinkered with the shape of the poem on the page with aural as well as visual considerations in mind.[17] A slavish obedience to line break, however, has led many an inexperienced reader (to the bored dismay of the listener) to intone each line as if it were a complete sentence; it has led many a younger poet—following perhaps his or her reading of Charles Olson's *Projective Verse*—to recite a poem in "that old singsong" that David Bromige complained about, "half rapt, half-assed."

The poet's determination in this century to control the sound of the poem notationally was no doubt largely responsible for the enthusiastic and widespread recourse to electronic recording once the technology became available. With the advent of cheap tape-recording, what Doris Sommer has called "the readerly will to appropriate a writer's position"[18] could turn to the poet's own reading for clarification and enlightenment, and the poet's own voice gains the status of Authentic Source. The listener can feel that he or she is now in touch with the genuine and originary poetic voice. However, such pursuit of the authentic (which I have elsewhere called the archaeological fallacy)[19] gives rise to some very real problems, not least because it establishes some readings as normative, and suggests that a "good" reading is timelessly stable, transcendent.[20] Thus the 1962 liner notes to the Caedmon record of Dylan Thomas reading Shakespeare and Webster comment that "All who have written of Dylan Thomas's recordings agree that the voice holds the absolute key to the works."[21] What would a late-twentieth-century audience make of Keats's cockney, I wonder.

On the evidence of tape-recordings, for instance, the opening of Louis Zukofsky's "So That Even a Lover" should properly be read

Little wrists,
Is your contént
My sight or hold . . .

That is invariably Zukofsky's voicing.[22] Zukofsky had one of the finest ears in the business, and in this poem—as in so many of his short lyrics—he is working for the tune. This does not mean, however, that a reading which substitutes "cóntent" for "contént" is inept or even inappropriately jars the tune: that "hold" in the third line suggests Zukofsky's awareness of that pun and its resonance in this context. No reading can be definitive—either reading opens up the poem.

That tiny voiced non-committal crux becomes, in the practice of a poet like Robert Grenier, a basic compositional tool. His fairly early poem "Warm," for instance,[23] exploits undecidability and is extremely difficult if not impossible to voice at all satisfactorily. The poem is designed, I think, not to be heard, but to be read with the eye. It's a very deceptive piece of writing, for it comes trippingly and easily off the tongue, it makes a very pleasing noise. But voicing the poem closes down its play of indeterminacies.

WARM

Bones in the child
child in the womb
womb in her
body in
bed in the room

room in the house
house in the
plain
moon
drifts

blackness
because we have
drawn curtains

It reads like a series of notations, hastily jotted down. It works so strongly for the eye that it is difficult to imagine any satisfactory reading aloud, save *possibly* to an audience that has the text before it. The use of line-break (is the "womb in *her*," for instance, or "in her *body*"?); the extreme recurrence of "in" (which appears in the first eight and the last line—i.e., nine times in this 13 line poem); the shifts or ambiguities in the parts of speech (is "drifts" a noun or a verb?); that "have" of line 13 (does it signify possession, or tense?); are the curtains open or shut? But it also reads—especially at the beginning—like a nursery rhyme, and it invites the voice to sing, or at least chant. The poem is, then, a really quite dense play of possibilities, the possibilities afforded by the eye playing with and against those afforded by the ear. A Zukofsky trick, maybe. Or Donne's. Or Shakespeare's.

Unsayability, in the sense I have been discussing, is a central feature of a great number of poems, of this and of earlier centuries. How curious, and how interesting, that Shelley's punctuation is so problematic. How important it was in the eighteenth century to pin Shakespeare's noise down. The attraction of firm punctuation is the attraction of the clear voice, which is in turn the attraction of the authentic and the sure: certainty is transcendent. But the unsayable casts doubt on the reader's and hearer's capacity to know, all uncertainty removed, without (and I borrow my phrasing from Doris Sommer) "allowing incapacity to float into the comforting, unmanageable mists of ambiguity" (264). The unsayable cripples masterful understanding by holding on to an inexplicable and perdurable residue. Its cultivation has important ethical and political implications, for it leaves us uncompromisingly face to face with the unknowable and different. It is the allure of the unsayable that has led so many poets to a courtship of the unpredictable, because the unpredictable disconcerts: Lyn Hejinian, Barrett Watten, Susan Howe, Robin Blaser, Rae Armantrout, Bruce Andrews; the extravagance of Robert Duncan, the economy of Lorine Niedecker. As Howe cogently and vividly has instructed and reminded us in *My Emily Dickinson* and elsewhere,[24] the last half of the twentieth century in especial has been the age of the stammering poet, groping for words, stuttering in quest of articulation, refusing the preset certainties of pattern. The stammerings of Billy Budd and the astonishing hesitancies of Emily Dickinson plumb us in the undecidability of language as it moves through us. They have become representative voices of the last half-century, along with Olson, say, especially in his emphysemic breathing through his poems. Or Jackson Mac Low, and his use of random or indeterminate procedures. Or Kathleen Fraser, and her incorporation of error into her text. And dozens upon dozens of others.

The voiced noncommittal crux is the voice of coming-to-speech, that moment on the threshold of speech where syntax as we have been taught it is thrown over as we come to words, as words come to us. As we move to utterance, the mind and the body cast for and negotiate possibilities, overriding if only momentarily the rhetoric of socially differentiated understanding, with nothing quite adequate to the exact event, never exactly sayable. Robert Grenier, in his well-known 1971 essay "On Speech," put it this way: "what now I want, at least, is the word way back in the head that is the thought or feeling forming out the 'vast' silence/noise of consciousness, experiencing world *all the time* . . . I want writing what *is* thought/where feeling is/*words are born.*"[25] Where words are born. A century and a half ago Whitman said of the American poet, in one of those extravaganza flourishes that informed and directed him, possessed him, and *thought* him through his 1855 *Preface,* that "Mississippi with annual freshets and changing chutes, Missouri and Columbia and Ohio and Saint Lawrence with the falls and beautiful masculine Hudson, do not embouchure where they spend themselves more than they embouchure into him"—and they stutter out again, disjointed inarticulate freshets of lists, fragments and piled clauses, heap upon heap of them. Almost, if not completely, unsayable. Voiced, tentative, noncommittal cruxes. Which make poems poems, whatever their ideological stripe. Good reading, bad reading: neither is wholly possible; either might bring us to the threshhold of speech. Strength of vocables: to bind.

Notes

Epigraphs. David Bromige, untitled contribution to "Voice // Voicing // Voices. A Forum on the Theme of Voicing," *O.ars 6/7 Voicing* (1989): 26; Edmond Jabès, *A Foreigner Carrying in the Crook of His Arm a Tiny Book,* trans. Rosmarie Waldrop (Hanover: Wesleyan UP/UP of New England, 1993) 15.

1. I have in mind the kind of reading described by Paul Metcalf: "incredibly bad. Stoned out of his mind, mumbling inaudibly, chain-smoking throughout the reading, begging drinks, ignoring all of us save for an occasional leer. . . . I'm told he grosses something like 90 thou a year for this sort of performance" (quoted by Jonathan Williams, "'Anyway, All I Ever Wanted To Be Was a Poet,' Said Leon Uris, With a Smile, As We Strode Together Into the Vomitorium," [*The Magpie's Bagpipe: Selected Essays,* Thomas Meyer, ed. (San Francisco: North Point, 1982) 74]). See also Williams's description of a reading in his "Take the Number 78 Bus to Helicon," ibid. 127–30.)

2. Charles Bernstein, "Artifice of Absorption," *A Poetics* (Cambridge: Harvard UP, 1992) 9.

3. John Cage, "Mureau," *M: Writings '62–'72* (Middletown, CT: Wesleyan UP, 1973) 35–56; Cage's reading of part of "Mureau" at St. Mark's Church, New York, 1 January 1975, is on the LP *Biting Off the Tongue of a Corpse* (Giorno Poetry Systems Records GPS005); Tom Raworth, "Survival," *West Coast Line* 7 (Spring 1992): 7–14; *Survival* (Cambridge: Equipage, 1994). Raworth read "Survival" at the Kootenay School of Writing, Vancouver, in autumn 1991.

4. *Dylan Thomas Reading from William Shakespeare's* King Lear *and John Webster's* The Duchess of Malfi (Caedmon TC1158).

5. *Keats and Shelley Read by Theodore Marcuse* (Lexington 7505). (Lexington Records was a division of Educational Audio Visual, Inc., New York.)

6. William Hazlitt, "My First Acquaintance with Poets," *The Complete Works of William Hazlitt,* P. P. Howe, ed., *Uncollected Essays* (London: Dent, 1933) v. 17, 118. The essay first appeared in Leigh Hunt's *The Liberal* 3 (1823).

7. Robert Duncan, "The Truth and Life of Myth," *Fictive Certainties* (New York: New Directions, 1985) 50.

8. Douglas Oliver, *Poetry and Narrative in Performance* (New York: St. Martin's P, 1989) x.

9. Gilles Deleuze and Félix Guattari, "Rhizome," trans. Paul Foss and Paul Patton, *Ideology and Consciousness* 8 (Spring 1981): 53, which was rephrased as "There is no ideal speaker-listener, any more than there is a homogeneous linguistic community" in *A Thousand Plateaus: Capitalism and Schizophrenia,* trans. Brian Massumi (Minneapolis: U of Minnesota P, 1987) 10.

10. For a preliminary discussion of the speech-perception of those born deaf, see Ivan Fónagy, *La Métaphore en Phonétique,* Studia Phonetica 17, (Ottawa: Didier, 1979) 111–120.

11. William Carlos Williams, "Landscape with the Fall of Icarus," *The Collected Poems: 1939–1962,* Christopher MacGowan, ed. (New York: New Directions 1988) v. 2, 386.

12. Bernard Lintott's was the first "responsibly edited" reprint of the *Sonnets* (Stephen Booth, *Shakespeare's Sonnets,* edited with analytic commentary [New Haven: Yale UP, 1977] 543); further and more scholarly editions appeared in 1766 (one edited by George Steevens, another by Edward Capell), and in 1780 (as part of Edmond Malone's great annotated edition of the complete works).

13. Booth, *Shakespeare's Sonnets,* 111. Among those accepting the 1609 punctuation is John Dover Wilson, who remarks that "as [Martin] Seymour-Smith insists, to impose a modern punctuation on the *Sonnets* would indubitably lead to misrepresentation" (*The Works of Shakespeare,* ed. John Dover Wilson, vol. 36: *The Sonnets* [Cambridge: Cambridge UP, 1966] cxxiv).

14. Laura Riding and Robert Graves, "William Shakespeare and E.E. Cummings," *A Survey of Modernist Poetry* (London: Heinemann, 1927). For a vigorous contrary view, see Booth, *Shakespeare's Sonnets,* 441–452.

15. Don Wellman, "Preface," *O.ars 6/7 Voicing* (1989): 1. Similar problems arise in the voicing of what I called the "apparent anapaests" opening line 10.

16. The semiotics of tone is extremely complicated, and is inextricably compounded with the question of whether all? some? of language is motivated rather than arbitrary. The notion that tone has a universal meaning attracted a number of modernist writers: Basil Bunting, for instance, was not alone in his belief that "it is perfectly possible to delight an audience by reading poetry of sufficient quality in a language it does not know" ("The Poet's Point of View," *Three Essays,* Richard Caddel, ed. [Durham: Basil Bunting Poetry Centre, 1994] 34). Bunting's practice of reading Goethe and Hafez to students in North American classrooms (at, for example, the University of British Columbia in 1970) has kinship with Zukofsky's adoption of

transliteration as a compositional principle in his and Celia Zukofsky's translation of *Catullus* (London: Cape-Goliard, 1969), and with others. The literature on the semiotics of tone is vast. I owe much to excellent discussions in David Appelbaum, *Voice* (Albany: State U of New York P, 1990); Ivan Fónagy, *La Vive voix: essais de psycho-phonétique* (Paris: Payot, 1983); Roman Jakobson and Linda Waugh, *The Sound Shape of Language* (Bloomington: Indiana UP, 1979); Reuven Tsur, *Toward a Theory of Cognitive Poetics* (Amsterdam: North-Holland, 1992); and—also by Tsur—*What Makes Sound Patterns Expressive? The Poetic Mode of Speech Perception* (Durham: Duke UP, 1992).

17. "Some Simple Measures in the American Idiom and the Variable Foot"—and especially the "Exercise in Timing" (*Collected Poems,* v. 2, 418–423)—confirm Williams's use of line break as a semantic, syntactic, and above all rhythmic control, though his recordings—most of them made after his stroke—don't usually follow the line-breaks.

18. Doris Sommer, "Textual Conquests: On Readerly Competence and 'Minority" Literature," *The Uses of Literary History,* Marshall Brown, ed. (Durham: Duke UP, 1995) 260. This is an extremely useful discussion, to which I owe a great deal; at one or two points in my essay my own phrasing echoes hers.

19. Peter Quartermain, *Disjunctive Poetics: From Gertrude Stein and Louis Zukofsky to Susan Howe* (New York: Cambridge UP, 1992) 124–25.

20. For a brilliant discussion of the hubristic aspects of the archaeological fallacy as it relates to the "authentic" performance of music, see Richard Taruskin, *Text and Act: Essays on Music and Performance* (New York: Oxford UP, 1995). In his introduction (14), Taruskin quotes the following from the article on "Performing Practice" in the *New Grove Dictionary of Music and Musicians* (14: 370): "The principle that the performers should be allowed some scope to 'interpret' the notation subjectively has been challenged successfully for the first time . . . with the advent of recordings and electronic means of fixing a composition in its definitive form once and for all."

21. The liner notes list five further LP recordings of Thomas reading his own work, plus a two-disk set of *Under Milk Wood* (TC 2005), and add: "At no former time in history has a poet's own voice been treasured and familiar in so many thousands of homes."

22. Louis Zukofsky, *Complete Short Poetry* (Baltimore: Johns Hopkins UP, 1991) 114. The Harry Ransom Humanities Research Center, University of Texas at Austin, has what may well be a complete collection of Zukofsky's taped readings.

23. Robert Grenier, "Warm," *Series: Poems 1967–71* (Oakland: This, 1978), 17; also *In The American Tree,* ed. Ron Silliman (Orono: National Poetry Foundation, 1986) 6.

24. Susan Howe, *My Emily Dickinson* (Berkeley: North Atlantic, 1985); *The Birthmark: Unsettling the Wilderness in American Literary History* (Hanover: Wesleyan UP and U of New England P, 1993).

25. Robert Grenier, "On Speech," *This* 1.1. (Winter 1971); also in *In The American Tree* 496–497.

Paradise of Letters

> We have an emotion towards the vegetable tuftings and ornaments of the earth.
>
> —Geoffrey Grigson. *The Englishman's Flora*

On 28 April 1529, at the sign of the Pot Cassé on the Petit Pont, just over two-and-a-half years after King François I of France had on 5 September 1526 by Royal Privilege granted him exclusive copyright for ten years, Geofroy Tory finished printing his attempt "to lead the unlearned to the contemplation and comprehension of well-formed letters."[1] Letters, he said, are "so noble and divine that they should not be in any wise misshapen, mutilated, or changed from their proper shape" (189). They should have the proportions of the human body, and in their "divine perfection" (63) should—like the human body—"stand in their requisite and proper aspect, upright and intact" so that they can be seen "face to face" (vi-vii).

On 17 February 1600, after almost eight years in prison in Venice and then in Rome, Giordano Bruno was burned at the stake for saying that "divinity is within us more than we ourselves are," that stars "have life in themselves," that planets, worlds, and the things within them, are all ensouled, and that "all of God is within all things."[2] Gaspar Schopp, an eyewitness, reports that at the stake, when he was offered the crucifix, Bruno in disdain turned away his face.

Tory's book is called *Champ Fleury.* Bruno was burned in the Campo dei Fiori. Two fields of flowers. *A Suite of Fleurons* and *Flowers and Flourishes* are the titles of two celebrated books on printing by John Ryder, typographer and book designer.[3]

~

Fields of flowers. When the death-god Hades carried off and raped Kore, she was playing with her friends in a sweet meadow, gathering the flowers of the rose and lilies, soft crocuses, beautiful violets, irises with hyacinths, and narcissus. This is an old, old story. Some 2,500 years later Milton following a later tradition would call that meadow "that faire field of *Enna,*" locating it as did Ovid in Sicily, and (retelling a story of perhaps equal antiquity) would describe Adam and Eve, in their amorous *jouissance* having lost the Garden of Eden by eating the "Bad Fruit of Knowledge," disporting themselves on a couch of

> Pansies, and Violets, and Asphodel,
> And Hyacinth, Earths freshest softest lap.

Flowers and flourishes, pleasure of what text.

"Flours were the Couch," Milton said, and

> There they thir fill of Love and Loves disport
> Took largely, of thir mutual guilt the Seale.[4]

Imperfection's celebration and attachment, pleasure and pain conjoined, stain sealed in lettered text. In his sequence of *Heroic Emblems* (cast concrete or carved stone in the grounds at Stonypath) Ian Hamilton Finlay modeled "The Divided Meadows of Aphrodite,"[5] where Empedocles's moving principles of Love and Strife, "equal in length and breadth to the four elements,"[6] are the source of all things. Some meadow! Some garden! At Stonypath the boundaries of garden, meadow, pasture, and moor blur and are permeable, and it is sometimes hard to distinguish where you are.

"What the hell's the difference," William Carlos Williams asked Ezra Pound somewhat impatiently on 22 May 1948, "between condemning the world from heaven or hell?"[7]

The word *paradise* has as antecedent, in Hebrew, *pardes;* in Zend (old Persian), *pairidaeza;* the first means a park or grove, the second, an enclosure. Fenced, perhaps, to ease the Blessed, that they be not disturbed by the doomed. In Arabic Persian *firdaus* is the word for both paradise and garden, and some time around the close of the tenth century Abu 'l Kasim Mansur—Firdosi—composing what became the national epic the *Sháh Námeh* (a poem twelve times the length of *Paradise Lost*), told the story of Tahúmers who brought letters into the world. Tahúmers was the Demon-binder *(Diw-bund),* who killed Ghú, the leader of the demons, at a blow. To save their lives, the surviving demons "taught him letters, and his eager mind with learning was illumined."[8] A transformation, a metamorphosis.

Letters, caught at the first in demonic light. The story of Kore comes from the *Homeric Hymn* to Demeter, whose daughter she was. In Phoenician the word *aleph* means ox, and the letter was made to look like its head—unless,

that is, it comes from the Egyptian *Apis,* the sacred bull. The wise men in ancient Egypt, thought Bruno, "knew God to be in things, and Divinity to be latent in Nature, working and glowing differently in different subjects and succeeding through diverse physical forms, in certain arrangements." He cited scorpions and vipers, onion and garlic, as examples.[9] One Greek myth says that when Cadmus, who founded Thebes in blood, brought writing into Greece, he placed Alpha first in the alphabet because the cow (which had led him to the site of his new city) is sacred to Demeter.

The cow is the first of essential things.

In the vale of Tempe (in Greece, between Mount Ossa and Mount Olympus), Zeus raped Io and then turned her into "a Cow as white as milke" to hide her from Hera, the goddess of flowers. This too is an old, old story, old when Homer told it, and often told since. As Arthur Golding retells Ovid's version (1567—book 1, lines 701–943), when Io tried to lift her hands, "she sawe she had no handes at all"; when she tried to speak, her lowing "did hir so affray, / That oft she started at the noyse, and would have run away."[10] When at last she saw her reflection in her father's stream, "she was agast" at her gaping jaws and sprouting horns "and from hir selfe would all in hast have fled." And when Inachus her father found her, and fed her sweet and tender grasses, "She as she kyst and lickt his hands did shed forth dreerie teares." Without speech she could not tell him, not even who she was, but she "printed" her name in the sand, "Two letters with hir foote," IO. A hoofprint. The letter *I* going through the *O*—a distress of letters—"from which name," Tory reminds his reader, "the country was called Ionia and its people Ionians" (20).

Geofroy Tory derived the whole alphabet from *I* and *O.* In his alphabet, letters are folded and enfolded, one in another—"E when properly designed and written contains within itself F & L" (98)—and as in his quest for human perfection he unpacks them, so does he unpack extensions: "the letter A," he says, "is made from the letter I" and is "a triangle, which is an odd number":

> The two feet of the A and the head make the said triangle; but it must be placed within a square, which is represented by the word Hyacinthus, which consists of four syllables, *Hy-a-cin-thus.* The ancients, wishing to demonstrate the extraordinary perfectness of their letters, formed and fashioned them according to the proper proportions of the three most perfect figures of geometry—the circle, the square, and the triangle. And because an odd number was always considered among the ancients as a lucky number, . . . they made their first letter in the image of an odd number placed upon the square, which is an even number, to give a good opening & fortunate approach. (26)

Plutarch recorded that the odd number is male, the even female; Tory, continuing his exploration of A, saw that "as by the conjunction of the male and female man is engendered, so by the conjunctions of letters syllables are made, and by the conjunctions of syllables, words. And speech" (26). He hoped that by his work in *Champ Fleury* "our language might well be enriched by certain fine flowers and figures of rhetoric" (3). Transformed.

Transformations, by which to read what has been written. "If it is assumed that the art of reading is confined to the printed page," the American architect Louis H. Sullivan wrote in about 1906, "we cannot go far. But if we broaden and quicken our sense of reading until it appears to us, in its more vital aspect, as a science, an art of interpretation, we shall go very far indeed. In truth there will be no ending of our journey; for the broad field of nature, of human thought and endeavor, will open up to us as a book of life, wherein the greatest and the smallest, the most steadfast and the most fleeting, will appear in their true value. Then will our minds have escaped slavery to WORDS and be at liberty, in the open air of reality, freely and fully to deal with THINGS."[11]

But "tell me," Virgil asks in the third eclogue, "in what countries are born flowers inscribed with the names of kings?" Hyacinthus, a pre-Hellenic god, was a beautiful boy beloved of Apollo, who accidentally killed him with a discus. His lamentation of grief, ἀιαῖ (alas! alas!), is written on the petals of the lily which sprang from his blood. In scientific language, the Linnaean name for the common English bluebell is *Endymion nonscriptus,* and the narcissus, as Athanassakis reminds us in his translation of *The Homeric Hymns,* "was the lure that led to the rape of Persephone and her sojourn in Hades."[12] In their old age Cadmus and his wife Harmonia were transformed into serpents and carried away by Zeus to a beautiful meadow at the western end of the earth, on the banks of Oceanus, where there is no snow, no storm, no rain, and the cool west wind breathes for ever: Elysium, which Hesiod thought of as the Islands of the Blest.

On 17 March 1962, Louis Zukofsky wrote to Cid Corman that a letter is solid, a syllable body. Some 35 years later Ron Silliman described Charles Olson's *Human Universe* as "a collection best known for its attempt to correlate poetic form with the functions of the human body."[13]

Extensions, then, of capability, which transcend, remind, and even inform. Think, Giordano Bruno enjoined the reader of *The Expulsion of the Triumphant Beast,* "think, thus, of the Sun in the Crocus, in the narcissus, in the heliotrope, in the rooster, in the lion; you must think of each of the gods for each of the species under the genera of the entity." For "to the extent that one communicates with Nature, so one ascends to Divinity through Nature."[14] Indeed, said Louis Sullivan, "most of us have, in less or greater measure, this gift of reading things. We come into it naturally."[15] How curious, and how apt, that the great manuscript collections of learning from which, in the Middle Ages, the young were inducted into the great tradition of Western knowledge, should have been called *Florilegia.* Collections of flowers. Anthologies. What Zukofsky in *Bottom: On Shakespeare* called An Alphabet of Subjects.

An alphabet. In 1901 Sullivan read the pier, the lintel, and the arch as "the three letters, which constitute the alphabet of our art." He saw balanced within the pier "the two great forces, the simplest rhythms of nature, to wit, . . . the Rhythm of Life . . . and the Rhythm of Death,"[16] allegorizing his art. Here's a cockney alphabet, as I remember it from my childhood. It's been around for quite a while, a hundred years or more, another distress of letters.

A for Orse
B for Mutton
C for Thighlanders
D for Dumb
E for Brick
F for Vescence
G for Indian
H for 'Imself
I for Novello

J for Oranges
K for Restaurant
L for Leather
M for Sis
N for Eggs
O for A Pee
P for Relief
Q for Tickets
R for Mo
S for Williams
T for Two
U for Me
V for La France
W for Mirror
X for Breakfast
Y for Usband
Z [i.e. *zed*] for The Last Time

Though it keeps shifting in some of its details and definitions, it's stayed pretty constant in its great variety of puns, in its play of techniques and expectations. *A* is not for "Orse" in the way in which *C* is for "Thighlanders"—and of course my introduction of *is* just there wrecks the alphabet and obliterates the transformations. "Some day," Georges Dumézil has observed, "it will be necessary to restore to the history of religions the idea of the symbol. . . . It is what permits one, if not to voice, at least to approximate, to delimit the nature of things, by substituting for the stiff and clumsy copula of identity, 'to be,' more flexible affinities: 'to resemble,' to have as an attribute or principal instrument,' to recall by an important association of ideas.'"[17]

Tory's letters invoke unseen cosmologies, hidden connections, and powers. They manifest and make visible metamorphoses akin to those of Bruno's Sun in the crocus. The transformations in the puns of the Cockney alphabet more than gesture towards similar potentials in their variety, as *for* shifts in quite remarkably Steinian or even Joycean ways and lets us glimpse a possible world of ciphers in which a doctrine of signatures might once more hold. Or doctrines.

There is, too, an archaeology in these sometimes quite complex puns and their reversals. In his *Dictionary of Slang and Unconventional English*, Eric Partridge, citing Ernest Weekley's *Etymological Dictionary of Modern English*, suggests that "Hell for Leather" comes from "all of a lather," which is what happens to a horse's skin when you ride it, drive it, too fast.[18] An archaeology of letters which informs, too, the verbal fancies of turn-of-the-twentieth-century travel writer Norman Douglas, where he finds the memory of a "snowy temple . . . embedded in the name of the village of Massa Lubrense *(delubrum).* A wondrous mode of survival, when one comes to think of it: a temple enshrined in the letters of a word whose very meaning is forgotten, handed down from father to son through tumultuous ages of Romans and Goths and Saracens, Normans, French, and Spaniards, and persisting, ever cryptic . . . after the more perishable records of stone and marble are clean vanished from earth."[19] Letters. Geofroy Tory proposed, on the basis of similar evidence, that Hercules, after building there, left a company of men-at-arms in Paris as settlers, after whom the city was named. They were, Tory says, "called *Parrhasians* from the name of their province of Greece . . . and by the change of A to I, the inhabitants of this city were, and are to this day, called Parrhisians" (15–16).

Letters. The alphabet is, like Bruno's cosmos, an enfolded universe of infinite extensions. In over 60 published works Bruno maintained that there is life on other planets and that each of us, each thing, is a universe, microcosm. An infinitude of infinitudes, yet in a finitude, and so a universe. A many and a one. An open and closed form, like the shape of A. Its stress.

Forgetting the distinctions between upper and lower case (to say nothing of the differences between fonts), Kenneth Goldsmith somewhat incautiously observed on 22 August 1998 that "one of the occupational hazards of being a text artist is that your work is going to look like everyone else's—there are only 26 forms that you can use."[20] About a century earlier E. Cobham Brewer was more in the right of it:

> the English alphabet will combine into more than twenty-nine thousand quatrillion combinations; that is, 29 followed by twenty-seven figures, as—
>
> 29,000,000,000,000,000,000,000,000,000.
>
> Yet we have no means of marking the several sounds of our different vowels: nor can we show how to pronounce such simple words as *foot* (pull and dull), *sugar* (father and rather), (gin and be-gin), *calm,* . . . and thousands of other words. . . . Take . . . *e,* we have *prey* (a), *met* (e), England (i), *sew* (o), *herb* (u), etc. The other vowels are equally indefinite.[21]

An alphabet. Letters. A range of possible sounds. A vocabulary. Vocabularies.

Tory sought the proportions of letters as reflected in those of "the natural body and face of the perfect man" (ii); he speaks again and again of "proper proportions" and "sovereign perfection." He thinks of history as a progress, a development, an improvement. "When one shall have treated of the letters," he said, "and another of the vowels, a third will appear, who will explain the words, & then will come still another, who will set in order the fine discourse" (xxiii). Not unlike Bruno, Tory claimed to have "excogitated and discovered rather by divine inspiration than by what I have seen written or heard" (38). He sought perfection, and saw it in unity and authority.

Perfection. Kathleen Fraser sees the quest for perfection in the poem as a crippling, an inhibition, and an imprisonment.[22] Perfection. Bruno sought it too, but protested "how powerful is the habit of believing and being brought up on certain opinions since childhood, in shutting off the most obvious things from the understanding."[23] I take that *certain* to mean *certainty,* and his protest one against crippling, inhibition, and imprisonment. Sullivan, speaking of "this gift of reading things," thought that "We come into it naturally; but, curiously enough, many are ashamed because it does not bear the sanction of authority, because it does not bear the official stamp of that much misunderstood word scholarship, a stamp, by the way, which gives currency to most of the notions antagonistic to the development of our common thinking powers."[24] In the history of writing, it seems that the less legible, the more coded and arcane, the letter, the more likely it is to be adopted by and reserved for Authority, for its exclusive use. The control of literacy by the Church. The reserved (secret) Magic of spelling, the power of correctness. In Bruno's view, "Authority usually binds and deceives in countless ways."[25] He saw perfection in diversity; in the unfolding of possibility.

A field of flowers, paradise, is a field of possibilities, transformations. On 20 January 1600 Pope Clement VIII personally presided over the congregation of nine cardinals, six coadjutors, and a notary, which examined Bruno for heresy, and nineteen days later, on 8 February, handed him over to the secular arm for burning. Of the 1,565 people tried for heresy before the Venetian inquisition in the sixteenth century, Bruno was one of only *five* actually sentenced to die, and to die by fire.[26] According to one account, his tongue was spiked before he was burned. Others say he was (merely) gagged. After the fire, his ashes were scattered to the winds in the Campo dei Fiori. On 7 August 1603 his writings were placed on the Index.

On 18 July 1870, Pope Pious IX presiding, the First Vatican Council enounced the doctrine of Papal Infallibility: "in consequence of the divine aid promised him in St. Peter . . . definitions of the Roman pontiff are themselves, and not in consequence of the Church's assent, irreformable." On 9 June 1889 some thirty thousand people came to the unveiling of H. Ferrari's statue of Bruno in the Campo dei Fiori. Pope Pious IX fasted and issued an address to be read in the churches, condemning the proceedings, and condemning Bruno as a man of "insincerity, lying and perfect selfishness, intolerance of all who disagreed with him, abject meanness and perverted ingenuity in adulation," a charlatan whose "own writings condemn him of a degraded materialism."

After the unveiling, Algernon Charles Swinburne called Bruno "A sacrifice to hate and hell."[27]

The power of the letter.

Bruno's statue broods over the Campo dei Fiori. It reminds us that in learning how to spell we have lost a vision of paradise.

Why would a word be a destination?

Notes

1. Geofroy Tory, *Champ Fleury,* trans. George B. Ives (New York: Grolier Club, 1927), 58. Hereafter cited parenthetically in text.

2. Giordano Bruno, *The Ash Wednesday Supper,* trans. Edward A. Gosselin and Lawrence S. Lerner (New York: Archon, 1977) 91, 155). Giordano Bruno, *The Expulsion of the Triumphant Beast,* Arthur D. Imerti, trans. and ed. (New Brunswick: Rutgers UP, 1964) 235.

3. John Ryder, *Flowers and Flourishes* (London: Bodley Head, 1976); *A Suite of Fleurons, or A Preliminary Enquiry into the history & combinable nature of certain printers' flowers* (London: Phoenix House, 1956).

4. John Milton, *Paradise Lost* IX, *Poetical Works,* Helen Darbishire, ed. (London: Oxford UP, 1958) lines 1040–43.

5. Ian Hamilton Finlay, "Heroic Emblems," illustrated Ron Costley; commentaries Stephen Bann, *Meantime* 1.1. (April 1977): 1–15.

6. G. S. Kirk and J. E. Raven, *The Presocratic Philosophers* (Cambridge: Cambridge UP, 1957) 250.

7. *Dear Ez: Letters from William Carlos Williams to Ezra Pound,* Mary Ellen Solt, ed. (Bloomington: Friends of the Lilly Library, 1985) 35.

8. Firdausí, *The Sháh Námeh,* trans. James Atkinson (London: Routledge, 1898) 5; there are several abridged translations into English, in which Firdosi's name is variously Romanized (sometimes by the same translator) as Ferdausi, Ferdowsi, Firdosi, Firdusi, etc. Not all include the story of Tahúmers.

9. Bruno, *The Expulsion* 237, 236.

10. Arthur Golding, *The. xv. Bookes of P. Ouidius Naso, entytuled Metamorphosis, translated oute of Latin into English meeter, by Arthur Golding Gentleman, . . . Im-*

prynted at London, by Willyam Seres, 1567. Reprinted as *Shakespeare's Ovid Being Arthur Golding's Translation of the Metamorphoses*, W. H. D. Rouse, ed. (London: Centaur, 1961).

11. Louis H. Sullivan, "What Is Architecture: A Study in the American People of Today," *Kindergarten Chats and Other Writings*, Isabella Athey, ed. (New York: Wittenborn, Schultz, 1947) 230.

12. *The Homeric Hymns*, trans. Apostolos N. Athanassakis (Baltimore: Johns Hopkins UP, 1976) 74n16.

13. Ron Silliman, "The Dysfunction of Criticism: Poets and the Critical Tradition of the Anti-Academy," *Poetics Journal* 10 (June 1998): 184.

14. Bruno, *The Expulsion* 236.

15. Sullivan, "What Is Architecture" 230.

16. Louis H. Sullivan, "The Elements of Architecture," *Kindergarten Chats and Other Writings*, Isabella Athey, ed. (New York: Wittenborn, Schultz, 1947) 124, 121.

17. Georges Dumézil, *Archaic Roman Religion, with an Appendix on the Religion of the Etruscans*, Philip Krapp, trans. (Chicago: Chicago UP, 1970) v. 1, 26.

18. Eric Partridge, *A Dictionary of Slang and Unconventional English from the Fifteenth Century to the Present Day* (New York: Macmillan, 1961).

19. Norman Douglas, *Siren Land* (1911) (London: Secker, 1929) 23.

20. Debra Bricker Balken, *Graham Gilmore and Kenneth Goldsmith: Whose Words?* (New York: Dorsky Gallery, 1998).

21. E. Cobham Brewer, *The Dictionary of Phrase and Fable: Giving the Derivation, Source, or Origin of Common Phrases, Allusions and Words That Have a Tale to Tell* (London: Cassell, Petter & Galpin, 1894) 37.

22. Kathleen Fraser, "Faulty Copying," *Translating The Unspeakable: Poetry and the Innovative Necessity* (Tuscaloosa: University of Alabama Press, 2000) 77–88.

23. Bruno, *The Ash Wednesday Supper* 99.

24. Sullivan, "What Is Architecture" 230.

25. Quoted in Giordano Bruno, *Cause, Principle & Unity: Five Dialogues*, Jack Lindsay, trans. (New York: International Publishers, 1962) 9.

26. Vincenzo Spampanato, *Vita di Giordano Bruno, con documenti editi e inediti* (Messina: Casa Editice G. Principato, 1921) 518.

27. Algernon Charles Swinburne, "The Monument of Giordano Bruno," *Astrophel and Other Poems* (London: Chatto and Windus, 1904) 6, 243–244.

Index